The Slipper Orchids

The Slipper Orchids

Catherine Cash

CHRISTOPHER HELM
A&C Black • London

Dedication

This book is dedicated to our Mother Earth and to all the humans who are committed to her protection, to stewardship, and to the healing of the growing scars on her beauty, bounty, and generous support of life in all its variety and mystery.

© 1991 by Timber Press, Inc.
All rights reserved.

First published in Great Britain by Christopher Helm (Publishers) Ltd, a subsidiary of A&C Black (Publishers) Ltd, 35 Bedford Row, London WC1R 4JH

ISBN 0-7136-8112-8
Printed in Hong Kong

Contents

List of Figures and Tables

Figures

Tables

Foreword

Those of us who grow orchids usually become infatuated with the popular *Cattleya* first. Gradually we realize there are more orchids than cattleyas. We try *Phalaenopsis, Oncidium,* and some of the more showy genera. The slipper orchids are considered bizarre, weird, and even ugly by some growers. Eventually, however, many of us become entranced by Paphs and Phrags.

The slipper orchids are surrounded with mystique. We read of the discovery of *Paphiopedilum spiceranum, P. fairrieanum,* and others of the Indian species. We are fascinated by the glossy texture, the hairs and warts. To delve into the accounts of the explorers is like reading a mystery novel—the single collection of *P. delenatii,* the elusive *P. rothschildianum* and *P. sanderanum* grip us with desire to unravel their secrets.

We admire the big round hybrids developed in Europe and continued in the United States. After a while we discover the charm of the species. Next, we yield to the primary hybrids which possess the allure of the wild parents but exhibit the vigor of hybrids. No other genera exhibit such diversity and adaptation to specific environments. We see evolution in a living laboratory in Asia where new discoveries are unfolding, such as the Chinese species *P. armeniacum, P. micranthum, P. emersonii,* and *P. henryanum.* On the South American continent we are amazed by the chance discovery of *Phragmipedium besseae* and its incredible beauty. We wait in anticipation for the debut of the next star, whether it be *Phragmipedium, Paphiopedilum,* or *Cypripedium.*

The author of this book has long held and shared her fascination with this orchid family. The book is not merely a collection of pretty pictures, although there is a wealth of pretty pictures, nor is it just a scientific discourse on the Cypripedioideae. It is a scholarly work of love for these plants that give us aesthetic beauty, intrigue, challenge, and satisfaction.

DON OSBORNE
Accredited American Orchid Society Judge
President, Piedmont Carolinas Orchid Society
President, North Carolina Orchid Society

Preface

The decision to write this book is the outgrowth of many years of deliberation. In 1972 my former husband and I wrote the Waters and Waters *A Survey of the Slipper Orchids* out of sheer desperation. At that time a growing number of articles about various species of Cypripedioideae had begun to appear in periodicals, but no books devoted exclusively to the group had been written. Each time we needed information on a particular species of our then near-complete collection of *Paphiopedilum* and *Phragmipedium*, it was a whole day's work to locate the pertinent reference.

Since that pioneer book, many changes have occurred in the slipper world and in my own life; my old collection of slippers was sold, while slipper popularity has increased a thousandfold. It is, in fact, safe to say that slipper orchids have come into their own in these 17 intervening years. In the past few years, I have begun to rebuild my slipper collection; on a larger scale, a number of fine books on slippers have appeared. Most important, many exciting new slippers have been discovered and made available to growers, while information has mushroomed.

In many ways the story of slippers is quite different from the one told in that first book, not the least of which is the difference in attitudes about hybrids. Not only have species regained their initial popularity in the interim, but the lion's share of interest in the hybrids is now focused on the novelty hybrids with their stronger alliances to species.

Thus, it is from a new perspective, both personally and with respect to these charming plants themselves, that I write today. I first believed I was merely embarking on a revision of the earlier book. Little did I realize the enormity of the changes in scope in the slipper world, nor that the book would come to be a total rewrite, bearing almost no resemblance to its predecessor. It has been a joy and a trial, a reward and a penance.

My wish for you, the reader, is that it be a challenge. I hope that these words widen your views, disturb your preconceived notions, create discussion and even argument. I know I can rely on slipper growers, above all others, to refute, to disagree, to question these words. You, my readers, have been foremost in my mind, keeping me honest, objective and self-critical. It is with great awareness of my limitations, especially my lack of experience with

Paphiopedilum, Phragmipedium, and *Selenipedium* in their native habitats, that I submit my writing to your scrutiny. You must keep me in mind as fundamentally a teacher with a lifetime of classroom exposition riding my coattails. Because I am also a scientist, and one whose more humanistic tendencies are only now beginning to emerge from the rigidity of slavelike devotion to objectivity and accuracy, I find I enjoy the occasional opportunity to wax subjective. At times, I take a stand on issues, such as conservation. Far more often, I prefer to present viewpoints, leaving you to decide for yourselves where truth lies. Some of you will feel I have occasionally given credence to humbug—perhaps that is so. Perhaps I have taken to the fence rather than making a needed stand at times. Above all else, I have respected your capacity to read, consider, question, evaluate, and choose your own stance.

My primary purpose throughout this book is to make and amplify connections. I have emphasized the relationships between allied species or variants of a single species. I freely acknowledge my tendency as a "lumper" rather than a "splitter." I have undertaken to link hybrids with the species stock from which they sprang. I have tried to illuminate connections between species and their environments, between habitats and cultural practices, between successful growers and the attention they give to their plants, between morphology and physiology, between taxonomy and evolution as they relate to kinship among species, between earlier views and more modern concepts in classification, and between the historical climates out of which major scientific milestones appeared and our current perceptions of slippers and their importance.

I trust I have succeeded in making broad connections both for myself and for you. Personally, I have made some very rewarding connections with other orchidists. I have delighted in passing many of their observations on to you. Subordinate in my two most important and most difficult relational goals has been to link the botanical/scientific aspect of slipper orchids to the horticultural point of view in a spirit of greater understanding for the increased enjoyment and success of both groups of slipper enthusiasts. In a small way, I have tried to associate the nuts-and-bolts mechanics of growing with the aesthetic aspects of being an orchidist. To some extent, and with particular reference to the chapter on hybrids, I have endeavored to link the past to the present—to illustrate how hybridization has developed as an outgrowth of the failures as well as the successes of the past. Further, I have attempted to link the present with the future in hybridization and technology as well as through emphasis on conservation of extant orchids.

If I have succeeded anywhere, it is my chief desire to have linked each reader with the urgency for active advocacy of and participation in global cooperation in conservation efforts—not just of orchids, but of all the wealth of living forms and the interactive systems supporting life—and to have underlined the ultimate connection, the certainty that, if we exploit part or all of our planet, the intricate web of life is threatened, jeopardizing the survival of every species including our own.

Thus, it is with a challenge to you to unite with other orchidists, and indeed other conservationists, on every continent in a cooperative and concerted effort directed toward conservation, improved communication, and a heightened enjoyment of our orchids, that I have written and compiled these pages. As the final decade of the twentieth century unfolds, I anticipate its inauguration of an improved climate of international cooperation in the conservation of slipper orchids as well as other rare, natural species, the rain forests, the oceans, and the atmosphere. I emphasize our shared responsibility to conserve not only the slipper orchids, but all endangered species and support systems. Conservation is essential to survival in its broadest sense. So, because the human species is the root of the threat of large-scale extinction as well as the only species capable of combatting that threat, we may no longer permit ourselves the complacency of ignoring our larger responsibility toward our planet—preserving its beauty and diversity along with its pragmatic, life-giving capacity.

Acknowledgments

Without the assistance of orchid friends, old and new, and many other generous individuals, this book could not have reached fruition. (The term "completion" is never applicable to a book on slipper orchids, as the field constantly grows!)

I owe gratitude to my editor, Richard Abel, for his patient and tireless guidance, and to the staff at Timber Press.

To my friends, American Orchid Society judge Don Osborne and grower Owen Holmes of Carter & Holmes, I owe gratitude for a great deal more than the slides and references which they made available to me; by example and through words of encouragement to me among a host of others, these two men have fostered and lived the highest ideals of orchidists.

The assistance of the staff at the American Orchid Society headquarters in West Palm Beach, Florida, in locating sources was an invaluable aid to me.

Dr. Atwood of the Orchid Identification Center at the Marie Selby Gardens in Sarasota, Florida, provided gracious assistance.

Miss Ann Moseley and the library staff at Cherokee County Public Library, Gaffney, South Carolina, located source materials and placed them at my disposal, while offering constant encouragement.

Emerson "Doc" Charles generously gave me a crash course in the intricacies he learned over a lifetime of experience in hybridizing slipper orchids and graciously provided many of the illustrations included herein. Doc's contributions and encouragement are gratefully acknowledged.

Richard Topper, Topper Orchids, Lexington, North Carolina, gave me an afternoon, showing me his orchids and his collection of transparencies; he sprinkled the afternoon with pithy comments about slippers and their lore, and made a number of his transparencies available to me.

Carson Whitlow of Adel, Iowa, took time to send references and transparencies, without which the chapter on *Cypripedium* could never have been written; he graciously read that chapter prior to publication, making observations and lending helpful suggestions.

Ray Rands, Malibu, California, courteously shared his familiarity with certain *Paphiopedilum* species by telephone.

Dr. Frank Stermitz and Dr. Louis Hegedus, both of the Chemistry Department of Colorado State University, lent their expertise as well as transparencies of *Phragmipedium.*

Dr. Bob Dressler of the Botany Department of the University of Florida graciously forwarded references and transparencies for use in the chapter on *Selenipedium.*

Dr. Jack Fowlie of La Canada, California, editor of *The Orchid Digest,* took time to point me in the direction of several elusive references.

Dr. Victor Soukup, Herbarium Director for the University of Cincinnati, provided numerous illustrations as well as the latest *Cypripedium* descriptions to come out of China. His invaluable contributions also presented me with an unprecedented challenge in dealing with species descriptions in Latin and Chinese.

A wealth of illustrations for the chapter on hybrids came from John Hanes, San Gabriel, California, and from Dr. William W. Wilson, Penn Valley Orchids, Wynnewood, Pennsylvania.

Mark Pendleton, Orchid Zone, Salinas, California, provided a slide of *Paphiopedilum sanderanum.*

Dr. Carlisle Leur of Sarasota, Florida, gave his permission for use of *Cypripedium* transparencies given to Hugh Waters and me many years ago.

All these contributors have my gratitude.

To Hugh Waters, with whom I coauthored the pioneer book on slippers in 1973, I extend thanks for his cooperation in waiving any rights to the information we accumulated jointly as I set about revising the first book. As it turned out, a rewrite was in order rather than a revision, although I gained from that first experience much of the courage to go on with this one.

My mother, Cynthia Cash, and my daughters, Beth Waters and Cassie Lipsey, lent their encouragement and unflagging support to my long hours at the keyboard. Without their love and concern, I would have found it far more difficult to meet the demands of this book.

To all those who have contributed materials or encouragement, I offer my heartfelt thanks. Writing about slipper orchids is a labor of love, the benefits of which extend to giver and receiver alike. The willingness of growers to lend time, transparencies, and their own personal viewpoints to this book is proof positive that the common goal of promoting this unique group of plants lives among us stronger than ever. I am grateful to everyone who joined me in the preparation of this book, as well as most humble about claiming authorship of what has clearly been a team effort. However, I accept full responsibility for the interpretations, whether accurate or in error, found within these pages.

CHAPTER 1

Introduction and a Caution

Choosing to grow slipper orchids imparts a certain distinction to the grower. The appeal of these orchids is by no means universal. Therefore, most orchid growers could be classed as either cypriphiles or cypriphobes. Although the latter may describe slippers as ugly, warty, snouty orchids, the dedicated slipper grower emphasizes quite different attributes: the infinite variety of form, the subtle coloring, the durable, waxen texture, the attractive foliage, the compact growth habit so desirable in greenhouses abulge with plants and the year-round bloom available from slippers. While displaying little of the frilly daintiness of *Cattleya* blossoms, slipper flowers exhibit a charm both elfin and grand. If beauty is indeed in the eye of the beholder, then how much more beauty resides in the eye of the grower? Few joys exceed that of showing off a specimen plant bearing 20 or more flowers, or that of displaying the first bloom on a hybrid of one's own making. Just as the mentality of orchid growers is eccentric to ordinary horticulture, similarly the mentality of the cypriphile is tangential to that of the typical orchidist. Yet in every respect, the pleasure of growing slipper orchids reflects the grower's humanity, creativity and individuality. For the cypriphile, all the aspects of horticulture—challenges and rewards alike—are heightened in the growing of slippers.

By way of introduction, it is important to circumscribe the group to which this book is devoted, to identify and to understand the intrinsic "cypness" which distinguishes the slippers from other orchids and unifies the 4 genera included in the subfamily Cypripedioideae—*Cypripedium, Paphiopedilum, Selenipedium* and *Phragmipedium*. I shall devote particular attention to the 2 genera usually cultivated in greenhouses, *Paphiopedilum* and *Phragmipedium*.

The subfamily Cypripedioideae was described by Lindley. As a taxon it is characterized as herbs lacking pseudobulbs or storage roots. The subfamily is considered to be primitive within the orchid family because of the presence of 2 fertile anthers—1 more than is typical for the majority of orchids. Floral structure is the definitive taxonomic feature, and that of the slipper orchids is distinctive both in appearance and composition.

1

FLORAL STRUCTURE

The most obvious feature of the slipper flower is the prominent saccate or pouched lip which resembles the toe of a slipper. The pouch functions as a trap for insects in the intricate process of pollination. However, documentation of pollination has been made for only a few of the species of this subfamily. Insects are attracted to the flower by visual and/or odorous stimulants originating at or around the staminode, the third, sterile anther. An attempt to land upon either staminode or pouch rim pitches the insect into the pouch, trapped by the treachery of the slippery-smooth surfaces of these apparent landing stages. Once inside the pouch, the insect encounters more smooth surfaces in the area of the inner wall adjacent to the aperture, but is provided with a ladder of hairs leading up the rear wall of the pouch. The insect is thus led to exit by crawling through 1 or the other of 2 narrow passageways, each of which is partially barred by 1 of the 2 fertile anthers. If the mechanism is successful, pollen adheres to the dorsal thorax of the escaping insect and is borne away to be placed upon the stigma of another slipper nearby, as the insect performs a second pouch-escape maneuver. However, an insect too small to serve as a pollinator may fail to dislodge the pollen, or it may carry the pollen to the exterior of the pouch, only to be unable to fly with the increased weight. On the other hand, an insect too large to be accommodated by the passageways is doomed to die within the pouch. The accompanying illustrations, Figures 1 and 2, identify both the names and the positions of the flower structures involved. Nectar is not known to be produced by slipper orchids. Flies are among the most common pollinators of *Paphiopedilum* and *Phragmipedium,* while bees typically pollinate *Cypripedium* and *Selenipedium.*

The calyx of slipper orchids is distinctive as well in that it normally consists of only 2 sepals: the dorsal sepal and a ventral sepal, also known as the synsepalum, formed as the result of the fusion of 2 lateral sepals. Located within the calyx is the corolla, consisting of 2 lateral petals and a third modified petal—the pouch.

Occasional peloria (the anomalous return by an irregular flower to the regular condition, i. e., a return to 3 sepals and/or 3 petals, which is the regular pattern in flowers of Monocotyledonae) restores the number of sepals to 3, in some *Paphiopedilum* hybrids. Likewise, certain *Cypripedium* species have poorly fused or unfused ventral sepals. In *Phragmipedium lindenii,* peloria restores the corolla to the standard 3 petals. This unique species is the only example of predictable peloria of the corolla in the subfamily, and its appearance is greatly modified by the presence of a petal in place of the pouch. Because of the close relationship between stamens and petals, it is not surprising that the flower of *P. lindenii* possesses a third fertile anther as well. Given the capacity for variability inherent in slippers and the artificially induced combinations of chromosomes of disparate species, anomalous flowers occur fairly frequently among complex hybrids. Perhaps the most astonishing of these is the extraordinarily uncommon flower possessing 3 pouches and no petals in its corolla.

These showy segments of the flowers are of great interest to growers. Their enormous diversity creates myriad variations on the theme of the standard slipper pattern. Sepals may exhibit stripes, dark blotches or suffusions of vivid and/or pastel colors. They range in form from the wide, flattened expanses typical of hybrid slippers to the narrower, arched and reflexed sepals of the species. Often they are adorned with undulate margins. Petals also vary in width, length and orientation. Their adornments include warts, hairs, stripes and marginal frills. Their presentation may be horizontal to pendulous, and they may exhibit varying degrees of corkscrew spiraling. Petals may curve forward as if to embrace the pouch or they may reflex. Petals of complex hybrids are usually quite broad, while those of many of the species are slender, and in a few species, extremely elongated. Various slippers exhibit

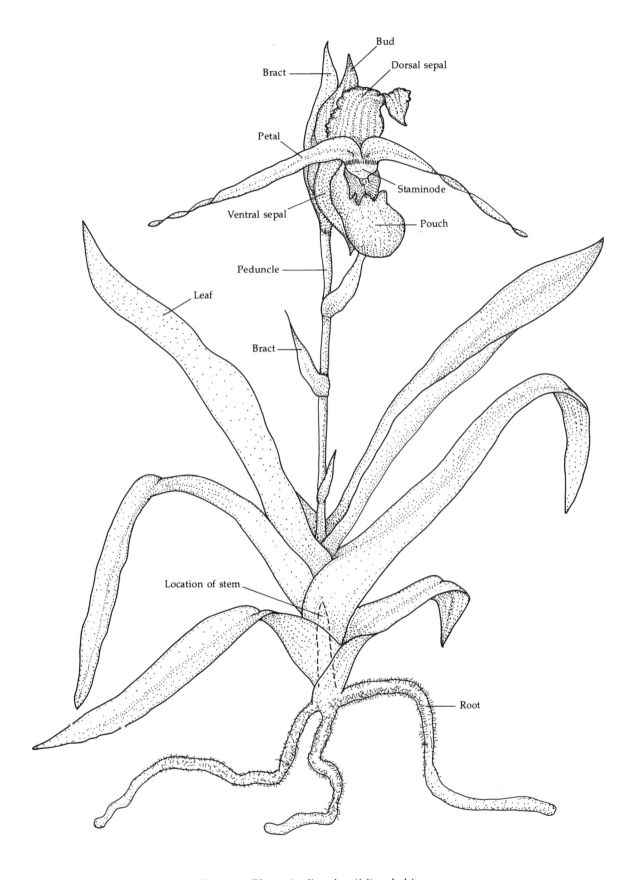

Figure 1. *Phragmipedium longifolium* habit.

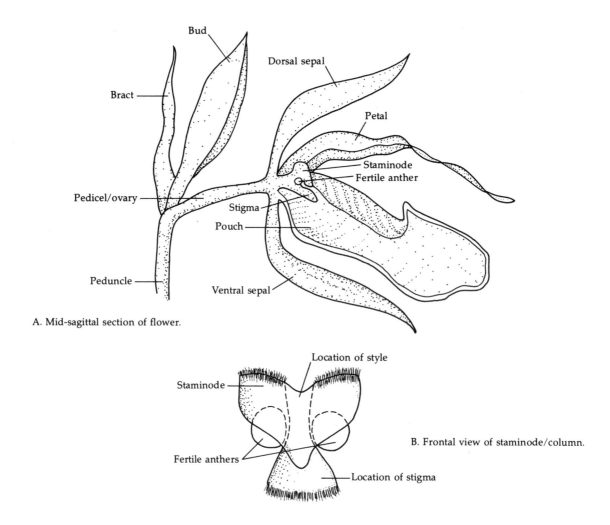

A. Mid-sagittal section of flower.

B. Frontal view of staminode/column.

Figure 2. *Phragmipedium longifolium.*

smooth, grooved or veined pouches in a wide range of shapes, colors and sizes. Pouch presentation varies from drooping to pugnacious. Staminodes are variously shaped, bossed or smooth, and mounted at a variety of angles, while staminodal coloration varies from rich to pale in hue. Color in the slipper orchids may be dull, yet in some individuals it is quite vivid. The single adjective which never applies to slipper color is gaudy. Texture varies from delicately thin in *Cypripedium* and *Selenipedium* to leathery or waxen in *Phragmipedium* and *Paphiopedilum*, where it approaches the texture of the sturdiest *Anthurium* blossoms. With few exceptions, even delicate slipper blossoms are quite long-lasting.

The reproductive structures are located within the 2 showy whorls of the flower. As is to be expected in the orchid family, fusion of reproductive parts is evident in these genera also. The 2 fertile anthers are fused to and situated laterally and just posterior on the prominent, median, sterile anther—the staminode. The stigma and style are also fused to the base of the staminode, and this entire reproductive assemblage is called the column. As is characteristic of orchids, the ovary is inferior.

Within the ovary, the locular condition and the placentation of ovules have received much attention, although their significance has perhaps been overemphasized. The trilocular (3-chambered, arranged around a central, columnar, placental tissue) ovary has been used historically as 1 of the definitive features delimiting the genera *Selenipedium* and *Phrag-*

mipedium while the unilocular (1-chambered, with placental, seed-bearing tissue only on the parietal walls) ovary has traditionally defined the genera *Cypripedium* and *Paphiopedilum*. According to Atwood (1984b), the disparity between the characteristic trilocular ovary with axile placentation, a primitive feature of the 2 genera indigenous to tropical America, and the contrasting condition of a unilocular ovary with parietal placentation in the other 2 genera is not a distinction as sharply delineated as was formerly believed. Based on his studies of ovaries of the 4 genera, Atwood concluded that ovarian structure grades from 1 condition to the other in many examples, supporting his view of the affinities between the unilocular *Cypripedium* and the trilocular *Selenipedium*. Atwood reports that cross sections used to define the genera have traditionally been cut from the median regions of ovaries, so that the 2 conditions contrasted clearly. However, when sections are cut from the distal regions of trilocular ovaries, the central axis is often found to be discontinuous. Moreover, sections cut from the basal portions of unilocular ovaries frequently reveal the vestiges of carpellate fusion in the presence of 2 or 3 locules.

Flowerscapes in the subfamily are varied, but less extravagantly so than the flowers themselves. Most *Cypripedium* and all *Selenipedium* bear cauline (belonging to the stem or arising from it) inflorescences; that is, flowerscapes are produced as the terminal portion of a leafy stem axis or as branches from it. Flowers are borne in a terminal raceme in *Selenipedium*, atop the canelike stalks of these enormous Central American orchids. In most species of *Cypripedium*, the stem converts from production of leaf buds and matures to bear 1 or more flowers atop the same axis. However, several species of *Cypripedium* lack distinct aerial stems and produce a peduncle from the center of a more or less acaulescent (stemless or having a shortened stem) whorl of leaves. These and some caulescent *Cypripedium* are typically unifloral; other species are bifloral or even multifloral. The favorite greenhouse genera, *Paphiopedilum* and *Phragmipedium*, bear peduncles from the center of an acaulescent, distichous (disposed in 2 vertical ranks) fan of conduplicate (folded lengthwise) leaves. All *Selenipedium* and *Phragmipedium*, as well as certain species of the other 2 genera, are multifloral. Multifloral racemes open simultaneously or successively, depending upon the species. Species of the subgenus *Cochlopetalum* of genus *Paphiopedilum* produce an indeterminate flowerscape which flowers continually over a period of 9–36 months. Among the various species in cultivation, the flower stalk may vary considerably in height, a matter of some concern where slippers are grown as cut flowers.

Orchidists who are less botanically oriented routinely refer to the *Paphiopedilum* flower stalk as a stem with perfect understanding among themselves. This custom is harmless and rarely causes confusion. However, within these pages, the term "stem" will be applied consistently to the leaf-bearing organ of the plant.

VEGETATIVE MORPHOLOGY

Roots. Roots of evergreen slipper orchids are covered with velamen, the specialized epidermal layer typical of the surface of most orchid roots. Velamen enables roots to absorb atmospheric moisture as well as liquid water. The roots of all slipper orchids function both to anchor the plant and to absorb water and nutrient minerals. The function of anchorage is of more import than is immediately apparent, particularly to nonterrestrial species of *Paphiopedilum* and *Phragmipedium* which cling to cliffs with nearly vertical rocky faces, or to trees, rocks or other soil-poor substrates. Growers bear these habitats in mind when repotting, and provide a free-draining medium in which the plants must be fairly tightly potted. In nature, roots of evergreen species, whether semiterrestrial, lithophytic or epiphytic, typically trap their own supply of humus as they cling to rocks or trees.

Slipper roots are relatively coarse and thick, measuring about 2–5 mm (⅛–¼ in.) in diameter. They are sparsely branched, if at all, reach lengths of 30–50 cm (12–18 in.), and are numerous on healthy plants. Young *Paphiopedilum* root tips are beige to ivory-white in color, while older portions become progressively darker brown and more furry.

Roots emerge from the rhizome, from the base of the fan, and, in some species, from the axils of the lower leaves of the fan. It is important to remember that fan growth usually outstrips the growth of roots, so that young fans may be dependent upon the parent plant for more than a year before sufficient roots are present to permit their removal to an independent existence.

Stems. The stem of *Paphiopedilum* and *Phragmipedium* is the smallest of their vegetative organs, and is subdivided into 2 structural and functional components. The main stem is the horizontal rhizome, basal in position, and typically located beneath the surface of the substrate. This is the fundamental stem, giving rise to roots, rhizomal branches and vertical branches which bear the leaves. The vertical stem of the 2 cultivated genera is extremely foreshortened, and may be thought of as a core, much like the core of a lettuce head. Its internodes are tightly compressed so that new leaves are borne immediately atop the preceding ones. The vertical stem typically bears a species-constant number of leaves, after which maturity is reached and the single bloom spike is generated. In some species and hybrids, buds which produce new fans also arise in the axils of the lower leaves of older fans. In such plants, proliferation of new growths is rapid, and large specimen plants are readily produced. *Paphiopedilum* Maudiae, an early primary hybrid, is an example. After several years of producing lush growth, *P.* Maudiae matures growths rapidly enough to remain in nearly constant bloom. This feature is but a sample of a host of reasons for its perennial popularity with growers.

Leaves. Within all 4 genera leaf variation from species to species may be best understood if we envision the characteristics arrayed along a continuum. The plicate (folded or ribbed longitudinally by the presence of several to many parallel veins) leaves of *Cypripedium* and *Selenipedium* are relatively thinner and more flexible than the conduplicate (midvein-keeled, folded into a V in cross section), coriaceous (leathery in substance) leaves of *Phragmipedium* and *Paphiopedilum*. On the thin end of the spectrum, *Cypripedium* leaves are thinner than those of *Selenipedium*. This is logical from an adaptive standpoint, due to their relatively shorter length which requires less support, and to the shorter span of time before abscission. Slight intrageneric variations in thickness occur among plicate-leaved species and, as might be predicted, even intraspecific variations can be detected between prairie populations and more protected stands of the same species. As a rule the evergreen genera bear thicker leaves, although thin-, intermediate- and thick-leaved species are to be found within *Paphiopedilum*. In this genus the combined factors of leaf substance and leaf length also determine whether leaves will be stiffly erect, prostrate, or even pendulous as is true of most cliff-dwelling and epiphytic species.

Some slippers have leaves with hirsute surfaces or margins, though the majority of leaves are bare. A large number of *Paphiopedilum* species are marked with purple anthocyanin pigment on the underside, and it is also only in this genus that characteristically tessellated leaves are to be found. The ratio of dark green to silvery pigmentation present in leaf tessellations is more or less characteristic of species and even of varieties of species. There are also many *Paphiopedilum* species with plain, green leaves devoid of any mottling. The leaves of 2 species of *Cypripedium* are densely spotted with liver-brown pigment. With those 2 exceptions, *Cypripedium*, *Phragmipedium* and *Selenipedium* leaves lack markings on their solid green surfaces.

With very few exceptions, slipper leaves are long and narrow. They lack serration, lobing or other marginal irregularities. *Cypripedium* species exhibit the greatest variation in leaf shape, including several species that bear broad, fan-shaped leaves which superficially appear to have serrate margins because of pronounced plication.

Veins may be prominent on the undersurface of leaves, creating exaggerated keeling in conduplicate leaves or a corrugated appearance in plicate leaves. Conversely, prominence of veins may be diminished in other species so that leaves are rather flattened.

As the photosynthetic organ of the plant, the critical importance of the leaf cannot be emphasized too strongly. As an aesthetic portion of the plant, the leaf is due its share of praise as well. In spite of their range of variations, leaves are distinctive and somewhat useful in identifying genera or even species. The leaf is a most useful indicator of the general health of the plant. This topic will be explored further in Chapter 2.

An introduction to the subfamily Cypripedioideae requires an overview of the 4 genera of which it is comprised. Additional discussion is found at the beginning of each of the 4 chapters devoted to a specified genus.

CYPRIPEDIUM

American wildflower aficionados are most familiar with *Cypripedium*, a circumboreal genus inhabiting the subarctic, temperate and subtropical regions of the Northern Hemisphere. For more than a century horticulturists called all the slippers "cypripediums" or "cyps," although usually the species in cultivation were indeed of other genera. This genus, the true "cyps," includes 30–50 species of deciduous perennials. These terrestrial species inhabit woodlands and meadows at many elevations, as well as the margins of bogs. The southernmost species are native to Mexico; the northernmost are found near the Arctic Circle in Alaska, Siberia and Canada. Vegetatively the typical *Cypripedium* bears an elongated leafy stem, as opposed to a fan of leaves, and its leaves are plicate or ribbed rather than conduplicate. The plant is perennial from a rhizome or rootstock, and flowers are borne only on mature plants. Immature individuals are usually restricted to fewer leaves nearer ground level. At the time of blooming, the axis extends to produce bracts and flower buds. Only a few species vary from this pattern by producing a peduncle for flowering, while all the true leaves are basal upon a short stem. The height of a blooming plant varies from only 10–12 cm (4–4.5 in.) in the smallest species to 30–85 cm (12–33 in.) among the larger well-known species, and up to 1.5 m (nearly 5 ft.) for the recently described *C. subtropicum*.

Cypripedium are deciduous, overwintering by means of their rhizome. There is considerable variation among species and populations as to the time of anthesis, depending both on elevational and/or latitudinal position with relation to season and on the plant's growth habit. Several species progress rapidly to blooming; others grow vegetatively for more than a month before the inception of buds. In all cases however, flowering occurs in spring and summer. Pollination is quickly followed by fertilization in this genus. Capsule production is both rapid and common in the majority of species. Chapter 3 is devoted to this genus.

PAPHIOPEDILUM

Paphiopedilum is by far the largest genus in the subfamily with nearly 70 known species. This genus inhabits a large part of Southeast Asia and many of the nearby islands. One or another of these species is adapted to the many diverse habitats of the region. Some are epiphytes but most are lithophytes, while a few are terrestrial. At least 1 species tolerates salt spray as a denizen of the shoreline. Many live perched on high mountain slopes or on the banks of deep ravines. Some thrive in steamy lowlands in the shade of dense vegetation. All enjoy high humidity for much of the year and relative protection from freezing temperatures. No members of this genus go into a true dormancy extending to leaf drop, although several tolerate seasonal cold or moderate drying. All the species can be induced to flourish in greenhouse conditions if care is taken to make use of the small microclimates which occur within glass walls.

Depending upon the species, the foliage of *Paphiopedilum* is green or tessellated, arranged in fans of leaves borne from a very short stem. Individual fans, or growths, persist for several years, flowering but once. They are easily distinguished as being immature, mature (in bud or flower), or older, nourishing growths with their spent bloom stalk in the center. Leaves are described as conduplicate or keeled. The leaf arrangement is distichous, referring to the 2 vertical ranks of leaves which create the fan-shaped configuration.

There is considerable variation in size of plants among the species of *Paphiopedilum*. Comparisons of individual mature growths eliminate any confusion regarding quantity, so that leaf length and breadth, as well as the number of leaves in a mature fan and how closely the leaves are appressed 1 above the other, are the determining factors in growth size. The dwarf "limestone paphs" have a leafspan of about 10 cm (4 in.). At the opposite extreme, large epiphytes often achieve a leafspan of about 1 m (40 in.). Height of mature growths varies both with leaf length and substance. Frequently, plants with long leaves stand only 25–30 cm (10–12 in.) high, due to the pendent nature of the elongated leaves.

Flowerscapes of *Paphiopedilum* emerge from the base of the youngest leaf and may bear 1–20 flowers. A few species produce a continual-bloom spike that opens successive flowers over many months while others bear a multiple-bloom spike of 2–20 simultaneous blossoms. Old, well-grown multiple-growth plants may bear up to 20 or more flowerscapes at a time creating a spectacular effect as a specimen plant, although each fan of leaves bears but 1 flowerscape during its life.

The height of the peduncle is another variable factor. Dwarf species may hold the blossom only 4 cm (1.5 in.) or so above the leaves, while the largest species produce inflorescences up to or exceeding 60 cm (24 in.) in height.

Certain species of *Paphiopedilum* appear to be frequently pollinated in nature, while others rarely produce capsules. Fertilization in this genus is typically delayed by slow growth of pollen tubes, which often lags several weeks behind pollination.

A judicious selection of species and hybrids of *Paphiopedilum* will ensure a year-round profusion of bloom to delight the heart of the grower with almost infinite variety. Hybridization within the group has created new forms and colors, vastly increasing the options available to growers. As a result of both careful breeding and polyploidy, the complex hybrids have come to vary from the species to a degree as spectacular as the variance observed among the diverse species. Chapter 4 is devoted to *Paphiopedilum* species; hybrids in the genus are discussed in Chapter 7.

SELENIPEDIUM

Selenipedium is a little-known genus of only 6 species, indigenous to the northern tropics of the Western Hemisphere. The genus has received minimal attention from botanists and horticulturists. Its meager horticultural merit as described below, together with its limited distribution in somewhat remote equatorial regions, account for its relative neglect. Cypriphiles are most familiar with this genus name because of its erroneous application to members of the genus *Phragmipedium*—a discrepancy which flourished during the 19th and early 20th centuries. However, very little nomenclatural confusion persists as a result of the early indiscriminate use of this genus name for the 2 tropical American genera. Although older orchid literature, including volumes of *Sander's List of Orchid Hybrids* through May, 1961, uniformly referred to plants of the genus *Phragmipedium* as *Selenipedium* until the mid-20th century, this usage fortunately appears to have been completely abandoned.

The true *Selenipedium* is a tall, canelike plant. Flowers are borne in profusion, but blossom size is almost comically small relative to the huge plants. For this reason the genus is considered to be unsuitable for horticulture and is rarely grown outside its native environs. Found in Central and South America, its reported habitats are at or north of the equator. Thus, the genus as presently known must be considered native to the Northern Hemisphere.

Selenipedium bear plicate leaves all along a stem axis which may reach heights of 1.5–5 m (5–17 ft.) or more. Head-high plants restrict greenhouse culture of this genus. Dressler (1981) reports that the stems branch. Although Rolph (1896) referred to the genus as deciduous, Atwood (personal communication) indicates that leafy canes persist for more than a year. In tropical climates which promote year-round growth, dieback of aerial stems is unlikely to occur annually. Because the genus has not been widely grown and studied, there is a dearth of ready information about its growth habit.

Racemes of 3–6 cm (1–2.5 in.) blossoms are produced from the axil of the uppermost leaf of each mature stem or branch. Flowers open successively over several months, so it is not unusual to see stalks simultaneously bearing buds, flowers and capsules. *Selenipedium* is discussed in greater detail in Chapter 5.

PHRAGMIPEDIUM

The genus *Phragmipedium* is composed of 14–22 species. All of them are prized by slipper enthusiasts as worthy of greenhouse culture. Almost as spectacular as the "paphs," and similar in vegetative and floral structure, *Phragmipedium* are native to Central and South America.

Fans of green leaves make up the growths. Leaves are borne on extremely shortened stem axes. As in *Paphiopedilum*, the peduncle emerges from the base of the youngest leaf at the center of the fan. The peduncles of *Phragmipedium*, however, are jointed, and all species produce multifloral scapes. With the exception of *Phragmipedium caudatum* and its allied species in the section *Phragmipedium* which bear 3–4 simultaneous flowers, the general pattern is successive flowering, although the older flowers often do not drop until shortly after the younger ones open. Typically, 3–7 flowers are produced per spike. The blooms are large in relation to the size of the plant. Often, they are showy, held on tall scapes of 15 cm to 1 m (6–40 in.) in height.

Phragmipedium are grouped into 3 foliar categories: large leaves of medium green, smaller leaves of medium green, and slender, sedgelike leaves of dark green. No species exhibit leaf tessellations. Leafspan among the large-leaved species ranges from 40–70 cm (15–30 in.); small-leaved species attain leafspans of 30 cm (12 in.) or less. As in the genus *Paphiopedilum*, the leaves are coriaceous, distichous and conduplicate.

Phragmipedium prefer lithophytic or humus-epiphytic habitats. The culture of this group is very similar to that of *Paphiopedilum*, differing primarily in the preference by *Phragmipedium* for a more acid pH and in their slightly higher fertilizer requirements. Light and temperature ranges for *Phragmipedium* most nearly approximate the bright and intermediate ranges suggested for *Paphiopedilum* culture in Chapter 2.

Hybridization of *Phragmipedium* began in the 19th century at about the time early *Paphiopedilum* hybrids were made, but although a number of primary and secondary crosses have been made, a complex *Phragmipedium* hybrid comparable to those of the genus *Paphiopedilum* has yet to be developed. It is not clear whether the genetics are vastly different, the induction of polyploidy is more difficult, or neglect by hybridizers is the cause, but the lag is obvious and the genus is worthy of the increased attention it is currently receiving.

Phragmipedium, like *Cypripedium*, have the briefest of delays between pollination and fertilization. Autogamy (self-fertilization), cleistogamy (self-fertilization within nonopening buds), self-sterility and other reproductive difficulties occur, however, within this genus. Species *Phragmipedium* are discussed in greater detail in Chapter 6; their hybrids are included in Chapter 7.

HYBRIDS

Hybridization has been a major part of the story of these delightful orchids over the past century, *Paphiopedilum* hybrids having substantially outnumbered the hybrids produced in any other orchid genus. Until recently, however, the emphasis in breeding was placed so exclusively upon *Paphiopedilum* that the other slipper genera were virtually ignored. The wealth of beautiful *Paphiopedilum* hybrids attests to the fortuitous marriage of man's creativity with the inherent slipper capacity for variability.

Investigators continue to pursue the causes behind the lack of success in intergeneric hybridization between *Phragmipedium* and *Paphiopedilum*. This incompatibility is a matter of considerable interest in light of the unusual degree of plasticity in intergeneric hybridization characteristic of the orchid family as a whole. To date, the slipper group has produced a single flowering specimen which may possibly be called an intergeneric hybrid, although conclusive proof remains elusive. Several other hybrids have been accorded registration as intergeneric hybrids, because they were grown from seed capsules resulting from intergeneric pollination. No flowering occurred in the majority of these cases, while, in those that did flower, the results have indicated that parthenogenesis (development of ova or ovules due to mechanical or chemical stimuli rather than to fertilization by a sperm) by the pod parent was responsible for the seed.

Carson Whitlow (personal communication) reports early progress in several crosses between *Cypripedium* and *Phragmipedium*. At this writing, he has protocorms of crosses between *Cypripedium reginae* and 2 *Phragmipedium*: *caudatum* and *sargentianum*. He reports germination in only 4 weeks at warmer temperatures than those to which *Cypripedium* typically respond. Moreover, he indicates that both the seed and the protocorms are larger than *Cypripedium* normally are although *C. reginae* is the pod parent. Whitlow is working with Jerry Fisher, who supplied *Phragmipedium* pollen and who has work in progress with *Phragmipedium* crosses using pollen of *Cypripedium kentuckiense*. Great anticipation surrounds these efforts.

Investigation has revealed a substantial disparity in chromosome size between *Phragmipedium* and *Paphiopedilum*. A fascinating puzzle awaits solution by researchers delving into the reasons for the lack of success with intergeneric hybrids among slipper orchids. Efforts to fuse somatic cells in tissue culture are included in the battery of techniques currently being applied to this problem, although success remains elusive.

With regard to the technique of tissue culture, the regrettable fact is that while this technique has been remarkably successful in many genera of orchids in providing the means for rapid and abundant vegetative reproduction of clones of plantlets from a meristematic bud, only marginal success has been reported to date in Cypripedioideae. Research funded by the American Orchid Society continues in an effort to unlock the avenues to all the potentials of tissue culture in this subfamily. Whitlow (personal communication) indicates that successful meristem propagation of *Cypripedium* may be in the vanguard of this avenue of progress. Further discussion of hybrids and of the technology and problems related to hybridization is found in Chapter 7.

GENERA, SPECIES, POPULATIONS, GENETICS, EVOLUTION, AND TAXONOMY

Throughout the natural world difficulties in naming the particular entities to be described and discussed remain consummate problems. Not only is the need to name and classify a thoroughly human one, but communication is extremely difficult in the absence of unique names. Although many lives have been devoted to taxonomy, great difficulties persist in the classifying and naming of living things. Few groups of organisms resist orderly classification more vigorously than do orchids. As a consequence, some historical perspective and discussion is required in order to enable the reader to better understand the particular taxonomic difficulties of this subfamily as well as my very personal approach to certain of them.

In the binomial system of nomenclature (generally attributed to Linnaeus who certainly popularized it, but actually orginated by Jean Bauhin, more than a century before Linnaeus's system—a system Linnaeus also modeled after John Ray), the first part of the assigned binomial is the genus name, delimiting the group. The second name is the species epithet (not capitalized, although this rule required subsequent standardization), setting forth the kind or the specific type. The system is ingenious, a logical approach to the task of creating order in diversity. Its aim is to show unity by linking similar species in the same genus while still recognizing the various kinds or types in existence. The concept grew so that each species was not only recognized as belonging to a certain genus, but related genera belonged to a family, similar families to orders, like orders to classes and classes to phyla, the major groupings of organisms in the plant and animal kingdoms.

The Binomial System of Nomenclature devised by Linnaeus is more than 2 centuries old, and it is still used today largely in the same way as originally conceived, although the *International Code of Botanical Nomenclature* (Stafleu, 1978) has been established to assist modern taxonomists in following evolving standards. While the Code has been helpful in maintenance of uniform standards, it has also curbed progress toward more enlightened taxonomic thought worthy of the 20th and 21st centuries. Because the work of Darwin and Mendel occurred subsequent to Linnaeus' taxonomic work, and because more profound comprehension of evolutionary and genetic principles continues to emerge out of the work of their modern-day counterparts, phylogeny and taxonomic thought have largely failed to keep pace with current concepts in botany and genetics. Taxonomic views in certain areas of expertise have been significantly modified by students of population genetics with the aid of computer-assisted statistical assessments of relationships among organisms. Such modifications have yet to be widely employed in sorting out the taxonomy of orchids, a task of great urgency if order is to be established in this large and unwieldy family.

Review of the historical impact of Linnaeus's system together with subsequent modifications to the original concept, will prepare the way for a clearer understanding on the part of the reader of the enormity of the task still to be accomplished. When *Species Plantarum* was published in 1753, the accepted concept of a species, whether plant or animal, was a very simple one of divine and immutable creation. Each kind of organism was believed to be an ideal or standard (uniform) type which could be established by proper description. Subsequently, it was believed that any specimen could be compared against the first-named type for identification and verification. Variations from the type were ignored or denied unless the variant was deemed to be sufficiently different to qualify as a new type or species. This attitude persists today to some degree, to the detriment of an improved understanding of the nature of orchids with their extraordinary reproductive pattern and large capacity for variability.

Until the appearance in 1859 of the revolutionary ideas published by Charles Darwin in *On Origin of Species,* no challenge to Linnaeus's system arose. The result of Darwin's and Wallace's joint emphasis on variability and its function in the evolutionary success of organisms would stimulate the formulation of modified concepts of the species, and would ultimately shatter the notion of immutability of species. Ideas were slow to change, so that well into this century the process of naming newly discovered organisms changed but little. However, basic concepts did change. Within the ranks of population geneticists the notion of an ideal type, created and immutable, did give way to a concept of variable, evolving, inter-breeding populations by 1930. The major difficulty persisting today lies in the failure to communicate the newer concepts into the mainstream thinking of many practicing taxonomists.

The major flaw in Darwin's work was a lack of understanding of genetics particularly as it applied to variations. He postulated that, given the enormous amount of variability he had observed, and given the fact that in every case known to him reproduction vastly exceeded the capacity of nature to support all the progeny, nature acted to select only the most successful of those variable individuals to survive and propagate their superior traits. He died perplexed by the persistence of great variability when he wrongly assumed that breeding created a blend of variable characteristics at the same time that nature consistently eliminated many variants. Darwin recognized the existence of a flaw in his reasoning. He saw that if his views were completely accurate, evolution must lead to uniformity, but he could find no evidence in nature of such a trend toward uniformity.

The work of Gregor Mendel on the laws of genetics, first published in 1865, would have done much to clarify Darwin's postpublication ideas and questions to Darwin himself had it not been lost in archival obscurity until De Vries and others unearthed it in 1900. When Mendel's work re-emerged, it stimulated much study and research, gradually becoming augmented by the emerging concepts of population genetics. Mechanistic views of evolution came to the forefront in the biological sciences by the 1930s—views which emphasized the variability inherent in species through active gene pools, and which invalidated the old immutable ideal type of the Linnaean concept. Unfortunately, not all taxonomists were prepared to accept this modern viewpoint, so taxonomic thinking has remained divided into 2 camps: the conservative, old-line proponents of only slightly modified Linnaean taxonomy, and those embracing the modern, statistical approach.

Taxonomists who accept the evidence of the existing variability as well as the preponderant emphasis of genetic and evolutionary evidence are no longer prepared to define the ideal type, to rely upon a search of the literature to be certain that a species has never been described before, or even to credit the validity of the species concept in many cases. Variability is so universally evident that its ubiquity has severely eroded the old species concept, thwarting every recent attempt to define precisely what a species is.

Nowhere is variability more apparent than in the orchid family. In any number of orchids collected from an interbreeding population, the number of variants is virtually equal to the number of individuals. Thus, not only is a species a highly variable and diverse assemblage of individuals, but frequently, what appeared to be 2 separate species is discovered to be unified by the presence of intergrading populations. Typically, the widest divergence occurs at the extremes of the geographical range, while intermediate forms intergrade between those extremes in mid-range. As understood today, this pattern is a reflection of the relatively predictable interactions within a gene pool.

Occasionally, 2 distinct but similar species are separated by a sea or a mountain range, so intermediate forms are lacking. Such an eventuality is a particularly common feature of *Paphiopedilum* native to the peninsulas and archipelagos of Southeast Asia. The mechanism by which 2 species develop from a single species is known as divergence; that is, a common ancestor once existed out of which certain highly variable populations diverged to become species A and species B, aided by geological or other agents which interrupted free interbreeding within the gene pool. In such a case, because of variable factors such as pollinator requirements or geological isolation of certain portions of the greater population, interbreeding between the extreme portions of the greater population ceases. Eventually, the intermediate forms as well as the common ancestral form may disappear. Today's assortment of *Barbata* species of *Paphiopedilum* provides examples of several degrees of the confusion created by such a possible spectrum of discontinuity. Isolation of 2 populations encourages diversification, whereas free gene flow within a cohesive population maintains a more unified population, however variable the gene pool. Once millennia have elapsed, it is rarely possible to determine at what precise point species A and species B had a common parentage, although a reasonably coherent picture of the events may frequently be inferred.

Furthermore, the variations within a species frequently appear to be no less extensive than the variations between the most similar examples of 2 closely related species. Biologists have been forced to the view that the species concept defies definition in any globally applicable sense. Thus many of them have come to regard it as merely an artificial construct which enables taxonomists to name organisms. However, such was the original purpose of classification—that ability to name, describe and communicate about an organism. Those disillusioned with the loss of the immutable species concept fail to recognize and appreciate the enormous beauty of an even more majestic concept—the orderly choreography of genes interacting in a gene pool, revealing the statistical, graphable changes which, more than defining the species in its 3 dimensions, also introduce the dimension of its fluctuation over time.

It is apparent that taxonomic undertakings in orchids are hazardous. Should one attempt to speak with authority, it is necessary to be aware that the old species concept has fallen to be replaced by one of variable, interbreeding populations. Since more than half of the species of slipper orchids were described before taxonomic thought began its own evolution to this view, and because the slippers themselves are evolving rather rapidly, much work must be done to mitigate the existing confusion in the taxonomy of this group. Criteria must be weighted for importance and agreed upon by the investigators. Descriptions must allow for a range of variability. Descriptions relying on dried, pressed herbarium specimens are particularly problematic because of the more or less spherical pouch and its deformations during preservation. Above all, the unity within slipper species must be envisioned just as clearly as the variability. The practice of raising every variant to species level creates the very confusion which makes communication more difficult, while perpetuating the old myth of immutability.

A relative few problems exist which make re-examination of genera urgent in the slipper orchids, calling for increased agreement on weighted criteria on a broader scale. *Cypripedium*, with its inclusion or exclusion of the genus *Criosanthes*, is a case in point which is examined in Chapter 3. An example of a more typical taxonomic dilemma is the uniquely cohesive group, subgenus *Cochlopetalum* of *Paphiopedilum*. On the species/variant level, it still defies the efforts of taxonomists to make order of its variability. See Chapter 4 for further discussion of this topic.

Nomenclatural changes reflecting 20th-century views of what is already known about slipper orchids are to be welcomed in order to resolve the numerous conflicts remaining as outgrowths of confusing synonymy. Incisive investigations based upon major criteria must be undertaken to further elucidate the degree and significance of relationships among slippers. Agreement must also be reached on the degree of divergence which may exist within any 1 species given its particular circumstances, especially as more new slippers are discovered. My personal bias which will be evident in the following chapters is that of "lumper" as opposed to "splitter." The reader will find that many of the horticulturally acceptable species names in *Paphiopedilum* and *Phragmipedium* have been engulfed as variant taxons within an augmented species. While this practice is no less arbitrary than the splitting off of each variant into separate species, it has the advantage of emphasizing both genetic relationships and the most current concepts of population genetics. Two operant disadvantages must be noted for the practice of lumping variants together: the economics of selling to growers who desire complete collections is enhanced with the proliferation of species. Thus, commercial interests support elevation of variants to species rank. Likewise, the honor of describing new species encourages some taxonomists to elevate variants to full species rank. It is an accepted fact that slipper orchids are actively evolving, although somewhat less so than orchids as a whole. Whether certain entities are actually modified sufficiently to warrant elevation from variant to species rank is the core of the debate.

Because of the mechanics of their pollination, orchid evolution progresses at a different pace than that of most plant families. Any seed capsule in any orchid genus, whether intraspecific or hybrid, potentially contains several hundred thousand seeds. The operative difference in orchid reproduction lies in the sheer numbers of possible combinations of the genes of only 2 parents. The apparent relative infrequency of slipper pollination in nature—the basis for the comment that slipper orchids are comparatively less active evolutionarily among orchids—applies more to *Paphiopedilum* than to the other 3 genera of slippers.

Virtually all the earlier confusion in nomenclature at the genus level has been resolved today, although debate waxes at the species/varietal levels. Whether to raise a variety to species rank in one instance, or to combine several species as varieties of a single species in another, is an ongoing question. It may be an inherently orchidaceous quandary to which there may be no clear solution given our current level of expertise.

This orchidaceous quandary stems from the fact that orchid reproduction is unique, or nearly so, in the plant kingdom, because of the sheer number of seeds produced per capsule. Furthermore, because of the massive pollinia which are transferred whole at pollination, each capsule is unique in representing nearly 100% of the possible randomly assorted gene combinations of only 2 parent plants. These features, so at variance with the reproductive strategies of plant families other than orchids, ensure that most of the possible random combinations of genetic alleles carried by the 2 parents are present within the seeds of a single capsule. The enormous plasticity in variation and natural selection which is thereby made manifest becomes a veritable laboratory for the investigative evolutionist, but is a nightmare for the taxonomist. In a grex (a group of offspring all originating from a single seed pod) of orchids, the range of variation may be so broad and complex as to give the appearance of many varieties or even several species. Taxonomists who study such variation under controlled conditions have a difficult enough task. When they attempt to make order of naturally segregating wild populations from a number of seed capsules, perhaps after natural selection has eliminated many of the intermediate forms over a wide geographic range, the necessity for a fresh approach to such a complex situation becomes all too apparent. Correct scientific interpretation of such a wealth of variation cannot emerge from studies which rely solely upon traditional morphological criteria. Rules, methods and perspectives which were adequate to unlock the mysteries of the rose and pea families are hopelessly inadequate when applied to the orchid family. The use of statistical techniques, electrophoresis and other sophisticated techniques of molecular biology may winnow some kernel of logic and order out of a degree of complexity which has become chaotic in the hands of the armchair taxonomist comparing morphological differences against a type specimen.

However, due to this plasticity or capacity to generate the maximum number of combinations of variable traits, the orchids are masters at exploiting the available niches in nature. Incorporated among the variations are many factors, some of which are more visible than others. A larger size or a more brightly marked corolla are of obvious competitive value as successful attractants to potential pollinators, and thus, as successful evolutionary strategies employed by a living population of orchids. But they are not necessarily more valuable than other, less visible, physiological factors. A vast complex of capabilities—to better compete for nutrients, to more effectively repel pests and predators, to regulate water loss more efficiently, to attract pollinators more consistently, to conserve energy in seed production—are of competitive and evolutionary significance and value. Therefore, these and other adaptive features, whether structurally obvious or not, must be identified, compared and evaluated in order to determine the degree of kinship within a group of orchids. Many of the nomenclatural problems in the orchid family will defy solution until investigators employ both functional and structural approaches, and until kinship is established upon genetic evidence rather than mere superficial resemblance.

Perhaps we lack answers to some extent because we are still asking archaic questions. The pertinent questions center on functions operating at a macromolecular level of which gross structure is at best a very imperfect reflection. Nonetheless, certainly some of the deficiency in our understanding should be ascribed to those investigators who allow a craving for distinction or fame to supercede their quest for fuller information. Severe gaps in our understanding have been widened by nomenclatural squabbles among students of the genera. The time has come for intense investigation performed in the spirit of pure scientific curiosity, objectivity and cooperation, and employing the most modern techniques, so that definitive solutions to perennial taxonomic problems may be derived. This sort of intense investigation is, in fact, in progress. At present, it still occurs in isolated bits and pieces, but the time is ripe for breakthroughs which will unite investigators in several branches of botanical study in a concerted effort to unlock the mysteries of the relationships among the slippers.

CONSERVATION OF ORCHIDS

Orchid conservation has been a concern since the early 19th-century importations for the English auctions. Time has not ameliorated the tendency for mankind to ruthlessly strip nature of her treasures. Quite the contrary, the combined pressures of technology and a mushrooming human population have broadened the threat to orchids until there exists today a multifaceted threat from all of mankind rather than merely from acquisitive horticulturists. Human nature is a curious mixture of attitudes. If the news were to be flashed over the media that the future survival of all life on earth is in jeopardy due to the behavior of a single species, active resistance to this threat would be mounted immediately, uniting the peoples of all nations against the offending species. But the fact that the enemy is mankind is neither news nor is it readily comprehended in many households. Our failure to govern war-making has captured the curiosity of generations of historians and philosophers. Our failure to govern our exploitation of the planet dismays ecologists and conservation-minded orchid fanciers alike. I submit that the fate of endangered orchids rests upon the whims—and/or decisions—of mankind. However, the fate of all species, including *Homo sapiens*, as well as of the planet at large is hardly less precarious.

It is difficult to determine whether the restricted range of several species of *Cypripedium* is a natural phenomenon or the result of man's encroachment. It is readily apparent that the dramatically shrinking ranges of particular species are due to the pressures of population growth and land development. At this writing a number of species are on conservation lists and efforts are being made to protect a few sites. Thanks to a handful of horticulturists and botanists who are unraveling the means of reliable propagation from seed, preservation through cultivation is currently underway. However, conservation-minded orchid growers are waging a battle against time and economic pressure, and the fate of several species in this genus is uncertain. The landmark accomplishments of Carson Whitlow and others in growing *Cypripedium* from seed offer the first rays of hope that the steady destruction of these natural beauties may be slowed or reversed.

A number of nurseries advertise *Cypripedium* plants for sale. Growers wishing to purchase plants are often misled by the statement that these specimens are "nursery grown." In no case is this statement literally true in the sense of nursery propagation; at most it indicates merely that plants have been held since their collection from the wild.

The threatened or actual extinction of many species in the widely cultivated genus *Paphiopedilum* is readily apparent. International trade in collections from wild populations of *Paphiopedilum* and *Phragmipedium* was forbidden as of 1 January, 1990 at the strength of the 91 member countries of the Convention on International Trade in Endangered Species of Wild Flora and Fauna (CITES). Although habitat exploitation for land development, charcoaling or other objectives is a significant factor and must be discouraged, the major inroads upon this genus have been made by unprincipled collectors who are motivated solely by profit. Therefore, I charge you, the grower, with your individual responsibility. Purchases of endangered *Paphiopedilum* species must be limited to plants propagated from the seed of established parents. Not only are such plants more likely to be vigorous in cultivation, but this is the single most effective means of combatting the heedless decimation of natural populations by unscrupulous collectors. When in doubt as to the status of wild species and/or the ethical practices of suppliers of plants, consult the literature or other growers. Ratification of CITES regulations will prove fruitless if growers create a climate which encourages poaching and black marketeering.

Orchid publications should assume the responsibility of screening advertisements placed by collectors and brokers to avoid complicity, however inadvertent, with firms of questionable integrity and thereby avoid indirect, though active, participation in the stripping of *Paphiopedilum* from their native habitats.

In no way should these comments be construed as a blanket indictment of orchid collectors and brokers. Many ethical growers and suppliers who wholeheartedly support conservation aims are in business. On the other hand, while not all species of *Paphiopedilum* are equally endangered, a marked imbalance in attitudes favoring exploitation over responsible stewardship still prevails.

No devoted grower lacks that acquisitive sense which is the author of greed, so the most effective place to control exploitation of wild populations is at the grassroots level. It is obvious that the behavior of hobbyists, however small their collections, sets in motion an economic demand to which commercial houses wish to cater. Whenever demand exceeds supply, the wild populations of species are the victims and the earth becomes a poorer place as each extinction occurs. The reader no longer has the luxury of wondering why someone doesn't do something. You must instead confront your participation in extinguishing species of *Paphiopedilum*. Protection is the shared responsibility of hobbyists, commercial growers, collectors, brokers, orchidists' organizations, publishers and governments. No individual or group may ignore this responsibility without culpability.

Selenipedium, the small genus of large plants, is well worth conservation. It is, however, endangered by the rampant deforestation of much of the American tropics. As a narrow endemic *S. steyermarkii* could be easily decimated by loggers in a week's work. Perhaps this has already happened. Estimates in the early 1980s indicated that tropical forests fell at the rate of 5000 acres/hour. Mindless exploitation by mankind has already damaged extensive portions of the planet. While efforts to convert forested areas to arable land appear laudable in Third World countries, the unyielding ecological processes dominating such ecosystems virtually preclude the production of arable soil required for successful agriculture.

It is presently unclear how extensively damaged *Phragmipedium* habitats actually are as a result of clear-cutting timber operations. There is concern that the expected frequency and extent of drought conditions subsequent to wholesale deforestation will lower water tables, inevitably parching innumerable populations of *Phragmipedium* and so radically reduce their numbers.

The concern we orchid growers face immediately is the formidable combination of ignorance, complacency and exploitation which permits the daily razing of vast reaches of the tropics—areas estimated to be as large as the state of Connecticut. Even in the absence of catastrophic global warming, these forests are amenable neither to reforestation nor to extended agriculture due to a complex network of ecological factors. Some ecologists have predicted that once the percentage of forested land drops below a critical level, whatever remains is doomed to extinction by the resulting harsh climatic changes consequent to the onset of the greenhouse effect—changes which may not be mitigated, controlled or reversed by any known means until they run their course, permanently changing the very nature of the planet. Orchidists must become better informed. It is not enough to only lend support; they must form the vanguard of conservation efforts in order that the long-term future of life on earth, including the many thousands of species of orchids, may be safeguarded.

Slipper orchids remain as fascinating today as they were more than 100 years ago when collectors sent huge shipments to the auctions, and thousands of pounds, British Sterling, were paid for a single unique plant. Those of us enamored by the slippers can find no challengers to their place of honor as the most intriguing group of plants in cultivation, as they lend themselves at every turn to increasing our aesthetic, intellectual and creative awarenesses. Together with the hundreds of thousands of other species, the slipper orchids have a legitimate claim to our support of efforts to preserve them from extinction. All cypriphiles worth their salt will invest money, time and energy in so laudable and crucial an effort.

CHAPTER 2

Growing Slipper Orchids

RECOMMENDATIONS FOR BEGINNERS

A great many facets of slipper-growing cannot be taught in any other school but that of experience. However, much guidance is available in orchid publications and from fellow growers. My first suggestion to a beginner is to join an orchid society. Without interaction with fellow orchidists, the path seems lonely and strewn with the remains of deceased orchids. The American Orchid Society is an ideal place to start. Although it is large and somewhat impersonal, its monthly bulletin is beautiful and helpful. Moreover, AOS provides its members with listings of the local affiliated societies, and it is on this more personal level that beginners find mentors and friendly assistance from experienced growers. Orchid growers are possibly an eccentric group of people. I have certainly met some entertaining and unusual characters in orchid societies. Never believe, however, that snobbery is common; it is the exception rather than the rule. You will find orchid growers generous with assistance and gifts of plants; indeed, orchid growers are often likened to pushers, trying to hook the world on their habit! Most growers enjoy their orchids intensely and willingly share their expertise, without a trace of superiority toward neophytes.

Keeping current with newly discovered species and available hybrids is an important part of becoming an experienced slipper grower. The journals are full of informative articles and advertisements. Beginners find that with exposure to such periodicals their familiarity with and usage of long nomenclatural terms of Latin and Greek origin become second nature. Moreover, illustrations and descriptions hone the beginner's ability to distinguish between adequate and truly exceptional flowers, while how-to articles offer advice borne of the personal experiences of fellow orchidists.

Among the most valuable aids in developing discrimination are attendance at and/or participation in orchid shows and acquisition of familiarity with judging criteria. These criteria are available from judges or from the AOS. They consist of points awarded for form, size, and color, as well as other factors. Lest readers become misled, I hasten to say that there are worthy flowers which are not award quality. On the other hand, a knowledge of the judges' criteria can prevent the beginner from purchasing inferior plants. Thus, while beginning growers want to avoid plants of poor quality, many good plants will still fall short of the 80–90 points required for a prestigious award. Point scores merely aid in the selection of flowers. There is no magic in them because progress is ever upward; thus plants which were awarded in past decades are today considered to be good, but no longer exceptional. It is from this older group that beginning growers may select fine specimens at reasonable cost.

Beginning growers have several concerns, including culture, plant quality, and most of all, their personal preferences and the constraints under which they cultivate their plants. Many learn through experience to restrict their initial purchases to the easily grown individuals in the slipper family. Guidelines can help beginners to select plants which will best tolerate guinea-pig status. My first recommendation is that you choose *Paphiopedilum* species which grow well at intermediate temperatures and require no rest periods. Included in this category are: *P. glaucophyllum* and its relatives, *P. barbatum*, *P. argus*, *P. javanicum*, *P. haynaldianum*, *P. sukhakulii*, *P. venustum*, *P. superbiens* (frequently listed as *P. curtisii*), *P. spiceranum*, and the members of the *P. insigne* complex. I believe that familiarity with the techniques of mainstream growing necessarily precede the mastery of the more stringent culture required by a minority of slippers.

The vast majority of hybrids also grow well at intermediate temperatures. The finest first plant for a beginner is *P.* Harrisianum 'G. S. Ball'. This is a particularly vigorous clone of the pioneer *Paphiopedilum* hybrid, and as a primary hybrid, it possesses vigor while lacking the sometimes bewildering genetic quirks exhibited by many of the complex hybrids. A personal experience will illustrate my faith in the tolerance shown by *P.* Harrisianum. This hybrid was among the first slippers I grew. I purchased the plant at a local greenhouse, finding to my chagrin that it was growing in garden soil composed largely of red clay. I was already aware of the need for aeration to slipper roots, so I marveled at its survival. It rewarded me almost immediately with a bloom and showed no ill effects from its sojourn in garden soil, adapting and flourishing in its new substrate. Although my *P.* Harrisianum may have been an unusually tolerant specimen, most of the primary hybrids are rather easy to grow. However, I predict difficulty with a certain few. Those with parentage in the section *Brachypetalum* of the *Brachypetalum* subgenus or with background in the *Coryopedilum* section of the subgenus *Paphiopedilum* should be avoided at first. The *Brachypetalum* group, including species epithets such as *bellatulum*, *concolor*, *godefroyae*, and *niveum*, are free-blooming but also subject to fungus problems and physiological difficulties. This group should be included only after the initial experience with slippers has yielded some success. The *Coryopedilum* group, including species epithets such as *rothschildianum* (for which *elliottianum* is a synonym), *sanderanum*, *stonei*, *philippinense*, and several others, is notoriously slow to adapt to new situations and begin flowering. Hybrids of this group retain some of this reluctance and, like the species, fail to provide the rapid gratification needed by beginners. For the most part, complex hybrids are suitable for beginners. There are exceptions, but reputable plant retailers provide open guidance about these problems if beginners inquire.

Beginning growers should familiarize themselves as much as possible with the morphology, habitat, and particular natural history of slipper orchids. A vast amount of published information is available, ranging over time from the *Manual of the Orchidaceous Plants* by Veitch (1887–94) to current articles in *The Orchid Digest*. The more knowledge at hand, the fewer the costly mistakes—this is a truism beginners cannot afford to ignore. In later years they will be able to look back and discover which errors were avoided through such study. Experience is the ultimate teacher, gradually bringing confidence and know-how. For the alert, prepared beginner, experience is achieved more quickly and at the least expense. In a remarkably short time, beginners find themselves speaking with assurance about their experiences, confidently asking intelligent questions of experienced growers, and thoroughly at ease in a fascinating, challenging, and rewarding new world of slipper orchids.

Personal preferences, above all, will mandate the beginner's selections of plants, although tastes may change throughout the pleasurable years of acquisition. Some growers will find the species less appealing at the beginning; others will be attracted immediately to their odd shapes and varied adornments. As a beginner, I found complex hybrids exceedingly dull, even remarking that once I'd seen one, I'd seen them all. In nearly every case, the grower's tastes broaden, and virtually all sorts of slippers become desirable.

Financially, the period of eclecticism is the danger period. Beginners never heed the warning, but I make it, nevertheless: beware of buying community pots and new divisions at a rapid pace. The expense of plants is only a small fraction of your overall cost. Increased expenses for pots, medium, fertilizer and above all, enlarged greenhouse space and increased utility costs are the inevitable results of heedless purchases. At repotting time, trade divisions or donate excess plants to the raffle table at your orchid society before the responsibility becomes unwieldy. Many growers reach the saturation point without realizing it, find the responsibility overwhelming, and lose motivation just as their increased expertise should be providing sustained gratification. For this reason, the first plant in my recommended list is *P. glaucophyllum*—a successive-bloom plant which provides the grower with long-term bloom, serving to ameliorate the urge to acquire more flowers. Like most pleasures, the pleasure of orchid growing is largely anticipation. When the orchid habit takes hold, beginning growers often find their anticipation leads them to make hasty choices. One of the best means of governing the acquisitive aspect of your anticipation is to provide yourself the opportunity of visiting a fellow orchidist, and perhaps receiving a gift division of a plant.

CULTURE

The culture of slipper orchids is both an art and a science. While requirements exist and recommendations may be made and quantified by measurements, the best culture is not necessarily by the book, no matter how authoritative. This chapter describes both optimum conditions and ranges of tolerance; the grower must do the rest. No one optimizes every growing condition, but successful growers have developed adaptations of recommended procedures or otherwise compensated for the constraints of their local environments, and so produce luxuriantly healthy slippers, prodigal with blooms.

A number of ingredients must be included in a recipe for successful growing of slipper orchids, but the first ingredient is the grower, and the real issue is the difference between the master grower and the unsuccessful one. All growers need a green thumb, but green thumbs are made—not born. After analyzing the characteristics held in common by the best growers I know, I find there is only one that consistently shows up: conscious attention to each plant on a regular basis. Growers of real genius literally commune with their plants on a daily to thrice-weekly basis, keeping every sense alert. They know each by name, usually without reference to labels. They note every change in each plant during the past year and, if memory fails, they consult their records. I recommend that every grower keep detailed records of repotting and division, fertilization and pest-prevention schedules. Even more importantly, records must be kept on each plant indicating date of purchase, number of growths purchased and number produced each year, pests and control required, bloom, and any other pertinent data. Ideally, photographs of the blooms are included as well. Intimacy with the plants and records which document both the progress of each plant and the growing techniques employed are required for successful culture.

The plants themselves have much to do with the grower's success as well. It is false economy to purchase plants of poor quality or questionable health, for the success of the grower and the health of the collection are both placed at risk. Economy may be practiced by judicious purchase of plants which are quite good but neither rare nor the latest discovery. A strategy of growers who have well-stocked collections is to trade growths with colleagues or to buy small plants for economy's sake.

Slipper orchids enjoy optimum conditions in their native habitats. Successful growers familiarize themselves with these conditions in order to determine the ranges of tolerance accepted by each species and any special requirements. They then create an environment for each plant which most nearly meets its needs. Among the conditions which must be duplicated or approximated are: ambience which includes temperature and humidity, substrate, moisture requirements, light intensity, and nutrients. This text provides general information concerning each of these conditions, but the reader should refer to Table 1 for specific details applicable to an individual *Paphiopedilum* species. Further discussion in the text not only amplifies the information in Table 1, but also includes repotting procedures and treatment for pests and diseases.

Meeting the needs of plants from exotic lands requires the grower to compare his latitude with the latitude of origin of a particular species in order to optimize available light, warmth and humidity. Whether these factors must be supplemented or decreased in cultivation depends on a careful comparison of the native habitat with the site of the greenhouse.

Because light influences greenhouse temperature, which in turn influences humidity and water requirements, and so on, growers find that different strategies are necessary for each greenhouse or even for different parts of the same greenhouse. Seasonal differences pertain to the care given a slipper collection because of these same interactions. A constantly shifting environment requires attention to a whole series of adjustments.

Table 1. *Paphiopedilum* culture.

Species	Temperature[1]	Light[2]	Water[3]	Nutrients[4]	Rest[5]
1. *acmodontum*	I	I	EM	T	None
2. *adductum**	I	I–H	EM	T–I	None
3. *ang thong*	I–W	I–H	EM	C	None
4. *appletonianum*	I	I	EM	T	None
5. *argus** †	I	I–H	EM	T–I	None
6. *armeniacum**	I–W	I–H	EM	T	None
7. *barbatum*	I	L–I	EM	T	None
8. *barbigerum*	I	I	EM	T	None
9. *bellatulum*	I–W	I–H	EM	C	None
10. *bougainvilleanum*	I	I	EM	T	None
11. *bulleninaum*	I	I	EM	T	None
12. *callosum*	I	I	EM	T	None
13. *charlesworthii*	I–C	I	EM	T	None
14. *ciliolare*	I	I	EM	T	None
15. *concolor*	I–W	I–H	EM	C	None
16. *dayanum*	I	L–I	EM	T	None
17. *delenatii*	I	I–H	EM	T	None
18. *druryi*	I	I	EM	T	None
19. *emersonii*	I	I–H	EM	T	None
20. *exul*	I	I	EM	T	None
21. *fairrieanum*	I–C	L–I	EM	T	None
22. *glanduliferum*	I	I–H	EM	T–I	None
23. *glaucophyllum*	I	I	EM	T	None

Species	Temperature[1]	Light[2]	Water[3]	Nutrients[4]	Rest[5]
24. godefoyae	I–W	I–H	EM	C	None
25. gratrixianum	I	I	EM	T	None
26. haynaldianum*	I	I–H	EM	T	None
27. hennisianum	I	I	EM	T	None
28. henryanum	I	I	EM	T	None
29. hirsutissimum	C	L–I	EM	T	None
30. hookerae	I	I	EM	T	None
31. insigne	I–C	L–I	EM	T	None
32. javanicum	I	I	EM	T	None
33. kolopakingii*	I	I–H	EM	T–I	None
34. lawrenceanum	I	I	EM	T	None
35. liemianum	I	I	EM	T	None
36. lowii*	I	I–H	EM	T	None
37. malipoense*	I–W	I–H	EM	T	None
38. mastersianum	I	I	EM	T	None
39. micranthum*	I–W	I–H	EM	T	None
40. niveum	I–W	I–H	EM	C	None
41. papuanum	I	I	EM	T	None
42. parishii* † †	I–C	I	EM–D	T	W
43. philippinense*	I	I–H	EM	T–I	None
44. primulinum	I	I	EM	T	None
45. purpuratum	I	I	EM	T	None
46. randsii	I	I–H	EM	T–I	None
47. richardianum*	I	I–H	EM	T	None
48. rothschildianum* † † †	I–C	H	EM	I	W
49. sanderanum*	I	I–H	EM	T–I	None
50. sangii	I–W	I	EM	T	None
51. spiceranum	I–C	L–I	EM	T	None
52. stonei	I	I–H	EM	T–I	None
53. sukhakulii	I	I	EM	T	None
54. supardii	I	I–H	EM	I	None
55. superbiens	I	I	EM	T	None
56. tonsum	I	I	EM	T	None
57. urbanianum	I	I	EM	T	None
58. venustum	I	I	EM	T	None
59. victoria–mariae	I	I	EM	T	None
60. victoria–regina	I	I	EM	C	None
61. villosum	I–C	I	EM	T	None
62. violascens	I	I	EM	T	None
63. wardii	I	I	EM	T	None
64. wentworthianum	I	L–I	EM	T	None

*Hanging basket culture recommended.

† Use slightly more fertilizer than normal; lower temperatures in December facilitate reliable flowering.

† † Cool and restrict water in winter; benefits from hanging basket culture.

† † † Cool treatment recommended in winter; hanging basket culture recommended year-round; typically should be potted up without division; hapuu added to substrate effective in safely delaying repotting for 3-year intervals.

[1]C = cool, 13–15° C (55–60° F); I = intermediate, 15–17° C (60–65° F); W = warm, 17–21° C (65–70° F). Temperatures described are night temperatures; ideal daytime temperatures are approximately 11° C (20° F) warmer.

[2]L = low light intensity, 1,200–2,000 foot candles; I = intermediate light intensity, 2,000–2,500 foot candles; H = high light intensity, 2,500–3,000 foot candles.

[3]W = wet, frequent watering; EM = evenly moist, allow compost to partially dry between waterings; D = dry, compost should be barely humid at watering time.

[4]C = extra calcium; T = typical fertilizer regimen; I = increased frequency and/or slightly increased concentration of nutrients.

[5]W = winter rest; see related note to determine the particular rest treatment required by individual species.

Ambience

The general quality of the atmosphere surrounding slipper orchids is controlled by its temperature, relative humidity and the concentration of pollutants. Ideally, the air should be free of most pollutants and in constant motion. The relative humidity should be 50–90%, and daytime temperature should be 20–35° C. (70–90° F.), averaging 11° C (20° F) higher than particular nighttime temperature requirements.

Air Quality and Circulation. Slipper orchids are adversely affected by most hydrocarbons, oxides of sulfur and other pollutants common in industrialized, metropolitan atmospheres. If a good air filtration system is feasible, pollution may be sufficiently reduced to enable growers to cultivate slippers in such areas.

Greenhouse air should be in constant motion, gently circulated day and night by fans. Adequate circulation not only promotes even distribution of heat and humidity, but also minimizes the likelihood of fungus outbreaks. The flow of air should be slow and gentle so that leaves are not disturbed. Fans should be mounted and their speed adjusted in such a way that drafts are created only in the upper layer of air while the lower layers are gently stirred.

Temperature. Slipper orchids are grouped by preference for night temperature into warm, intermediate and cool types. (See Table 1 for specific information.) Place reliable thermometers at several locations in the greenhouse to determine the ideal site for placing plants. All 3 types of slippers may be grown in the same house using this strategy.

Plants in the warm group require a night temperature of 17–21° C (65–70° F). Included in this group are a very few species of *Paphiopedilum*. The vast majority of species and hybrids of *Paphiopedilum* and *Phragmipedium* belong to the intermediate group and thrive at a night temperature of 15–17° C (60–65° F). The cool group, consisting of a few species of *Paphiopedilum*, requires night temperatures of 13–15° C (55–60° F).

The standard night temperatures given are optimal. Plants can survive temperatures slightly above or below optimum with ease. Cool-growing species may fail to set buds if grown at a warmer night temperature during a critical winter rest season, but they will suffer no long-term ill effects from brief aberrations in temperature which fall within the range of 5–21° C (40–70° F). As a general rule limit the duration of the aberrant temperature when the deviation is more than 3° C (approx. 5° F) from the optimum range. However, all other considerations being optimal, plants tolerate indefinitely deviations within 3° C of optimum with a minimum of ill effects. Temperature deviations which coincide with major drops in relative humidity are far more damaging to plant tissues.

Elevated day temperature is a problem for greenhouse growers. In virtually every case ventilation must be automatic, and for best growing conditions the thermostat should be set to keep day temperatures below 35° C (90° F). Below the 40th parallel ventilating fans usually run continuously during the sunny days of the year exhausting both heat and humidity. Evaporative coolers are essential in desert climates and are highly recommended elsewhere in the southern latitudes or above 40°S, in the Southern Hemisphere.

The essential factors in maintaining proper temperature ranges for slippers are these: 1) keep night temperatures within or near the optimal ranges, and 2) allow day temperatures to rise at least 11° C (20° F) above night temperatures. Growers cultivating slippers under lights must pay particular attention to the second factor, although this day/night differential occurs readily in modern greenhouses.

Humidity. In humid climates of the latitudes bordering the tropics, humidity exhausted by the ventilating fan may be sufficiently replaced by wetting the aisles and floor several times each day. In the summer season a cooling mist of water directed on plant surfaces is beneficial during the daylight hours prior to late afternoon. Growers will do well to remember, however, that slippers should not be misted in the 2–4 hours before sunset, especially on overcast days, because evaporation virtually ceases at dusk, and moisture retained in the crowns promotes damage by fungi.

Growers who depend upon the humidity of exterior air being brought into the greenhouse by the action of a ventilating fan must be reminded that the subsequent heating of fresh air once inside an even warmer greenhouse will lower the relative humidity. Thus, some supplementary humidity must be supplied year-round no matter how humid the climate. In arid climates culture of slippers is virtually impossible without an adequate humidification system.

Maintaining relative humidity at 50–90% is of enormous value in preserving a healthy ambience for slipper orchids, so a good hygrometer is a wise investment. Not only is high humidity characteristic of their native habitats, but it is the single greatest mitigating factor should temperatures accidentally soar or plummet, because of power failure or other misadventure.

An explanatory word regarding relative humidity is in order at this point. By definition it is the amount of dispersed water vapor in the air at a given temperature relative to the amount of water vapor which air at that temperature is able to absorb. Thus, 100% relative humidity (saturation) usually prevails during rainstorms. Warming the air directly increases its moisture-holding capacity and thus lowers its relative humidity. Conversely, cooling air lessens the amount of water vapor which it is capable of holding so relative humidity rises. Dew is a phenomenon which occurs overnight as the earth and the air above it cool. When dew-point or saturation (100% relative humidity) is reached, subsequent cooling forces humidity out of its dispersed, vaporous state to condense as droplets of liquid water. These droplets accumulate on cool surfaces as dew.

Slipper growers must be aware of how shifts in temperature alter the relative humidity within a greenhouse or on a light bench. Cold weather generates the greatest drops in humidity because air is constantly being warmed to a greater extent. As drier, winter air is warmed, moisture must be dispersed into it in order to maintain a constant relative humidity. Automatic misting systems supply the necessary moisture quite well, but hosing the floor 1 or more times each day is adequate in humid climates.

A misting system is a worthwhile investment for growers who have several hundred plants or more. The summer function of cooling (water absorbs a tremendous amount of heat as it moves into a vaporous state) is as desirable as the humidification function. Growers with large collections which require both operations find a misting system to be essential. Lacking such, the grower is required to be in attendance virtually hourly during seasonal extremes.

Light Intensity

Light is absolutely essential to all green plants, but different species have differing tolerances for light just as they do for heat and other culture variables. Most of the variables discussed in this chapter interact with each other, and light intensity is no exception. Light is the major source of daytime heat in all greenhouses and, therefore, the available light influences not only temperature but humidity and watering schedules as well.

Light intensity is a function of both latitude and season. It increases directly as one moves nearer to the equator or as midsummer approaches. The more perpendicular the rays which strike a surface, the more intense the light and its resultant effects. The 2 genera of slippers which are cultivated in greenhouses are indigenous to tropical latitudes and, therefore, adapted to modified levels of the most intense light received on earth. Shading is applied to orchid greenhouses to approximate light levels of tropical shade of varying depths. Despite their northerly latitude English growers have historically produced some of the world's most beautiful slipper orchids. These northern latitudes where the sun's rays always strike at a more oblique angle present growers with both the problem of reduced light intensity and that of more extreme variations in length of day. Yet, obviously, such conditions lend themselves to successful culture of slippers. The success of the English is a tribute to growers who have summoned their ingenuity and skill to compensate for such grave constraints.

Optimum light for healthy slippers ranges from moderately bright to low, filtered light, and varies with the species or cultivar. As a rule, large-leaved, epiphytic species of *Paphiopedilum* and their hybrids require moderate light, while small-leaved, lowland slippers thrive in more shade. (Refer to Table 1 for detailed information concerning particular species which may deviate from this generality.) *Phragmipedium* require moderate light and rarely flower under low light conditions.

A practical method for determining whether plants are receiving optimum light is to hold your hand about 75 cm (2.5 ft.) above the surface of the bench and examine the shadow which is cast. If the shadow is apparent but with indistinct margins, the light intensity is in the proper general range. A light meter gives a more accurate measure of light intensity, and permits the finetuning needed for particular species.

Based on optimum light intensity, slippers belong to 1 of 3 groups. The high intensity group, although not by any means sun-loving, thrives at 2,500–3,500 footcandles of light. Plants requiring medium light intensity should be grown at 2,000–2,500 fc., and the low intensity slippers prefer 2,000 fc. or less.

Greenhouse shading is necessary to prevent scorching of slipper leaves and severe physiological imbalances resulting from the effects of strong light. The shading required varies with climate, season and the latitude—both of the native habitat of the plants and that of the greenhouse location. Furthermore, in temperate zones shading must be increased in summer and decreased in winter to simulate the steady light levels typically found under canopy in the tropics.

Once the grower has applied shading to the greenhouse, tested light intensity by hand or meter, and installed his slippers, the task of monitoring light intensity has only begun. Winter snows and rains gradually wash shading applications off the glass, so as the sun moves toward a more nearly vertical position in the spring, shading must be renewed to protect slippers from its harsh rays. The observant grower monitors leaf color routinely throughout the year. Dark green leaves with a bluish cast indicate excessive shade, illustrating what is called "soft" growth. Such plants are at increased risk of fungus attack. Light yellowish green leaves indicate that the plants are being grown at their upper tolerance for light intensity. Although "hard" growth enables plants to resist fungus disease more consistently than does "soft" growth, it exerts excessive stress upon the plants' water regulations. Both extremes must be avoided. Plants grown from mid-range to near the upper limits of their optimum range of light intensity perform best. Look for green leaves that have little or no blue or yellow cast to their coloration, bearing in mind, of course, the slight, specific variations which occur naturally in leaf color. Adjust shade to achieve a true green in developing fans, and replace shading as necessary.

Fine tune light intensity by hanging epiphytic slippers over the benches on which shade-loving species are kept. If necessary, place the low light plants underneath the bench, but exercise great care for it is easy to ignore them. In my experience, plants placed under the bench are forgotten, neglected, and rapidly dispatched by fungal organisms.

Watering

The amount and quality of water are critical factors, as is the frequency of watering. There are few hard-and-fast rules, and at best, the generalizations are vague.

Water quality is of great importance. Growers, especially in southwestern United States, should consult their agricultural agent to determine whether harmful levels of alkalis and/or salts are present in their water supply. All growers should be aware that water fit for human consumption is not necessarily safe for slipper orchids. Hard water, with a minimum of other salts besides calcium carbonate, is excellent for *Paphiopedilum* but may be too alkaline for *Phragmipedium*. The majority of *Paphiopedilum* inhabit limestone outcrops in nature and profit from the addition of calcium carbonate to the potting medium. The presence of dissolved calcium carbonate in hard water is a positive factor for this genus. However, toxicity to lime and other alkalis is a consideration in *Phragmipedium* culture. Growers should note that many otherwise harmless salts present in water may accumulate and cause a problem over time. High levels of fluorine, chlorine and sulfur ions should be avoided.

Use of certain water softeners and deionizers may lead to problems as great as those solved by these means. The sure way to solve problems of water quality lies in testing water and following the advice of your agricultural agent. Where water quality is so adverse as to preclude the growing of slippers, collection of rain water is an alternative worth trying. The first of any rainfall should be discarded, because of the presence of air pollutants rinsed out by the initial precipitation.

Water pH is another important quality to be measured. This concept is not difficult to understand at a practical level although it might seem so to those lacking a chemistry background. Water contains dissolved minerals which may produce acidity or alkalinity. Simply stated, pH is a measure of the acidity or alkalinity of a solution. Expressed on a scale from 0 to 14, pH is most acid at 0, neutral at 7, and most alkaline at 14. Moreover, advancing from 8 to 9 on the scale, for example, does not mean that a solution is 1 unit more alkaline, but in fact, each number moved on the scale raises or lowers pH by a power of 10. In other words, a pH of 9 is 10 times more alkaline than a pH of 8. Living organisms function best at or near neutral, the optimum ranging from 6.7–7.3 for most forms. *Paphiopedilum* prefer a pH of 7–7.3, so the addition of small quantities of oystershell, agricultural lime or other soil-sweetening agents to the substrate is beneficial as a neutralizer for the acidity of bark and peat in the substrate as well for as the acidity which may be present in the water supply. Moisture applied to the substrate will become acid without these additions. However, it may be necessary to add small quantities (10–15 parts per thousand) of white vinegar to hard water before watering *Phragmipedium* as the pH required by that genus is 6.7–7.

The obvious importance of understanding pH in living systems lies in avoiding a caustic environment and approximating the optimum pH, but more subtle relationships exist as well. The occurrence of physiological reactions hinges on the activity of enzymes which in most cases run a set of reversible reactions. For example, at a certain pH the digestive enzymes break down food molecules, but at a slightly different pH the very same enzymes are able to resynthesize the complex molecules from their component parts. Thus, the relevance of pH to the metabolism of living things and the importance of providing the optimum pH are evident. The grower's role is not one of painstaking accuracy, however. Maintaining pH within near-normal parameters is adequate because organisms regulate their own pH on the physiological level.

The amount of water provided slippers is important and hinges upon frequency of watering. For the sake of having a point of reference, once or twice a week is a reasonable frequency for watering slippers in most instances. However, beware of this generalization, and work toward maintaining even moisture around the slipper roots. For instance, during a period of severe cold or high wind, the humidity levels may drop sufficiently to require watering an unusual 3 times a week. The roots must not be allowed to become dry as desiccation means certain death for the root system, and plants will be severely set back by root loss should they survive the ordeal. Conversely, constantly soggy roots rot away producing the same end result. The beginner may find the concept of even moisture around the roots confusing, but need not be intimidated. The conditions for which growers strive are perfect drainage to obviate sogginess, and humid air spaces adjacent to the roots. The loose medium in which slippers are potted solves the problem of soggy wetness providing the medium has not decomposed. Perfectly drained plants can be watered daily with no danger of rotted roots. Therefore, growers are advised to repot slippers at 2 year intervals.

Factors other than potting interval affect the rate at which potting medium dries. Through their impact on humidity levels, temperature and air circulation have a directly proportional effect upon drying. The grower should accommodate his watering schedule to the season of the year to some degree. Pot size affects drying inversely; small pots dry more rapidly than large ones. Humidity also has an inverse relationship to drying—the higher the relative humidity, the slower the rate of drying. The amount of humus or peat in the potting medium has a direct bearing upon the water-holding capacity of the medium. Alert growers routinely lift pots feeling for water weight as a means of checking moisture content, and then adjust their watering routines accordingly as the pots feel lighter and dryer at varying rates during different times of the year.

A final caution about the means of watering is needed. A hose is acceptable, but I recommend that jet nozzles be avoided. I use a water-breaker nozzle which gives plants a gentle shower from time to time. If water is applied late in the afternoon use of an automatic device which puts a water spider outlet in each pot, or handwatering with a narrow-spouted watering can is necessary to avoid water standing in the crowns overnight. Pots must never stand in saucers full of water unless gravel is used to hold the pots above water level. Allowing slippers to habitually stand in puddles only encourages root decay. Avoid standing water around buds or in pouches of flowering slippers, as well, because bud blast or blossom drop is predictable within days should this caution be neglected.

Potting

Many factors are involved in potting slippers, including technique, frequency, medium used, choice of plastic or clay pot, pot size, and division of plants. Diversity of opinion on this broad subject is limited solely by the number of slipper growers times the number of variable factors. The aim of this section is to set forth several sets of factors which have intrinsic relationships, to show the rationale behind these relationships, and to encourage the grower to devise his own set of compatible variable factors.

Technique is governed by the choice of medium and the type of pot used. Regardless of those choices, the new pot should be only 2–5 cm (1–2 in.) larger than the previous one. Allow room for 1–3 new growths to mature per existing growth. Plants should not be potted deeper than they were, and the base of the fan of leaves should sit just at the surface of the medium. Dead roots should be removed. Particles of medium which adhere to live roots should be gently removed from the surface. In short, disturb live roots as little as possible. Some effort should be made to replace roots in the pot in the same orientation as they previously grew so as to minimize shock. Pot tightly; tamp the mix around the roots firmly enough so that the plant does not wobble loosely in the pot. Be sure to wet the mix thoroughly before beginning the repotting process as roots will be dried and killed if placed in a bone-dry medium. Finally, a finished product is replaced on the bench only when the identification label has been marked with the repotting date and firmly affixed to plant, pot or stake.

Frequency of potting varies with the medium selected. In general, the finer the texture of the medium, the more rapidly it decomposes. Thus, depending upon particle size, frequency may vary from 1.5–3 years. In most cases the maximum of 3 years should be reserved for media composed largely of nondegradable materials such as cinders or lava rock or resistent hapuu (fern fiber). The vigilant grower observes the rate and degree of decomposition of medium and repots as necessary. Although beginners may reason that it is wise to repot annually to reduce or avoid the problems of sogginess and decomposition, the fact is that plants usually experience some shock from being repotted, and this shock should be minimized.

One caution must be observed with regard to changing from one potting medium to another: slippers frequently lose some or all of their roots when placed in a different type of substrate. Therefore, if a change in medium is desired, make the change by degrees. Use some of the old recipe in making up the new mix and accustom plants to the new medium by gradual stages over a period of years.

Dividing. At repotting time, growers must decide whether to divide or to simply pot up to the next size. The issue of division of slippers must be considered in light of the grower's purpose. Commercial growers divide plants as frequently as possible in order to increase inventory, but hobby growers usually prefer to grow plants with multiple growths both for show and as a means of conserving bench space.

A plant consisting of several old growths, each of which bears 1 or more younger growths, may be divided with ease at repotting time by allowing the rhizome to separate itself into several clusters of plants. Rhizomal deterioration at the site of the oldest growths often divides the plant automatically. If the rhizome must be mechanically separated, growers may cut or break it. If cutting, use a clean, sharp knife, exercising care to reclean the knife thoroughly in a fungicidal solution before moving along to the next plant. Among growers there is little agreement as to the superiority of cutting over breaking of rhizomes. My preference is breaking, unless excessive force is required. Very tough rhizomes are best cut to avoid bruising of tissues.

Separate plants into naturally occurring clusters and avoid removing young fans that have not developed an adequate root system. Treat the cut surfaces with a fungicide, pruning sealant, and/or a mild rooting hormone. With the exception of the fungicide, these applications may be omitted under most circumstances. My schedule permits time for repotting my collection of plants during summer days when heat and humidity reach their maximum; therefore, I apply benomyl because conditions are so favorable for fungal invasion of freshly opened tissues.

Repotting. Many growers use broken crocks in the bottom of the pots, but I find this practice both tedious and unnecessary. Modern-day potting media drain well without the use of crocks, and the use of pots of moderate depth creates the same conditions quite well. If used, crocks must be cleaned well before each reuse or discarded. I am not convinced that the benefit is worth the trouble of scrubbing them.

The choice between clay pots and plastic pots is less critical in repotting slipper orchids than it is among other genera of orchids due to the small size of slippers. Only rarely is a slipper too large to be manageable in a heavier clay container, or large enough to tip over easily in lightweight pots. Cleaning plastic pots for reuse is extremely easy. Aeration of roots is somewhat improved by the use of clay, but its porosity is equally disadvantageous in its retention of salts and fungus spores. I use plastic pots exclusively, but my reason is merely that it is convenient and clean. Having also grown slippers in clay pots, I find either type of pot produces good results.

Much disagreement exists among growers about when to repot slippers. At one extreme are those who insist that slippers must be repotted after blooming, while a few growers confidently insist upon repotting before blooming occurs. The vast majority probably repot whenever busy schedules permit. Beginners should avoid repotting before blooming because only adept fingers are capable of avoiding mechanical damage to buds. Furthermore, shock can cause bud blast in the event of root damage. However, the most important element in the whole matter is to get the repotting done on a schedule governed by substrate condition. Loss of a bud is minor in comparison to loss of an entire plant through neglect of repotting.

Substrate. There are many types of potting media which growers in turn modify to suit their particular needs. If the mix in use gives good results, stick with it. While most growers are constantly on the alert for a better mix, hoping always to grow bigger, better slippers, the mix used is one of the least critical of the culture variables. Two mixes having rather different merits are worthy of comment: Off mix and UC mix. Modifications are possible with either.

Off mix is widely used for *Cattleya* orchids and available premixed from many dealers. Off mix consists of bark, perlite, fiber, peat and an assortment of nutrients. Modified Off mix containing seedling-grade bark is the most suitable for growing slippers. Its major disadvantage is that particle size of seedling-grade bark is relatively large, so potting firmly in such a medium requires skill. The larger particles readily resist decomposition for 2 years, however, and this is a major advantage. I use modified Off mix, consisting of 4 parts seedling fir bark, 1 part redwood fiber, 1 part perlite and 1 part peat. To this basic mix, I add 1 part of a nutrient mixture composed of 2 parts oystershell or other coarse lime source, 1 part Mag-Amp, 1 part Osmocote 13–13–13, and a slight dusting of Micromax for trace minerals. With this rich mix of slow-release nutrients present, it is still necessary to fertilize with high-nitrogen applications during the spring and summer months, to counterbalance the activity of microorganisms which utilize nitrogen in the process of decomposing the bark. Of course, when preparing mix for *Phragmipedium*, the oystershell must be omitted.

The UC mix differs from the Off mix primarily in texture. As it was initially developed by the University of California, it was composed of inert ingredients, but it easily lends itself to modifications which include nutrients. The base mix is 1 part coarse sand, 3 parts ground fir bark and 3 parts rice hulls, having a particle size about twice that of coarse coffee grounds. The texture of the UC mix greatly facilitates potting. However, the surface-to-volume ratio is so increased by the small particle size that decomposition is quite rapid. All nutrients must be provided, so growers usually incorporate oystershell into the mix at a rate of 1 part. Additions of bone and blood meal, potassium sulfate, lime, Mag-Amp, cottonseed meal or other nutrient sources are needed, if growers wish to avoid adding some soluble fertilizer to the watering regime each week. As in the case of Off mix, even when additional nutrients are incorporated, additional applications of high nitrogen fertilizer are required during the spring to compensate for nitrogen depletion by microorganisms. A slow-release nutrient supplement prepared following the same formulation as that given for the Off mix supplement in the preceding paragraph, can be added to the UC mix as 1 part. Frequency of watering is reduced by use of UC mix because of its texture and smaller air spaces. Because of its compact quality, some growers restrict use of UC mix to clay pots. However, plastic pots are completely compatible with UC mix as long as watering schedules are adjusted properly. The single feature of UC mix which limits its flexibility is the speed with which it decomposes, once this process begins. Growers must repot within a month or so of a somewhat suddenly precipitated change in the substrate.

The addition of charcoal to potting media is an option upon which growers rarely agree. The pro-charcoal faction swears by it, while others insist that, having gotten by so well without it, there is no need to bother. Undoubtedly, charcoal is an antistagnation agent, and when repotting is performed on schedule, there is no obvious need for such an agent. If there is the slightest doubt about the prompt repotting of plants, the presence of 1 part charcoal in the medium is advisable, especially as charcoal does not decompose.

Repotting begins when clean pots, tools and premoistened medium are all assembled. Plants should be inspected for live pests and signs of recent damage, as scrutiny of the basal regions is facilitated during repotting. Afterwards, old mix and all weeds should be discarded since these materials create a site for pests to breed if left underneath benches. This waste material is useful as garden mulch, however, or as an ingredient in a compost heap where pests are killed by the heat of fermentation.

Nutrients

Successful growers devote considerable attention to the general principles involved in meeting nutrient needs of slipper orchids. There are all-purpose, complete and incomplete, organic and inorganic fertilizers, and both the quality and quantity of the nutrients contained may vary drastically. Choices include fertilizers that are applied as slow-release solids and those that are applied in solution. The quantity required and the proper season for application are also matters for concern. A few commonsense guidelines will clear away much confusion. Some fundamental knowledge of which nutrients are available in a fertilizer, as well as the function of each, is invaluable to growers.

Fertilizer labels display an N–P–K ratio. This ratio is a listing by weight of the available percentages of the 3 major ingredients. Thus, in a bag of 10–10–10 lawn fertilizer weighing 100 lbs., 10 lbs. are N or nitrogen compounds, 10 lbs. are P or phosphates, and 10 lbs. are K or potassium salts. The remaining 70 lbs. are inert earths in some fertilizers, or are calcium carbonate (lime) in others. The 70% dilution of the active ingredients is necessary to prevent scorching of plant tissues by the application of a dry fertilizer. Fertilizers designed to be dissolved in water are diluted by the quantity of water to be mixed in. For a soluble product a 30–10–10 ratio indicates that 30% of the prepared solution is nitrogen sources, 10% is phosphorus, another 10% potassium salts, while the remaining 50% is water.

The N–P–K ratio is vital information for the grower. With this knowledge and an understanding of the nutrient role of each of these elements, the fertilizer best suited to a particular purpose can be selected. Nitrogen promotes vigorous growth of vegetative organs. Young seedlings, single growth plants or any plants grown just for foliage should be fertilized with a nutrient mixture that is proportionally higher in nitrogen. Commercial growers, therefore, apply somewhat more nitrogen when fertilizing slippers than do hobby growers. The presence of bark in the substrate, and the resultant depletion of nitrogen by microorganisms decomposing the bark, is another factor increasing the quantity of nitrogen required. Seasonal demands must also be considered, as nitrogen is more rapidly depleted in spring, when daylength increases and growth accelerates.

The role of the second element in fertilizer, phosphorus, is the promotion of flowering and fruit production. The hobby grower thus selects a fertilizer which is proportionally high in phosphate content to induce the maximum number of growths to mature and flower.

The third element, potassium, promotes sturdy cell structure and, consequently, tougher plant parts. Weak flower stalks and limp leaves may, for example, indicate a need for a slightly increased amount of potassium, although water stress, insufficient light or certain physiological conditions produce similar symptoms.

The preceding explanation is an entirely practical and simplistic overview of N–P–K ratios as they relate to plant requirements, so the reader may wish to obtain further information about the roles of these 3 elements in plant nutrition for specific purposes or needs.

The role of each of the minerals in the N–P–K ratio is only the beginning of the nutrient story, however. Availability of nutrients to plants is a major criterion in selecting a fertilizer. Nutrients must be soluble in water in the form of ionizing mineral (inorganic) salts to be absorbed by the plant cells. Solubility of the nutrient is critical; greater solubility makes for greater availability to plants, but it also increases the risk of scorching tissues should excessive quantities be applied. Inorganic nitrogen is rather freely soluble. Therefore, applications of nitrogen should be made at lower strengths and greater frequency to provide the amount of nitrogen necessary for both slippers and decomposition microorganisms while still avoiding tissue burn. Availability of much of the nutrient content of organic fertilizer (nitrogen-rich urea and ammonia are exceptions which cause nitrogen burn if applied in concentrations comparable to those of bone meal and other organic nutrients) is delayed by the necessity for decomposition to inorganic form by the action of microorganisms.

Most forms of phosphates are poorly soluble. Calcium phosphate in bone meal, for example, has been estimated to persist undissolved in the substrate without yielding more than 5% of its nutrients over the 2 year period before repotting! The phosphate source known as super-phosphate is the most soluble, although risk of scorching is still minimal because its solubility is considerably lower than that of either nitrogen or potassium salts.

Potassium sources are largely soluble and readily available. Apply with caution to avoid scorching of roots with potash and other compounds of potassium. As in the case of nitrogen, recommended usage is frequent applications of dilute strength.

Required nutrients are not limited to the 3 elements listed in N–P–K ratios. Growers should be aware that certain fertilizers may be limited to those 3, or to N–P–K plus lime, so careful reading of labels is mandatory. Fertilizers with no more nutrient minerals than those 3 are called incomplete fertilizers. Reliance on them results in malnourished plants.

The sources of calcium and magnesium are carbonates and sulfates. Lime, the carbonate source, is both a nutrient and a pH regulator. It is relatively poorly soluble. The sulfate forms are more freely soluble. Of course, lime should be avoided in the culture of *Phragmipedium* because of pH requirements.

The amounts of additional kinds of nutrients required by plants are so small that these minerals are referred to as trace elements. Iron, sulfur, zinc, copper, nickel and molybdenum are but a few of those which have been shown to be necessary to the health of plants in trace quantities. Few or none of these elements are present in an incomplete inorganic fertilizer. Supplements are available commercially; seaweeds are excellent sources of trace minerals, but should be purchased rather than scavenged because of the possibly toxic level of sea salt. Fish meals and emulsions are reliable sources of trace elements. Organic fertilizers, though not immediately available to plants in most cases, usually are a reliable source of trace minerals.

Because the list of nutrients is tediously long, and lest the reader become convinced that solubilities must be memorized, it is appropriate at this point to bring some order and common sense into this discussion. Use a complete inorganic fertilizer weekly, at one-half the recommended strength if the substrate lacks nutrients. With nutrient-enriched media use it once each month together with frequent but dilute applications of 30–10–10 during spring and summer. Reduce all applications to less than half this frequency during the darker winter months. Be sure calcium carbonate is available in the substrate, year-round, for *Paphiopedilum*.

Some growers prefer to use a cheaper, incomplete inorganic fertilizer. It should be applied at the appropriate intervals depending upon the nutrients present in the substrate. Trace minerals must then be supplied by watering with solutions of fish emulsion, violet water (a solution prepared by steeping manure in a vat of water), or some commercial source of trace minerals.

I use the modified, nutrient-enriched version of the Off mix recommended in the previous section and limit applications of fertilizer solutions to just a very few in spring. I hand-water 4–5 times with 30–10–10, mixed ½ strength, and at least once with a solution of fish emulsion. The rest of the year, I apply only water without proportioners or other encumbrances.

Above all, the reader is cautioned to practice moderation in fertilizer application since slipper orchids as a group are never heavy feeders. Half-strength dilutions are always recommended, while many growers maintain that very infrequent applications provide success even in nutrient-poor substrate.

Some controversy exists about the virtues of foliar feeding. I believe that there is some merit in an occasional application of weak fertilizer to leaves on early spring mornings, but it may be that I merely enjoy performing the task sufficiently to convince myself the plants actually benefit from it. I can offer no documentation on the efficacy of foliar feeding of slipper orchids, but I do reiterate that late afternoon foliar moisture encourages fungal attack.

Another generality applies to the varying requirements for nutrients among the groups of slippers. Species of *Paphiopedilum* require the least fertilizer; hybrids of that genus need slightly more. The species and hybrids of *Phragmipedium* use the largest quantity of nutrients, requiring amounts closely approximating the quantity of fertilizer typically applied to orchids in general. Seedlings are usually given slightly more frequent applications of dilute high-nitrogen fertilizers for promotion of rapid growth. All slippers may be considered as low to moderate users of nutrients. A rule of thumb is to dilute fertilizers to half the strength recommended for nonorchid plants.

Pests and Diseases

The relative freedom of slipper orchids from pests and diseases in comparison to other plants is one of their more gratifying characteristics. As a consequence, growers are able to maintain beautiful, healthy foliage with a minimum of care. The grower's major task in keeping slippers free of parasites and predators lies in maintaining a clean greenhouse environment. Clean glass and benches along with floors kept clear of detritus discourage proliferation of insects, mites and fungi. Pots should be kept free of *Oxalis* and other weeds in the course of routine housekeeping aimed at preventing pest problems. Destruction of potential breeding sites for infectious organisms eliminates much of the risk of attack and saves the time, effort and expense of combating pests. Thus, growers who routinely employ pest-prevention measures have more attractive greenhouses and spare themselves many labors.

Obviating the use of pesticides is not only beneficial to the environment, but to the health of the grower as well. I cannot emphasize too strongly the urgency of exercising care in the course of pest-prevention programs to avoid unnecessary inhalation of or skin contact with poisonous chemicals. Protective clothing and masks are wise precautions against accidental exposure to toxic levels of sprays used in the confined atmospheres of greenhouses. Taking time to bathe immediately after pesticide use is recommended.

Careful reading of pesticide labels is mandatory to determine toxicity to humans, livestock, particular pests, and even to certain plants. The irony of killing or severely damaging a valued plant through use of a pesticide which has no toxicity for the pertinent parasite is obvious.

Mites. Spider mites and, occasionally, other mites attack slipper orchids. Because these 8-legged pests are only distantly related to insects, many insecticides are ineffective against them. Further, mites readily develop immunities to miticides, so prepared growers, particularly those who live in warmer climates, stock an arsenal of miticides. These persistent and prolific pests challenge the ingenuity of growers everywhere. It is important to recognize them early and to initiate a prompt and exhaustive campaign against them.

Infestations of spider mites occur primarily, but not exclusively, during the hot summer months. The minute individuals usually inhabit the undersurfaces of leaves. Appearing to the naked eye as a powdering of red dust, the mites may go undetected until they have built small webs among the leaves or even until the leaves are damaged and marked with a silvery stippling.

Early detection and faithful attention to a spray regimen are equally important because of certain features of the mite life cycle. The speed with which they mature and reproduce is a direct function of the ambient temperature. At temperatures above 22° C (80° F), new hatchlings reach maturity and lay eggs in the span of 3 days or so. A succession of 3 or more applications at 3-day intervals, varying the miticide used each time, is the most effective means of control. This regimen insures that each newly hatched generation is eradicated as soon as it emerges and becomes vulnerable to spraying. Care must be taken so that miticide makes contact with the undersurfaces of leaves, and droplets of spray drain down to penetrate into the crevices between overlapping leaves in a fan. All surfaces, including the pot rims and the substrate, should be thoroughly saturated with the miticide. Spray at least twice more after visible infestation is over because an individual mite is virtually invisible yet capable of reinfesting the entire bench in a week. Furthermore, eggs are resistant to miticide, so spray must reach the hatchling at the right time. There are slow-release preparations consisting of microencapsulated particles of pesticide, some of which is released each time plants are misted or watered over a period of several weeks. Such products are useful for 1 of the several applications used in combating mites. Systemic products which poison the plant and make it toxic to the predator are valuable, but create a problem in the environment at large. Disposal of dead leaves and potting medium directly into vegetable garden soil could pose a hazard to human health. Long-term consequences of the use of systemic pesticides are still being studied.

Growers must be aware when handling infested plants that contaminated skin and clothing promote spreading of mites to uninfested plants. If possible, isolate infested plants in quarantine until leaves are clear of mites. Never underestimate the lethal potential of organisms in this group for they are insidious and voracious predators.

Scale. Several scale insects prey upon slippers, including soft brown scale, Boisduval scale and hemispherical scale. These organisms are more visible than mites and, therefore, more easily detected by vigilant growers. Scale insects are, however, well-protected by their outer coverings so that removal of adults requires wiping leaves clean. Contact insecticides are effective against juveniles, and systemic insecticides are useful in killing adults and preventing crawlers from establishing themselves as armored adults. Eggs of most types resist all insecticides.

An infestation by scale is an indication that a grower has neglected the daily close scrutiny of plants which distinguishes top-notch growers. One bout with these tenacious, armored insects provides sufficient motivation to reform lax habits, although a single bout is a rare occurrence. Most commonly, scale tends to recur periodically, until benches and floors are completely cleaned and all detritus is removed. Cleaning leaves and rhizomes by hand is painstaking and time-consuming work, but overlooking just 1 live organism is sufficient to reinfest the plants. Recommended prevention requires use of a systemic insecticide. The application must be renewed periodically to maintain strength. Treatment of an infestation is laborious, and may be avoided if preventive housekeeping is practiced in combination with vigilance and temporary quarantine of newly acquired plants.

Resistance to insecticides is a problem among the various species of scale. Good insecticidal soaps are among the safest products, although resistance to them may build up rather quickly. Growers should employ a variety of insecticides considered safe for slippers in their battle against scale.

Mealy Bug. This ubiquitous pest is unsightly and potentially damaging, but is, perhaps, the easiest to detect and vanquish. Some species of mealy bugs bear live young while others lay eggs in cottony masses. Control of this insect is relatively easy. Most insecticides are efficacious in killing the organisms, and 2–3 sprays at 5–7 day intervals should eliminate subsequent hatchlings.

Occasionally, however, mealy bugs become tolerant of particular insecticides. A thorough washing of plants in a sudsy bath followed by a low-force rinse with a jet nozzle is effective in eliminating persistent mealy bugs.

Snails and Slugs. Slipper roots are not as delectable to these pests as are those of other orchids. Damage to roots, fans and blooms is rare.

Molluscan pests are best eliminated by products which contain metaldehyde. I avoid the arsenic-laced snail bait products; not only do the pellets grow unsightly molds when moistened, but they seem to be irresistible to dogs. One experience of dosing a dachshund with an emetic was enough to send me in search of a different product. Metaldehyde must be handled with the same care used in dispersing other pesticides. Its advantages are its lack of attractiveness to pets, coupled with overnight death to snails and slugs that come into contact with it. Victims of metaldehyde poisoning should be disposed of in keeping with the same rules for safe handling and disposal of pesticides.

Growers interested in organic pest control find marked success with the use of shallow containers of beer to attract and kill snails and slugs. In any case, dead snails and slugs must be removed from the greenhouse and disposed of—a distasteful task.

Fungal and Bacterial Diseases. These infections are the major cause of concern to slipper growers. Plants already weakened by prior neglect or pest attack are particularly susceptible to infection and rapid death. Both proper sanitation practices and adequate air circulation belong in a regimen of prevention against the decay organisms which attack slippers. Here again the grower's vigilance may determine the life or death of valued plants. A tendency of these microorganisms to become tolerant or resistant to fungicides dictates that a spectrum of fungicides is superior to a limited selection.

Brown rot caused by species of *Erwinia* is the most common of the bacterial rots. Infection frequently begins at leaf tips, and may be transmitted by pests or mechanical damage. The infected area turns brown and soft and may be punctuated with translucent blisters. It spreads downward toward the base of the leaf at a variable rate of speed, and may invade an entire growth or, by spreading through the rhizome, may eventually destroy the whole plant.

Treatment of early infections involves the environment as well as the ailing plants. Following a thorough housecleaning to remove breeding sites for fungi and bacteria, spray the entire greenhouse with benomyl. Plant care involves excision of the leaf well behind the infected portion, and dusting the cut surface with an effective fungicide. When the disease has progressed to an entire growth, more drastic treatment is required to protect the rhizome from infection. All infected parts must be removed, borderline material must be trimmed away, and only clean, healthy tissue retained. Knives must be scrupulously disinfected, and transmission by contaminated hands and clothing must be avoided. The apparently healthy remainder of the plant should be soaked in a Natriphene solution for an hour, and then repotted in fresh medium. Dispose of all contaminated medium carefully. Keep the newly potted remnant away from uninfected slippers for at least a month, and grow it marginally drier than usual. Avoid placing the invalid plant under the bench or in any deep shade. Also avoid subjecting it to either harsh light or severe drying.

Brown rot is more likely to attack during periods of increased heat and humidity, or when there are seasonal changes in heat, light or humidity. Constant vigilance is called for especially in summer and autumn. Standing water in the crowns of plants and more frequent insect bites conspire with heat and humidity at this time to maximize the opportunities for infection to occur.

Bud blast and root loss may be fungal or bacterial in nature, but this is not well-documented. Much loss of buds and roots is currently ascribed to physiological responses by the plants, although some is due to unknown cause. At the stage of emergence from the crown, bud blast may be the result of water damage. Subsequent blasting is often a response to the presence of minute quantities of certain hydrocarbon gases in the air. The cause is especially puzzling in light of the frequency with which only 1 of 2 buds on the same plant blasts. Root loss from rotting in soggy medium is obviously fungal in nature. However, prevention of this rot is as simple as regular repotting. Treatment afterwards should include soaking in Natriphene and/or dusting with a fungicide. Root loss associated with shock at repotting in different medium is not believed to be disease-related.

Virus. Although suspected in some instances, the presence of viral bodies in slipper cells has not been demonstrated. Until clear evidence is produced, certain deformations or color breaks may be considered to be either viral in origin or to be part of a quite different genetic disturbance. However, unless virus is shown to be absent from slippers, growers are well-advised to use only clean knives, pots and other implements when tending their slippers.

In summary, I wish to emphasize that slipper culture must be a labor of love. It must never become so arduous as to tempt growers to postpone necessary care. Each grower discovers a personal approach to the most efficient and productive culture methods from experience combined with comparing notes and sharing useful cultural practices with other growers. Beginners gain much valuable information from experienced growers, while their mentors benefit from increased confidence and enthusiasm through sharing their expertise. These mutual exchanges are among the priceless fringe benefits enjoyed by slipper growers.

CHAPTER 3

The Genus *Cypripedium*

The genus *Cypripedium* consists of approximately 40 species, all of which are deciduous and require a period of winter dormancy. Not found in greenhouse culture, these slippers are grown where climate permits in garden culture by wildflower enthusiasts, but are best left in natural sites protected from collectors and land developers. Many of the species are difficult to naturalize; transplantation is all too frequently fatal. While asymbiotic culture of *Cypripedium* from seed is a technique in its infancy, it is the preferred cultural practice for it is the only means of conserving wild populations which offers a ray of hope for the survival of many species of this genus.

The genus is circumboreal with several species ranging from above the 15th parallel in the Northern Hemisphere to the Arctic Circle. Most of the genus is found at or north of the 30th parallel, preferring temperate to subarctic climates, although Yunnan, Taiwan and several other major Asian ranges lie between the 20th and 30th parallels. Three species are notable exceptions: *Cypripedium irapeanum* and *C. dickinsonianum*, allied tropical species of Mexico and Guatemala that are anomalous in the Western Hemisphere by virtue of their southerly location, and *C. subtropicum*, a Tibetan species. All 3 exhibit similarities to the genus *Selenipedium* in their elongated, canelike aerial stems and their floriferousness.

The vegetative structures of this genus exhibit the greatest variety to be found in the subfamily Cypripedioideae and range from acaulescent or virtually stemless plants bearing 2–3 basal leaves to plants producing many leaves about an upright axis. Leaves are dimorphic in many species, and distinguishable either as basal, sheathing leaves frequently dry and brown, or as open foliar appendages. Both the number of leaves present and the leaf shape are highly variable from species to species. Height ranges from a few centimeters (4–6 in.) to 1.5 meters (approx. 5 ft.) and is drastically expanded since publication of *C. subtropicum* Chen & Lang sp. nov. in 1986.

Mature plants flower during spring or summer, either bearing a peduncle from the center of a basal whorl of leaves or extending the leaf-bearing axis as a floral stalk. The species which produce a peduncle are more likely to be unifloral.

Enormous diversity in preference of habitat is exhibited within the genus, and wide intraspecific habitat tolerance is a feature of certain species. The variety of habitats includes low acid bogs, upland coniferous forests, prairies and meadows, deciduous and mixed forests, roadsides, river basins and limestone outcrops. A few species are endemic to a small region, while others are widespread on 1 or more continents. For example, the *C. calceolus* complex is fairly ubiquitous and thrives in many types of habitats across North America, Europe and Asia, while *C. californicum* is very restricted in both habitat and range.

Cypripedium are perennial from a rhizome. Both the leaves and the aerial stems, if present, are deciduous. Leaves are thin, plicate, and green without tessellation, with the exceptions of *C. margaritaceum* and *C. wumengense* which bear spotted leaves. Fairly large, leaflike bracts subtend the flowers of all but a few species.

One of the most interesting characteristics found in several of the slippers of this genus is the production of a contact irritant, cypripedin, by the abundant glandular hairs of flowers, stems and leaves. Persons sensitive to this toxin react with skin eruptions resembling those caused by poison ivy (*Rhus radicans*). *Cypripedium irapeanum*, *C. calceolus*, and *C. reginae* are among those reported to produce the irritant. Fortunately, not everyone is susceptible. It is not surprising, however, that clumps of *C. calceolus* remain ungrazed by cattle and other herbivores.

Several species of *Cypripedium* yield a drug which, in powder or liquid form, has been used to treat such nervous disorders as neuralgia, hysteria, epilepsy and chorea, as well as joint inflammation resulting from scarlet fever, according to Correll (1950). *Cypripedium calceolus* is the major source plant, and the same volatile oils which irritate skin may be the active ingredients of the drug. The annual consumption of this drug is currently negligible.

More than 2 centuries ago, Linnaeus named and described the genus *Cypripedium* from 2 Greek words meaning "Aphrodite" and "foot," out of which grew the term "Aphrodite's shoe" and later, "Lady's Slipper." He defined the genus from a specimen of *C. calceolus*. For many years this genus name was used by early collectors and growers to encompass all known slipper orchids. Long after botanists had established the 4 genera of slipper orchids and in fact, until the 1960s growers continued to refer to all slippers as "cyps."

Within *Cypripedium* several taxonomic questions should be addressed. The generic status of *C. arietinum* R. Brown, for example, is currently under review. Atwood (1984b) proposed that this species be placed in the genus *Criosanthes* Raf., based upon its 2 lateral sepals, spurred lip, antherlike staminode, and a difference in epidermal cell size. This change may be justified, but the rather ephemeral bloom of *C. arietinum* is a variant feature which provides an evolutionarily valid reason to set this species apart. The characteristics which Atwood cites as the foundation for his proposed isolation of this species are all morphological, all primitive, and appear to have little bearing upon the competitive success of the species. Production of flowers which last but a day or 2 is a trait indicative of an evolutionary advance over species with longer lasting flowers, and is a critical adaptation with major implications for the success or failure of the species. In my opinion, the ephemeral flower lends more significant weight to the argument for reclassification of *C. arietinum*. Perhaps conservatism in reclassification at genus level is the wisest course until exhaustive genetic studies have elucidated relationships in the genus to a far finer degree. The occurrence of unfused lateral sepals in *C. reginae* and in other species to a lesser degree supports the advisability of delaying such a decision, pending further study. Atwood (personal communication) expressed a degree of reconsideration of his proposal, after 5 years' retrospective, stating that in light of the responses it had elicited from other students of the genera, separating this species seemed to have generated more confusion than it had resolved.

A different sort of dilemma arises with regard to *C. calceolus* L. Several varieties of this widespread species have been described. Because of strong similarities between this species and several other named species, *C. calceolus* must be considered to be a complex. Furthermore, while there is interest in elevating 1 or more of its varieties to species rank, there is an equally acceptable opinion that other currently discrete species may deserve inclusion within the complex. Until the true relationships are revealed, feelings run high and eventually reputations among taxonomists may be at stake if the disputed species/varieties remain unresolved for several decades. For the sake of clarity within these pages, I have treated the species as a complex incorporating the aforementioned variants. It seems to me to be an efficient way of sidestepping controversy so as to get information across without having to choose or defend either viewpoint. I suggest that electrophoretic data be gathered, examined and tabulated, and that scientists then sit down and define the degree of divergence in nucleic acids, alkaloids and other molecular cell components required to establish species rank. Determination of the relative importance of ecospecific criteria is equally imperative. Only such an orderly method can provide the rest of us with evidence—as opposed to opinion or conjecture—with which to resolve taxonomic disputes.

Our understanding of *Cypripedium*, in particular, is obscured to a greater degree because it was the first of the 4 genera in the subfamily to be described, so early errors proliferated and became more deeply imbedded in complexity. See the description of *C. vernayi*, listed at the end of the chapter, as an example of a probable error persisting in the literature today. The need for clarification of the number of species within this genus is urgent. There may be as few as 35 species or as many as 50. A thorough taxonomic revision is required to eliminate the redundancy and confusion created by the existence of several synonyms for many of the species. In actual fact, it is often difficult to determine which binomials represent a discrete species and which are merely synonyms. This chaotic situation is but one facet of a many-faceted problem confronting taxonomists.

Attempts to investigate Asian species have been hampered by obstacles such as near extinction, political barriers and false trails laid by early collectors to preserve their finds from rivals. However, the past decade has provided opportunities for substantial contributions to the body of knowledge about Asian species. These contributions must be expanded and incorporated into a more profound understanding of the genus.

Until recently, hybrids in this genus were largely restricted to a few natural ones because, although several artificial hybrids were reportedly produced and grown in England and elsewhere, records of those hybrids were allowed to fall into obscurity. Correll (1950) listed as natural hybrids × *C. Andrewsii* from *C. candidum* and *C. calceolus*, as well as × *C. Favillianum* from the same parentage, although a different variant form of *C. calceolus* is incoporated into each hybrid. If *C. candidum* is indeed an alba form of *C. calceolus*, these hybrids deserve a closer look before being accorded true hybrid status. Darnell (1930) dicusses *C. Barbeyi* (*calceolus* × *macranthum*) as a vinicolor hybrid.

Neglect of man-made hybrids of *Cypripedium* is due to both the difficulty in cultivating many species and the problems with propagation from seed, but advances are possible. As growing this genus from seed becomes more practical, it seems likely that the culture of the species will become sufficiently lucrative to inspire limited interest in commercial hybridization. During this decade, Whitlow (1988b) has pioneered artificial hybridization in this genus. Further discussion of his contribution is found in Chapter 7.

As an impetus toward the resolution of the taxonomic chaos in *Cypripedium* and in anticipation of a thorough revision of this genus, I submit a preliminary structure which both illustrates the alliances among the various species and complexes and reflects some degree of taxonomic integrity. The structure I have devised is as follows:

Subgenus *Criosanthes*
       Cypripedium arietinum R. Brown
           Syn. *Arietinum americanum* Bech.
           Syn. *Criosanthes arietina* (R. Brown) House
           Syn. *Criosanthes borealis* Raf.
           Syn. *Cypripedium plectrochilum* Franch.

Subgenus *Cypripedium*
   Alliance *Cypripedium*
      C. calceolus L.
          var. *kentuckiense* Reed
             Syn. *C. furcatum* Raf.
          var. *parviflorum* Salisb.
          var. *planipetalum* (Fern.) Morris & Eames
          var. *pubescens* Willd.
      (related binomials: *C. alternifolius* St. L., *C. cruciatum* Dulac., *C. hirsutum* Mill, *C. marianus* Krantz., *C. parvulum* Fedde., *C. vaganum* Cockl. & Baker)
      C. candidum Muhl. ex Willd.
      C. cordigerum D. Don
      C. henryi Rolfe
          Syn. *C. chinense* Franch.
      C. microsaccus Kraenzl.
      C. montanum Dougl. ex Lindl.
          Syn. *C. occidentale* Wats.
      C. shanxiense S. C. Chen sp. nov.

   Alliance *Corymbosa*
      C. fasciculatum Kell. ex S. Wats.
          Syn. *C. knightae* A. Nels.
          Syn. *C. pusillum* Rolfe

   Alliance *Macrantha*
      C. amesianum Schltr.
      C. corrugatum Franch.
          var. *obesum* Franch.
      C. fasciolatum Franch.
          (possibly including *C. franchetii* Rolfe sensu Breiger)
      C. himalaicum Rolfe
          Syn. *C. pulchrum* Ames & Schltr.
      C. lanuginosum Schltr.
          Syn. *C. lanuginosa* Schltr.
      C. macranthum Sw.
          Syn. *C. franchetii* Rolfe
          var. *albiflorum* (Makino) Ohwi
          var. *rebunense* (Kudo) Ohwi
      C. speciosum Rolfe
      C. thunbergii Bl.
      C. tibeticum King ex Hemal.
      C. ventricosum Sw.
          Syn. *C. manchuricum* Stapf

C. wilsoni Rolfe

C. yunnanense Franch.

Alliance *Flabellifolia*

C. acaule Ait.

Syn. *C. humile* Pursh.

Syn. *C. nutans* Schltr.

Syn. *Fissipes acaulis* Sm.

C. bardolphianum W. W. Sm. & Farrer

Syn. *C. nutans* Schltr.

var. *zhongdianense* S. C. Chen var. nov.

C. debile Reichb. f.

Syn. *C. cardiophyllum* Franch.

C. ebracteatum Rolfe

C. elegans Reichb. f.

C. farreri W. W. Smith

C. formosanum Hay.

C. japonicum Thunb.

Syn. *C. cathayanum* Chien.

C. margaritaceum Franch.

Syn. *C. fargesii* Franch.

C. micranthum Franch.

C. palangshanense Tang & Wang

C. wumengense S. C. Chen sp. nov.

Alliance *Guttatum*

C. guttatum Sw.

var. *guttatum* Sw.

var. *yatabeanum* Makino

(related binomials: *C. orientale* Spreng., *C. variegatum* Georyi, *C. calceolus*
var. *variegatum* Falk., *C. wardii* Rolfe)

Alliance *Obtusipetala*

C. californicum A. Gray

C. dickinsonianum Hagsater

C. flavum Ward

Syn. *C. luteum* Franch.

C. irapeanum Llave & Lex.

Syn. *C. molle* Lindl.

Syn. *C. splendidum* Scheid.

C. passerinum Richards.

C. reginae Walt.

Syn. *C. album* Ait.

Syn. *C. canadense* Michx.

Syn. *C. spectabile* Salisb.

C. subtropicum Chen & Lang sp. nov.

When in devising this structure I have regrouped species which were placed in former sections, I have deliberately avoided use of those section names. However, when I have only added to existing sections, I have retained the old name, as in my Alliance *Cypripedium*. My attempt to group those species most closely allied employs an infrastructure which I have called an "alliance." The reader should not infer that such a grouping is an accepted taxon nor should it be construed as anything more than an indication of interspecific similarities. At the current informational level, the term *alliance* refers to an assemblage of similar species, and should not be confused with a *complex*—a group of variants within a highly variable species. Due both to the difficulty of precisely defining a species and to the immense body of information yet to be discovered about most of these species, however, certain cases exist in which an alliance may in the future be determined to be a complex or vice versa.

The alliance designated *Obtusipetala* may represent a taxon, or it may be divisible on the basis of the number of flowers produced. In the latter case, *C. flavum*, *C. passerinum*, and perhaps, *C. reginae* would remain together, leaving the exceptionally multifloral species set apart in an alternate alliance, perhaps called *Multiflora*.

The alliance which I have called *Flabellifolia* contains a subgroup of species which produce no floral bracts, including *C. ebracteatum*, *C. margaritaceum*, *C. micranthum* and *C. wumengense*. This alliance may therefore be further divisible on the basis of such a criterion, pending evaluation of a spectrum of criteria. Likewise, there are additional criteria awaiting discovery in all these alliances.

The intention of my proposed restructuring of the genus is threefold: to create cohesive groups illustrating relationships, to promote understanding by horticulturists and to stimulate taxonomic discussion. Intensive morphological, cytological and biochemical investigations are sure to reveal much valuable data which will further clarify interspecific relationships adequately for taxonomic revision into valid sections.

The remainder of the chapter is devoted to discussions of the species of *Cypripedium* arranged alphabetically by species name. Each consists of varietal names and synonyms where applicable, range and habitat information, a description of vegetative and floral structures, cultural notes, data on time of flowering and common names. Color plates illustrate many of the species.

Arietinum americanum Bech. See *Cypripedium arietinum* R. Brown.

Criosanthes arietina (R. Brown) House. See *Cypripedium arietinum* R. Brown.

Criosanthes borealis Raf. See *Cypripedium arietinum* R. Brown.

Cypripedium acaule Ait.   PLATES 1 & 2

GEOGRAPHIC DISTRIBUTION *Cypripedium acaule* is a native of eastern North America. Ranging from Alabama northward into eastern Canada and Newfoundland, it follows generally the course of the ancient Appalachian range. However, it extends not only into the eastern Piedmont but westward into the northern Plains states and the central Canadian provinces.

HABITAT This species is found in pine forests, hardwood forests, coastal sand hills, acid bogs and swamps at a variety of elevations. While habitats diverge widely in temperature and moisture levels as well as latitudinal and elevational climate zones, the 2 constants in this wide variety of sites are shade and soil acidity. Abundant humus and good soil aeration appear to be consequent conditions of the shaded, acid habitats which support *C. acaule*.

CULTURAL NOTES Efforts to transplant this lovely orchid to wildflower gardens rarely succeed. Growers watch with gradually diminishing hope as carefully tended plants produce only vegetative growth during the first season after transplanting. Only rarely does a plant send up an emergent bud for a second season. Most growers gather a large portion of the humus from the wild site in an attempt to improve their prospects for a successful transplant but to no good end.

The reader is discouraged from digging this species because of poor success rates and shrinking wild populations. Occasionally, wildflower nurseries advertise this species. Rest assured that these plants are dug from their native sites rather than from a cultivated nursery bed, so ordering plants from these sources is inadvisable.

If, however, a population of these orchids stands in the path of a bulldozer, it is good for a grower to understand that transplanting success hinges upon mulching underneath the leaves with pine needles. The broad, basal leaves positioned so close to the surface of the soil tend to collect mud-splash and to trap excessive humidity which condenses overnight to form droplets on their undersurfaces. This unfortunate combination encourages attack by fungus and pests, and coming close on the heels of transplanting shock, it routinely weakens the plants beyond their ability to recover and become established. The presence of a thick mulch of pine needles promotes underleaf aeration and drying, prevents mud-splash and increases the success rate of transplantation.

DESCRIPTION As one would expect given the specific epithet *acaule*, the vegetative plant is very nearly stemless. The rather large, basal leaves are dark forest green in color, strongly ribbed (plicate) by the parallel veins, and possessed of a silvery luster on the lower surface. The elliptical to ovate leaves reach lengths of 10–25 cm (4–10 in.) and widths of 4–15 cm (1.5–4 in.). The entire plant bears glandular pubescence.

Mature plants produce a peduncle bearing a large, showy flower hooded by a large bract. Very rarely is the peduncle bifloral. Inflorescences reach heights of 20–45 cm (8–18 in.), and the individual, nodding flowers are typically 6–7 cm (2.25–2.75 in.) long by 5–6 cm (2–2.5 in.) wide.

Sepals and petals are greenish yellow to khaki in color, broader at the base and tapered to acute points. The dorsal sepal is narrow and arches deeply over the pouch. The synsepalum is fully connate. Both dorsal and ventral sepals measure 3–5 cm (1–2 in.) in length. The twisted petals are up to 7 cm (3 in.) in length. Their presentation is pendulous, thereby narrowing the overall width of the flower.

The showy pouch varies in color from rich magenta to pale pink in the typical flower. The *alba* form possesses a white pouch which may bear a blush of pink or a suffusion of pale green. The 2 forms may inhabit the same general area but very rarely share the same site. The pouch is usually veined in a darker color and bears a velvety pubescence. The most distinctive identifying feature is the slitlike aperture, a vertical fissure bisecting the frontal surface of the inflated, elongate pouch. Measuring about 5 cm (2 in.) in length, the pouch is the focal point of the flower.

Both *C. japonicum* and *C. formosanum* bear a resemblance to this slipper in that their pouch apertures are partially slitlike.

FLOWERING SEASON From mid-April in the South through late July in the upper reaches of its range.

COMMON NAMES Pink Moccasin Flower, Pink Lady's Slipper and Stemless Lady's Slipper are among the most frequently used common names for *C. acaule*. Correll (1950) provides a longer list of common names for this species and several others described in this chapter.

Cypripedium album Ait. See *C. reginae* Walt.

Cypripedium alternifolius St. L. See *C. calceolus* L.

Cypripedium amesianum Schltr.

C. amesianum is reported to be closely allied to *C. himalaicum*.

GEOGRAPHIC DISTRIBUTION This slipper is native to western Sichuan Province, China.

HABITAT *C. amesianum* inhabits thickets and wooded areas at elevations of 3,000 m (10,000 ft.).

CULTURAL NOTES I have no knowledge of this species in cultivation nor am I aware that it has been imported by growers. See cultural notes for *C. cordigerum* for information relating to Himalayan species.

DESCRIPTION The plant consists of a rhizome bearing an aerial stem 30–45 cm (12–18 in.) tall. The stem, which is erect to arching, typically bears 2 elliptic, acute, hirsute leaves that measure 7.5–13 cm (3–5 in.) in length.

The flower is usually solitary, quite large and measures about 6 cm (2.5 in.) across. The oblongate dorsal sepal is apically acute; the synsepalum is similar but apically bidentate.

The petals are oblongate-lanceolate with ciliate, undulate margins. The bulbous labellum is proportionally large. Flower color is reddish violet with tessellations of a deeper purple.

FLOWERING SEASON June and July.

Cypripedium arietinum R. Brown   PLATES 3 & 4

Atwood's (1984b) proposed reclassification of this species to a separate genus as *Criosanthes arietina* (R. Brown) House has been discussed in the introductory comments in this chapter.

Cypripedium plectrochilum Franch. is a binomial in use for the Asian populations. Whether this binomial is synonymous or representative of a well-defined but related Asian species is unclear at present, but synonymy is believed to be the case.

GEOGRAPHIC DISTRIBUTION Native to North America and Sichuan, China, *C. arietinum* shares both its range and its habitat with *C. reginae* including northeastern United States, the northern Plains states and the eastern Canadian provinces. Many of the sites listed on older herbarium specimens are no longer extant, and *C. arietinum* is an endangered species.

HABITAT Temperature is a critical factor in the habitat of this slipper. Plants rarely survive where soil temperature exceeds 25° C (76° F) during the summer. In China *C. arietinum* is found at elevations of 4,000–5,000 m (12,000—15,000 ft.); in North America it is never found south of New York State.

Moisture is not a limiting factor. The plant thrives in both boggy situations and on upland slopes. Well-aerated humus soils associated with coniferous biomes, and the consequent acidity and low levels of nutrients in these habitats, provide the most suitable conditions for this slipper. Although frequently found in dense shade, it tolerates bright conditions where heat buildup is minimal.

The Asian populations are reported from dry pine forests at elevations of 2,600–3,200 m (9,000–11,000 ft.).

CULTURAL NOTES Because *C. arietinum* is in critical danger of extinction in many North American sites, it is not recommended that concerned cypriphiles attempt more than site protection at present. The ephemeral flowers never last but a few days, nor are they showy enough to warrant collection and decimation of the species merely because it is rare and curious. Even when reliable cultivation techniques are developed, and successful propagation from seed is commonplace, efforts to conserve this species by transplanting will still provide only slight protection. Residents of warm climates must refrain from all attempts to grow this species.

DESCRIPTION The vegetative plant is relatively tall and bears 3–5 leaves upon a twisted stem which averages about 35 cm (14 in.) in height. The stem and leaves bear glandular hairs. The lower half of the stem is covered by several tubular brown sheaths; the upper portion bears the photosynthetic leaves.

Elliptical in shape, the plicate leaves are minimally pubescent, dark green in color, and 5–10 cm (2–4 in.) long by 2–4 cm (1.75–2.5 in.) wide.

The main axis elongates to become a unifloral flowerscape. A large erect bract subtends the flower, only distally arching over the nodding blossom. The fragrant, pubescent flower is composed of 3 sepals, 2 petals and the spurred lip. The free lateral sepals place *C. arietinum* among the most primitive species of *Cypripedium*. Superficially, *C. reginae* bears little resemblance to *C. arietinum* but frequently exhibits no more than basal fusion of its lateral sepals. The close proximity in habitat of these 2 species and their commonality in unfused lateral sepals is probably merely parallel or convergent development in more than 1 trait. Investigation is needed to determine the ramifications of these coincidental similarities between *C. arietinum* and *C. reginae*, if they do in fact exist, and to determine whether additional traits exhibit parallelism.

The free sepals are concave, arching forward, and their color ranges from khaki to purple or aubergine, with green streaks and margins. The dorsal sepal is widest and hoods the pouch; it measures 1.5–2.5 cm (0.6–1 in.) in length and 0.5–1 cm (0.2–0.37 in.) in width. The pair of lateral sepals and the paired petals are slender and similar in size and appearance, 1.5–2 cm (0.5–0.75 in.) long by 0.5 cm (0.2 in.) wide. These 4 segments exhibit some undulation and twisting along their length.

The lip is unique in that it appears partially inflated and bears a slender spur, a nipplelike projection which grows downward in the direction opposite to the pouch aperture. The 2 petals and the spurred pouch combine to suggest the lowered head of a charging ram; curving forward upon a nodding flower, the petals resemble horns, and the spurred, pilose pouch suggests face and beard. The labellum is unique, also, by virtue of the prominent hairs surrounding the aperture and extending down the frontal portion. Pouch color is white adjacent to the orifice but becomes pink to magenta on its lower surfaces. The rich coloring is introduced in a veined pattern where it adjoins the white rim, and the color gradually suffuses to rose veined with magenta. The labellum measures roughly 1.4–2.5 cm (0.5–1 in.) vertically and about 1.5 cm (0.6 in.) horizontally. The staminode is unusual by virtue of its remarkable similarity to the fertile stamens, although staminodal pollen production has not been reported.

FLOWERING SEASON May to August depending upon latitude and elevation.

COMMON NAMES The petals and uniquely spurred pouch are responsible for the common name Ram's Head Orchid. The likeness is so splendid that not only is there no other common name, but the species epithet, *arietinum* is Latin for ramlike.

Cypripedium bardolphianum W. W. Sm. & Farrer

S. C. Chen (1985) lists *C. nutans* Schltr. as a synonym for this species, although Atwood (1984b) states that Breiger puts *C. nutans* close to *C. acaule* Ait.

GEOGRAPHIC DISTRIBUTION Native to western China, this dwarf species often grows with *C. flavum*.

HABITAT This species inhabits shady montane forests, rooting in mossy leafmold.

CULTURAL NOTES Carson Whitlow (personal communication) indicates that some importation of this species has occurred. See notes on its habitat and also cultural notes under *C. cordigerum* for guidelines on cultivation.

DESCRIPTION The stem stands 6–7.5 cm (2.5–3 in.) above the rhizome. The paired glabrous leaves are oblongate with rounded apices, and measure 5 cm (2 in.) in length.

The solitary flower measures only 2.5 cm (1 in.) across. Sepals and petals are pale green. The dorsal sepal is ovate with a rounded apex. The elliptic ventral sepal is bidentate apically. The spreading petals are lanceolate and no longer than the sepals. The orange-hued pouch is verrucous; typically ovoid, it is frequently deformed. Darnell (1930) reports that this species emits an unpleasant odor.

S. C. Chen (1985) compares *C. bardolphianum* var. *bardolphianum* with a form from Yunnan Province which he published as var. *zhongdianense* S. C. Chen var. nov. He mentions minor differences in the sepals and peduncle and describes his variant as more densely pubescent.

FLOWERING SEASON June and July.

Cypripedium calceolus L.

At present this species must be considered a complex, and a number of taxa must be included pending definition of their actual relationships. For convenience I have left the species which are named separately, the alba taxa in this complex, standing as separate species. The reader is referred to *C. candidum* and *C. montanum* in this chapter for further information on the alba forms. See also the following related Asian species: *C. cordigerum*, *C. henryi*, and *C. microsaccus*.

GEOGRAPHIC DISTRIBUTION Widely distributed in Europe, Asia and North America, this species is more like a polymorphic and ecospecific complex than a clear-cut species. The complex embraces variations in size, fragrance, color and number of blossoms per inflorescence, but when viewed as a group the differences are somewhat less impressive than are the similarities. *C. calceolus* is truly circumboreal. It is reported from the entire eastern region of the North American continent above the Florida peninsula, and is widespread in the Pacific Northwest as well as the Canadian provinces. The species has been reported at lower elevations in the Himalayas, from the British Isles, and according to Schrenk (1981), large populations are found in the Black Forest region of nothern Europe. Slyusarenko (1981) writes, "*Cypripedium calceolus* L. is widespread in the USSR—from the western frontier to the islands of the Far East."

HABITAT *C. calceolus* as a complex is at home at most elevations and in most conditions. Unlike many other species, it is not acid-loving; certain of the forms prefer limestone outcrops as their substrate. Some populations are located in the Louisiana Delta near sea level; still others find a suitable habitat at elevations of 2,700 m (9,000 ft.) or more in the Rocky Mountains. An extremely wide variety of habitats is occupied by this species, including open meadows, dense coniferous forests, pine thickets, dry slopes, sphagnum bogs overlying calcareous rock strata, the arid plateaus of Arizona, the rain forests of British Columbia and the rock-strewn coastal lowlands of Newfoundland. Although forms in this complex are among the most amenable to naturalization in the genus, forms from one extreme of the range should not be shipped for transplanting to the opposite extreme without regard for ecospecific requirements.

CULTURAL NOTES If transplanted locally, this species naturalizes with ease in wildflower gardens. No special care is required, although it is advisable to place specimens in a stable area where they are unlikely to be disturbed by subsequent planting and cultivation.

C. calceolus var. *kentuckiense* is a notable exception to this rule. Victor Soukup (personal communication) relates that plants of this large, beautiful variety were washed away from a locale in his garden, and when retrieved several thousand feet downstream and replanted, thrived better than the undisturbed plants. He believes that disturbance stimulates this variant, and reports that it is typically found growing in sandy-silt soils which become crumbly dry but not hard.

Ellipsoid seed capsules are readily produced, so obtaining seed for propagation is less difficult than for many other species.

DESCRIPTION According to Correll (1950), there are 4 distinct forms of *C. calceolus* found in North America. Correll called all 4 entities by the same name, *C. calceolus* var. *pubescens*, and considered the 4 entities to be intergrading forms. Atwood (1985a) takes a quite different stand, giving 3 of these entities full species rank and placing the fourth at varietal level. More will be said about Atwood's position below. The type specimen was described by Linnaeus in *Species Plantarum* in 1753. The forms which are common in the southern United States are *C. calceolus* var. *pubescens* Willd., a large, fragrant, typically unifloral form; *C. calceolus* var. *parviflorum* (Salisb.) Fernald which is smaller and produces 2–3 small flowers per scape; and an entity called *C. kentuckiense* Reed or *C. furcatum* Raf., an exceptionally large form of the complex reported from sections of southern and central United States. The latter, which I prefer to call *C. calceolus* var. *kentuckiense*, ranges from pale hues to particularly dark coloration. A discussion of its characteristics has been published by Atwood (1984a) as *C. kentuckiense* C. F. Reed. The fourth form, *C. calceolus* var. *planipetalum* (Fern.) Morris & Eames, is indigenous to northern latitudes.

Dr. John Atwood, Director of the Orchid Identification Center of the Marie Selby Gardens of Sarasota, Florida, has published detailed information on the *C. calceolus* complex as a whole (1985a). He calls the first entity *C. pubescens* var. *pubescens*, the second *C. parviflorum*, the third *C. kentuckiense*, and the fourth *C. pubescens* var. *planipetalum*. As his study has spanned 2 decades and his qualifications as an orchid taxonomist are unexcelled, it has been difficult to elect to emphasize the closer relationship among these plants in the face of his evidence to the contrary.

Among the salient features recognized by Atwood is data on pouch aperture size variations among sympatric plants of *C. kentuckiense* and *C. pubescens*, as he names what I consider to be 2 variants. Size variation in pouch aperture leading to pollination by different species of bees is certainly one of those significant factors which serve to drive species to diverge and become 2 species. Atwood (1985a) further gives his rationale for allowing the *C. pubescens* taxon to include both the typical form and var. *planipetalum*; according to his observations, the 2 forms intergrade in Colorado and freely hybridize in Michigan and Wisconsin. He further states that the smaller size, richer pigmentation of segments, and absence of intergrading forms fully distinguishes *C. parviflorum* from the rest of the complex. Readers who wish to satisfy their curiosity about the taxonomic status of this complex are referred to the 1985 *Proceedings: The Eleventh World Orchid Conference* for further details. Closely related, according to Atwood (1985a), are the white-lipped taxa *C. montanum* and *C. candidum*, which are routinely considered to be species in their own rights.

For the purposes of this work, a general description of *C. calceolus* var. *pubescens* Willd. is presented as a standard against which variant forms will be compared for the sake of brevity and clarity. The vegetative plant reaches heights of 45–60 cm (18–24 in.) and bears 3–5 broadly elliptical, acute leaves. The leaves are strongly plicate and basally clasp the stem. Leaf length is 15–20 cm (6–8 in.), and the width may be up to 10 cm (4 in.) at the broadest portion. *C. calceolus* var. *pubescens* is typically unifloral, but bifloral scapes are not uncommon. The flowers are hooded by a large bract that measures 4–10 cm (1.5–4 in.) long and 2–4 cm (0.75–1.5 in.) wide at the midpoint.

The sepals and petals vary from yellowish green to aubergine or madder purple. The dorsal sepal is ovate, acuminate and frequently undulate. Held well over the pouch orifice, it measures 4–5 cm (1.5–2 in.) in length and 3–6 cm (1.25–2.5 in.) in width. The fused synsepalum is occasionally bidentate at the tip. Its shape is oblong-lanceolate, and it measures 3–8 cm (1.25–3 in.) in length and 2–3 cm (0.75–1.25 in.) in width.

The petals are linear-lanceolate and twisted, 6–8 cm (2.25–3 in.) long and 1–2 cm (0.37–0.75 in.) wide at the broadest point. The inflated pouch is white, cream or yellow, typically golden yellow. Veins of magenta cross the outer surface of the pouch, and spots of the same color adorn the inner pouch surface. The lower lateral surfaces of the pouch are frequently blotched with large spots ranging in color from peach to red. The pouch is 3–6 cm (1.25 2.5 in.) in length and exhibits a nearly circular pouch aperture which is corrugated about the rim.

C. calceolus var. *parviflorum* Salisb. is distinguished by having less pubescence and bearing flowers roughly half the size of those of var. *pubescens*. In fact, in the dimensions of all the parts of the plants, this variant is approximately half the size of var. *pubescens*. Among populations I have observed, var. *parviflorum* has less purple pigmentation in sepals and petals and tends more toward yellowish green, olive or khaki in sepal color. Atwood (personal communication) believes that there may be species-rank differences between northern and southern populations of this form found in the United States. This variant typically produces 2–5 flowers per stalk.

C. kentuckiense Reed is the third form of the complex. I prefer to include it as a variant of *C. calceolus*, and in so doing, inevitably become embroiled in the conflict which has erupted in the 1980s with regard to this plant. One contingent of orchidists insists that the correct name is *C. furcatum* Raf., and that controversy is far from resolved. However, the more serious debate centers upon whether this taxon should be taken out of the *C. calceolus* complex and elevated to separate species rank. In fact, my position in including it as a variant form of *C. calceolus*, rather than as a separate species, is extremely controversial. This form is distributed from northeastern Kentucky, through Tennessee into northern Louisiana and the Texarkana region, and northward into the Plains States. *C. calceolus* var. *kentuckiense* bears the strongest resemblance to var. *pubescens*, but routinely exceeds its size in both vegetative and floral parts by some degree. The sepals and petals are generally darker than those of var. *pubescens* and, typically are deepest mahogany brown or madder purple. The lips, by contrast, are pale yellow or cream, and in many populations the lip has a greater inflation of its distal portion with dorsiventral flattening occurring in the pouch of most individuals. This is a striking flower, and a distinctive form. Illustrations routinely fail to do it justice. However, one of the most striking features of both the flower and the vegetative plant is its close resemblance to *C. calceolus* var. *pubescens*.

Carson Whitlow (personal communication) and Victor Soukup (personal communication) feel strongly that var. *kentuckiense* deserves species rank. They cite fragrance differences and a strong likelihood of other physiological differences from the rest of the *C. calceolus* complex. Soukup indicates that it consistently flowers 10 days later than other forms of *C. calceolus* and on longer peduncles. Variance in flowering time effectively isolates this form from participation in the larger gene pool, and serves to drive the divergence process. Perhaps the strongest argument in favor of species rank for this form is its discrete habitat/range preferences; it tends to occupy wetter habitats in portions of the south central United States. If it is not already a discrete species, it will so diverge in the future by virtue of its several isolations from interbreeding with the greater gene pool.

C. calceolus var. *planipetalum* (Fern.) Morris and Eames is a northern form described from Alaska, Newfoundland and northern regions of Europe and the USSR as well as from the lower latitude of the mountains of Colorado. It has shorter petals and sepals with blunt tips and displays little or none of the twisting which is characteristic of the petals of other forms. The sepal margins of this variety also exhibit little undulation. Sepal and petal coloration tends toward aubergine, and pouch color is typically yellow, although alba lips appear in every form of the complex. According to Atwood (1985a), the ventral sepal of this form is frequently bifid for a quarter of its length, a trait which sets it apart from the rest of its complex.

At this point in the discussion of the complex, the question of inclusion of *C. candidum* and *C. montanum* as alba forms of the complex arises. Upon morphological criteria alone, there are few grounds for excluding them from the complex, so I call the reader's attention to both of these species (listed separately in alphabetical order) in concurrence with Dr. Atwood's (1985a) opinion. However, for the sake of clarity, I shall let each stand as a separate species as they have stood for so many years.

Descriptions of the taxa of the *C. calceolus* complex abound. Diligent students might collect specimens from hundreds of sites and make a reasonable case for separating this complex into dozens of species and variants. I contend that while the authors of such descriptions and revisions might win personal distinction, the distinctions between the plants themselves would, nonetheless, be arbitrary and artificial in most cases in light of the existence of intermediate forms. Certainly, this group of *Cypripedium* is endowed with a large degree of variability. Just as emphatically, the intrinsic unity within the complex must be acknowledged.

Because the plants of this complex are vigorous and responsive to cultivation, there are grounds for believing a solution to the enigma represented by the complex will soon be achieved. Data gathered and tabulated to elucidate genetic and ecological relationships will create an understanding far surpassing the current concepts based so precariously upon primarily morphological criteria. Until a fresh approach is taken with this complex, confusing taxonomic opinions will continue to proliferate.

C. montanum Dougl. ex Lindl. (see alphabetical listing) is like the var. *pubescens* described here, in overall appearance. Various structures are quite similar in size and shape. However, if the alba labellum is not sufficient to distinguish it from the complex, there is a distinct ecospecific narrowness in this taxon: it prefers mountainous habitats.

A second white-lipped species, *C. candidum* Muhl. ex Willd., is to all appearances an alba form of the Small Yellow Lady's Slipper, *C. calceolus* var. *parviflorum*. Both these white-lipped taxa are described separately within this chapter.

FLOWERING SEASON Full anthesis from April in the Deep South through August in the extreme north.

COMMON NAMES The Yellow Lady's Slipper, Yellow Moccasin Flower, Venus' Shoe and a host of names of European origin are applied to this lovely orchid. In England, it is called the Common Lady's Slipper. Unfortuately, the present-day applicability of the adjective common is slight for this and many orchids.

Cypripedium calceolus var. *variegatum* Falk. See *C. guttatum* Sw.

Cypripedium californicum A. Gray   PLATE 9

GEOGRAPHIC DISTRIBUTION The range of this species is limited to northern California and southern Oregon.

HABITAT Upland marshes host natural populations at elevations of 400–1,500 m (1,400–5,000 ft.). The species is found in association with another endemic plant, the carnivorous *Darlingtonia* or cobra plant. Occurring on wet banks of ravines or on spring-drenched open slopes, *C. californicum* is typically found in open woods along small streams at the base of mountains. As a narrow endemic, it is not amenable to cultivation.

CULTURAL NOTES I have no personal knowledge of this species in cultivation. Its status in the wild with respect to both its relative abundance and its natural habitat must be carefully evaluated by a prospective grower before endangering wild specimens, if, indeed, it is not under protection as an endangered species.

DESCRIPTION This species bears glandular pubescence throughout and measures 25–120 cm (10–48 in.) in height. Five or more plicate leaves sheath the stem and are held at an approximate 45° angle to the vertical. Borne alternately, the leaves are broadly ovate and acuminate, 7–16 cm (2.5–6 in.) in length and 2–7 cm (0.8–2.5 in.) in width. The uppermost leaves are smaller than the lower ones, becoming more lanceolate and acute, and grading into the size and shape of the bracts of the inflorescence. The floral bracts are larger than the flowers.

Each inflorescence bears 3–12 flowers and, in this respect as well as in locular structure, *C. californicum* resembles *C. irapeanum*. According to Atwood (1984b), the extensive flowerscape of these 2 species and the ovary which exhibits some transitional characteristics are the features which link the *Cypripedium* with the genus *Selenipedium*. *C. subtropicum* Chen and Lang sp. nov. and *C. dickinsonianum* Hagsater (see alphabetical listing) are notable for the characteristics linking them to the 2 aforementioned species and *Selenipedium* as well.

The sepals are tan to brownish yellow. The dorsal sepal is elliptical and concave, measuring approximately 2 cm (0.75 in.) long by 1 cm (0.37 in.) wide. The synsepalum is entirely connate in some individuals and bidentate in others. In color, shape and size it is similar to the dorsal sepal.

The petals are held well back and flat and are yellow-green in color. Petal length is approximately 2 cm (0.75 in.) and the width, which is only 0.5 cm (0.125 in.) at the base, tapers along the length to a blunt point.

The lip is white, roundly inflated, and measures 2.5 cm (1 in.) in length and width. Pouch markings consist of small brown spots or a rose blush.

FLOWERING SEASON Late May to July.

COMMON NAMES California Lady's Slipper is the only common name in global use.

Cypripedium canadense Michx. See *C. reginae* Walt.

Cypripedium candidum Muhl. ex Willd.   PLATE 10

The reader is referred to the introductory passage of this chapter and to the descriptions of *C. calceolus* and *C. montanum* for a broad view of the large complex of which this species is a member.

GEOGRAPHIC DISTRIBUTION *C. candidum* is found in New York, Pennsylvania, New Jersey, westward through the Great Lakes states as far as the Dakotas, and southward into Kentucky and the middle Great Plains states. It is also known from as far south as Alabama and northward into the Canadian province of Ontario. Never a dense colonizer, the plant occurs sparsely in most sites. It is cultivated in gardens in England where, according to Correll (1950), it was first introduced in 1826.

HABITAT Commonly associated with limestone strata, this is a cool-climate species which is unusual among slippers in its ability to thrive on open prairies. It also grows protected by thickets or in wooded areas. Tolerant of dry habitats, it is more likely to be found in damp humus.

CULTURAL NOTES See the habitat notes above for guidelines. This species is amenable to naturalization in cooler climates.

DESCRIPTION Mature, flowering plants stand 30–40 cm (12–16 in.) tall. The erect stems appear deceptively thick due to the basal sheathing leaves which are held nearly erect and loosely clasping the stem for their entire length. Above the basal leaves 2–4 lanceolate leaves grow stiffly at an acute angle from the stem. An unusual feature of these free leaves is their midrib which is more pronounced than the other parallel veins; the midrib's prominence thus ordains that the leaves are both conduplicate and plicate. They measure 10–20 cm (4–8 in.) in length and 2.5–5 cm (1–2 in.) in width. The floral bracts are smaller and more elliptical but otherwise similar to the upper leaves. The entire plant is sparsely covered with glandular hairs.

A feature of this species which, along with its smaller size, distinguishes it from *C. montanum* is the flowering of *C. candidum* prior to full vernation. Leaves of the larger, montane species are fully expanded before anthesis.

The typically solitary flower measures 6–7 cm (2.3–2.5 in.) in height and 4–6 cm (1.5–2.3 in.) in width. Sepals and petals are olive green to khaki, while the pouch is white. Dorsal and ventral sepals are elongate and acuminate. They exhibit undulate margins and are subconduplicate. The dorsal sepal is 2–3 cm (1 in.) long and 1–2 cm (0.5 in.) wide. The ventral sepal is just slightly smaller in proportions.

Petals are linear and twisted, held in a slightly pendulous orientation. They measure 3.5–4.5 cm (1.25–1.75 in.) in length and 0.5–1 cm (0.25–0.37 in.) in width.

The glossy white pouch bears some maroon veining. It is longer than wide and held nearly perpendicular to the stalk. Distally it is roundly inflated with a circular orifice. Its inner surface is pubescent.

The overall appearance of the flower is suggestive of an alba form of *C. calceolus* var. *parviflorum*. It is known to hybridize naturally with 2 variants of *C. calceolus*. However,

Atwood (1985a) distinguishes between white-lipped forms of *C. calceolus* var. *parviflorum* (which he calls *C. parviflorum*) and *C. candidum* on the basis of closely spaced vascular bundles in the leaves of the latter, and refers to those reinforcing vascular bundles as adaptations made to its windy, prairie habitat.

FLOWERING SEASON April to July.

COMMON NAMES *C. candidum* is called the Small White Lady's Slipper, Silver Slipper and White Moccasin Flower.

Cypripedium cardiophyllum Franch. See *C. debile* Reichb. f.

Cypripedium cathayanum Chien. See *C. japonicum* Thunb.

Cypripedium chinense Franch. See *C. henryi* Rolfe

Cypripedium cordigerum D. Don   PLATE 11

According to Darnell (1930) and Atwood (1984b), this species is most closely allied to *C. calceolus*. A brief description was written by R. E. Arnold and published in *The Orchid Review*, February 1939. The most detailed description of this species is Pradhan's (1986). In comparing it with European specimens of *C. calceolus*, he outlines particular distinctions between the 2. Having no firsthand knowledge of *C. cordigerum*, I have relied heavily on his account in the following contrast of the 2 species. However, parenthetical comments are mine.

1. **Pouch shape.** *C. calceolus* has a rounded to elliptical, apically bulbous lip, whereas that of *C. cordigerum* is more dorsiventrally flattened with a blunt apex and somewhat bilobed in appearance. (Pouch shape varies among the North American entities included in the *C. calceolus* complex; the reader is referred to the discussion of that complex for further information, and to Atwood [1985a]).

2. **Shape and orientation of petals.** Petals of *C. calceolus* are spiral, linear-lanceolate, and 1.5 times longer than the petals of *C. cordigerum* which are devoid of twisting and oblong-cordate in shape.

3. **Pigmentation of sepals and petals.** According to Pradhan, the perianth of *C. calceolus* is chocolate brown while that of *C. cordigerum* is yellow-green. (Pale greenish sepals and petals are frequently seen on North American specimens of *C. calceolus*, however.)

4. **Staminodal shape.** *C. calceolus* bears a keeled staminode which is oblong-obtuse in shape, while that of *C. cordigerum* is rounded dorsally and oblong-cordate.

5. **Comparison of length of dorsal sepals with labellar length.** *C. calceolus* has a dorsal sepal which is nearly equal in length to the length of the lip, while the dorsal sepal of *C. cordigerum* is about 1.5 times the length of the pouch.

6. **Labellar color.** In Pradhan's experience of labellar color, *C. calceolus* is bright yellow (see *C. calceolus* for a discussion of allied taxa with white pouches and forms with white or cream pouches), while that of *C. cordigerum* is white.

The reader is referred to Pradhan for further particulars. However, it should be borne in mind that Pradhan is comparing Eurasian forms of *C. calceolus* with *C. cordigerum*; because of long-standing reproductive isolation between the former and its North American relatives, certain particulars will require additional comparisons before definitive differences between these 2 entities are completely outlined.

GEOGRAPHIC DISTRIBUTION This species is reported from Kashmir and Simla in the Himalayas of India through Nepal and into Bhutan.

HABITAT Growing at 2,600–3,700 m (9,000–12,700 ft.) elevation, *C. cordigerum* occurs in dappled shade of open slopes in association with rhododendron, grasses and juniper.

CULTURAL NOTES Pradhan (1986) states that Himalayan *Cypripedium* are amenable to rock garden culture north of the 30th parallel (or south of that parallel in the Southern Hemisphere) providing that snows occur regularly and that acid conditions can be established. He recommends a winter temperature of 5° C (40° F) or less and a summer temperature of 15° C (60° F). Pradhan further recommends a substrate consisting of 2 parts loam, 2 parts coarse leaf mold, 1 part coarse sand and 1 part chopped sphagnum, kept moist at all times.

DESCRIPTION The pubescent stem reaches heights of 20–60 cm (8–24 in.) and bears several leaves which vary from lanceolate to suborbiculate with acute apices. Leaf length is 7.5–15 cm (3–6 in.). The scape produces a large foliose bract subtending a single large flower measuring 10 cm (4 in.) across. Sepals and petals are greenish white. The labellum is white with orange hairs on the infolded margins.

FLOWERING SEASON July and August.

Cypripedium corrugatum Franch   PLATE 12

Closely related to *C. tibeticum*, this species is possibly synonymous with *C. ventricosum*, or it may even be a variant of *C. tibeticum*. Among the Asian species, there is an urgent need for further study to dispel the confusion among species, variants and synonymous binomials.

GEOGRAPHIC DISTRIBUTION *C. corrugatum* and its variant *obesum* are native to western Yunnan Province, China.

HABITAT This species prefers open, montane meadows and the perimeters of pine forests. Elevations of 2,900–3,200 m (10,000–11,000 ft.) support its populations.

CULTURAL NOTES See *C. cordigerum*.

DESCRIPTION The leafy stem rises 18–30 cm (7–12 in.) above the rhizome. Leaves are oblongate and acute with ciliate margins and measure 10–12.5 cm (4–5 in.) in length.

The solitary flower is subtended by a large bract. The horizontal spread of the flower is up to 10 cm (4 in.). Sepals and petals range from green, suffused with chestnut brown and veined with purple, to maroon purple. The acute dorsal sepal is ovate-oblongate. The ovate ventral sepal is bidentate at its apex.

Petals are acute and ovate-lanceolate. The pouch is spheroid with pronounced corrugations about the infolded margin. The lip is deep maroon with near black venation. The pouch of var. *obesum* is larger than that of the type.

FLOWERING SEASON June.

Cypripedium cruciatum Dulac. See *C. calceolus* L.

Cypripedium debile Reichb. f.

GEOGRAPHIC DISTRIBUTION *C. debile* is indigenous to China and Japan.

HABITAT Dappled shade of open woods at elevations of 1,450 m (5,000 ft.) or more is the preferred habitat of this slipper.

CULTURAL NOTES Widely cultivated in Japanese gardens, this species is not believed grown in English or North American gardens. Moist, acid woods earth and cooler climates promote successful cultivation.

DESCRIPTION This dwarf species produces a weak, arching stem bearing a pair of leaves. The leaves are subopposite, cordate-triangular in shape and glabrous. They measure 4–5 cm (1.5–2 in.) in length, are nearly sessile, and arise about midway up the stem.

A single small flower of pale greenish yellow is produced some distance above the bract; it measures about 4 cm (1.5 in.) across. Sepals and petals are pale green. The acute dorsal sepal is lanceolate and curves forward to shield the pouch aperture. The ventral sepal is lanceolate as well. The spreading petals are broadly lanceolate. The creamy white pouch is broadly inflated, has a corrugate lip margin, and is dotted and veined with purple or liver brown.

FLOWERING SEASON June and July.

Cypripedium dickinsonianum Hagsater

Described as recently as 1984, this species is closely related to *C. irapeanum* and grows conspecifically with it in at least 1 area of Mexico. It is easily distinguished from *C. irapeanum* by the smaller size of its flowers which barely measure 3.5 cm (1.5 in.) longitudinally. However, it perhaps should be considered a variant form of the larger species, although no intermediate forms are presently known. Cultural differences and growth habit distinctions, as well as differences in staminodes, add support to the case for allowing this taxon to stand at species rank for the present.

Hagsater (1984) reports that this species is autogamous (self-fertile), bears abundant capsules, and is observed while in flower to hold the pollinia in contact with the stigma.

GEOGRAPHIC DISTRIBUTION The state of Chiapas in Mexico hosts this species.

HABITAT Growing in cedar forest at 1,500 m (5,100 ft.), it appears to be restricted to the high, level Maseta Central of Chiapas.

CULTURAL NOTES Importation is not recommended, as no great success has been demonstrated in the cultivation of this species or the related *C. irapeanum* in nearby Mexican locations. Asymbiotic seedlings which can be shipped with phytosanitary certificates should be readily available from this autogamous species in the near future as should capsules for seedling culture outside Mexico.

DESCRIPTION The densely hirsute stem stands up to 30 cm (12 in.) above the rhizome. The oblong-lanceolate leaves are hirsute as well and distributed spirally along the stem. The lower leaves measure up to 5.5 cm (2.3 in.) long, but leaf length diminishes farther up the stem, grading into the foliose bracts which subtend the 5–6 flowers produced along the upper third of the axis.

The flowers are concolor bright yellow with a flush of red inside the pouch. The dorsal sepal is elliptic, shortly acuminate, pubescent upon the reverse, and sparsely pubescent upon the face. It measures 1.8 cm (0.75 in.) long by 1 cm (0.4 in.) wide. The dorsal is moderately concave and hoods the pouch aperture. The ventral sepal is similar though slightly longer and narrower, entirely connate, and pubescent on its outer surface.

The petals are elliptic-lanceolate, apically obtuse, and sparsely pubescent upon both surfaces. They curve forward very slightly and exhibit an approximate 30° decline from horizontal. The pouch is obovoid and sculpted by its veins. Spots of red occur on its inner surface, visible through the translucent fenestrations of the labellar wall. Its outer surface is glabrous and glossy.

FLOWERING SEASON May and June.

Cypripedium ebracteatum Rolfe

This species is placed in an alliance with *C. acaule, C. japonicum, C. formosanum, C. margaritaceum,* and others. Further study of it and its allies which produce no bracts may indicate the need for establishing a separate group for bractless species.

GEOGRAPHIC DISTRIBUTION Western Yunnan Province, China is the reported range of this species.

HABITAT *C. ebracteatum* occurs at 2,600–3,200 m (9,000–11,000 ft.) in dry pine woods.

CULTURAL NOTES See cultural guidelines accompanying *C. cordigerum.*

DESCRIPTION *C. ebracteatum* is an acaulescent species bearing 2 leaves which are suberect, ovate to suborbiculate, and apically obtuse. Leaf length is 10–11.5 cm (4–4.5 in.).

The flower is borne singly upon an erect, pubescent scape at a height of 15–20 cm (6–8 in.). The rather small flower measures only 3 cm (1.25 in.) across. The dorsal sepal is elliptic-ovate and apically acute. The ventral sepal is narrower but otherwise similar. Petals are lanceolate and acute. The well-inflated labellum is broad frontally. Flower color is greenish yellow overlaid with maroon mottling.

FLOWERING SEASON June.

Cypripedium elegans Reichb. f.

Along with *C. ebracteatum*, this species is allied with *C. acaule, C. japonicum,* and the other acaulescent and/or orbicular-leaved species. Its floral bract separates it from the ebracteate members of the alliance.

GEOGRAPHIC DISTRIBUTION *C. elegans* is a dwarf species reported from the Himalayas of Sikkim, Bhutan and Tibet. It is also reported from Yunnan Province, China.

HABITAT This species inhabits stony soil in partial shade of thickets. Pradhan (1986) states that its grassy habitat makes it prone to grazing.

CULTURAL NOTES Refer to cultural information under *C. cordigerum.*

DESCRIPTION Having the habit of *C. formosanum,* this species bears 2–3 suborbiculate leaves upon a stem which is only 2.5–4 cm (1–1.5 in.) in height below the leaves. The small leaves are subopposite and only 2.5–5 cm (1–2 in.) in length.

The small flower measures about 2.5 cm (1 in.) across and is borne singly upon a scape which is approximately 4 cm (1.5 in.) in height. The apically acute dorsal sepal is oblong-lanceolate and strongly hoods the pouch aperture. The short lateral sepals are only basally connate with spreading apices. The ovate petals are apically acute. The pouch is sub-spheroid with a triangular aperture. Flower color is quite similar to that of *C. ebracteatum.* The yellow-green ground color is striped with red upon sepals and petals, and suffused with rich red over the labellum. The overlying color may be brown in some individuals.

FLOWERING SEASON July.

Cypripedium fargesii Franch. See *C. margaritaceum* Franch.

Cypripedium farreri W. W. Smith

C. farreri exhibits affinities with the *C. japonicum* group, although it also possesses certain features in common with the *C. calceolus* group. In the absence of conclusive evidence, I have placed this species in the same alliance as *C. japonicum.*

GEOGRAPHIC DISTRIBUTION *C. farreri* is reported from Yunnan Province, China.

HABITAT Growing in leaf mold and forest shade, this species forms colonies on limestone cliffs at elevations of 2,300–2,600 m (8,000–9,000 ft.).

CULTURAL NOTES See *C. cordigerum* for cultural guidelines.

DESCRIPTION This is a large-flowered dwarf species. The slender stem reaches heights of up to 20 cm (8 in.). Two leaves arise about midway up the stem; they are ovate-lanceolate, apically acute, thin in texture, and bear ciliate margins.

The solitary, fragrant flower measures 9 cm (3 in.) across. Its dorsal sepal is ovate and apically obtuse. The elliptic synsepalum is apically bidentate. The twisted petals are linear-lanceolate and spreading. The pouch is subspheroid with a small aperture.

Flower color is greenish yellow and striped with maroon on sepals and petals. The glossy pouch is ivory with infolded margins of rich maroon.

FLOWERING SEASON June.

Cypripedium fasciculatum Kell. ex S. Wats.   PLATE 13

  C. knightae A. Nels. is described by Darnell (1930) as a small, allied species restricted to Colorado and Wyoming. Since the described differences are minor ones of size, and since *C. fasciculatum* is known to be size-variable, it is probable that *C. knightae* is merely a synonym. *C. pusillum* Rolfe is another synonym for *C. fasciculatum*.

GEOGRAPHIC DISTRIBUTION Wyoming, Montana, Idaho, Colorado, Utah, California, Oregon and Washington are the sites of record.

HABITAT *C. fasciculatum* is found in coniferous forests and shrubby thickets. It prefers higher elevations and tolerates varying degrees of moisture ranging from dry slopes to boggy areas of spring drainage. This slipper prefers acid soils.

CULTURAL NOTES This species is not widely cultivated and should not be attempted in warmer climates where winter snow is only an occasional event.

DESCRIPTION This species is unusual in its overall appearance and unique in bearing a cluster of terminal flowers. The flowering plant stands up to 30–35 cm (12–13 in.) in overall height at anthesis. It bears 2 subopposite leaves at a height of about 15–20 cm (6–8 in.). The leaves are plicate, broadly ovate, obtuse or rounded at the tips, and measure 5–10 cm (2–4 in.) in length by 3–6 cm (1.3–2.7 in.) in width. The base of the stem is enclosed by brown sheaths.

  The floral axis extends approximately 10–15 cm (6–8 in.) above the 2 leaves and bears a corymbose raceme of 2–4 flowers. The flowers are typically concolor dark purple, although forms with pale greenish yellow flowers are known as well.

  The dorsal sepal is lanceolate and acuminate. It measures 1.5–2.5 cm (0.5–1 in.) long and 3–6 mm (0.125–0.37 in.) wide. The apically bifid ventral sepal is slightly shorter and wider than the dorsal sepal.

  The flat petals are broadly lanceolate and acuminate, measuring 1.5–2.5 cm (0.5–1 in.) long and 0.6–1.7 cm (0.2–0.5 in.) wide. The elongate, ladlelike pouch is roundly inflated distally. It measures just over 1 cm (0.5 in.) in length and less than 1 cm wide (0.25 in.). Deeply infolded margins bound the subcircular pouch orifice.

FLOWERING SEASON April through August, depending on elevation.

COMMON NAMES Clustered Lady's Slipper is the most widely applied common name for this species. It reflects the species epithet *fasciculatum*, which means "bundle" or "cluster."

Cypripedium fasciolatum Franch.

  C. franchetii Rolfe is given as a synonym. This is probably an incorrect judgment as the flowers of *C. franchetii* are significantly smaller than those of *C. fasciolatum*. Inclusion of *C. franchetii* as a variant form of *C. fasciolatum* seems a more apt placement. Both of these taxa are a part of the *C. macranthum* alliance.

GEOGRAPHIC DISTRIBUTION This species is reported from Yunnan Province, China. *C. franchetii* is reported from Sichuan Province, China.

HABITAT Mixed and pine forests at elevations of 2,000–3,200 m (7,000–11,000 ft.) provide the niche preferred by this species.

CULTURAL NOTES See *C. cordigerum* for general guidelines to the culture of Himalayan *Cypripedium*.

DESCRIPTION The rather large flowers measure up to 11.5 cm (4.5 in.) across. The sepals are yellow, veined with purple. The long, slender, twisted petals are similar in color. The labellum is a rich rose magenta veined with deep purple. Some concolor purple flowers are reported with venation which is almost black.

  The flowers of the smaller taxon, var. *franchetii*, are only about 4.3 cm (1.75 in.) across. This variant is noted for its increased pubescence as well.

FLOWERING SEASON June (both variants).

Cypripedium flavum Ward   PLATE 14

      C. luteum Franch. is a synonym.

GEOGRAPHIC DISTRIBUTION *C. flavum* is native to China, where it is considered common and abundant. It inhabits portions of Yunnan, Sichuan and Hubei Provinces, and is believed to be still abundant along the Chinese-Tibetan border.

HABITAT This species grows at high elevations of 2,700–3,400 m (8,800–11,000 ft.). It typically occurs near glacial runoff channels rooted in mossy tufts on almost pure limestone substrate in pine forests and thickets on north-and east-facing cliffs.

CULTURAL NOTES This species was cultivated in England during the 19th Century, although it is uncertain whether any of those earlier domestic populations are extant today. Recent collections have been made from the wild, so that this species has reappeared in cultivation. Refer to *C. cordigerum* for information promoting successful culture.

DESCRIPTION All parts of this species are pubescent with the exception of the corolla (petals and labellum). The erect stem reaches heights of 30–45 cm (12–18 in.). Strongly plicate leaves sheath the stem; the 4–5 leaves are broad and dark green.

      The solitary flower is often concolor chrome yellow with amber venation of the glossy labellum, although some individuals exhibit duller coloration. Flower width is 6–9 cm (2.25–3.5 in.).

      The dorsal sepal is ovate and apically acute, curving forward over the labellar aperture to assume a nearly horizontal position. The synsepalum is concave and closely appressed to the undersurface of the labellum.

      The petals are held flat and horizontal in orientation. Apically they reflex to some degree. They are elliptic-lanceolate with acute apices. The labellum is subspheroid and somewhat flattened dorsiventrally.

FLOWERING SEASON May and June.

COMMON NAMES This beautiful species was given the appellation Proud Margaret by the 19th-century explorers of western China. It would be misleading to indicate that this is a common name in the normal sense of the term, however, as the species is neither known nor cultivated widely by Westerners, nor is this name in use by the indigenous population.

Cypripedium formosanum Hay.   PLATE 15

      This species is a member of a rather large alliance, including, in the Occident, *C. acaule* and several related Asian taxa. See also *C. japonicum*.

GEOGRAPHIC DISTRIBUTION Endemic to the northerly half of the island of Taiwan above the 24th parallel, this species is found at high elevations of 1,500–2,000 m (5,000–6,700 ft.) in fairly isolated populations in the wild. However, it thrives in cultivation at sea level and intermediate elevations.

HABITAT *C. formosanum* inhabits steep slopes of shale which are prone to frequent slides. Dense shade is never an attribute of its habitat because stands of trees fail to establish in such conditions. Plants root in humus and receive constant moisture from seepage between the fissile shale layers. The species is temperature tolerant and prefers acid conditions and bright shade.

CULTURAL NOTES Provide bright conditions, adequate drainage, a soil rich in humus with added peat moss for acidity, and ample moisture. Mulch fairly heavily to insure success with this species in a wildflower garden.

DESCRIPTION Bearing a strong resemblance to *C. japonicum*, *C. formosanum* is most similar to *C. acaule*, in the West. It is a large species producing a solitary 10 cm (4 in.) blossom atop a 20–30 cm (8–12 in.) stalk. The base of the stem is sheathed by 2–3 green leaves and topped by 2 large, subopposite, fan-shaped plicate leaves. The leaf margins appear serrate due to the deep corrugations created by the parallel veins. The maximum width achieved by the leaves reaches 20–25 cm (8–10 in.), while the length is typically nearer 15 cm (6 in.). The pair of leaves is a vivid apple green color and creates a striking contrast for the delicate pink blossom.

The dorsal sepal is white and daintily spotted with minute flecks of rich pink near its base. Typically concave, it hoods the pouch and measures 5–6 cm (2–2.4 in.) in length by 2–2.5 cm (1 in.) in width. The ventral sepal is similar in color, size and shape.

The rather flat petals are slightly longer than the sepals, but bear similar pink spotting. They are held in a forward and pendulous position. The large, teardrop-shaped pouch is well-inflated and measures 6–7 cm (2.5–3 in.) in length by 4–5 cm (1.5–2 in.) in width. Delicately creamy white, it is surmounted by a rich pink staminode while its infolded margins bear veins and suffusions of rosy pink. The pouch aperture is slitlike proximally as in *C. acaule*, but distally it widens to a teardrop-shaped orifice suffused with pink color all about its margin.

FLOWERING SEASON After the snows melt, mid-February at sea-level, typically in March and April at higher elevations.

COMMON NAMES No Western-equivalent common names are known, although for convenience it is referred to as the Formosan Lady's Slipper.

Cypripedium franchetii Rolfe sensu Breiger. See *C. fasciolatum* Franch. and *C. macranthum* Sw.

Cypripedium furcatum Raf. See *C. calceolus* var. *kentuckiense* Reed.

Cypripedium guttatum Sw.   PLATE 16

GEOGRAPHIC DISTRIBUTION Widely distributed, this species has been found as far north as the Arctic Circle. It occurs in the Pacific Northwest, the western Canadian provinces, the Yukon, Alaska, Siberia, Japan, China, Manchuria, and east-central USSR. The type locality of var. *guttatum* is Japan. This variant is also independently established in the North American sector of its range. Although var. *yatabeanum* is largely Asian, the 2 varieties coexist and intergrade in the Aleutian archipelago and other intermediate parts of their range.

HABITAT *C. guttatum* is commonly found in meadows and grasslands, on the slopes of mountains, and occasionally in open birch woods or in thickets. It requires moisture during the growing season and can be found at elevations from sea level to 4,000–5,000 m (13,700–17,000 ft.).

CULTURAL NOTES Cultivation is not considered realistic in any but the colder climates. Bright conditions and ample moisture are required.

DESCRIPTION The plant is 15–35 cm (6–14 in.) in height. It bears glandular pubescence and brownish articulated hairs. The stem is covered basally with 2–3 tubular sheaths. It bears 2 alternate leaves arising at short internodes above the sheaths. The leaves are plicate and suberect, broadly elliptical and acuminate, 7–15 cm (2.75–6 in.) long by 2.5–6 cm (1–2.5 in.) wide. The foliose floral bract measures 2.5–3 cm (1–1.4 in.) long by 1.5 cm (0.3 in.) in width.

The solitary flower is white or cream and richly spotted with brown or purple. The dorsal sepal is ovate and acute, deeply concave and hoods the pouch in var. *yatabeanum*, while the dorsal of var. *guttatum* is erect. It measures 2–3 cm (1 in.) in length and 1.5 cm (0.5 in.) in width. The synsepalum is bidentate at its tip and is the smallest of the floral segments, measuring 1.5 cm (0.5 in.) long and 6–8 mm (0.25 in.) wide.

The petals are broad at their attachment narrowing to a blade with rounded or obtuse tips. Petal margins are subundulate. The length of the petals is approximately 1.5–2 cm (0.5–0.75 in.), and at their broadest point the width is 7–9 mm (0.25–0.3 in.). The labellum is roundly inflated with a broad orifice. It closely resembles certain *Paphiopedilum* pouches and is noticeably bucket-shaped. Pouch length varies from 2–2.5 cm (0.75–1 in.) and width averages about 1 cm (0.37 in.).

This species is notable for its excellent waxy substance. *C. guttatum* var. *guttatum* Sw. bears flowers of white marked with rich rose or magenta splotches, while *C. guttatum* var. *yatabeanum* Makino produces greenish to yellowish cream flowers spotted with tan to mahogany brown.

FLOWERING SEASON June to August, varying with both elevation and latitude.

COMMON NAMES *C. guttatum*, in agreement with its specific epithet, is called the Spotted Lady's Slipper.

Cypripedium henryi Rolfe   PLATE 17

C. henryi is synonymous with *C. chinense* Franch. These taxa are attributed by Atwood (1984b) to the *C. calceolus* alliance.

GEOGRAPHIC DISTRIBUTION Sichuan and Hupei, China.

HABITAT A montane species of undetermined elevational preference, *C. henryi* prefers the dappled shade of shrubby habitats or open woods.

CULTURAL NOTES Collectors and other visitors to the habitat have made recent reports of extant populations of this species. Some limited importation has occurred as well. For cultural guidelines, see the general information under *C. cordigerum*.

DESCRIPTION The pubescent stem rises 45–60 cm (18–24 in.) above the rhizome. It bears 4–5 elliptic, acute leaves which are strongly plicate and measure 10–20 cm (4–8 in.) in length.

The scape bears 2–4 flowers with yellow green segments and creamy white to yellow pouches. The flowers are quite large and measure 9 cm (3.5 in.) across. Each is subtended by a foliose bract. The acute dorsal sepal is ovate to broadly lanceolate. The ovate ventral sepal is bifid apically. The petals are linear-lanceolate. The pouch is subspheroid.

FLOWERING SEASON June.

Cypripedium himalaicum Rolfe

This species is included in the rather large assemblage of species allied to *C. macranthum* Sw. *C. pulchrum* Ames & Schltr. is a synonym.

GEOGRAPHIC DISTRIBUTION *C. himalaicum* is reported from the Lachen Valley, in Sikkim, India, from the Chumbi Valley in the western mountains of Bhutan, from Nepal and western China. *C. tibeticum*, likewise, is found in the Lachen Valley, as are Indian species of *Paphiopedilum*.

HABITAT Inhabiting the perimeters of forests and thickets, this species flourishes in association with shrubs and grasses on limestone rock at elevations of 3,000–5,300 m (10,000–18,200 ft.). It grows conspecifically with *C. tibeticum*.

CULTURAL NOTES See *C. cordigerum*.

DESCRIPTION The stems reach heights of 30–45 cm (12–18 in.). Basally sheathed with dried scales, the stems are leafy above. The elliptic-lanceolate leaves, typically 4 in number and unequal in length, are strongly plicate. The variable leaf length is 7.5–10 cm (3–4 in.). Leaf margins are undulate and ciliate.

Petals and sepals are yellow green and striped with red or liver brown. The broadly ovate dorsal sepal is concave and hoods the pouch aperture. The ventral sepal is apically bidentate. The pendulous petals are linear-lanceolate. The lip is subspheroid and compressed laterally. Its aperture is small and deeply corrugated. Lip color is maroon purple. Its infolded margins exhibit a creamy white border but become yellow green spotted with red within.

FLOWERING SEASON May through July.

Cypripedium hirsutum Mill. See *C. calceolus* L.

Cypripedium humile Pursh. See *C. acaule* Ait.

Cypripedium irapeanum Llave & Lex.   PLATE 18
    This species is undeniably related to the recently described *C. dickinsonianum* with which it lives conspecifically in Chiapas, Mexico. The precise nature of the alliance is presently undetermined. Although it is probable that these taxa will be ranked as variants of a single species, within this text they stand as described—2 separate species.
    GEOGRAPHIC DISTRIBUTION *C. irapeanum* has the most southerly range in the genus. Widely distributed, it is found throughout the mountains of the southern states of Mexico and in much of montane Guatemala.
    HABITAT This species inhabits well-drained slopes of high mountains and plateaus at elevations up to 3,300 m (11,300 ft.). The soil is heavy red clay but not acid. Plants generally colonize bright localities with limestone or volcanic ash in the substrate, receiving rainwater only in the wet spring and summer months. It is unclear whether the winter dormancy is associated with both freezing and drying, in all localities. Seepage is likely to be a factor of the habitat, mitigating the dry season's harshest effects.
    In most sites, the only shade for these plants is provided by grassy flora which stand about the same height as the orchids.
    CULTURAL NOTES This species is quite difficult in cultivation. Importation is not feasible because of the near certainty of death as a result of bare-root shipping and quarantine procedures. Local cultivation is rarely successful, and it is not clear whether water pH is responsible or if there are other factors involved.
    DESCRIPTION *C. irapeanum* is one of the tallest members of the genus, reaching heights of 75 cm (29.5 in.) or more. The stem bears 6–16 leaves. Lower leaves are significantly larger with size decreasing up the stem and grading into the size of the large floral bracts. Leaf length ranges from 20 cm (8 in.) to only 8–10 cm (3–4 in.). The ovate-lanceolate blade is widest at midleaf, and width varies from 6–8 cm (2.3–4.125 in.) on the lower leaves to only 2–4 cm (0.75–1.5 in.) on the small, upper leaves. Leaf arrangement is spiral. The foliose floral bract is 4–6 cm (1.5–2.3 in.) long by 1.5–3 cm (0.5–1.25 in.) wide and is a rich green color, as are the leaves.
    The inflorescence consists of 1–8 large, showy flowers of concolor yellow with wide, flat segments. The dorsal sepal is broadly ovate, acute, and measures 2–3 cm (1 in.) in length by 1.5–2 cm (0.5–0.75 in.) in width. The synsepalum is similar in all respects.
    The petals are ovate-lanceolate, acute, and measure 2.5–3.5 cm (1–1.5 in.) long by 1.5–2 cm (0.5–0.75 in.) wide. The labellum is spherically inflated with deeply infolded side lobes. It bears numerous crimson dots on its outer surface.
    FLOWERING SEASON July and August.
    COMMON NAMES There is no English equivalent, but the species has been called "pichahuastle."

Cypripedium japonicum Thunb.   PLATE 19
    The following species are considered to be related, perhaps in a more loosely knit group than the other alliances: *C. formosanum, C. margaritaceum, C. acaule, C. ebracteatum, C. elegans,* and *C. micranthum. C. cathayanum* Chien. is a synonym for this species.
    GEOGRAPHIC DISTRIBUTION *C. japonicum* is, of course, native to Japan. Much of its range there is thought to be artificial, that is, due more to human intervention than to former glaciations or other natural phenomena. It is common throughout the islands, except for the northern reaches of Hokkaido, and is found at intermediate and lower elevations. It is most abundant near populous regions. This species has also been reported from China on the Asian mainland.
    HABITAT Preferring dappled shade, *C. japonicum* flourishes in bamboo thickets and in forests of *Cryptomeria,* Japanese Cedar. It prefers well-drained soils and lower elevations. Therefore,

the lower slopes of mountains are choice sites. Japan's rainy season during June and July is an essential element of the habitat. This slipper is widely cultivated in Japan.

CULTURAL NOTES See habitat information above.

DESCRIPTION This species closely resembles *C. formosanum*, although it differs in that is possesses a richer floral color. The leaves of both species are distinctively fan-shaped, and held some distance up the stem. Their flowers also are similar in shape.

When in flower *C. japonicum* stands approximately 40 cm (18 in.) tall. The 2 subopposite leaves are borne midway up the stem and, as in *C. formosanum*, are broader than long, corrugate-plicate, fan-shaped and measure 15–20 cm (6–8 in.) in length by 20–30 cm (8–12 in.) in width. The radiate venation produces ridges; there is no strong midvein. The color is apple-green.

The pubescent peduncle bears a solitary flower subtended by a foliose floral bract. The bract is lanceolate and acute, measuring 4–6 cm (1.5–2.5 in.) in length and 2.5–3 cm (1–1.25 in) in width.

The dorsal sepal hoods the pouch, and like the ventral sepal and petals, is a pale yellow green. Sepals and petals are undulate, lanceolate and acute. The dorsal sepal is approximately 2–2.5 cm (0.75–1 in.) long and 1.5–2 cm (0.5–0.75 in.) wide. The ventral sepal is proportionately smaller. The petals are longer, measuring 2.5–3.5 cm (1–1.3 in.) in length, but no wider than the sepals. The pouch is pink to deep rose and bears a slitlike aperture proximally which widens to an enlarged, teardrop-shaped orifice distally. The rim of the orifice is corrugated by the pouch venation. The entire outer surface of the labellum is deeply veined.

FLOWERING SEASON April and May.

COMMON NAMES This slipper has no English common names, but in Japan is called "Kumagaya's herb." The name is derived from the resemblance of the labellum to the bustle worn by this ancient warrior.

Cypripedium knightae A. Nels. See *C. fasciculatum* Kell. ex S. Wats.

Cypripedium lanuginosum Schltr.

C. lanuginosum Schltr. (syn. *C. lanuginosa* Schltr.) is a dwarf species which is also allied to *C. himalaicum*.

GEOGRAPHIC DISTRIBUTION Western China.

HABITAT A montane species, *C. lanuginosum* prefers wooded sites. Its habitat is very similar to that of *C. himalaicum*.

CULTURAL NOTES See *C. cordigerum*.

DESCRIPTION The vegetative and floral parts of this species are densely pubescent, and it is this characteristic which suggested the species epithet. Growing from a rhizome, the slender hirsute stem reaches heights of 15–25 cm (6–10 in.) and bears 2–3 leaves. The pubescent leaves clasp the stem basally; they are elliptic, acute apically. Leaf length is 7.5–11.5 cm (3–4.5 in.).

The solitary flower measures approximately 6 cm (2.5 in.) across. The erect dorsal sepal is elliptic-ovate and apically acute. The elliptic synsepalum is connate to its acute apex. The petals are spreading, lanceolate and apically acute. The labellum is ovoid. Flowers are greenish yellow in ground color and overlaid with maroon stripes on the sepals and petals, while the pouch is suffused with liver to aubergine.

FLOWERING SEASON August.

Cypripedium luteum Franch. See *C. flavum* Ward.

Cypripedium macranthum Sw. PLATES 20 & 26

This Oriental slipper is allied to many other Asian species, making up yet another alliance including *C. corrugatum*, *C. fasciolatum*, *C. himalaicum*, *C. lanuginosum*, *C. speciosum*, *C. thunbergii*, *C. tibeticum*, *C. wilsonii* and *C. yunnanense*.

GEOGRAPHIC DISTRIBUTION Japan, Korea, Manchuria, northern China, Kamchatka, Siberia and eastern Europe all list this species among their flora.

HABITAT *C. macranthum* inhabits both northern latitudes and regions of higher elevations. This showy slipper prefers cold climates, tolerates summer heat poorly, and thrives in bright light. It is typically reported from grassy mountain slopes.

CULTURAL NOTES See habitat information above. See also cultural guidelines under *C. cordigerum*.

DESCRIPTION Achieving a height of 30–50 cm (12–20 in.), this species bears 5–7 spirally arranged leaves upon a pubescent stem. The flower is typically solitary; bifloral individuals occur rarely. The leaves are ovate-lanceolate and acute, strongly plicate, sheathing the stem. Lowermost leaves are largest, reaching lengths of up to 20 cm (8 in.) and widths of 8–10 cm (3.5–4 in.). Upper leaves grade down in size to near that of the leaflike floral bract which measures 6–10 cm (2.25–4 in.) in length by 4–6 cm (1.75–2.25 in.) in width.

The typical flower reaches overall dimensions of 7–9 cm (3 in.) and is a concolor pink, fuschia or purple. A white-flowered var. *albiflorum* is known, while *C. macranthum* var. *rebunense*, an endemic of Rebun Island in Hokkaido, is a rare yellow-flowered form.

The concave dorsal sepal hoods the labellar orifice. Broadly ovate and acute, its dimensions are 4–5 cm (2 in.) in length by 3–4 cm (1.25–1.5 in) in width. The ventral sepal is much smaller, measuring 2.5–3 cm (1–1.25 in.) long and 1.5–2 cm (0.5–0.75 in.) wide.

The petals are flat, curving forward around the belly of the labellum. Lanceolate and acuminate, they measure 3–4.5 cm (1.25–1.75 in.) in length by 1–1.5 cm (0.3–0.6 in.) in width. The pouch is large and roundly inflated. The venation creates corrugation about the aperture.

FLOWERING SEASON May and June.

COMMON NAMES As is true of several Asian species, there is no English common name. However, the Japanese call it "Atsumori's herb" in commemoration of an ancient warrior.

Cypripedium manchuricum Stapf. See. *C. ventricosum* Sw.

Cypripedium margaritaceum Franch. PLATE 21

C. fargesii is considered to be synonymous with this species. Part of the large *C. japonicum* alliance, *C. margaritaceum* belongs to the bractless portion of this alliance. *C. wumengense* is a newly described species which has many features in common with *C. margaritaceum*. See *C. wumengense* for details of the parallels and differences between these 2 species.

GEOGRAPHIC DISTRIBUTION *C. margaritaceum* is reported from Yunnan Province, China.

HABITAT This montane species prefers moist, well-drained limestone slopes in pine or mixed forests at elevations around 3,400 m (11,000 ft.). It was observed by Lancaster (1982) growing on limestone on the eastern flank of the Lijiang Range.

CULTURAL NOTES This species has been imported on a limited basis and is being cultivated in cooler climates. See habitat information above. See also *C. cordigerum* for general cultural information.

DESCRIPTION Prior to Chen's publication of *C. wumengense* in 1985, the foliage of *C. margaritaceum* was unique in the genus in bearing spotting. The 2–3 suberect, acauline leaves, strongly ribbed and suborbiculate like those of *C. japonicum*, are striking in appearance due to the roughly circular, sometimes overlapping, spots of liver maroon liberally dotted over them.

The leaves measure up to 15 cm (6 in.) across.

The scape is only 15 cm (6 in.) tall. Its lack of height, in conjunction with its large leaves, gives the flower the appearance of nestling in a spotted bowl.

The solitary, bractless flower is yellow green with purple stripes on the sepals and petals and spotting or suffusion of purple on the pouch. The segments are covered with purple pubescence as well.

Sepals and petals are ovate, apically acute and concave. Their forward orientation embracing the pouch creates the appearance of a partially opened bud, even at full anthesis.
FLOWERING SEASON May.

Cypripedium marianus Krantz. See *C. calceolus* L.

Cyprepedium micranthum Franch.

This species is closely allied to *C. margaritaceum* and the several bractless members of the *C. japonicum* alliance.
GEOGRAPHIC DISTRIBUTION *C. micranthum* is reported from Sichuan Province, China.
HABITAT Habitat information is very limited, but it is known to prefer open mixed forest.
CULTURAL NOTES See *C. cordigerum*.
DESCRIPTION Nearly acaulescent, the stem rises not more than 2 cm (0.75 in.) above the rhizome. Two leaves, subopposite in position and measuring up to 10 cm (4 in.), are borne upon the foreshortened stem. In shape, the leaves are oblongate; in color, they are deep green. They stand semierect creating a funnel from which the short scape arises.

The pubescent scape extends approximately 9 cm (3.5 in.) above the leaves and bears a solitary flower without a bract. The flower measures up to 6.5 cm (2.5 in.) across. The floral segments are yellowish green, while only the lip bears purple blotches. The apically acute dorsal sepal ranges from ovate-oblongate to broadly lanceolate. The synsepalum is broadly lanceolate and bidentate at the apex. The petals are ovate and acuminate; the purple-blotched pouch is obovoid.
FLOWERING SEASON May and June.

Cypripedium microsaccus Kraenzl.

This species is a member of the *C. calceolus* alliance.
GEOGRAPHIC DISTRIBUTION The Primorski region of Siberia is host to *C. microsaccus*.
HABITAT Living at or near sea level, this species inhabits the marshy perimeters of rivers and lakes.
CULTURAL NOTES Probably not currently in cultivation, this species should be attempted only in cold climates. Ample moisture is a critical factor in its cultivation.
DESCRIPTION *C. microsaccus* produces pubescent, leafy stems up to 30–45 cm (12–18 in.) in height. The 4–6 pubescent, ovate-oblongate leaves measure up to 15 cm (6 in.) in length.

The bifloral scapes bear a large foliose bract beneath each flower. Flowers measure 6 cm (2.3 in.) across. The sepals are pinkish brown and lanceolate; the ventral sepal is apically bidentate. The petals are aubergine in color, linear-lanceolate and twisted. The pouch is quite short, roundly inflated and yellow in color.
FLOWERING SEASON June.

Cypripedium molle Lindl. See *C. irapeanum* Llave & Lex.

Cypripedium montanum Dougl. ex Lindl.   PLATE 22
This species is part of the large alliance which includes *C. calceolus*. According to Atwood (1985a), it should also be considered as part of the close complex of *C. calceolus*.

GEOGRAPHIC DISTRIBUTION As one would expect from its specific epithet, this species is distributed in mountainous regions. Found in the western United States and Canada, it has been reported from Montana, Idaho, Wyoming, California, Oregon, Washington, Alberta, British Columbia, Vancouver Island and Alaska.

HABITAT Preferring wooded montane slopes at intermediate to high elevations, *C. montanum* thrives from 1,500 m (5,000 ft.) up to subalpine levels. Not only is it is pH tolerant, but it tolerates moist or dry soils and varying levels of canopy from dense to bright shade. Cool temperatures are, however, critical. Moist, open, deciduous woods provide the most frequently colonized habitat.

CULTURAL NOTES This species is not difficult within climatic constraints. See habitat information above.

DESCRIPTION The slender, erect plant stands 30–35 cm (12–14 in.) high when in flower; immature individuals rarely exceed 25 cm (10 in.). The alternate leaves number 4–6 and sheath the stem. They are ovate-lanceolate and acute. They grade smaller in size as they progress up the stem to near the size of the floral bracts. The largest, lowermost leaves are 5–16 cm (2–6.5 in.) long and 2.5–8 cm (1–2.75 in.) wide. The plant is sparsely pubescent throughout. Unlike *C. candidum*, the other white-lipped ally of *C. calceolus* which flowers while its leaves are still developing, *C. montanum* goes into anthesis only after the leaves have fully expanded.

An erect flowerstalk bears 2–3 well-spaced, fragrant flowers which strongly resemble the flowers of *C. calceolus* except that the labellar color is white. The sepals and petals are held well out from the pouch, although the apex of the dorsal sepal hoods the pouch, and the petals are pendulous. Sepals and petals are khaki to brown or aubergine. All these segments exhibit some marginal undulation.

The dorsal sepal is more or less broadly lanceolate and acute. It measures 3–6 cm (1.2–2.3 in.) in length and 1–1.5 cm (0.25–0.5 in.) in width proximally, tapering distally to a slender point. The ventral sepal is often apically bidentate and is similar in length and width to the dorsal sepal.

The narrow, twisted petals become pendulous and curve minimally toward the front of the pouch. They attain lengths of 4.5–7 cm (1.75–2.75 in.) and rarely exceed 0.5 cm (0.125 in.) in width.

The labellum is roundly inflated, although dorsiventrally flattened and bears a strong resemblance in shape to a bedpan. Venation on the pouch produces deep grooves. Pale suffusions of pink or purple may adorn the pouch, or the color may be cream or dazzling white. The inner surface of the pouch is marked with dots and veins of magenta.

FLOWERING SEASON May to July.

COMMON NAMES Often called the Mountain Lady's Slipper, it is also known as the Large White Lady's Slipper.

Cypripedium nutans Schltr. See *C. acaule* Ait. See also *C. bardolphianum* W. W. Sm. & Farrer.

Cypripedium occidentale Wats. See *C. montanum* Dougl. ex Lindl.

Cypripedium orientale Spreng. See *C. guttatum* Sw.

Cypripedium palangshanense Tang & Wang

GEOGRAPHIC DISTRIBUTION This species is indigenous to northwest Sichuan Province, China.

HABITAT The habitat data of the 1936 publication of this species is quite limited, revealing only that it grows at an elevation of 2,200 m (7,550 ft.).

CULTURAL NOTES See *C. cordigerum*.

DESCRIPTION The plant reaches a height of 12 cm. (4.75 in.), bearing a pair of opposite leaves at midstem. The suborbicular leaves are glabrous, 5 cm. (2 in.) in both length and width.

The solitary, nodding flower is deep purple and is subtended by a lanceolate bract measuring 2.5 cm (1 in.) long by 0.8 cm (0.3 in.) wide.

The dorsal sepal is narrowly lanceolate and apically acuminate. It measures 2 cm (0.75 in.) long by 0.4 cm (less than 0.25 in.) wide and cups forward to hood the labellar aperture. The apically bidentate ventral sepal is similar but more than twice as wide.

The lanceolate petals are held obliquely; apices are acuminate. They measure 1.8 cm (0.75 in.) long by 0.6 cm (0.25 in.) wide. The small labellum is obovoid and measures 1 cm (0.3 in.) long by 0.6 cm (0.25 in.) wide.

FLOWERING SEASON June.

Cypripedium parvulum Fedde. See *C. calceolus* L.

Cypripedium passerinum Richards.   PLATE 23

GEOGRAPHIC DISTRIBUTION This species is restricted to northern latitudes of the North American continent, and is known to occur very near the Arctic Circle, perhaps within it. It also occurs at high elevations, but is indigenous only in the Canadian provinces and Alaska, never having been reported from any of the contiguous 48 states.

HABITAT *C. passerinum* inhabits moist, evergreen forests and littoral zones. It clings to steep banks of ravines and flourishes just as well in gravelly outwash plains. It apparently tolerates acid humus or calcareous substrates equally well. Cold soil temperatures are essential for its success. Populations thrive at elevations up to 2,400 m (8,200 ft.).

CULTURAL NOTES This species is not currently maintained in cultivation. Climate restrictions severely limit possibilities for success.

DESCRIPTION The erect stem measures 20 cm (8 in.) tall in the unbloomed state, and up to 30 cm (12 in.) in height when in flower. Its lower section is nearly concealed by the 3–5 leaves which sheath it and remain subconvolute around it. The leaves are ovate-lanceolate and obtuse to acute. Leaf length is 5–16 cm (2–6.5 in.) and the width is 1.5–5 cm (0.75–2 in.). The elliptic floral bracts measure 6–8 cm (1.25–3 in.) in length and up to 2 cm (0.75 in.) in width.

The nodding, fragrant flowers are typically solitary. The dorsal sepal is olive to apple green, broad and concave. The degree to which the dorsal hoods the pouch and its orifice is so pronounced that the upper surface of the labellum can be seen only by peering into the cavern of the dorsal. It measures 1.5–2 cm (0.75 in.) in length and 1–1.5 cm (0.5 in.) in width. The lateral sepals vary in degree of fusion from nearly separate to bidentate at the very tip. Whether as a single ventral sepal or a pair of laterals, these structures always appress themselves closely to the undersurface of the labellum. When separate the sepals spread at about a 30° angle, and each is elliptic and acute, 1–1.5 cm (0.5 in.) long and rarely more than 0.5 cm (0.125 in.) wide. A well-fused synsepalum is equal in length to a lateral sepal but approximates the width of the dorsal sepal.

The white petals are suffused with pale green, flat and curved forward as if to embrace the pouch. Linear-elliptic to oblongate, they bear bluntly obtuse apices. Petals are 2 cm (0.75 in.) in length and less than 0.5 cm (0.125 in.) wide. The pouch is broadly but not spherically inflated, varying in color from white with minute purple spots to rose with purple spots. The spotting is most dense upon the lower pouch surface beneath its chin. At the aperture, the margins are deeply infolded.

FLOWERING SEASON June to August.

COMMON NAMES The Sparrow's Egg Lady's Slipper is an apt common name for this species.

Cypripedium plectrochilum Franch. See *C. arietinum* R. Brown.

Cypripedium pulchrum Ames & Schltr. See *C. himalaicum* Rolfe.

Cypripedium pusillum Rolfe. See *C. fasciculatum* Kell. ex S. Wats.

Cypripedium reginae Walt. PLATES 24 & 25

An occasionally used synonym is *C. spectabile* Salisb. Even more obscure synonyms are: *C. album* Ait. and *C. canadense* Michx.

C. reginae is the only species of slipper orchid to be selected as a state flower in the United States, having been so honored by the state of Wisconsin.

GEOGRAPHIC DISTRIBUTION *C. reginae* occurs widely in central and eastern North America. It is reported throughout the Appalachian region from Alabama northward to Nova Scotia and Newfoundland. Found westward as far as Saskatchewan, this species is fairly abundant throughout the Great Lakes states and southward to Missouri. Native also to western China, *C. reginae* has even been reported by Eric Hagsater (personal communication) in Mexico, near Monterray, Nuevo Leon.

HABITAT This delicately beautiful species inhabits both boggy areas and dry upland slopes. It is particularly abundant in the Great Lakes region in balsam-spruce-tamarack bogs. It thrives equally well in meadow grasslands, narrow fingers of prairie and mossy woods. It frequently grows in proximity to *C. arietinum* and *C. calceolus*.

CULTURAL NOTES *C. reginae* is difficult to cultivate. While its natural conditions of temperature, soil pH, moisture and light are all readily duplicated by gardeners, a further unknown barrier frequently defeats attempts at culture. Correll (1950) postulates that fungus attacks bring about the death of transplanted individuals. Although this species is amenable to cultivation, the secret of success is elusive. Heavy mulching is recommended.

DESCRIPTION This showy species is quite large, reaching heights of 35–85 cm (14–33.5 in.) when in flower. The erect stem bears 3–7 leaves. Ovate to elliptic and acute, the leaves are strongly plicate with hirsute margins and veins. Glandular hairs prevail throughout. The large, ribbed leaves measure 10–25 cm (4–10 in.) in length and 6–15 cm (3.3–6 in.) in width.

The inflorescence bears 1–4 large flowers subtended by large, foliose bracts. Bracts are elliptic to lanceolate and acute, 6–12 cm (2.3–4.75 in.) long and 2.5–5 cm (1–2 in.) wide.

The white sepals and petals are held well back and flat. The broad dorsal sepal is ovate, 3–5 cm (1.3–2 in.) long and 2–3.5 cm (0.75–1.5 in.) wide, hooding the labellum only slightly. The synsepalum is similar in shape and somewhat smaller, measuring 3–4 cm (1.2–1.5 in.) in length by 2–3 cm (1 in.) in width. Not uncommonly, the ventral sepal is deeply bifid, almost separate as 2 free lateral sepals.

The petals are ovate-lanceolate, acute to obtuse, and measure 2.5–4 cm (1–1.5 in.) in length by 1–1.5 cm (0.5 in.) in width. The pouch is broadly inflated and corrugated by its venation. Its typical color is white with a pink blush, but rose to magenta suffusion is also observed. Rarely an albino flower (Plate 25) with a white pouch is seen. The veins, which are typically colored rose or magenta, remain white in these rare specimens as well.

The unusual feature of this flower, and a quite primitive characteristic, is the presence of a trilobed stigma. Peloria occurs occasionally in *C. reginae*, producing a flower with 3 petals and no pouch.

The source of the contact irritant produced by this species is reported to be the glandular hairs on the epidermis. Some evidence exists to indicate the presence of raphides (bundles of needle-shaped crystals) as well. Victims of the skin eruptions resulting from contact with this species report that the potency of the irritant increases over the growing season, reaching its maximum only when seed capsules are present.

FLOWERING SEASON May and June, in the United States; as late as July in the Canadian Provinces.

COMMON NAMES Showy Lady's Slipper, Queen Lady's Slipper and Large White Lady's Slipper are among the most frequently used common names for this species.

Cypripedium shanxiense S. C. Chen sp. nov.

Chen (1983) describes this species as having an affinity nearest *C. henryi* Rolfe and belonging to Section *Cypripedium*.

GEOGRAPHIC DISTRIBUTION This slipper is found in Shanxi Province, China.

HABITAT Preferring semishade in meadows, this species is found at elevations of 950–2,300 m (3,250–7,900 ft.).

CULTURAL NOTES Cultural practices described for *C. cordigerum* should be effective.

DESCRIPTION The plant stands 40–55 cm (16–22 in.) tall. The stem is erect, pubescent and sheathed basally with 3–4 leaves. Above the basal leaves, 3–4 free leaves arise which are elliptic-lanceolate, apically acuminate and arranged alternately. They measure 7–15 cm (2.75–6 in.) in length by 4–8 cm (1.6–3.2 in.) in width. All the leaves are sparsely pubescent with ciliate margins.

The inflorescence bears 1–3 flowers. A bifloral inflorescence is the norm. Foliar bracts subtend the flowers. The bracts measure 5.5–10 cm (2.2–4 in.) long by 1–3 cm (0.3–1.2 in.) wide. The purple flowers measure approximately 4 cm (1.6 in.) across.

The lanceolate dorsal sepal measures 3–3.5 cm (1.2–1.3 in.) long by 1 cm (0.6 in.) wide. Apically, it is more or less tailed or strongly acuminate. The ventral sepal is similar but shorter and apically bidentate.

The glabrous, linear-lanceolate petals are similar in length to the sepals but measure only 0.7 cm (0.25 in.) in width. The labellum is small and subglobose, measuring 1.6–2 cm (0.6–0.75 in.) long by 1.3 cm (0.5 in.) wide.

FLOWERING SEASON May and June.

Cypripedium speciosum Rolfe

This slipper is allied with *C. macranthum*.

GEOGRAPHIC DISTRIBUTION *C. speciosum* is native to Japan.

HABITAT According to Darnell (1930), this species sparsely inhabits forested regions.

CULTURAL NOTES I have found no cultural information for this species.

DESCRIPTION Aerial stems rise 20–40 cm (8–16 in.) above the rhizome. Densely pubescent, the stout stems bear a few pale green, pubescent leaves. The lower leaves are broadly ovate. Those borne higher up the stem become progressively more oblongate or broadly lanceolate, grading into the large foliose bracts. Leaf length is 5–15 cm (2–6 in.).

The solitary flower measures 7.5 cm (3 in.) across. Creamy white to pale blush pink petals and sepals exhibit rosy crimson spotting basally with venation of the same deep color. The dorsal sepal is broadly ovate or subcircular. Apically, it curves over the orifice of the pouch. The ventral sepal is oblongate and bifid apically. The long showy petals are pendulous and lanceolate. The subspheroid pouch is unsculpted by veins or corrugations; however, its blush-pink color is lined with venation of deep crimson. The margin of the orifice is pure white rimmed with crimson.

FLOWERING SEASON May to July.

Cypripedium spectabile Salisb. See *C. reginae* Walt.

Cypripedium splendidum Scheid. See *C. irapeanum* Llave & Lex.

Cypripedium subtropicum Chen & Lang sp. nov.

Discovered in 1980, this species was published in 1986 together with a discussion of its similarity in growth habit, inflorescence and column to *Selenipedium*. The authors included their assessment of the phylogeny of *Cypripedium* and its descent from *Selenipedium*, as well as a recommendation for further study of relationships in thier publication. Perhaps more an example of parallel evolution than evidence to support phylogenetic claims, this species is, nonetheless, intriguing.

Chen and Lang (1986) place *C. subtropicum* in a new section, Section *Subtropica* sect. nov. Its similarity to other multifloral species such as *C. californicum* and *C. irapeanum* illustrates the need for intensive phylogenetic, molecular and genetic investigation in this group in order to clarify relative taxonomic positions. I have included it in the alliance with *C. irapeanum*, although not adopting the section name suggested by Chen and Lang (1986).

GEOGRAPHIC DISTRIBUTION The published locality is Xizang, the Chinese name for Tibet.

HABITAT Living at 1,400 m. (5,000 ft.), this species is found in alder forests.

CULTURAL NOTES Cultural information is unavailable.

DESCRIPTION A short, thick rhizome produces erect stems reaching heights of 1.5 m (60 in.). The stem bears a multifloral, terminal raceme of flowers each of which is subtended by a small lanceolate bract. The terete, pubescent stems are thick and measure as much as 1 cm. (0.35 in.) in diameter of dried specimens. The base of the stem is sheathed with 5–6 closely appressed leaves; 9–10 erect free leaves arise alternately from the upper stem. The free leaves are prominently veined, elliptic-lanceolate in shape, and measure 21–33 cm (8.25–12.5 in.) long by 7.7–10.5 cm (3–4.3 in.) wide. Pubescence occurs along the venation. Leaf margins are sparsely ciliate.

The inflorescence produces up to 7 flowers. Bracts and pedicels are adorned with black hair. The flowers are golden yellow with reddish brown to purple blotches upon the lips.

The elliptic dorsal sepal measures 3.5–3.9 cm (1.3–1.5 in.) long by 2.2–2.5 cm (1 in.) wide. Apically acuminate, it bears black hairs upon its reverse surface and ciliate margins. The ovate-elliptic synsepalum cups forward. Apically bidentate, it also exhibits marginal cilia and black hairs on the reverse.

The oblongate petals measure 3–6 cm (1.25–2.3 in.) long by 0.9–1.1 cm (0.3 in.) wide. Black hairs adorn the reverse surfaces as well as the proximal portions of the frontal surfaces. The labellum is held nearly horizontal, thrust pugnaciously forward. Obovoid to ellipsoid in shape, it measures 4–4.6 cm (1.5–1.75 in.) long and about 3 cm (1.2 in.) across. Its outer surface is glabrous. The aperture is oblongate. The very small staminode is held rather distant from the column, in this species.

FLOWERING SEASON July.

Cypripedium thunbergii Bl.

C. thunbergii belongs to the *C. macranthum* alliance.

GEOGRAPHIC DISTRIBUTION Japan hosts this species.

HABITAT Semishade at forest perimeters provides the favored site for *C. thunbergii*.

CULTURAL NOTES There is a dearth of cultural or habitat information about this species.

DESCRIPTION The sturdy stem rises 30–45 cm (12–18 in.) above the rhizome and bears numerous leaves, the bases of which overlap the stem as well as the leafbase of the next superior leaf. Apically acute, the leaves are broadly oblongate and strongly plicate, measuring 10–15 cm (4–6 in.) in length.

The scape bears a large foliose bract beneath the solitary flower. Bifloral scapes are rare in this species.

The large flower measures 7.5 cm (3 in.) across and 5 cm (2 in.) vertically. Concolor rosy pink, only the pouch exhibits maroon reticulations. The erect dorsal sepal is lanceolate and acute. The synsepalum is narrow and bidentate apically. The spreading petals are linear-lanceolate. The labellum is spheroidally inflated.

FLOWERING SEASON June and July.

Cypripedium tibeticum King ex Hemal.

  This member of the *C. macranthum* alliance may come to be ruled synonymous with *C. corrugatum* or a variant form of it.

GEOGRAPHIC DISTRIBUTION Reports place this species in western China and Tibet.

HABITAT A true alpine species, this plant grows among grasses at elevations of over 3,500 m (12,000 ft.).

CULTURAL NOTES See *C. cordigerum.*

DESCRIPTION The erect stem stands 7.5–45 cm (3–18 in.) in height and bears 3–4 leaves, whose bases sheath the stem. The strongly plicate, nearly glabrous leaves bear ciliate, undulate margins. Measuring 6–15 cm (2.5–6 in.) in length, they are acute and ovate-oblongate.

  The large nodding flower is borne singly, and measures 7.5–15 cm (3–6 in.) across. Sepals and petals are blush pink in ground color overlaid with tessellations of rich maroon. Pouch color is deep maroon purple. The acute dorsal sepal is ovate and arches over the labellar aperture. The ventral sepal is bifid apically. The elliptic petals bear undulate margins and typically clasp the pouch in a semiopen attitude. The subglobose pouch bears corrugations about the infolded lip margins.

FLOWERING SEASON July and August.

Cypripedium vaganum Cockl. & Baker. See *C. calceolus* L.

Cypripedium variegatum Falk. See *C. guttatum* Sw.

Cypripedium variegatum Georyi. See *C. guttatum* Sw.

Cypripedium ventricosum Sw.   PLATES 26 & 27

  C. manchuricum Stapf is illustrated and discussed in the *Botanical Magazine*, Tab. 9117 of 1927, as a new species. It is clear from the account that it is synonymous with the older *C. ventricosum*.

GEOGRAPHIC DISTRIBUTION *C. manchuricum* was described as native to southeastern Siberia; *C. ventricosum*, according to Slyusarenko (1981), is found throughout the USSR. Over the years, it has been reported from various sites in eastern Asia.

HABITAT Thriving in damp sites bordering hardwood and mixed forests, in montane meadows and shrubby thickets, and preferring moist humus as a substrate, it is most abundant in river basins.

CULTURAL NOTES See habitat information.

DESCRIPTION The pubescent stem stands up to 60 cm (24 in.) tall, typically bearing 5 broadly elliptic leaves. The leaves are apically acuminate and sheath the stem basally. Rarely bifloral, the typical specimen bears a solitary flower. The ovate dorsal sepal is apically acuminate. It hoods the pouch and measures 3–6 cm (1.25–2.3 in.) long by 2–2.5 cm (0.75–1 in.) wide. The synsepalum is similar in size and shape. Both sepals are ciliolate basally, otherwise glabrous. Sepal color varies from greenish through white to rose, red or purple.

  C. ventricosum bears linear-lanceolate, acute petals which are held just below horizontal and curve around the pouch. The petals are pubescent proximal to the pouch and measure 3–6 cm (1.25–2.3 in) long by 1 cm (0.3 in.) wide. The pouch is broadly inflated and corrugated, with a small oval aperture. It varies from globose to a somewhat flattened elongate-obovoid shape. Its overall dimensions are 3–5 cm (1.25–2 in.). Pouch color typically agrees with the flower color, although the margin of the orifice is quite pale. In fact, the flower color is highly variable and includes white, cream, rose, purple, and bicolored white and rose/red specimens. Individuals which are collected from forested sites tend to produce smaller flowers of darker hue, while the meadow specimens achieve significantly

larger size with magnificent pouches exhibiting enormous color variety.
FLOWERING SEASON May and June.

Cypripedium wardii Rolfe. See *C. guttatum* Sw.

Cypripedium wilsoni Rolfe
GEOGRAPHIC DISTRIBUTION This species grows in Sichuan Province, China.
HABITAT *C. wilsonii* prefers deep forest shade at an elevation of about 2,100 m (7,300 ft.).
CULTURAL NOTES See the recommendations for *C. cordigerum*.
DESCRIPTION The pubescent stem reaches heights of 30–37.5 cm (12–15 in.), and bears numerous sheathing leaves. The pubescent free leaves are ovate, apically acute and strongly plicate. They measure 7.5–15 cm (3–6 in.) long by 5–12.5 cm (2–5 in.) wide.

The large solitary flower measures 15 cm (6 in.) across. The ground color of the segments is yellow; sepals and petals are striped with liver brown, while the pouch is blotched with the same brown color. The acute dorsal sepal is ovate; the ventral sepal is slightly narrower and apically bidentate. The spreading petals are narrowly oblongate and apically acuminate. The lip is ovoid and corrugated about the aperture.
FLOWERING SEASON June.

Cypripedium wumengense S. C. Chen sp. nov.
Although described in 1985 as a new species, this ebracteate taxon may well be a variant form of *C. margaritaceum* with which it shares not only its overall geographic range but the unusual possession of liver brown spotting of its foliage. However, without firsthand knowledge it is unwise to consign such a newly described taxon to inclusion within an existing species even on the basis of so singular a characteristic. Chen (1985) enumerates the following ways in which *C. wumengense* varies from *C. margaritaceum*:
1. The sepals and petals of *C. wumengense* are glabrous in contrast to the pubescence of those same segments in *C. margaritaceum*. In addition, these segments of *C. margaritaceum* clasp the belly of the lip, while they are held in a more open orientation according to the description of *C. wumengense*.
2. The lip of *C. wumengense* is smaller and verrucous (warted). Carson Whitlow (personal communication) adds that the lip of *C. margaritaceum* is quite fleshy, shallow dorsiventrally, and circular in outline.
3. The foliage of *C. wumengense* is longer than wide, while that of *C. margaritaceum* is typically wider than long.
GEOGRAPHIC DISTRIBUTION *C. wumengense* is reported from Yunnan Province, China.
HABITAT Found at 2,900 m (9,950 ft.), this species inhabits the western slopes of Mt. Wu Meng in the shade of shrubby growth where it roots on calcarous outcrops.
CULTURAL NOTES No information beyond the habitat description is currently available.
DESCRIPTION The plants reach a height of 22 cm (8.6 in.) with the stems arising from a very small rhizome. The basal portion of the erect stem is sheathed by several leaves; the 2 open leaves are arranged alternately and held erect. The leaves are ovate-elliptic, apically mucronate, and measure 11–13 cm (4.3–5.2 in.) long by 6.5–7 cm (2.5–2.75 in.) wide. Green with purple-brown spots, the leaves are glabrous and bear prominent veins.

The solitary flower is composed of segments held well back and open; it measures 6–7 cm (2.3–2.6 in.) across and arises without a bract. Pigmentation of dried specimens takes on a stippled-striated appearance, exhibiting regular purple striations.

The broadly ovate, apically mucronate dorsal sepal measures 3.5 cm (1.4 in.) long by 2.8 cm (1.2 in.) wide. The elliptic synsepal is only briefly bidentate at the apex, and measures 4 cm (1.5 in.) long by 2 cm (0.75 in.) wide. Both sepals bear ciliate margins but are otherwise glabrous.

The glabrous petals are held in an open and horizontal position. Oblongate-spathulate in shape, they bear ciliate margins and obtuse-mucronate apices. Petal length is 4 cm (1.6 in.) while the width is about 1.5 cm (0.6 in.). The small; subglobose labellum measures about 1.6 cm (0.65 in.) in diameter. Its orifice is subcircular.
FLOWERING SEASON April and May.

Cypripedium yunnanense Franch.
    C. yunnanense is allied to *C. macranthum.*
GEOGRAPHIC DISTRIBUTION This species is native to Yunnan Province, China.
HABITAT Dry pine forests provide medium to dense shade for this species. Further habitat information is not available.
CULTURAL NOTES See *C. cordigerum.*
DESCRIPTION The sparsely pubescent stem stands approximately 30 cm (12 in.) tall, bearing 3–4 leaves. Apically acuminate, the leaves are narrowly oblongate and pubescent beneath; they measure 7.5–10 cm (3–4 in.) in length.
    The solitary flower is subtended by a large lanceolate bract and measures 6 cm (2.5 in.) across. The sepals and petals are white striped with purple. The acuminate dorsal sepal is oblongate; the ventral sepal is ovate. The acute petals are elliptic-lanceolate. The ovoid pouch is rosy purple with darker purple venation.
FLOWERING SEASON June and July.

Fissipes acaulis Sm. See *C. acaule* Ait.

Several binomials found in the literature have been excluded from these species descriptions as it is presently unclear which are valid species names and which are synonyms. They are sure to be taxa of one alliance and/or complex or another, but whether they are variants or synonyms of better-known species or discrete species in their own rights remains obscure. Several of these obscure binomials represent plants indigenous to the Orient, and are acknowledged to be cloaked in the mystery still surrounding many of the plants of that region. The list includes *C. calcicola* Schltr., *C. compactum* Schltr., *C. smithii* Schltr., *C. turgidum* Sesse & Moc., and *C. vernayi* F. K. Ward. Of these, *C. vernayi* is discussed briefly, below.
    F. Kingdon Ward wrote in *TheGardeners' Chronicle* (1938) of his discovery of *C. vernayi* and gave a compelling, if informal, description. He places the species in the eastern Irrawaddy in Burma at an elevation of 1,460 m (5,000 ft.), where he found it in bloom in late November. Stating that he climbed a tree to retrieve the first specimen from high upon the trunk, he describes the common habitat as terrestrial and semishady on moist cliffs with an eastern exposure. His description is vivid, if incomplete. The 30-cm (12-in.) stem is wooly and white. The green leaves are leathery in texture and measure 30–38 cm (12–15 in.) in length. The flower measurement is 12.5 cm (5 in.) both vertically and across. Floral ground color is apple green. Both sepals are blotched centrally with maroon brown. The striking petals are green below the midvein and maroon above with no blending between the 2 regions of color. Pouch color is buff or pale green, suffused with a blush of red. No mention is made of more than a solitary flower per growth. Shapes and most measurements of vegetative and floral structures are omitted from the preliminary description. There can be no doubt of Ward's singular pleasure in his discovery, although I question its generic placement. It seems highly likely that this specimen is a *Paphiopedilum* rather than a *Cypripedium.* This conclusion is based on several points:

1. At the time of its discovery, the use of the genus name *Cypripedium* was virtually universal.
2. The November flowering time is inconsistent with the genus *Cypripedium*, while entirely consistent with *Paphiopedilum*.
3. Perhaps the most telling evidence in the account resides in its epiphytic habit, the leathery leaf texture, and the bicolor petals—3 traits quite typical of the genus *Paphiopedilum* but not of *Cypripedium*.

Thus, although it is probable that *C. vernayi* has been invalidly placed in this genus, it remains in the literature on *Cypripedium*, so must be discussed here. Based on the available evidence, *C. vernayi* may be synonymous with *P. villosum*.

In conclusion, there is little necessity to reiterate the genuine need for exhaustive taxonomic investigation and revision within this genus. Most richly variable of the Cypripedioideae in floral and vegetative morphology and in habitat exploitation, this genus presents the botanic community with a monumental challenge: to increase our commitments both to a better understanding of and a greater will to preserve these unique orchids.

It is clear that much must be done in order to insure the future of this genus. The fate of several species, if not the whole genus, has been jeopardized. Within the past decade, renewed horticultural emphasis has been placed on *Cypripedium*. In addition, renewed concern for protection of the genus is evident. Both these changes occurred primarily through the improved capacity to grow these slippers from seed, a forward step which will enable growers to enjoy these slippers without resorting to wholesale collection from wild populations. This development, which promotes the genus and permits a ray of hope for its survival, also fosters hybridization within the genus.

Among the species indigenous to North America, most are enrolled on endangered species lists. Restricted endemics, such as *C. californicum*, are particularly vulnerable to careless land management policies. Several species, including *C. acaule*, are subject to overcollection in North America. Without active concern on the part of cypriphiles, many species will vanish into extinction.

CHAPTER 4

The Genus *Paphiopedilum*

When the genus *Paphiopedilum* came into cultivation in England before 1845, it created a sensation from which the ripples continue to spread unchecked. New species and varieties continue to be discovered, and expanding circles of growers the world over still respond with boundless enthusiasm, striving to amass complete collections. The history of the discovery and cultivation of this genus is replete with revealing stories of human nature. The greed and rapacity of early collectors and growers is legend. Rival orchid houses employed the entire spectrum of dirty tricks in their pursuit of more and rarer slippers. Natural habitats were exploited or stripped, in the interest of exclusive possession of the latest and best of this genus. Regrettably, many of these practices continue today, so it is probable that several species survive only in cultivation.

The genus is cultivated worldwide, and the popularity of *Paphiopedilum* species and hybrids continues to increase. A well-grown slipper collection provides a year-round profusion of blossoms which is unparalleled for variety and aesthetic appeal. The subtleties of markings, shape, color and foliage create a fascination which among growers is both infectious and incurable.

Fortunately, taxonomic revisions in the genus *Paphiopedilum* have kept pace with new discoveries and the improved understanding of evolutionary trends more effectively than in the other slipper genera. Thus, this genus may be conceptualized fairly easily in spite of its large number of species. These Asian species exhibit, however, a dismaying range of varietal differences, so the relative generic clarity does not extend to comparable order at the species level. As a consequence, there is considerable disagreement as to the number of species in the genus. The count now varies from as few as 60 species to as many as 80 depending upon whose interpretation of the species is consulted.

For the purposes of this work, Atwood's (1984b) treatment of the genus is the primary taxonomic guide. Subsequent modifications in Cribb's (1987) monograph are incorporated to accommodate species discovered during the last decade, as well as to simplify the wealth of variant forms raised to species rank by some students of the genus. A few additional species are described since Cribb's work as well.

I differ from Cribb in incorporating the *Cochlopetalum* as a subgenus in accordance with the revision by Karasawa & Saito in 1982. My decision is based less upon the variance in chromosome number cited by Karasawa and Saito than upon the unique characteristic of successive bloom. Therefore, within this chapter the genus is organized accordingly:

Subgenus	Section
Brachypetalum	*Brachypetalum*
	Parvisepalum
Cochlopetalum	
Paphiopedilum	*Coryopedilum*
	Pardalopetalum
	Paphiopedilum
	Barbata

For the sake of clarity, the genus name *Paphiopedilum* is used routinely, but note is made of the rank when using the name *Paphiopedilum* at subgenus or section rank.

My tendency in dealing with the species is to group varieties together where possible without losing the sense of the species rather than to elevate varieties to species rank. However, since ready recognition by both botanists and horticulturists is my prime objective, I have incorporated an extensive list of binomials within the appropriate subgenera to encompass species/varieties less than certainly placed, as well as to include binomials in common though probably erroneous usage.

The genus *Paphiopedilum* is organized into 3 subgenera, the largest of which are subdivided into sections. Species are grouped into the appropriate subgenus and section, where applicable, based on available geographic and morphological criteria, primarily. The species included are:

Subgenus *Brachypetalum*
    Section *Brachypetalum*
        P. ang thong Hort.
        P. bellatulum (Reichb. f.) Stein
        P. concolor (Lindl.) Pfitz.
            var. *conco-bellatulum* Hort. (intergrade)
        P. godefroyae (Godefroy-Lebeuf) Stein
          var. *leuchochilum* Rolfe
            Syn. *P. leuchochilum* (Rolfe) Fowlie
        P. niveum (Reichb. f.) Stein
    Section *Parvisepalum*
        P. armeniacum Chen & Liu
        P. delenatii Guill.
        P. emersonii Koopowitz & Cribb
        P. malipoense Chen & Tsi
        P. micranthum Tang & Wang

Subgenus *Cochlopetalum*
    P. glaucophyllum J. J. Smith
        Syn. *P. victoria-regina* (Sander) M. Wood subsp. *glaucophyllum* (J. J. Smith) M. Wood
      var. *moquettianum* J. J. Smith
        Syn. *P. moquettianum* (J. J. Smith) Fowlie

Syn. *P. victoria-regina* (Sander) M. Wood subsp. *glaucophyllum* (J. J. Smith) M. Wood var. *moquettianum* (J. J. Smith) M. Wood

P. liemianum (Fowlie) Karasawa & Saito

Syn. *P. chamberlainianum* (Sander) Stein subsp. *liemianum* Fowlie

P. primulinum M. Wood & Taylor

Syn. *P. chamberlainianum* (Sander) Stein subsp. *liemiana* Fowlie forma *primulinum* (M. Wood & Taylor) var. *flavum* Fowlie nom. illeg.

var. *purpurascens* (M. Wood) Cribb, comb. et stat. nov.

Syn. *P. chamberlainianum* (Sander) Stein subsp. *liemianum* Fowlie forma *primulinum* (M. Wood & Taylor) Fowlie var. *flavescens* Fowlie nom. illeg.

P. victoria-mariae (Sander ex Masters) Rolfe

P. victoria-regina (Sander) M. Wood

Syn. *P. chamberlainianum* (Sander) Stein

Subgenus *Paphiopedilum*

Section *Coryopedilum*

P. adductum Asher

P. glanduliferum (Blume) Stein

Syn. *P. praestans* (Reichb. f.) Pfitz.

Syn. *P. bodegomii* Fowlie

Syn. *P. gardineri* (Guill.) Pfitz.

var. *wilhelminae* (L. O. Williams) Cribb, comb et. stat. nov.

P. kolopakingii Fowlie

var. *topperi* Hort.

Syn. *P. topperi* Hort.

P. philippinense (Reichb. f.) Stein

Syn. *P. laevigatum* (Batem.) Pfitz.

var. *roebelenii* (Veitch) Cribb, comb. nov.

P. randsii Fowlie

P. rothschildianum (Reichb. f.) Stein

Syn. *P. elliottianum* (O'Brien) Stein

P. sanderanum (Reichb. f.) Stein

P. stonei (Hook.) Stein

var. *candidum* (Masters) Pfitz.

var. *platytaenium* (Reichb. f.) Stein

P. supardii Braem & Loeb

Section *Pardalopetalum*

P. haynaldianum (Reichb. f.) Stein

P. lowii (Lindl.) Stein

P. parishii (Reichb. f.) Stein

var. *dianthum* (Tang & Wang) Cribb & Tang

P. richardianum Asher & Beaman, sp. nov.

Section *Paphiopedilum*

P. barbigerum Tang & Wang

P. charlesworthii (Rolfe) Pfitz.

P. druryi (Bedd.) Stein

P. exul (Ridl.) Rolfe

P. fairrieanum (Lindl.) Stein

var. *bohlmannianum* Matho

Syn. var. *album* Hort.

P. gratrixianum (Masters) Guill.
    var. *affine* De Wild.
P. henryanum Braem, sp. nov.
P. hirsutissimum (Lindl. ex Hook.) Stein
    var. *chiwuanum* (Tang & Wang) Cribb, comb. et stat. nov.
    var. *esquirolei* (Schltr.) Cribb, comb. et stat. nov.
P. insigne (Wall. ex Lindl.) Pfitz.
    var. *maulei* Hort.
    var. *sanderae* Hort.
    var. *sanderanum* Hort.
    var. *variegatum* Hort.
P. spiceranum (Reichb. f. ex Masters & T. Moore) Pfitz.
P. villosum (Lindl.) Stein
    var. *annamense* Rolfe
    var. *boxalli* (Reichb. f.) Pfitz.

Section *Barbata*
P. acmodontum Schoser ex M. Wood
P. appletonianum (Gower) Rolfe
    Syn. *P. hainanense* Fowlie, sp. nov.
    Syn. *P. wolterianum* (Kraenzl.) Pfitz.
P. argus (Reichb. f) Stein
P. barbatum (Lindl.) Pfitz.
    var. *nigritum* (Reichb. f.) Pfitz.
        Syn. *P. nigritum* (Reichb. f.) Pfitz.
P. bougainvilleanum Fowlie
P. bullenianum (Reichb. f.) Pfitz.
    Syn. *P. amabile* Hallier
    Syn. *P. amabilis* (Hallier) Merrill
    Syn. *P. johorense* Fowlie & Yap
    Syn. *P. linii* Schoser
    Syn. *P. robinsonii* (Ridl.) Ridley
    Syn. *P. tortisepalum* Fowlie
    var. *celebesense* (Fowlie & Birk) Cribb, comb. et stat. nov.
P. callosum (Reichb. f.) Stein
    var. *sublaeve* (Reichb. f.) Cribb, stat. nov.
        Syn. *P. sublaeve* (Reichb. f.) Fowlie
        Syn. *P. thailandense* Fowlie
P. ciliolare (Reichb. f.) Stein
    Syn. *P. superbiens* (Reichb. f.) Stein subsp. *ciliolare* (Reichb. f.) M. Wood
P. dayanum (Lindl.) Stein
    var. *burbidgei* (Reichb. f.) Pfitz.
        Syn. *P. burbidgei* (Reichb. f.) Pfitz.
    var. *petri* (Reichb. f.) Rolfe
        Syn. *P. petri* (Reichb. f.) Rolfe
P. hennisianum (M. Wood) Fowlie
    Syn. *P. barbatum* (Lindl.) Pfitz. subsp. *lawrenceanum* (Reichb. f.) var.
        hennisianum M. Wood
    var. *fowliei* (Birk) Cribb, comb. et stat. nov.
        Syn. *P. fowliei* Birk

P. hookerae (Reichb. f.) Stein
    Syn. *P. schoseri* Braem
    var. *volonteanum* (Sander ex Rolfe) Kerch.
P. javanicum (Reinw. ex Lindl.) Pfitz.
    var. *virens* (Reichb. f.) Pfitz.
    Syn. *P. purpurascens* Fowlie
    Syn. *P. virens* (Reichb. f.) Pfitz.
P. lawrenceanum (Reichb. f.) Pfitz.
    Syn. *P. barbatum* (Lindl.) Pfitz. subsp. *lawrenceanum* (Reichb. f.) M. Wood
    var. *hyeanum* Reichb. f.
P. mastersianum (Reichb. f.) Stein
P. papuanum (Ridl.) Ridley
    Syn. *P. zieckianum* Schoser
P. purpuratum (Lindl.) Stein
P. sangii Braem, sp. nov.
P. sukhakulii Schoser & Senghas
P. superbiens (Reichb. f.) Stein
    Syn. *P. curtisii* (Reichb. f.) Stein
P. tonsum (Reichb. f.) Stein
P. urbanianum Fowlie
P. venustum (Wall.) Pfitz. ex Stein
    Syn. *P. pardinum* (Reichb. f.) Pfitz.
P. violascens Schltr.
    var. *gautierense* J. J. Smith
P. wardii Summerh.
P. wentworthianum Schoser & Fowlie
    Syn. *P. denisii* Schoser

Natural hybrids exist within the genus *Paphiopedilum*, but they, like natural pollination, are poorly studied and apparently somewhat limited in occurrence. At the present level of ignorance, an exhaustive list is most likely to increase errors at the expense of factual information, so only a few examples are given here.

Paphiopedilum × Kimballianum (*rothschildianum* × *dayanum*) should be a spectacular hybrid given its parentage; having no personal knowledge of this hybrid, I list it for information only. *Paphiopedilum* × Shipwayae (*hookerae* × *dayanum*) is found in the same general area of Borneo as *P.* Kimballianum and the parents of these 2 hybrids. *P.* × Burbidgei, once considered a hybrid of *P. hookerae* × *P. javanicum*, is probably a form of *P. dayanum* from the same site on or near Mt. Kinabalu.

Paphiopedilum × Siamense (*callosum* × *appletonianum*) was described by Rolfe as early as 1890. Much information is needed about its natural habitat and the pollinator, among other features of this interesting hybrid. Other than its name, very little is known of *P.* × Frankeanum (*tonsum* × *superbiens*).

The hybrids known from India appear to have been subjected to considerable scrutiny over the years. Among these are *P. venusto-insigne*, *P. spicero-venustum*, and the more recently described *P.* × Pradhanii (*fairrieanum* × *venustum*).

The rest of this chapter is devoted to descriptions of the species of *Paphiopedilum* which are listed alphabetically within the appropriate subgenus and/or section. The discussion of each species consists of a description, range and habitat information, and the names of varieties, forms and subspecies, where applicable, as well as synonyms in common usage. No common names are included with descriptions as none are in routine use. Cultural notes are included for species which diverge significantly from the mainstream of slipper culture, although additional particulars are given in Table 1, Chapter 2. Refer to Cribb (1987) for an excellent treatment of the histories of publications and ensuing debates about the validity of various taxa and binomials.

SUBGENUS *BRACHYPETALUM*

The entire subgenus is calcicolous, so these slippers have long been called the limestone paphs. Culturally and morphologically distinctive, the subgenus includes those species which have a rounded flower bearing wide, typically overlapping segments.

With the introduction of species from southwest China during the 1980s, it has been necessary to revise and subdivide this subgenus. *Paphiopedilum delenatii* Guill. was pulled from its uneasy alliance with the earliest members of the subgenus and placed in a new section, *Parvisepalum*, along with the recently introduced *P. armeniacum* Chen & Liu, *P. emersonii* Koopowitz & Cribb, *P. malipoense* Chen & Tsi, and *P. micranthum* Tang & Wang.

Subgenus *Brachypetalum*, section *Brachypetalum* therefore consists of: *P. bellatulum* (Reichb. f.) Stein, *P. concolor* (Lindl.) Pfitz., *P. godefroyae* (Godefroy-Lebeuf) Stein and *P. niveum* (Reichb. f.) Stein. Though the status of *P. ang thong* Hort. as variety or hybrid remains unresolved, it is included here along with an intergrade form called *P. concobellatulum*.

Section *Brachypetalum*

The range of the typical section is from northern Malaysia eastward to Thailand, Indo-China, northeast Burma and southwest China. The plants are small and often referred to as the dwarf slippers. All have tessellated leaves. Inflorescences bear 1–3 flowers and rarely exceed 13 cm (5 in.) in height. Flowers are rounded with overlapping sepals and petals. Their color ranges from rose through cream to yellow with spots or blotches of maroon commonly occurring on the segments. The texture is excellent. The pouch is typically the smallest segment. Flowering occurs in late spring and throughout the summer.

Paphiopedilum ang thong Hort.   PLATE 28
The status of this slipper is uncertain. Having been variously described as a hybrid of *P. niveum* with *P. bellatulum* or *P. godefroyae*, as a variety of *P. godefroyae* or of *P. niveum*, or as a species in its own right, *P. ang thong* is shrouded in taxonomic ambiguity. No extant populations of the putative parents live in sufficient proximity at the present time for hybridization to have been of recent vintage. Pollination of *Paphiopedilum* in nature has been sparingly studied, and no pollinating insect has been postulated to have persisted in bearing pollen some 5,000 km (3,250 mi.) in order to accomplish this feat.

Superficially, the flower resembles both *P. niveum* and *P. godefroyae*. Cribb (1987) writes that his comparative studies place this form well within the range of variation for *P. godefroyae*, so he includes it as a cultivar of that species. Whether *P. ang thong* is species, variety, or hybrid, bear in mind that it occupies a discrete habitat, and that it has achieved some level of natural individuality. For this reason, Cribb's judgment that it is a cultivar seems ill-advised. I concur with Cribb (1987) that *P. godefroyae* is an actively evolving taxon; however, *P. ang thong*, whatever its status, is comparable in its genetic activity and variability. Moreover, the distributional evidence favoring species rank for this entity is difficult to refute.

GEOGRAPHIC DISTRIBUTION This form is indigenous to the Ang Thong Islands off the east coast of Thailand.

HABITAT The plants thrive in dappled and bright shade on limestone outcrops of the rocky hillsides of the islands.

CULTURAL NOTES *P. ang thong* is more easily grown than some other members of its section as it requires no rest period. Provided with calcium carbonate in its substrate, warm temperatures and moderate-to-bright light, this slipper may otherwise be given general *Paphiopedilum* care.

DESCRIPTION The plant is fairly small. The 4–6 leaves vary from 7.5–15.5 cm (3–6 in.) in length by 3–4.5 cm (1.2–1.75 in.) in width. Leaf color is deep green marked with tessellations of pale grayish green above; the undersurface is light green with purplish mottling.

The pubescent inflorescence is tall for this group, up to 13.5 cm (5 in.) in height, and bears 1–2 concave flowers subtended by small bracts. Flower color is satiny white spotted with maroon on all segments, although variability provides for both a pristine, unspotted form and another bearing maroon spots in a linear arrangement.

The dorsal sepal is broadly ovate and measures 2.5–3.5 cm (1–1.3 in.) in length by 2.5–4 cm (1–1.5 in.) in width. The ventral sepal is similar but somewhat smaller.

Petals are oblong to elliptical and may recurve; margins may be undulate. Petal measurements are 3.5–5.5 cm (1.3–2.2 in.) in length by 2.5–3 cm (1–1.2 in.) in width. The labellum is ellipsoidal or egg-shaped with involute margins and measures 2.5–3.5 cm (1–1.3 in.) in length.

FLOWERING SEASON Summer.

Paphiopedilum bellatulum (Reichb. f.) Stein   PLATE 29

GEOGRAPHIC DISTRIBUTION This species has been collected from several sites in central and eastern Burma and in Thailand.

HABITAT *P. bellatulum* inhabits limestone outcrops, preferring crevices in which humus collects. Clumps are found at elevations of 1,000–1,500 m (3,400–5,100 ft.) in dappled shade or even in open sun.

CULTURAL NOTES Well worth extra attention, this species responds to careful culture and grows to fill its pot at a moderate speed. Along with the other members of the subgenus, it must have a source of calcium carbonate in the substrate. Oyster shell, a very light top-dressing of agricultural lime applied quarterly or semiannually, or even crocks of broken concrete and mortar provide the necessary calcium carbonate. *P. bellatulum* is not a heavy feeder.

Seedling grade fir bark or other large particle medium should be used when potting; use of compact potting media such as UC mix may encourage root decay under warm temperature conditions.

For most of the year, warm night temperatures should be maintained (17–19° C or near 65° F). This species must never be placed under the bench or in a still, heavy atmosphere as the warmth must be offset by bright conditions and excellent air movement to prevent fungus attack.

Growers who have failed to flower this slipper should take note of its requirement for a rest period from December–February. During these months the amount and frequency of watering should be reduced to the minimum amount required to maintain roots. Night temperature should be allowed to drop slightly as well throughout the rest period. For the remainder of the year, this species should receive ample water and standard temperatures for warm-growing species.

DESCRIPTION The leaves are dark green with pale tessellation above and a pale green undersurface that is heavily spotted with anthocyanin (purple pigmentation). Leaves usually number 4–5 on mature growths. They are oblong to elliptic and reach a length of up to 15 cm (6 in.) and a width of 5 cm (2 in.).

The pubescent peduncle bears a single large flower at a height of only 2–4.5 cm (1.75–2.75 in.). Bifloral inflorescences occur rarely. A small conduplicate bract subtends the concave flowers which are composed of large sepals and petals, with a small pouch. Their color varies from white to creamy yellow; large blotches of maroon mark the segments, with the exception of the labellum which bears smaller dots of maroon. The flowers are large in comparison to the size of the plant.

The dorsal sepal is concave and visibly wider than long; it measures 3–3.5 cm (1.25–1.5 in.) in length by 3.5–4.5 cm (1.5–1.75 in.) in width. The synsepalum is deeply concave and smaller than the dorsal; it measures approximately 2 cm (1.75 in.) long by 2.5 cm (1 in.) wide.

The petals are broad and concave, ovate to elliptic, rounded at the apices, and measure 4.5–6.3 cm (1.75–2.5 in.) in length by 2.5–4.5 cm (1–1.75 in.) in width. The small pouch is egg-shaped, narrowly inflated and measures 2.5–4.5 cm (1–1.75 in.) in length. Pouch margins are involute.

FLOWERING SEASON Summer, fall, and at various other times when exceptionally well-grown.

Paphiopedilum conco-bellatulum Hort. (intergrade).

At the time of this writing, the existence of an entity called *P. conco-bellatulum* Hort. (intergrade) is creating some interest among growers and botanists. Chinese in distribution, it was first discussed by Fowlie in 1985. Illustrations show the typical pouch of *P. concolor* accompanied by profuse spotting typical of *P. bellatulum*. Variance in sepals and petals intergrades between the 2 species. Mark (1987) states that its blooming season is earlier than either of the species, a characteristic that may be explained by factors of latitude and climate. The fact of its earlier anthesis indicates that it is removed from interaction in the gene pool of the greater group, even if geographical range permits; thus, divergence is inevitable. The resolution of this entity's place as an important transitional link in the understanding of slipper evolution awaits the gathering and processing of more evidence. At present it is most conveniently considered as a variant form of *P. concolor*. See *P. concolor* (Lindl.) Pfitz.

Paphiopedilum concolor (Lindl.) Pfitz.   PLATE 30

GEOGRAPHIC DISTRIBUTION This species has the widest range of all in the subgenus. It occurs in 2 areas in southeast Burma, on the Birdsnest Islands off Thailand, in both North and South Vietnam, and in Cambodia, Laos and Yunnan Province, China. Mark (1987) writes that it also grows in Guangxi in western Canton.

HABITAT *P. concolor* grows as a lithophyte or terrestrial on coastal limestone cliffs. It tolerates dense shade to bright, reflected light at low elevations from sea level to 1,000 m (3,400 ft.). Its roots cling to rocks and tree roots collecting detritus, and are reported to take purchase in sandy substrate as well. Cool breezes prevent stagnation in the sites populated by this species.

CULTURAL NOTES This species requires less shade than formerly believed, as do many members of its section. Perfect drainage is also essential. Lack of success with *P. concolor* is most frequently due to failure to repot on schedule, thereby subjecting the root system to excessive moisture. It requires no rest period, however, and is easily maintained and flowered with routine care.

DESCRIPTION Growths consist of 4–6 leaves, tessellated above and bearing purple spotting on their undersurfaces. The leaves reach lengths of up to 14 cm (5.5 in.) and widths of up to 4 cm (1.5 in.).

The pubescent peduncle bears 1–2, rarely 3, flowers at a height of up to 8 cm (3 in.). The large, pubescent flowers are subtended by bracts. Typically, they are yellow and finely spotted on all segments with maroon dots, but rare cream and white forms are also known.

The dorsal sepal is broadly obovate, 2.5–3.5 cm (1–1.3 in.) long by 3.3 cm (1.25 in.) wide. The smaller, concave synsepalum is ovate to subcircular and measures 2–3 cm (0.75–1.25 in.) in both length and width. The petals are elliptic and nearly twice as long as their width, measuring 3.7–4.3 cm (1.5–1.75 in.) in length by 2.5 cm (1 in.) in width. Their apices point downward so that they fail to overlap the dorsal sepal to the extent typical of other species of the section. The ellipsoidal labellum is slightly more pointed at its distal end than are pouches of other members of the section. It measures 3.5–3.8 cm (1.5 in.) in length. Pouch margins are involute.

FLOWERING SEASON Summer.

Paphiopedilum godefroyae (Godefroy-Lebeuf) Stein   PLATE 31

This species includes a named variety, var. *leuchochilum* Rolfe, which has been raised to species rank by Fowlie (1975c), based upon both its geographic distribution and its distinctive white pouch. Because this species is highly variable and, according to Cribb (1987), includes *P. ang thong* as well, it should be viewed as an actively evolving complex. In this text var. *leuchochilum* is recognized at varietal rank in concurrence with Cribb's evaluation.

GEOGRAPHIC DISTRIBUTION This species has an extensive range, including South Vietnam, Burma and southern Thailand as well as the Birdsnest Islands in the Gulf of Thailand. Var. *leuchochilum* is collected from the eastern coast of Thailand in the region of the Isthmus of Kra, and from adjacent islands.

HABITAT *P. godefroyae* inhabits coastal limestone cliffs at low elevations where it occasionally receives salt spray. In many of its locations, it is exposed to full sun for part of each day and receives bright shade and/or reflected light from the surface of seawater throughout most of the day. Humidity is consistently high, rarely falling below 85%. Day/night temperature variation is pronounced. *P. godefroyae* and its variant root in humus-filled crevices in the limestone. They favor northward-facing slopes.

CULTURAL NOTES This species receives a rest period during January, February and March in its natural habitat. At this time night temperatures drop to approximately 13° C (55° F), while moisture is reduced to the minimum tolerated by roots of this genus. The plant thrives upon the culture peculiar to this section, including warm temperatures, bright light and ample moisture during the balance of the year. Excellent drainage and alkaline pH are year-round constants.

DESCRIPTION *P. godefroyae* grows in clumps, as do the other members of its section. A growth consists of 4–6 leaves which measure 13–14 cm (5–5.5 in.) in length by approximately 3 cm (1–1.2 in.) in width. Their dark green upper surfaces are tessellated with pale grayish green, while the light green undersides are densely spotted with purple.

The inflorescence bears 1–2 flowers subtended by conduplicate bracts; it stands erect and is pubescent throughout.

The concave flowers are rose to white with maroon spotting on all segments. They are large for the size of the plant, measuring 5–7.5 cm (2–3 in.) across. Var. *leucochilum* is described as lacking spotting upon the lip.

The dorsal sepal is almost twice as wide as long, measuring 2.5–3 cm (1–1.2 in.) long by 3–3.8 cm (1.2–1.5 in.) wide. The synsepalum is nearly circular and measures approximately 3 cm (1.2 in.) across. The petals are rounded as well, often retuse or notched at the tip, and measure approximately 3–5 cm (1.2–2 in.) in length and width. The pouch is somewhat pointed at the apex and is 2.5–3.5 cm (1–1.3 in.) long with involute margins.

FLOWERING SEASON Summer.

Paphiopedilum leuchochilum (Rolfe) Fowlie. See *P. godefroyae* (Godefroy-Lebeuf) Stein.

Paphiopedilum niveum (Reichb. f.) Stein   PLATE 32

GEOGRAPHIC DISTRIBUTION This species is native to the Langkawi Islands off the west coast of the Malay Peninsula; to Penang, a nearby island; and to the Tambelan Islands west of Borneo near Singapore.

HABITAT *P. niveum* grows in crevices of calcareous outcrops where it is rooted into detritus. It inhabits both shaded, hilly sites and exposed rocks of the coastal zone where salt spray drenches the plants. Elevations are sea level to 200 m (700 ft.). Humidity is uniformly above 70%; rainfall is heavy from May to mid-December.

CULTURAL NOTES In its native habitat, *P. niveum* experiences somewhat drier conditions from December through mid-April. For this reason it should be rested for at least 4 months (December–March) in cultivation and receive minimum water and slightly lowered temperature. Light intensity should be increased during the resting period. Ample water and other cultural needs typical of this section apply during the remainder of the year. The substrate must always be alkaline, of course.

DESCRIPTION The growths are clustered and consist of 4–6 leaves. The upper surface of the leaf is dark green, mottled with grayish green. The underside is deeply pigmented with purple. Leaves reach lengths of 10–20 cm (4–8 in.) and widths of 2.5–3.8 cm (1–1.75 in.).

The erect, pubescent peduncle bears 1–2 flowers well above the foliage at heights of 5–25 cm (4–10 in.).

The flowers are white and usually dotted with purple near the centers. The broad dorsal sepal measures 2.5–3.5 cm (1–1.3 in.) in length and 3–5 cm (1.2–2 in.) in width. The synsepalum is narrower, reaching a width of approximately 2.5 cm (1 in.). The long petals overlap the sepals and are held in a nearly horizontal position. They measure 3.5–3.8 cm (1.3–1.5 in.) long by approximately 2.5 cm (1 in.) wide. The labellum is small and ellipsoidal with involute margins about the orifice. It measures 2.5–3 cm (1–1.2 in.) long.

FLOWERING SEASON Early to mid-summer.

Section *Parvisepalum*

This is a section composed of 5 species from southwest China and Vietnam. All 5 are narrow endemics. Only *Paphiopedilum delenatii* has been in cultivation for many years. The other 4 species are recent introductions, having been exported from China since 1982, although several of the species were described as early as the 1950s.

With the exception of *Paphiopedilum emersonii*, which has plain green leaves devoid of tessellation above or anthocyanin pigmentation beneath, the species in this section are noted for their unusually heavily tessellated, remarkably leathery leaves.

Consistent with the subgenus *Brachypetalum*, the species in section *Parvisepalum* are calcicolous and thrive in the warm night temperature range, although they are generally tolerant of intermediate temperatures. Richard Topper (personal communication) indicates that while these species have been reported from rather high elevations, they typically do not flower when grown under cool temperatures.

The pouches of 3 of the 5 species are roundly inflated and unusually large for the genus; the exceptions are *P. delenatii* and *P. emersonii* with well-inflated pouches of average size. The 3 large-pouched species, *P. armeniacum*, *P. malipoense*, and *P. micranthum*, are further distinguished by their stoloniferous habit (producing runners or extended rhizomes), bearing plantlets at some distance from the parent plant, as opposed to generating the clustered growths so characteristic of the genus.

Species in this section differ further from those in section *Brachypetalum* in the production of longer peduncles. In this feature, the diverse alignment within *Parvisepalum* shows up once more; the peduncles are typically uniforal in the stoloniferous, large-pouched species, although they are often bifloral in *P. delenatii* and occasionally so in *P. emersonii.*

Clearly, *P. delenatii* exhibits traits characteristic of both sections as they are presently structured. Likewise, *P. emersonii* seems to link the 2 sections through the same set of traits, although its green leaves distinguish it strongly from all the other species in the subgenus. It is anticipated that future discoveries will shed new light on the subgenus as well as on the place of *P. emersonii* with its plain green leaves.

The initial response of orchidists to the introduction of the 4 new species in this section was one of intense interest. New shapes and colors delighted growers, but the ensuing speculation about the phylogeny of the new species was of far greater interest among botanists. Possession of granular pollen by several of the new species, the stoloniferous growth habit, and the position of bracts tended to suggest that this group of slippers might be a phylogenetic link between *Paphiopedilum* and *Cypripedium.* However, the ease of hybridization with *Paphiopedilum,* the conduplicate, predominately tessellated leaves of extremely leathery substance, the locular condition of the ovary, and most anatomical features serve to link these plants firmly to the genus *Paphiopedilum.* The presence of intermediate or *Cypripedium*-like traits is easily understood as evidence of parallel evolution, examples of which are found throughout the plant kingdom.

This section exemplifies the desirable qualities which drive humans to excessive avarice. *P. delenatii* is believed to be very limited, if not extinct, in its natural environs, and *P. armeniacum* and *P. malipoense* are likely to be completely stripped from their habitats before the end of their first decade in cultivation.

Paphiopedilum armeniacum Chen & Liu
PLATE 33

The species epithet *armeniacum* means "apricotlike." It was applied to the species as the earliest reports indicated that the color of the flowers was apricot. Individuals flowered in North America appear to range in color from pale lemon yellow to rich egg-yolk yellow and are devoid of any pigmentation in the peach to coral range. Koopowitz and Hasegawa (1986) suggest that Mandarin apricots are more yellow in color than their western counterparts and thereby created false expectations. It is possible, however, that at some time a flower of peach to orange hue will appear in this species. Growers who have been disappointed in the color of this species are unaware of the intense longing experienced by early growers for a pure yellow *Paphiopedilum.* Upon its introduction, this species created a justifiable sensation on its own merits.

GEOGRAPHIC DISTRIBUTION This species is known from 1 site in Yunnan Province, China.

HABITAT Found well inland, this slipper inhabits limestone hills near streams. Very little is known of its habitat.

CULTURAL NOTES *P. armeniacum* responds to general *Brachypetalum* care including warm night temperature, alkaline substrate and moderate-to-abundant water and light. However, this and other recently introduced species in section *Parvisepalum* appear less susceptible to fungus attacks, tolerate somewhat cooler night temperatures, and overall, are easier to grow than section *Brachypetalum.* According to Richard Topper (personal communication), this species thrives at night temperatures of 14–15° C (62–65° F) and prefers daytime temperatures up to 38° C (94° F); this is contrary to the earlier reports of cool habitats.

Growers should be aware of this species' tendency to run, so should take care to protect and nurture the tips of stolons where new growths appear. The long rhizomes must not be allowed to grow down to be trapped between or beneath the pots for this will damage or destroy new growths. Generally, a runner produces a plantlet from the drainage hole in the pot. This suggests that moss-lined hanging baskets constructed of slats or wire mesh provide the cleverest solution to growing stoloniferous species.

DESCRIPTION Growths are not clustered but are spaced up to 15 cm (6 in.) apart on a rambling rhizome which may exceed 20 cm (8 in.). The stolon is sheathed with bracts which are spaced at rather long internodes. It arises beneath the soil level and grows downward for several centimeters before turning horizontally to emerge to the surface, where it produces a new fan some distance from the parent plant. A growth consists of 5–7 boldly tessellated leaves measuring 6–12 cm (2.3–4.75 in.) long by 2–2.5 cm (0.75–1 in.) wide. The lower surface of the leaves is densely mottled with purple.

The pubescent peduncle bears a solitary large flower and stands 24–25 cm (9.5–10 in.) tall. The flower is subtended by a bract. The concolor yellow flower bears some minute, purple dots inside the pouch and basally on the petals. Its segments bear pubescence over the proximal portions.

The dorsal sepal is ovate and acute measuring 2.5–5 cm (1–2 in.) long by 1.5–2.5 cm (0.6–1 in.) wide. The synsepalum is smaller, ovate and acute. It is bicarinate (doubly keeled) and measures 2–3.5 cm (0.75–2.3 in.) in length and 2–2.5 cm (0.75–1 in.) in width.

The petals are ovate to subcircular and measure 3–5.3 cm (1.2–2.2 in.) long by 2.5–3.3 cm (1–1.3 in.) wide. Basally, the petals are pubescent and bear a sparse stippling of maroon. The pubescent labellum is well-inflated though longer than wide. Its texture is thin and translucent. It bears purple spotting on the involute margins and measures 4–5 cm (1.6–2 in.) in length.

FLOWERING SEASON Summer through late fall.

Paphiopedilum delenatii Guill.   PLATE 34

According to Koopowitz and Hasegawa (1986), a yellow-flowered *P. delenatii* var. *aurea* is reported to exist in Vietnam.

GEOGRAPHIC DISTRIBUTION North Vietnam is the documented source of this species, although locations in the central portion of Vietnam have been reported as well as Yunnan Province, China.

HABITAT Habitat descriptions are vague at best. Preferring detritus-filled crevices in limestone rock at lower elevations, this slipper appears to inhabit valleys and/or foothills of the mountainous regions of North Vietnam. Whether extant populations persist in the wild is an ongoing question.

CULTURAL NOTES Cribb (1987) writes that the plants presently in cultivation are probably all derived from a selfing of a single plant which survived in France during the first half of the 20th century. It is significant, given the amazing success early growers had with newly introduced slippers, that all but 1 plant of this species failed in cultivation. Its unusually high mortality rate earned it a reputation as extremely difficult to grow. However, in the past 20 years many seedlings have been produced through inbreeding and selfing of the individuals of that early French grex, so that *P. delenatii* has gradually become both available and acknowledged as easier to grow and flower than some species of section *Brachypetalum*.

This species should receive moderate light, intermediate to warm night temperatures, good air circulation, perfect drainage, and just enough water to keep it evenly moist. It requires calcium carbonate in the substrate.

DESCRIPTION Growths are produced in clumps and consist of 6–7 leaves. The leaves are dark green, tessellated above with pale green; dense purple pigment mottles the undersurfaces. In length, the leaves grow to 11 cm (4.3 in.), and the width ranges from 3–4 cm (1.25–1.5 in.).

The pubescent inflorescence bears 1–2 flowers and stands up to 23 cm (9 in.) in height. The large, pink, pubescent flower is subtended by a bract.

The dorsal sepal is ovate and acute, measuring 2–3.5 cm (0.8–1.3 in.) in length by 2–2.5 cm (0.8–1 in.) in width. The sharply acute ventral sepal is similar in dimensions.

Petals are broadly elliptic or subcircular with rounded apices. They measure 3.5–4.5 cm (1.3–1.75 in.) long by 2.5–3.5 cm (1–1.3 in.) wide. The broadly inflated labellum is ellipsoidal to spherical, 2.5–4 cm (1–1.5 in.) in length, and blushed with pink or rose. The pouch of *P. delenatii* is no larger than is typical in *Paphiopedilum*, in contrast to the enlarged, globose pouches of *P. armeniacum*, *P. malipoense*, and *P. micranthum*.

The staminode of this lovely species is worthy of note. It has the appearance of a shield, quartered diagonally; the quarters are colored alternately maroon and gold.

FLOWERING SEASON Spring and early summer.

Paphiopedilum emersonii Koopowitz & Cribb   PLATE 35

GEOGRAPHIC DISTRIBUTION Unconfirmed reports place this species in Ghuizhou Province, China. Richard Topper (personal communication) indicates that the Chinese borders with Tibet and North Vietnam are likely sites for this species.

HABITAT Habitat information is sketchy. Emerson "Doc" Charles (personal communication) reports that the species grows along creek banks in an area subject to frosts. He further states that he has seen colonies growing across a creek from a population of *Paphiopedilum henryanum*, a recently-discovered taxon (see *P. henryanum* in this chapter). Loamy soil is a feature of the habitat, according to Koopowitz and Hasegawa (1988).

DESCRIPTION Growths consist of 4–5 long leaves, measuring up to 25 cm (10 in.) in length and 3–4 cm (1.25–1.5 in.) in width, and devoid of all but the faintest tessellation or purple pigmentation. This species is unique in the subgenus for its plain green leaves.

The pubescent inflorescence bears 1–2 white flowers and stands erect at a height of 11.5 cm (4.5 in.). The flowers are subtended by white bracts of a papery texture. The subcompanulate flowers are large for the size of the plant and subsucculent in texture.

The elliptic to ovate dorsal sepal hoods the pouch and reflexes its lateral margins. White in color, it measures 4–4.5 cm (1.5–1.75 in.) in length and approximately 3 cm (1.25 in.) in width. The ventral sepal is subcircular and obtuse to rounded at the apex. It measures 3.5 cm (1.5 in.) in length and in width. Both sepals are conduplicate and pubescent.

The broad petals curve forward as if to clasp the belly of the pouch. Pink at their bases, they fade to white distally. Their shape is ovate to subcircular with obtuse to rounded apices. Pubescent throughout, they measure up to 4.5 cm (1.75 in.) in each dimension. The white lip, which is smaller than the pouches of stoloniferous species in this section, is rugose with involute margins. Its expanded toe is liberally spotted with creamy tan spots. Broadly inflated, it measures 3–3.5 cm (1.25–1.5 in.) in length. An even more remarkable feature is the presence of translucent fenestrae in the pouch, windows through which light does not so much penetrate to the bowl of the labellum as do interior pigmented spots show through to the outer surface.

As is the case in other species of the section *Parvisepalum*, the staminode is a striking feature of the flower. The shape is that of a slender, elongated trapezoidal shield, virtually a diamond which has had its lower point extended to about twice the length of the upper point, although actually both points are severely truncated. A side view of the staminode reveals that it curves forward as it emerges from the upper column surface, exhibiting a backward curve at an approximate 30° angle which begins just below its maximum width. The ground color is ivory with longitudinal stripes of butter yellow and crimson laterally positioned on either side of a deep median groove.

FLOWERING SEASON Spring and early summer.

Paphiopedilum malipoense Chen & Tsi   PLATE 36

GEOGRAPHIC DISTRIBUTION *P. malipoense* is among the species recently imported from Yunnan Province, China.

HABITAT Growing on rocky outcrops, this species lives in the shade of mixed hardwood and softwood forests on mountainous slopes at a reported elevation of 1,300–1,600 m (4,500–

5,500 ft.). Richard Topper (personal communication) believes that the preferred warm temperatures are inconsistent with these elevations, and suggests instead that collectors have attempted to draw a trail away from a site nearer sea level.

CULTURAL NOTES Refer to comments under habitat for temperature recommendations. See *P. armeniacum* for suggestions as to ideal methods for potting stoloniferous species.

DESCRIPTION *P. malipoense*, like *P. armeniacum*, produces growths from an elongate underground rhizome, spaced some 15–25 cm (6–10 in.) apart. The 7–8 leaves measure 10–20 cm (4–8 in.) in length and 2.5–5 cm (1–2 in.) wide, and stand nearly erect. They are dark green, boldly tessellated with pale green above and heavily spotted beneath with purple pigmentation.

The pilose inflorescence is the tallest in the subgenus and bears a large, solitary, concolor apple green flower at a height of 30 cm (12 in.) or more. A bract subtends the flower.

The dorsal sepal is teardrop-shaped and apically acuminate. Its length is nearly twice its width; it measures approximately 4.5 cm (1.75 in.) long by 2.3 cm (0.8 in.) wide. The synsepalum is bidentate at the tip and bicarinate; otherwise, it is very similar to the dorsal sepal.

The apically acute petals are similar in shape and size to the sepals. They are pubescent on the inner surface and bear narrow stripes of maroon from the base to within a few millimeters of their tips. The large labellum is subspheroid with corrugations at the involute margins. It is spotted maroon within and translucent so that the spots are visible through the pouch walls. It measures approximately 4.5 cm (1.75 in.) in length.

The staminode of *P. malipoense* is unique in the genus in that its upper portion is starkly white and pubescent, while the lower portion is deepest maroon, glossy and rugose.

FLOWERING SEASON Fall and winter.

Paphiopedilum micranthum Tang & Wang   PLATE 37

Described as early as 1951, the type for this species appears to have been either an aberrant flower or a mechanically opened bud. Chen and Liu redescribed it, in 1982, from a normal specimen. Thus, we find that this species, which bears the specific epithet *micranthum* meaning "small flower," is actually a quite large-flowered species with an enormous labellum. However, according to Cribb (1987), there are 2 forms of this species: the flowers of the normal form are about the same size as others in the section, while a probable tetraploid form has flowers nearly double the size of the normal form.

GEOGRAPHIC DISTRIBUTION Yunnan Province, China, very near the Vietnamese border, is the source of this and the other newly-introduced species in this section.

HABITAT Limited habitat information is available. This species prefers limestone outcrops, as do the related species of the subgenus.

CULTURAL NOTES See *P. armeniacum* for suggestions as to potting of stoloniferous species.

DESCRIPTION Growths are produced from an underground rhizome and each consists of 4–5 leaves. The foliage is very dark green and mottled with pale green above; the undersurfaces are densely spotted with purple. Leaves reach a length of 5–15 cm (2–6 in.) and a width of 1.5–2 cm (0.6–0.75 in.).

The pubescent peduncle is erect and bears a solitary flower of delicate texture at heights of 9–20 cm (3.5–8 in.). The flower is peach to pink with maroon veins upon sepals and petals. There is considerable yellow blended with the rosy pink of the sepals and petals, while the labellum is pink to deep rose. The labellum is enormous in proportion to the other segments, giving this species a distinctive appearance.

The dorsal sepal is ovate and acute, measuring 1.5–2.6 cm (0.6–1 in.) in length and 1.7–3 cm (0.7–1.25 in.) in width. Basally, the color is yellow; reticular veins of rose create a network across the dominant, parallel rose veins, and rose suffuses the margins as well. The bicarinate synsepalum is apically bidentate. Its color and dimensions are similar to those of the dorsal.

The petals are subcircular and acute to rounded at the apex. The veining and coloration is similar to that of the dorsal sepal, although the marginal bands of rose color are somewhat wider. Petals measure 2–3.5 cm (0.75–1.25 in.) in length and 2.5–3.5 cm (1–1.25 in.) in width. The pouch is broadly inflated, ellipsoid, pale to deep rosy pink, and 5–9 cm (2–3 in.) long. Its margins are involute and rugose. Purple spotting adorns the inner pouch walls.

The longitudinally conduplicate staminode of *P. micranthum* is worthy of note as a distinctive, identifying feature. Its colors are pink and yellow.

It should be noted, also, that this species is highly variable so that in both color and size some forms may be inferior to the description just given.

FLOWERING SEASON Fall and winter.

SUBGENUS *COCHLOPETALUM*

The morphological characteristic for which this subgenus is named is the corkscrew twist of the petals, which is reminiscent of the spiraled shells of certain snails. For this reason, the name *Cochlopetalum*, meaning "snail-shell petal," is appropriate. These slippers are among the easiest to grow and flower. No special care is required for any of the taxa included, so general intermediate *Paphiopedilum* care will insure success. For particulars, refer to Chapter 2.

All the members of the subgenus bloom continually over a period of months or years. The indeterminate flowerscape drops the senescent flower as a new bud begins to open so that 2 simultaneous flowers are present only briefly, if at all. Bracts persist, marking the site of each previous flower. The rachis acquires a zigzag configuration after several flowers have been produced and abscissed. Individual flowers are quite long-lasting, and up to 20 flowers may be borne on a scape, so that a single inflorescence may continue to flower for more than a year. On multigrowth plants, 2 or more young flowerscapes may begin to bloom before the eldest ceases to flower. Inception of flowering may occur at any time of the year, but is more likely in summer.

This subgenus is sufficiently different from other *Paphiopedilum* on several criteria to warrant more than sectional rank. Karasawa's karyological studies of the genus in the late 1970s (see Cribb, 1987) indicate that species in this genus have lost a chromosome from the typical *Paphiopedilum* genome. Therefore, in this subgenus 2n = 30–37, with the numbers being primarily derived by centric fission from a base of 2n = 25, while the characteristic *Paphiopedilum* base genome is 2n = 26, which gives typical genomes in the balance of the genus of 2n = 26–32. Identification of basal genomes involves careful study of chromosomes to determine the number which are unique and those which appear to be duplicates. Chromosome number may also be augmented in some species by the fragmentation of previously existing chromosomes so that short severed arms are subsequently perpetuated as discrete chromosomes.

The criterion which in my opinion is paramount in raising this group to subgenus rank, however, is the characteristic of successive flowering upon a more or less indeterminate inflorescence. This characteristic is not only unique in the genus but is of dramatic significance as a reproductive strategy, since it places the plants in a unique reproductive category. Reproductive strategies always involve some ratio of energy investment in vegetative versus reproductive activity. Thus, the heavier proportion of energy invested in reproduction by species of subgenus *Cochlopetalum* must be given serious consideration as a major factor in the ecological and evolutionary character of the entire taxon.

Consideration must, of course, be given to both geographical and morphological features of the subgenus, although these alone may not be sufficient to raise the group in rank from section to subgenus. Like the flowers of the subgenus *Paphiopedilum* (in which Cribb places *Cochlopetalum* at sectional rank), the petals are more than twice as long as they are broad, and the side-lobes of the pouch are the only portions which are involute. However, the short, ciliate, more or less horizontal, helical petals display a pattern unique to the genus. Furthermore, the similarities among the forms within the group indicate that this taxon is only moderately advanced beyond the stage of a complex, although it is well into the processes of divergence and speciation and still rapidly evolving. The narrowness of this taxon's distribution in Java and Sumatra, lends credence to this line of reasoning.

Differences between the taxa included in this subgenus are quite small, and among certain species/subspecies/varieties the differences are known to be not only inconsistent but to include intermediate gradations. The taxa clearly demonstrate their cohesion as 1 larger taxon. The difficulty lies in determining which of these taxa are species and which are subspecies, varieties and/or forms. It may well be that we are a millennium too early for making such decisions, and that in fact the populations have only begun to sort themselves out.

Subgenus *Cochlopetalum* is indeed remarkable for its intergrading variability within a cohesive and easily recognized overall pattern. Thus, while variability links 1 putative species with the next through the presence of intergrading characteristics, it is justifiably difficult to standardize definitive species characteristics within this group or to precisely identify certain individuals. The evidence from the historical perspective, which should provide a stable base for comparison, is weak given the development of taxonomic concepts which have superceded the old Linnaean concepts. Additionally, recent evidence coming from wild populations through collectors and importers is incomplete and diffuse. Hobby growers, taxonomists, and even collectors who deal with native populations behold such an array of slight variations among the individuals in a population, and so many links between the so-called species of this subgenus that, at present, even the accepted criteria are based upon assumptions which may be erroneous. Difficulties in classifying orchids using the old Linnaean concepts were pointed out in Chapter 1. Atwood (personal communication) adds that many of the early type descriptions have been shown to be inexact as they were made from dried, pressed specimens wherein pouch deformation, poor color retention and a myriad of mechanically induced, apparent aberrations led to false assumptions.

Chromosome studies and electrophoretic assays performed in laboratories remote from collection sites cannot be definitive because the initial identification of study material is dissociated from wild populations and thus subject to error. It is obvious that, should specimens used in chromosome study be misidentified, the results compound the probability of additional error and become authoritatively misleading rather than definitive. To make matters worse, variations such as pouch shape, spotting and other superficial, purely morphological criteria become artificially magnified in importance, although they are only poorly significant, genetically and evolutionarily speaking, primarily as evidence of the variational whimsy of the random genetic assortment which occurs in freely interbreeding wild populations of these taxa.

Thus, I conclude that until chromosome studies as well as electrophoretic and other molecular assays of biochemical contents are performed on specimens freshly collected from wild populations, and until ecotypes and/or hybrid swarms are identified and statistically assorted *in situ*, the present confusion will persist, enhanced rather than mitigated by the amassing of so-called definitive characteristics. At present, it is impossible to determine which claims have the greater validity when conflicting identifications are made in subgenus *Cochlopetalum*. Far too frequently, the definitive characteristics are suspect for the reasons cited above, and because of the additional chaos of misinformation generated by collectors protecting their sites.

Precisely because the taxa included in this subgenus appear to be rapidly evolving and unstable, and because much of the published information has failed to take into account subtle intergradations so that misinformation has been built upon rather than eliminated, these taxa are incapable of precise placement at this time. Thus, this intrinsic property of the subgenus requires that certain decisions be made rather arbitrarily. Cribb's (1987) interpretation of this group of slippers is well-documented and is used at species rank and below within these pages.

Paphiopedilum chamberlainianum (Sander) Stein. See *P. victoria-regina* (Sander) M. Wood.

Paphiopedilum chamberlainianum (Sander) Stein subsp. *liemianum* Fowlie forma *primulinum* (M. Wood & Taylor) Fowlie var. *flavescens* Fowlie nom illeg. See *P. primulinum* M. Wood & Taylor var. *purpurascens* (M. Wood) Cribb, comb. et stat. nov.

Paphiopedilum chamberlainianum (Sander) Stein subsp. *liemianum* Fowlie forma *primulinum* (M. Wood & Taylor) Fowlie var. *flavum* Fowlie nom. illeg. See *P. primulinum* M. Wood & Taylor.

Paphiopedilum chamberlainianum (Sander) Stein subsp. *liemianum* Fowlie. See *P. liemianum* (Fowlie) Karasawa & Saito.

Paphiopedilum glaucophyllum J. J. Smith   PLATES 38 & 42

This species has a variant, var. *moquettianum* J. J. Smith, which is discussed secondarily under this entry. Because the chromosome numbers of the species and the variant are dissimilar (*P. glaucophyllum* has been counted at both 2n = 36 and 2n = 37, while the taxon identified as var. *moquettianum* is 2n = 34), and both the evolution of the plant and its taxonomy are fluid, this is an excellent example of a species and its variant which are less than certainly placed at the present time.

Furthermore, *P. glaucophyllum* is so closely allied to *P. victoria-regina* (Sander) M. Wood, known horticulturally as *P. chamberlainianum* (Sander) Stein, that Wood (1975) considers *P. glaucophyllum* to be a subspecies of *P. victoria-regina*.

GEOGRAPHIC DISTRIBUTION *P. glaucophyllum* is found in central to eastern Java and in Sumatra. Var. *moquettianum* is more often seen in southwest Java.

HABITAT *P. glaucophyllum* clings to volcanic slopes at elevations from 200–700 m (700–2,400 ft.), in a region which receives abundant rainfall throughout the year. This species must be considered more lithophytic than terrestrial. The habitat of var. *moquettianum* receives slightly less rainfall.

DESCRIPTION *P. glaucophyllum* produces clustered growths consisting of 4–6 fairly large leaves. The leaves are 20–30 cm (8–12 in.) long and approximately 5 cm (2 in.) wide, with bristles along the proximal margins. The upper surface varies from plain green to very faintly tessellated, while the lower surface is densely spotted with purple.

The pubescent inflorescence bears 20 or more successive flowers. Two flowers are open at the same time only very briefly, if at all; when this happens, the older flower is at the point of abscission as the younger one unfolds. In this and other species of the subgenus the occurrence of previous flowers is marked by persistent, green, nodal bracts all along the rachis, at intervals of approximately 5 cm (2 in.). Older inflorescences develop a zigzag appearance associated with these successive nodal markers.

The dorsal sepal is cream to green, flushed with yellow green in the center, and veined with maroon. The dorsal is ovate to subcircular, obtuse, and pubescent on the back surface. It measures 2.5–3.5 cm (1–1.5 in.) in length by 3 cm (1.25 in.) in width. The ventral sepal is similar but smaller.

The petals are white with deep rose to maroon spots, and bear fascicles of eyelashlike hairs along their margins. Petals are held nearly horizontally and twist at least 1 full turn, usually 1.5 turns. Linear in shape, they measure 4.5–5 cm (1.8–2 in.) in length and only 0.9–1 cm (0.3 in.) in width.

The pouch is longer than broad, measuring approximately 4 cm (1.5 in.) in length by 2–2.5 cm (0.75–1 in.) in width. In color, the pouch is pink to lavender and dusted with a fine stippling of maroon.

Vegetatively, var. *moquettianum* is somewhat larger. It bears slightly larger flowers, lacking maroon veining but finely speckled with purple on its dorsal. The variant is generally less floriferous.

FLOWERING SEASON Anytime; more likely summer.

Paphiopedilum liemianum (Fowlie) Karasawa & Saito   PLATE 39

P. liemianum is often found listed as a subspecies of *P. chamberlainianum*. This placement is invalid, both because the latter binomial is a synonym, and because true species rank for this taxon is justifiable based upon its distinctive foliar characteristics, narrow geographic range, and chromosome number (2n = 32), which varies from that of *P. chamberlainianum* or, more accurately, *P. victoria-regina*, with 34 chromosomes.

GEOGRAPHIC DISTRIBUTION This species is found in the northern portion of the island of Sumatra.

HABITAT *P. liemianum* clings to the roots of trees perched upon steep ravines in the limestone hills at elevations of 600–1,000 m (2,100–3,400 ft.). It receives dappled shade and ample moisture. Monsoons provide heavy rainfall during autumn and again, but less relentlessly, in June. Located just north of the equator, there is little year-round variation in day length. Volcanic mountains alter the climate significantly by channeling prevailing winds and precipitation over the region inhabited by the slippers. Seepage provides moisture during drier months.

DESCRIPTION The growths are composed of 4–6 large leaves which are green above and barred beneath with distinct stripes consisting of rows of maroon dots. Bristles emerge from the margins of the leaves. Leaf measurements are 15–25 cm (6–10 in.) in length by 3–5 cm (1.2–2 in.) in width.

The many-flowered inflorescence produces large flowers successively over an extended period of time. The peduncle and rachis are both pubescent. Each flower is subtended by a persistent bract.

The ovate dorsal sepal has a creamy white border surrounding a green center. The margins are ciliate, and pubescence covers the outer surface. The dimensions of the dorsal sepal are 3–3.5 cm (1.2–1.3 in.) long by 2.5–4 cm (1–1.5 in.) wide. The synsepalum is narrower, yellow green, ciliate, and pubescent on the outer surface. It measures 3 cm (1.2 in.) in length and 2.5 cm (1 in.) in width.

The twisted, ciliate petals are held very nearly horizontally and recurve slightly. They are cream to white, spotted with purple, and linear. The petals measure 4–5 cm (1.5–2 in.) long by only 0.7–1 cm (0.25–0.3 in.) wide. The inflated labellum is rosy lavender spotted with minute purple dots. Lip length is 4–4.5 cm (1.5–1.75 in.), while the breadth is only 2.5 cm (1 in.).

FLOWERING SEASON Summer and continuing for 10–18 months.

Paphiopedilum moquettianum (J. J. Smith) Fowlie. See *P. glaucophyllum* J. J. Smith var. *moquettianum* J. J. Smith.

Paphiopedilum primulinum M. Wood & Taylor PLATE 40

P. primulinum var. *purpurascens* (M. Wood) Cribb, comb. et stat. nov. is a more highly pigmented variant form, which, at present, shall be left at the rank recently given it by Cribb (1987) in his monograph. Traditionally, however, the more pigmented taxon has been placed at specific rank, while the entity with reduced pigmentation (*P. primulinum*) has been placed subordinately as a variant with an *album* designation. In this case, the albinistic entity was described first, and priority of naming, under the *International Code of Botanical Nomenclature*, usually prevails. Var. *purpurascens* is discussed secondarily in this entry.

GEOGRAPHIC DISTRIBUTION A small area in the north of the island of Sumatra is the source of this species.

HABITAT *P. primulinum* grows at elevations of 400–500 m (1,400–1,700 ft.) in bright shade under the canopy of a dwarf forest. Limestone underlies the humus in which the plants take root. Annual rainfall is rather high, with wet and dry seasons dominating this equatorial zone rather than warm and cool seasons.

DESCRIPTION Both the vegetative organs and the flowers of this species and its variant are small in comparison to other members of the subgenus. Leaves are narrow and green; 4–7 of them make up a growth. Tessellations and purple pigmentation are absent, although the margins are hirsute.

The pubescent flower spike bears a succession of greenish yellow flowers, each subtended by a persistent bract.

The ovate dorsal sepal is green and bears pubescence on its outer surface and cilia upon its margins. It measures 2.5 cm (1 in.) in length and width. The ventral sepal is similarly colored and adorned. Its dimensions are 2.5–2.7 cm (1 in.) long by 1.2–1.5 cm (0.5–0.6 in.) wide.

The yellow petals are twisted and ciliate. They may be horizontal to slightly drooping. Their appearance is striking in this subgenus due to the lack of spotting. In length, they reach 3.3 cm (1.3 in.), while their width is 0.7–0.8 cm (0.25 in.). The lemon yellow pouch is elongate and inflated at the tip. It measures 3.4–3.5 cm (1.3 in.) in length by 1.5–2 cm (0.6–0.75 in.) in width.

Var. *purpurascens* is similar in size to *P. primulinum* but is faintly flushed with purple on the labellum and bears some purple spotting on the petals. Slight purple mottling is typically present on the undersides of the leaves.

FLOWERING SEASON Initiated in spring and summer, continuing for up to a year.

Paphiopedilum victoria-mariae (Sander ex Masters) Rolfe PLATE 41

GEOGRAPHIC DISTRIBUTION This species has been collected from locations in west central and south Sumatra.

HABITAT *P. victoria-mariae* clings to steep, noncalcareous lava cliffs at elevations of 1,500–2,000 m (5,100–6,900 ft.) where it receives abundant rainfall and deep shade. Its roots are anchored in acid peat moss. Located just south of the equator, its temperature range is 13–24° C (56–75° F). April-September is the period of cooler temperatures and somewhat drier conditions, although rainfall is seldom less than 15 cm (6 in.) per month. Most of the over 450 cm (approx. 200 in.) of rainfall occurs during October-March, together with the higher temperatures.

DESCRIPTION The leaves of this species are large, tessellated above and basally spotted with purple beneath. They achieve lengths of 25–30 cm (10–12 in.) and widths of 5–7 cm (2–2.75 in.). Their margins are hirsute basally. This species is somewhat rhizomatous.

The pubescent inflorescence bears 20 or more successive flowers and reaches lengths of 1–1.3 m (39–50 in.). Not infrequently, a sterile bract intersects the peduncle. Persistent green bracts subtend each flower. The rachis must frequently be staked or tied to an overhead support as it elongates with age.

The ovate dorsal sepal bears a cream or pale yellow margin and has a rich green center striped with veins of maroon. Cilia adorn the margin; the back surface is pubescent. The dorsal measures 2.5–3 cm (1–1.2 in.) in length and width. The synsepalum measures only 2–2.5 cm (0.75–1 in.) in length and 1.5 cm (0.6 in.) in width; it is densely pubescent upon its outer surface.

The petals are twisted and bear eyelashlike hairs upon their margins. In color, the petal margins are reddish purple or reddish brown, while the central portion is green or cream with narrow red veins. The dimensions of the linear petals are 3–4 cm (1.2–1.5 in.) long by 0.5–1 cm (0.25–0.3 in.) wide. Held horizontally, they recurve to a variable degree. The pouch is not broadly inflated, but is long and tapering, 3–4 cm (1.2–1.5 in.) in length by 2–2.5 cm (0.75–1 in.) in width. Purple in color, the labellum of *P. victoria-mariae* is characterized by Cribb (1987) as unique in the subgenus for its distinctive green pouch rim, with the sole spotting on the entire flower to be found upon the side-lobes of the pouch. However, Richard Topper (personal communication) identifies this taxon with or without spotting based on the presence of an elongate, tapered pouch.

FLOWERING SEASON Spring or summer, continuing for many months.

Paphiopedilum victoria-regina (Sander) Wood   PLATE 42

This species has been known far and wide as *Paphiopedilum chamberlainianum* (Sander) Stein. The reader is referred to Cribb's (1987) monograph, which provides insights into the rationale for the change of binomials after over 80 years.

GEOGRAPHIC DISTRIBUTION *P. victoria-regina* comes from northern Sumatra.

HABITAT Epiphytic on tree roots and lithophytic on restricted limestone outcrops among sandstone cliffs, this edaphic species thrives at elevations of 700–2,000 m (2,400–6,900 ft.), in bright shade with abundant moisture. Seepage provides moisture year-round. At the higher elevations, mists are ubiquitous, and the climate is that of perennial springtime. At the lower elevational extremes, the colonies are more plentiful, because of the wider availability of limestone substrate.

DESCRIPTION The green leaves are large, spotted basally with anthocyanin beneath, and measure 30–40 cm (12–16 in.) long by 5–7 cm (2–2.75 in.) wide.

The indeterminate inflorescence extends up to 60 cm (24 in.) in length and bears 20 or more flowers, each of which is subtended by a persistent green bract.

The dorsal sepal is ovate to subcircular and measures 2.5–3 cm (1–1.2 in.) in either dimension. The margins are undulate to smooth and yellow green to cream in color. Centrally, the dorsal sepal is suffused with deeper green and veined with dark maroon stripes. The ventral sepal is similarly marked but narrower, and measures 2.8–3 cm. (1.2 in.) long by 2 cm (0.75 in.) wide. Both sepals are pubescent on their outer surfaces.

The spiral petals are held horizontally and bear numerous cilia upon their margins. Their color is yellow to cream. Typically, they are spotted and veined with dark purple. The petals measure 4 cm (1.6 in.) in length and 2 cm (0.75 in.) in width. Recurving occurs at the petal apices of most individuals. The lip is roundly inflated distally, but is longer than wide, measuring 4 cm (1.6 in.) in length by 2 cm (0.75 in.) in width. Pouch color is pink with a white margin, and dense purple dotting marks the outer surface.

FLOWERING SEASON Spring and summer, continuing for up to 2 years.

Paphiopedilum victoria-regina (Sander) M. Wood subsp. *glaucophyllum* (J. J. Smith) M. Wood.
See *P. glaucophyllum* J. J. Smith.

Paphiopedilum victoria-regina (Sander) M. Wood subsp. *glaucophyllum* (J. J. Smith) M. Wood var. *moquettianum* (J. J. Smith) M. Wood. See *P. glaucophyllum* J. J. Smith var. *moquettianum* J. J. Smith.

SUBGENUS *PAPHIOPEDILUM*

Subgenus *Paphiopedilum* is composed of 4 sections: *Coryopedilum* and *Pardalopetalum*, both with simultaneously flowering multifloral inflorescences; and *Paphiopedilum* and *Barbata*, both typically unifloral. (The *Cochlopetalum* group as discussed above is given separate subgenus rank, rather than included as a fifth section of subgenus *Paphiopedilum*, because of its genome of $2n = 25$ and its successional flowering habit.)

The petals of subgenus *Paphiopedilum* are longer than wide. The side-lobes of the pouch are infolded. The species in this subgenus have varying numbers of chromosomes, but the base genome is $2n = 26$.

Section *Coryopedilum*

The species in this section are among the largest in the genus and are characterized as having straplike leaves devoid of tessellations. The inflorescences bear several flowers simultaneously. The petals are long and tapering, usually pendulous, twisted and warted along their margins. The section name is attributable to the helmet-shaped pouches of the flowers.

Some of the most desirable and most difficult species in the genus belong to section *Coryopedilum*. An excellent example of the difficulties to be encountered is the significantly slower maturation rate of the growths of *P. rothschildianum* (Reichb. f.) Stein. This characteristic extends the interval before an inflorescence is produced by a year or more, thus retarding flowering primarily on young, newly collected or poorly established plants. For striking flowers, however, the members of this section are unparalleled. The successful flowering of *P. rothschildianum* is unanimously described by growers as well worth the protracted delay. Fortunately, once the plants in this section become established and/or mature, their flowering is rewardingly regular.

Refer to Cribb (1987) for the rationale behind the binomials included in this section as species/subspecies/varieties/forms and those that are considered merely synonymous. His account is excellently documented, and his arguments are well-taken, although some binomials routinely used by horticulturists unfortunately become invalid.

Paphiopedilum adductum Asher   PLATE 43

Introduced into cultivation in 1980 as *Paphiopedilum elliottianum* sensu Fowlie, this taxon was described as a new species in 1983. Refer to Cribb (1987) for a detailed summary of its origins and taxonomic placement. Without firsthand knowledge of this species, I rely heavily upon his descriptive passage as well.

P. adductum does not have a reputation for ease of flowering. Rands (personal communication) indicates that he has not received shipments of this species bearing spikes, and that even after several years of acclimatization in greenhouse culture, most plants are still unflowered. Several clones have received awards in September-December. Richard Topper (personal communication) states that this species flowers in April and May in North Carolina.

GEOGRAPHIC DISTRIBUTION Mindanao, in the Philippine archipelago, is the home of this endemic species.

HABITAT Plants are found on slopes growing at elevations of 1,250–1,350 m (4,300–4,600 ft.) rooted loosely in humus.

DESCRIPTION The moderately large, green leaves reach a length of 25 cm (10 in.) and a width of approximately 4 cm (1.5 in.).

The inflorescence bears 2–3 flowers in an arching spray extending 20–30 cm (8–12 in.). Florally, this species most resembles *P. rothschildianum*, but is distinct in several particulars, notably the reduced staminode of *P. adductum*, as well as its narrower, unciliated, pendulous petals. The 2 taxa also occupy divergent ranges.

The dorsal sepal is overlaid with stripes of maroon upon a greenish yellow or cream ground color. Ovate and acuminate, it measures 5–6.5 cm (2–2.5 in.) long by 2.3–3.2 cm (1–1.25 in.) wide. The ventral sepal is similar but slightly longer.

The slender, tapered petals are pendulous. Proximally, they are yellow or cream and spotted with maroon; the distal portions are uniformly flushed with maroon. In length, the petals measure 8–15 cm (3.2–6 in.), while the width is less than 1 cm (0.25 in.). The labellum is pale cream or yellow beneath, suffused and veined with maroon frontally. Its length is 3.8–4.7 cm (1.5–1.8 in.), while its width is 1.5–2 cm (0.6–0.75 in.).

The staminode of this species is worthy of note because of its atypically small size. It is described as insufficient to provide a trap mechanism for normal insect pollination, although it in no way prevents the occurrence of pollination.

FLOWERING SEASON Autumn, possibly spring.

Paphiopedilum bodegomii Fowlie. See *P. glanduliferum* (Blume) Stein.

Paphiopedilum elliottianum (O'Brien) Stein. See *P. rothschildianum* (Reichb. f.) Stein.

Paphiopedilum gardineri (Guill.) Pfitz. See *P. glanduliferum* (Blume) Stein.

Paphiopedilum glanduliferum (Blume) Stein   PLATE 44

Growers seeking information about *Paphiopedilum praestans* (Reichb.f.) Pfitz., a widely used but subsequent synonym for this taxon, must read Cribb (1987) for historical details of nomenclature. *P. praestans* is a synonym for this species, due to its publication subsequent to *P. glanduliferum* (Blume). The unusual situation here involves a name which seems new to horticulturists though it was given to one of the earliest slippers described. *P. bodegomii* Fowlie is unpublished, having no type sheet; however, it is another binomial rather widely used for this taxon. A third and, according to Cribb, mistakenly used binomial has been applied to this species: *P. gardineri* (Guill.) Pfitz. Refer to Cribb (1987), Kennedy (1979) and Asher (1981c) for further study of the nomenclatural complexities of this taxon.

Distinctions between var. *glanduliferum* (Blume) Stein and var. *wilhelminae* (L. O. Williams) Cribb, comb. et stat. nov. are incorporated within the following description. The diversity is perhaps great enough to support separation into 2 species, and such action may be taken in future.

GEOGRAPHIC DISTRIBUTION The range of this species includes western New Guinea and the adjacent islands. Var. *wilhelminae* is found in both the east and west New Guinea highlands.

HABITAT Fairly divergent habitats characterize the variants of this species. *P. glanduliferum* is a denizen of low elevations from sea level to 200 m (700 ft.) and grows on calcareous outcrops. Populations flourish in bright sun to full shade. Poorly rooted in humus or occasionally epiphytic, the plants prefer excellent drainage.

Var. *wilhelminae* differs from the typical form in occurring at higher elevations of 1,700–

1,800 m (5,900–6,200 ft.), in heavy soil near rivers or lakes. Several colonies have been discovered growing in full sun.

DESCRIPTION The type plant produces clumps of growths, each bearing 4–6 leaves. The leaves reach lengths of up to 40 cm (16 in.) and widths of 3.5–5 cm (1.4–2 in.). By contrast, the leaves of var. *wilhelminae* are smaller, and according to Cribb (1987), the growths are not clustered, but are borne upon a short rhizome.

The flowerscape extends 30–50 cm (12–20 in.) in length and bears 2–5 large flowers, each subtended by a bract which strongly resembles a small sepal.

The dorsal sepal is ovate and acute, measuring 5–5.5 cm (2–2.2 in.) long by 2.5–3 cm (1–1.2 in.) wide. Its color is yellow with prominent purple stripes. The synsepalum is smaller but otherwise similar. Both sepals are pubescent upon their reverse surfaces.

The linear petals are yellow veined with maroon, and their orientation is spreading to pendulous. Their margins are sparsely fringed with cilia, proximally undulate and verrucous. They measure 9–10 cm (3.5–4 in.) in length by 1 cm (0.25 in.) in width. Typically, the petals are helical. The pouch measures 5–5.5 cm (2–2.25 in.) long by approximately 2 cm (0.75 in.) wide. It is yellow, flushed and veined with maroon.

Var. *wilhelminae* bears smaller flowers than those of the typical variety. Most frequently, marginal warts are absent from the petals as well.

FLOWERING SEASON Summer.

Paphiopedilum kolopakingii Fowlie

PLATES 45 & 46

The newly introduced *P. topperi* Hort. is included within this taxon as an albinistic variant. According to Richard Topper (personal communication), the plants of var. *topperi* are consistently larger and more floriferous than the outstanding *P. kolopakingii*.

GEOGRAPHIC DISTRIBUTION This species comes from central Kalimantan on Borneo.

HABITAT Documentation of the habitat of this recently discovered species is poor. According to Fowlie (1984b), it was collected from behind police borders near the headwaters of the Barito River in central Kalimantan. Its type location is described as rocky (possibly serpentine) cliffs over gorges at 600 m (2,000 ft.).

DESCRIPTION This species is quite large and uniquely floriferous. The 8–10 fleshy leaves per growth stand nearly erect and measure 40–60 cm (16–24 in.) in length and 6–8 cm (2.3–3.2 in.) in width.

The inflorescence extends 40–70 cm (16–28 in.) and bears 6–14 simultaneous flowers which, although small for the section, produce an outstanding display unparalleled in the genus. The bracts subtending the flowers are white to cream and veined with maroon. They strongly resemble the dorsal sepals, thus augmenting the already opulent display.

The dorsal sepal is cream with narrow veins of maroon. Ovate and acute, it measures 4.3–6.5 cm (1.75–2.5 in.) in length by 2.5–3.5 cm (1–1.5 in.) in width. The synsepalum is similar, although smaller and bicarinate.

The petals are ivory to green, slightly veined with maroon, and measure 5–7 cm (2–2.75 in.) long by 0.7–0.9 cm (0.25–0.3 in.) wide. Pendulous and linear, they lack ciliar fringing, spots and warts; the distal portions may exhibit some twisting. The pouch is tawny to ocher with darker veins. Pointed at the apex, it measures 4–6 cm (1.5–2.3 in.) long by 2.2–2.8 cm (0.8–1.2 in.) wide.

Var. *topperi* is primarily ivory white, striped on its segments with green, and green-flushed upon the pouch. It may produce as many as 20 flowers per spike on well-grown plants.

FLOWERING SEASON July.

Paphiopedilum laevigatum (Batem.) Pfitz. See *P. philippinense* (Reichb. f.) Stein.

Paphiopedilum philippinense (Reichb. f.) Stein   PLATE 47
    Binomials associated with this species include the synonym *P. laevigatum* (Batem.)
Pfitz., and the valid var. *roebelenii* (Veitch) Pfitz. described within the text.
GEOGRAPHIC DISTRIBUTION *P. philippinense* grows in the Philippines and on islands near Borneo.
Var. *roebelenii* is known only from the Philippine island of Luzon.
HABITAT Bright, breezy conditions in coastal regions provide the site for natural colonies of
this species. Limestone outcrops are the substrate of choice. Warmth and humidity are abundant at the low elevations of sea level to 500 m (1,700 ft.).
DESCRIPTION The large plants bear 7–9 straplike green leaves which achieve lengths of 15–50
cm (6–20 in.) and widths up to 5–6 cm (2–2.5 in.). The leaves are subsucculent in texture with
a glossy luster.
    The pubescent inflorescence stands erect and bears 2–5 flowers of variable size. It
reaches heights of up to 50 cm (20 in.). Each flower is subtended by a bract.
    The dorsal sepal is white, striped with maroon. Ovate and acute, it measures 4–5 cm
(1.5–2 in.) long by 2–2.5 (1.75–2 in.) wide. The synsepalum is similar in all respects. Both
sepals are pubescent upon their outer surfaces.
    The petals of *P. philippinense* are elongate and pendulous; proximally, they are adorned
with maroon warts along the margins. Petal margins are also ciliate, and where the warts
occur, the cilia are arranged in tufts growing out of the warts. In color, the linear petals are
yellow basally, gradually darkening to maroon for most of their length and fading to pale
green at their apices. Petal length varies from 6–13 cm (2.3–5.2 in.) while the width is only 0.5
cm (0.25 in.). The petals go through 1 complete spiral from base to apex typically.
    The helmet-shaped labellum is yellow to tawny buff in color and is typically veined
with green. It is rather small, measuring 3.5–4 cm (1.3–1.6 in.) long by 2–2.5 cm (0.75–1 in.)
wide.
FLOWERING SEASON Late winter or spring.

Paphiopedilum praestans (Reichb. f.) Pfitz. See *P. glanduliferum* (Blume) Stein.

Paphiopedilum randsii Fowlie   PLATE 48
GEOGRAPHIC DISTRIBUTION This species grows on the northern end of Mindanao in the
Philippine archipelago.
HABITAT Plants are epiphytic or humus terrestrials in dense forests at 400–500 m (1,400–1,700
ft.) elevation. Day and night temperatures vary little, ranging around 15–21° C (60–70° F).
DESCRIPTION The leaves of *P. randsii* are pale green with yellow margins. They vary from 15–30
cm (6–12 in.) in length and reach approximately 5 cm (2 in.) in width.
    The pubescent inflorescence bears 3–5 flowers, each subtended by a bract. The entire
structure reaches heights of 25–40 cm (10–16 in.).
    The dorsal sepal is white, veined with maroon, and pubescent on the outer surface.
Ovate and acute to subacute, it measures approximately 4 cm (1.5 in.) long by 2 cm (0.75 in.)
wide. The ventral sepal is similarly marked, measuring only 3 cm (1.2 in.) long by 2 cm (0.75
in.) wide.
    The petals are also white veined with maroon. Linear in shape, they exhibit no spiraling.
They are short, for the section, and pendulous with rounded apices. Their margins are
fringed with cilia. The petals reach lengths of 3.8–4.5 cm (1.5–1.75 in.) and an approximate
width of 0.5 cm (0.25 in.). The labellum is yellow or tawny buff in color veined with green.
Apically, a shallow groove bisects the pouch not quite producing lobes. The lip measures
2.5–3.2 cm (1–1.3 in.) in length and 1–1.5 cm (0.3–0.6 in.) in width.
FLOWERING SEASON Summer.

Paphiopedilum rothschildianum (Reichb. f.) Stein   PLATE 49

Cribb (1987) has effectively destroyed every argument for retention of the binomial *P. elliottianum* (O'Brien) Stein, in correct usage. In light of his evidence, growers may wish to relabel such specimens as *P. rothschildianum*.

GEOGRAPHIC DISTRIBUTION This endemic species is found only on the slopes of Mt. Kinabalu in northern Borneo.

HABITAT Clinging to steep, serpentine cliffs, this slipper tolerates both sunny and shady sites at elevations of 600–1,200 m (2,000–4,100 ft.). The plants are exposed to cool night temperatures in the spring in conjunction with the heavy downpours brought on by the winter monsoons. Plants typically overhang pools or flourish in the spray from waterfalls.

CULTURAL NOTES A late spring-flowering species in nature, *P. rothschildianum* is considered slow rather than difficult to flower in cultivation, being more likely to flower in early to mid-summer under glass.

This species has acquired an undeserved reputation for difficulty of flowering. Far from being mysterious, shy, recalcitrant, or any of the other adjectives carelessly ascribed to it, *P. rothschildianum* is a reliable, free-blooming species almost always bearing spikes in some developmental stage in the wild. The difficulties experienced by growers are understandable given improved knowledge of this plant and its easily-met requirements that differ rather sharply, however, from those of most other species or hybrids of this genus. As is apparent from study of the habitat notes, humidity is an important factor in good culture.

Growths of this species are known to mature slowly. Especially during acclimatization to a new environment or while a specimen is small or root-deprived, *P. rothschildianum* must be considered unlikely to flower on a regular, annual schedule. Upon becoming established, it blooms reliably. Becoming established, however, means somewhat more than it does in other more typical slippers. Because the growths may require up to 3 years to reach maturity, and because premature division may interrupt the complex hormonal processes involved in maturation, this species must always be maintained as a multigrowth plant. Once a multigrowth plant is established, and the individual new growths are progressing toward maturity, the plant may be considered a reliable bloomer. Contrary to these recommendations, Richard Topper (personal communication) states that particular clones of this species flower well on only 1 growth. These clones must be considered the exception rather than the rule.

Division of plants of this species should be undertaken only after several growths have matured, flowered and begun to produce offshoots. When dividing, distinct clusters of growths should be maintained intact for best results. Potting *P. rothschildianum* in a medium rich in small chunks of fern fiber (hapuu) will provide for minimal disturbance to an established plant, by extending the safe intervals between repotting to up to 3 years. Repotting should be carefully undertaken when spikes are approximately 5–10 cm (2–4 in.) long. The rationale for this timing is that it precedes initiation of new growths by a significant period of time so that interruption of the maturation cycle is less likely. If bud blast is a major concern, repotting should not be delayed after flowering by more than a week. Offshoots are initiated as full anthesis is achieved, even before the leafy shoots are externally visible.

Attention to cool temperatures during late winter and spring months is essential to induce regular flowering. This species does not require a full-fledged rest period complete with drying-off as the cool winter months in its native habitat are extremely wet. High humidity is a year-round feature of the natural habitat.

Conditions suitable for *Cattleya* orchids—including intermediate temperatures, large-particle medium, intermediate light, adequate humidity, brisk air movement and slightly more fertilizer than is usually applied to slippers—are also suitable for growing *P. rothschildianum* successfully. Incorporation of the winter cooling into this routine should insure well-grown and well-flowered specimens. By hanging the plants above the slipper benches the grower is able to optimize several of these special requirements in 1 step. Increased light and warmth (the temperature factor must be mitigated during the winter months, however) combine with improved air circulation from this higher vantage point.

The majority of the hybrid offspring of this species benefit from this same special treatment as they grow almost as slowly as *P. rothschildianum*. There are exceptions, however, and in each case some modification of these special cultural requirements is not only adequate but may be optimal to certain of these hybrids.

DESCRIPTION Growths are clustered, and mature growths bear very large leaves, measuring up to 60 cm (24 in.) in length and 5 cm (2 in.) in width.

The erect inflorescence bears 2–4 flowers, each subtended by a bract. The height of the inflorescence may reach 45 cm (18 in.).

The dorsal sepal is pale green, cream, or yellow and striped with purple. Ovate and acute, it reaches 6.6 cm (2.6 in.) in length and approximately 4 cm (1.5 in.) in width. The ventral sepal is similar but reduced in size.

The outspread petals are held just a few degrees below horizontal. They reach lengths of up to 12.5 cm (5 in.) producing an overall flower width of 24–30 cm (10.5–12 in.). The flowers are unique in the genus for their petal span. Petals are linear and tapered with rounded apices. Their width is only 1.2–1.5 cm (0.5–0.6 in.). Yellow or cream, the petals are striped with maroon. The margins are undulate and ciliate proximally. The pouch is approximately 5.7 cm (2.25 in.) long by 2.2 cm (0.8 in.) wide. It is yellow to tawny and suffused with maroon.

FLOWERING SEASON Early, mid- or late summer.

Paphiopedilum sanderanum (Reichb. f.) Stein   PLATE 50

P. sanderanum was a rare species following its discovery in 1885, then lost altogether, and only recently rediscovered. Its habitat is known today, and there is reason to anticipate its widespread cultivation from seedlings in the near future.

Having no firsthand knowledge of this species, my description relies heavily upon Cribb (1987) and older sources. Like Cribb, I am intrigued by the elongated petals and the possibility that they function as a ramp for pollinators. This same function has been postulated for the petals of *Phragmipedium caudatum* and the other members of its section, making field observation, such as Atwood's (1985c) study of the pollination of *P. rothschildianum* in Sabah, necessary for all of these long-petalled species as well as for the subfamily as a whole.

GEOGRAPHIC DISTRIBUTION This species is endemic to Sarawak in Borneo.

HABITAT Southeast-facing cliffs, shaded except for morning sun, are preferred by *P. sanderanum*. This species is a humus lithophyte upon calcareous rock, loosely rooted in the detritus collected in crevices. The elevations of its habitat range from 150–600 m (500–2,100 ft.). Precipitation is ample; seepage moistens the roots during drier seasons and humidity is constantly high. Air movement, preventing stagnation, is also a constant feature of the habitat.

DESCRIPTION The pendulous, straplike leaves are uniformly dark green. They reach lengths of 30–45 cm (12–18 in.) and a width of approximately 5 cm (2 in.).

The pubescent inflorescence is held in a moderately ascendant attitude. It extends to 45 cm (18 in.) or more in height and bears 2–5 flowers subtended by bracts.

The acute dorsal sepal is lanceolate. Its color is yellow heavily striped with deep maroon. It measures 4.8–6.5 cm (2–2.5 in.) in length by 1.3–2.5 cm (0.5–1 in.) in width. The bicarinate synsepalum is smaller, measuring 3.5–6 cm (1.5–2.3 in.) in length by 1–2 cm (0.3–0.75 in.) in width. In shape and color it is very similar to the dorsal. Both sepals are pubescent on their outer surfaces.

The unique petals of *P. sanderanum* set this species apart in the genus. Pendulous and ribbonlike, they extend for 30–90 cm (12–35.5 in.) in length, while their width is only 0.7–1 cm (0.25–0.3 in.). Basally, the petals are cream to yellow in color, warted and ciliate on the undulate margins and spotted with maroon. They taper and twist along their length and become deep maroon in color throughout the distal three-quarters.

The labellum is flushed with maroon above and yellow below its pointed apex. It measures 4.8–5 cm (2 in.) in length and 1.5–2.5 cm (0.6–1 in.) in width.

FLOWERING SEASON May.

Paphiopedilum stonei (Hook.) Stein   PLATE 51

Several varieties of *P. stonei* have been described, including var. *platytaenium* (Reichb. f.) Stein, var. *candidum* (Masters) Pfitz., and the invalid var. *stictopetalum* Wood which, according to Cribb (1987), is *P. Alice*, a hybrid of *P. stonei* × *P. spiceranum*. Although Cribb suggests that it may be a natural hybrid, this hybrid could only have occurred artificially because of the enormous geographic barriers separating Borneo from the Himalayan home of *P. spiceranum*. Furthermore, while *P. stonei* may delay its flowering until fall, when the earliest flowers of *P. spiceranum* appear, it most often blooms in summer, making natural hybridization an even more remote possibility. Distinctions between the species and the natural variants are discussed below.

GEOGRAPHIC DISTRIBUTION Sarawak, on Borneo, is the location of this endemic species.

HABITAT This species grows at elevations of 60–500 m (200–1,500 ft.) where it clings to calcareous cliffs. A minimum of humus collects about its roots, and it frequently roots in lithophytic mosses. Rather dense forest provides moderate shade over the northeastern faces of ravines and riverine valleys preferred by this species. Near-constant air movement is an important factor in the environment. Heavy rainfall occurs during the fall and winter months, associated with winter monsoon winds; early spring is drier, while July-August is predictably dry. According to Fowlie (1986), the majority of the colonies are situated so as to catch seepage, mist and condensation, effectively utilizing year-round water supplies.

DESCRIPTION The green, strap-shaped leaves are large, reaching lengths of up to 70 cm (28 in.) and widths of 5 cm (2 in.).

The arching to nearly erect inflorescence rises to 70 cm (28 in.) in height and bears 2–4 flowers, each of which is subtended by a bract.

The dorsal sepal is white and typically bears a pair of vertical stripes of blackish maroon, 1 on either side of the midvein. The reverse side is often heavily stained with maroon. Var. *candidum* lacks pigmentation of the sepals. In shape, the dorsal sepal is ovate to subcordate, apically acute, measures 4.5–5.7 cm (1.74–2.25 in.) long by 3–4.4 cm (1.25–1.75 in.) wide, and is deeply keeled. The ventral sepal is similar but smaller.

The elongate, spreading petals arch downward distally. They are linear and tapering, measuring 10–15 cm (4–6 in.) in length and 0.4–0.8 cm (0.25–0.3 in.) in width. Var. *platytaenium* is noted for its wide petals which are up to 2 cm (0.75 in.) wide. The distal portions of the petals exhibit some twisting. Proximally, sparse ciliar fringing of both margins is typical. In color, the petals are yellow, proximally spotted and barred with maroon, while the distal portions are stained maroon. The labellum is yellow or cream beneath, flushed rose frontally, and veined with maroon. It measures 5 cm (2 in.) or more in length by 2.8 cm (1.2 in.) in width.

FLOWERING SEASON Late summer and early autumn.

Paphiopedilum supardii Braem & Loeb   PLATE 52

Lacking firsthand knowledge of this species, I rely upon the descriptions provided in Cribb's (1987) monograph and by Asher (1988).

This slipper bears a strong overall resemblance to *P. rothschildianum*. Cribb (1987) writes that it is most closely allied to that species. However, it differs in the petals which, rather than extending nearly horizontally, curve as if the lower margins failed to keep pace as the upper ones elongacted. The petals are unique in the genus for their characteristic curling.

Many growers in the United States and elsewhere have purchased this species under the unpublished binomial *P. devogelii*.

GEOGRAPHIC DISTRIBUTION This species is endemic to southeast Kalimantan in Borneo.

HABITAT Found growing as a lithophyte at elevations ranging from 600–960 m (2,000–3,300 ft.), this species lives shaded except for morning sun.

DESCRIPTION The dark green leaves reach lengths of up to 55 cm (21.5 in.) and are 3.5–5.5 cm (1.3–2.2 in.) wide. The erect inflorescence bears 3–4 flowers at a height of up to 45 cm (18 in.). The ovaries are sheathed by large bracts which resemble the ventral sepal.

The ovate dorsal sepal tapers to an acute apex. Maroon stripes overlay a cream or buff ground color which is sometimes faintly suffused with green. Its dimensions are approximately 5.5 cm (2.2 in.) in length by 2.5 cm (1 in.) in width. The synsepalum is similar, although the maroon stripes are considerably narrower.

The pendulous petals of *P. supardii* are of the same pale color as the sepals, with spots and bars of maroon. The proximal margins are warted, undulate and ciliate. Toward the apices, the petals are helical through at least 1 turn. A curiously inequilateral elongation of their superior and inferior margins gives them a curled, almost deformed appearance. Petal dimensions are 8–9 cm (3.2–3.5 in.) in length by 0.7–0.9 cm (0.25 in.) in width. The pouch is pale creamy buff beneath, flushed with maroon frontally. It measures approximately 4.5 cm (1.75 in.) long by 1.5–1.8 cm (0.6–0.75 in.) wide.

FLOWERING SEASON Spring and early summer.

Paphiopedilum topperi Hort. See *P. kolopakingii* Fowlie.

Section *Pardalopetalum*

The 4 taxa in this section form an uneasy alliance. In fact, section *Pardalopetalum* as it is structured here is a clearly delineated taxon of 3 species with the addition of a fourth species and its variant which were formerly placed in a monotypic section, *Mystropetalum*. Geographically and morphologically, 3 of the 4 species are clearly allied, although sufficiently divergent on both criteria to warrant species rank for each. *P. haynaldianum* (Reichb. f) Stein and *P. lowii* (Lindl.) Stein, despite their resemblances, are obviously distinct from each other as the long-accepted components of the section. However, while the inclusion of *P. parishii* (Reichb.f.) Stein appears somewhat arbitrary by virtue of its geographic alienation from the other 2 species, the recently described *P. richardianum* Asher & Beaman provides morphological intergradations which tend to mitigate grounds for questioning such a decision. I raise the question, however, of the eligibility of *P. parishii* for reinstatement at monotypic status (formerly in section *Mystropetalum*) based upon its occurrence as the sole multifloral species of *Paphiopedilum* found well inland upon the Asian continent. This species and its variant, var. *dianthum* (Tang & Wang) Cribb & Tang, are relics of an ancient relationship with the rest of section *Pardalopetalum*, and when the morphological and geographical evidence is viewed critically, the divergence is perhaps sufficient to justify separate sections.

Paphiopedilum haynaldianum (Reichb. f.) Stein   PLATES 53 & 54

GEOGRAPHIC DISTRIBUTION This species is found on the Philippine islands of Luzon and Negros.

HABITAT Plants cling to rocks and trees or root loosely in humus on cliffs at elevations from sea-level to 1,400 m (4,800 ft.). The seasonal extremes include warm monsoon rains during the summer months and near-freezing temperatures during the drier winter. Even the winter months, however, provide substantial humidity and rainfall. In spring, high daytime temperatures occur, averaging 32° C (90° F). Bright light is received year-round by most colonies.

DESCRIPTION The large strap-shaped leaves are yellowish green. They reach lengths of up to 45 cm (18 in.) and widths of approximately 5 cm (2 in.). Tessellation is absent.

The arching to suberect inflorescence extends to 50 cm (20 in.) in length and bears 2–4 flowers. Each flower is subtended by a rather large bract; bracts and flower stalk are pubescent.

The dorsal sepal is cream to white, suffused with yellow green in the center, boldly spotted with maroon basally, and suffused marginally with pale purple. Obovate or elliptical in shape, it appears slender due to the pronounced basal reflexion of its lateral margins. It measures 3.5–6.4 cm (1.3–2.5 in.) long by 1.5–2.5 cm (0.6–1 in.) wide. The elliptic ventral sepal is yellow green and basally spotted with maroon. Apically bidentate, its dimensions are 2.5–4.5 cm (1–1.75 in.) in length by 2–2.5 cm (0.75–1 in.) in width. Both sepals are pubescent upon the reverse sides.

The spathulate petals arch and execute a quarter spiral. Their apices may be acute or obtuse. Petal color is yellow green and boldly spotted with maroon proximally. The distal margins are flushed rose or purple. The pouch is khaki colored, veined darker green and bears a frontal flush of purple which varies in intensity from clone to clone. It measures 3.5–4.5 cm (1.3–1.75 in.) in length and 2–2.5 cm (0.75–1 in.) in width.

Plate 54 illustrates an albinistic variant which has not received taxonomic attention; it has no type sheet, geographic range or other particulars, and is possibly a horticultural cultivar.

FLOWERING SEASON Late winter and early spring.

Paphiopedilum lowii (Lindl.) Stein   PLATE 55

GEOGRAPHIC DISTRIBUTION This widely distributed species is found in the Malay Peninsula, Sumatra, Java, Borneo and the Celebes.

HABITAT Occasionally found growing in humus or lithophytically, this species is typically epiphytic. It prefers elevations of 250–1,600 m (860–5,500 ft.) and colonizes wooded mountain slopes as well as ravines. It appears equally successful in the shade of rain forest canopy or in sites receiving some direct sun each day. As an epiphyte, its roots are never subjected to constant saturation even during the monsoon months of summer. Winter brings some drying along with cooler, although always moderate, temperatures.

DESCRIPTION The large yellow green leaves are strap-shaped and suberect. They measure 25–45 cm (10–18 in.) long and 2.8–6 cm (1.1–2.3 in.) wide.

The inflorescence is arching to suberect, extends to 50 cm (20 in.) in height, and bears 3–7 flowers. Large bracts subtend the flowers. Both peduncle and bracts are pubescent.

The dorsal sepal is pale green, suffused with brownish purple at the base. Keeled by its midvein and ovate in shape, it appears deceptively narrow due to reflexing of its basal margins. Its dimensions are 3.3–3.5 cm (1.3 in.) long by 2.5–3.2 cm (1–1.3 in.) wide. The smaller ventral sepal is bicarinate and elliptical, pale green in color. Sepal margins are undulate and ciliate.

The spathulate petals typically execute 1 full spiral. Their margins are ciliate. Petal color is pale yellow proximally, overlaid with purple spotting, while the distal region is rosy purple. Petals measure 5–9 cm (2–3.5 in.) long by 1.5–2 cm (0.6–0.75 in.) wide. The labellum is khaki colored and measures 3.5–4 cm (1.3–1.6 in.) long by 2.5 cm (1 in.) wide.

FLOWERING SEASON Spring or early summer.

Paphiopedilum parishii (Reichb. f.) Stein

As discussed in the introduction to *Pardalopetalum*, *P. parishii* is a newcomer to this section with a vast geographic gap separating it from the other members. Morphologically, there are a number of ways in which this species differs from the rest of the section. The dorsal sepal and the pouch are the features which are most typical of the section.

A variant of this species, perhaps an ecological subspecies, is var. *dianthum* (Tang & Wang) Cribb & Tang. Both its range and appearance vary from the type as outlined within the text below.

GEOGRAPHIC DISTRIBUTION *P. parishii* has a range extending from eastern Burma to western and northern Thailand and barely into southern China. Var. *dianthum* ranges from the eastern end of the distribution of the type into Yunnan Province, China. Frequently individuals collected in northern Thailand and southern China are, according to Cribb (1987), intermediate between the 2 variants.

HABITAT *P. parishii* grows as an epiphyte or a lithophyte in medium shade at elevations of 1,250–2,200 m (4,300–7,600 ft.). The roots frequently take hold in mossy substrate or in the roots of epiphytic ferns. Summer monsoons from May-October follow high spring temperatures. During late fall and winter drier and cooler conditions prevail, but roots receive moisture from fog and occasional rain. Temperatures reach 32–35° C (90–94° F) during the warmest months of spring, with nightly drops to 10–15° C (50–60° F); the coolest temperatures occur during autumn and winter, bringing highs of 22–23° C (77–80° F) and overnight lows at 5–10° C (42–50° F.). Fairly brisk breezes usually dry the moisture from the crowns of plants in the wild before darkness falls.

Var. *dianthum* typically perches atop limestone outcrops as a lithophyte, although it occasionally elects an epiphytic existence.

CULTURAL NOTES *P. parishii* prefers a winter rest period with the amount of water restricted and night temperatures reduced to 4–6° C (the low to mid–40° F range). Not a shy bloomer, this species will often flower without a rest period, although with optimum conditions, growths mature and flower far more reliably.

DESCRIPTION *P. parishii* bears 5–8 large, deep green leaves per growth. They reach lengths up to 45 cm (18 in.), and are unusually broad, measuring 4–7.5 cm (1.5–3 in.) in width. Typical of epiphytic species, the leaves are held in a pendulous manner.

The arching to suberect inflorescence is densely pubescent, papillose in var. *dianthum*. It achieves heights of 30–50 cm (12–20 in.), bearing 3–7 showy flowers. Flowers of var. *dianthum* are somewhat larger but are borne on a shorter flowerscape in comparison with those of the type.

The dorsal sepal is elliptic and measures 3.5–4.5 cm (1.3–1.75 in.) in length by 2–3 cm (0.75–1.3 in.) in width. Its color is pale to medium green with darker veins. Reflexing of the basal margins occurs to some degree. The apex curves forward over the pouch. The bicarinate synsepalum is ovate and held back at an angle from the undersurface of the pouch. Apple green in color, it measures 2.5–4 cm (1–1.6 in.) in length by 1.5–3 cm (0.6–1.3 in.) in width.

The ribbonlike petals are pendulous, tapered and twisted. Superficially they resemble the petals of species in section *Coryopedilum*. Close scrutiny reveals the features which make them unique; the apices bear velvety tufts of pubescence, and are cupped or ladle-shaped. Petal color is green proximally with pubescent maroon warts; the distal half is uniformly dark maroon. Petal dimensions are 5–9 cm (2–3.5 in.) in length by only 0.7 cm (0.25 in.) in width. The pouch tapers to a narrow apex and measures 3–4.5 cm (1.25–1.75 in.) long. In color, it is yellow green to deeper green, flushed with brownish purple.

FLOWERING SEASON Late spring and summer.

Paphiopedilum richardianum Asher & Beaman, sp. nov.   PLATE 58

This newly described taxon, itself a narrow, insular endemic, in no way assists in eliminating the geographic difficulties associated with inclusion of *P. parishii* in section *Pardalopetalum*. However, its floral morphology and coloration provide a transition between the established members of the section and the recently included *P. parishii*, although the petals are not typical of the latter. Asher and Beaman (1988) write that *P. richardianum* is most closely allied to *P. lowii*.

GEOGRAPHIC DISTRIBUTION This species is from Sulawesi in the Celebes.

HABITAT The type locality is at an elevation of 1,100–1,200 m (3,800–4,100 ft.), near the town of Palu which is on Palu Bay, on the northwest shore of the island. The area receives heavy rainfall associated with monsoon winds. Very few particulars are available with regard to this 1988 addition to the genus.

DESCRIPTION The strap-shaped leaves ally this species with *P. lowii* and others of the section.

The pubescent flowerscape bears 2 or more flowers, each of which is subtended by a bract.

The dorsal sepal is lanceolate and hoods the pouch aperture; it exhibits little or no lateral reflexion. It measures 4 cm (1.75 in.) long by 2.5 cm (1 in.) wide. The lower lateral margins are widely stained with dark maroon, while narrow stripes of the same color traverse the apple green center and apex. The synsepalum is smaller than the dorsal. Its color is apple green with narrow maroon margins basally.

The pendulous petals are subspathulate and twisted. The ground color is greenish ivory; proximally, several maroon spots are situated along the margins, while maroon veins gradually coalesce to suffuse the distal margins and apex broadly with maroon. Petal dimensions are up to 8 cm (3 in.) long by 1 cm (0.3 in.) wide. The labellum has a broad and shallow toe; pronounced auricles rise above the V-shaped anterior rim. Chestnut brown suffuses all but the greenish toe. The pouch measures 4 cm (1.6 in.) in length.

FLOWERING SEASON January, May, and November; smaller plants only in November (Richard Topper, personal communication).

Section *Paphiopedilum*

Species in this section have green leaves devoid of tessellations and bear solitary flowers. Seven of the 10 species included in this section are closely allied by virtue of their staminodal characteristics. Several of these appear to be well-derived species from an ancient complex, exhibiting evidence of kinship in overall color and morphology; they include *P. exul* (Ridl.) Rolfe, *P. insigne* (Wall. ex Lindl.) Pfitz., *P. gratrixianum* (Masters) Guill., and *P. barbigerum* Tang & Wang. In modern times *P. insigne* is geographically remote from the other 3.

Synonyms are included in the listing for the sake of clarity, so that growers seeking details about a particular favorite may locate the pertinent text even while employing an invalid appellation. According to Cribb (1987), *P. affine* De Wild. is a synonym of *P. gratrixianum*, but it is treated here as a variant. A closely related newcomer in this section is *P. henryanum* Braem, sp. nov. Only recently discovered growing near colonies of *P. emersonii*, its appearance gives the immediate impression of an early complex hybrid *Paphiopedilum*. Smaller alliances found within this section are discussed within the pertinent text below.

Paphiopedilum affine De Wild. See *P. gratrixianum* (Masters) Guill.

Paphiopedilum barbigerum Tang & Wang — PLATE 59

The description of this species is taken largely from Cribb (1987). It is a member of the *P. insigne* complex.

GEOGRAPHIC DISTRIBUTION This species was collected in southwest China, from the border region between Guizhou and Guangxi.

HABITAT There is a dearth of information about the environs in which this species grows. It is described merely as a terrestrial.

DESCRIPTION The linear green leaves are suberect and lack tessellations above, although purple pigmentation occurs at the bases of the undersides. They measure 8–20 cm (3.2–8 in.) in length by 0.7–1.5 cm (0.25–0.6 in.) in width. Mark (1987) describes them as needlelike.

The unifloral peduncle is erect, up to 20 cm (8 in.) in height, and pubescent. The dorsal sepal is ovate to subcircular, white at the margins, and flushed green centrally with nerves or veins of pink. There is no spotting upon the dorsal sepal. It measures approximately 3 cm (1.25 in.) in both length and width. The synsepalum is oblongate and measures 2.5–3.5 cm (1–1.5 in.) long by 1–1.5 cm (0.3–0.6 in.) wide. Both sepals are hirsute upon the back surface.

The petals are buff with cream margins. Oblong to spathulate, they are hirsute proximally with undulate margins. Petal dimensions are 3.5–4 cm (1.3–1.6 in.) in length by 0.9–1 cm (0.3 in.) in width. The glossy labellum is reddish amber to ocher in color. The toe is shallow and broad, deeply cut to a V at its frontal margin, and prominently auricled. It measures approximately 3 cm (1.25 in.) long.

FLOWERING SEASON October to December.

Paphiopedilum charlesworthii (Rolfe) Pfitz. — PLATE 60

A small alliance, consisting of this species, *P. spiceranum* (Reichb. f. ex Masters & T. Moore) Pfitz., and *P. druryi* (Bedd.) Stein, gives evidence of a closer association in the past. Geographically close to *P. spiceranum*, this species is less like the other 2 in morphological characters.

GEOGRAPHIC DISTRIBUTION This slipper is indigenous to the Shan states of Burma, near Lake Inle.

HABITAT Growing at elevations of 1,200–1,700 m (4,100–5,800 ft.), it roots on west- and northwest-facing slopes, clinging to rocks and trapping detritus. It is generally situated in bright shade. The climate is moderate with summer highs approaching 27° C (80° F), while winter brings temperatures just below freezing. Rainfall is heavy during summer but rarely absent altogether in winter. Frequently this species grows sympatrically with *P. spiceranum*.

DESCRIPTION The green leaves are slender and marked with purple spotting beneath. They measure 12–15 cm (4.75–6 in.) long by 2–2.5 cm (0.75–1 in.) wide. Growths occur in compact clumps.

The inflorescence bears a solitary flower of great beauty at a height of 15 cm (6 in.). The peduncle is pubescent, as is the bract which subtends the flower. Both are green spotted with purple.

The dorsal sepal is the captivating segment of the flower. Almost twice as broad as it is long, its color is pink with deeper pink venation. The margins pale to white with soft pink veins and reflex to some degree basally. The dorsal measures 4.5–5.5 cm (1.75–2.25 in) in length by 5.5–7 cm (2.25–2.75 in.) in width. The synsepalum is considerably narrower, elliptic, and acute. It measures approximately 4 cm (1.5 in.) long by 2–3 cm (0.75–1.2 in.) wide. Its color is pale green veined with ocher.

The spathulate petals are pale yellowish green veined with reticular patterns in ocher. They are held horizontally and curve forward as if to embrace the pouch. They measure 4–4.5 cm (1.5–1.75 in.) long by 1–1.5 cm (0.3–0.6 in.) wide. The pouch is ocher flushed with pink and veined with brown. The inner surface is hirsute. It measures 3.5–4.5 cm (1.3–1.75 in.) in length by 2.5–2.8 cm (1–1.2 in.) in width. The pouch orifice is large.

FLOWERING SEASON Autumn.

Paphiopedilum druryi (Bedd.) Stein   PLATE 61

GEOGRAPHIC DISTRIBUTION *P. druryi* is unique in its range as the solitary species located in the extreme southern tip of India and separated from its nearest related species by a tremendous subcontinental mass. It is a narrow endemic in the Travancore Hills.

HABITAT Although occasionally epiphytic upon roots of shrubs, this species typically grows in bright shade as a terrestrial at 1,500 m (5,100 ft.) in poor soil over calcareous rock. Shrubs, low palms, grasses and sedges provide the only shade during summer months, although this vegetation shrivels and provides little shade during the dry season. The winter season is dry, particularly so since deforestation. During these months, day and night temperatures swing between high and low extremes. Because of proximity to the equator, daytime highs approach 35° C (90° F), while overnight lows drop to around freezing. Monsoon rains interspersed with dense fogs occur from April through November and bring constant downpours during mid-summer.

The natural habitat of *P. druryi* has been altered severely by deforestation, according to Mammen and Mammen (1974). Cribb (1987) believes that this species is doomed in the wild, if not already extinct. During the dry winters, the region has become exceedingly susceptible to fire in addition to the increased probability of stripping by collectors.

DESCRIPTION *P. druryi* grows upon a strong, woody rhizome which is reported to exceed 5 m (195 in.) in length. The growths are clustered, and leaves are large in this species, measuring 15–45 cm (6–18 in.) in length by 2.5–5 cm (1–2 in.) in width. Purple spotting adorns the basal undersurfaces of the leaves.

The pubescent inflorescence is erect to suberect and bears a solitary flower at a height of up to 25 cm (10 in.). A large, spotted bract subtends the flower.

The dorsal sepal is yellow or greenish yellow with a striking midline stripe in maroon or brownish maroon. It conspicuously hoods the pouch aperture. Elliptic to ovate in shape, its margins are ciliate and subundulate; it measures 3–4 cm (1.25–1.6 in.) long by 2.5–3 cm (1–1.25 in.) wide. The greenish yellow synsepalum bears a few stripes of brownish maroon. It is ovate and smaller than the dorsal. Both sepals are pubescent on their outer surfaces.

The petals bear a midline stripe of maroon which contrasts beautifully with their primrose yellow color. They are held just below horizontal, and their spathulate apices frequently twist upward a quarter turn assuming a supinate position. Petal margins are undulate and reflexed. Pubescence and purple hairs adorn the petals primarily in the proximal portion. Petals measure 4–4.5 cm (1.5–1.75 in.) long by 1.5–2 cm (0.6–0.75 in.) wide. The pouch is yellow or tawny, and measures 4–4.5 cm (1.5–1.75 in.) long by 1.3–1.5 cm (0.5–0.6 in.) wide.

FLOWERING SEASON Late winter and early spring.

Paphiopedilum exul (Ridl.) Rolfe   PLATE 62

This species closely resembles *P. insigne* and belongs in its alliance.

GEOGRAPHIC DISTRIBUTION *P. exul* grows on both the east and west coasts of the Malay Peninsula, in Thailand.

HABITAT Inhabiting limestone outcrops, populations occupy northern and northeastern exposures on cliffs, from sea level up to 50 m (160 ft.). Full sun to bright shade, high humidity and warm temperatures with a minimum at 21° C (70° F) and a maximum at 35° C (95° F) mark the habitat of *P. exul*. Monsoon rains occur for half the year during May–December. Relative humidity remains at approximately 85% during the dry season, so condensation of mist provides moisture to the roots for those months.

DESCRIPTION The leaves are yellowish green and unmarked on either surface. Their dimensions are 25–35 cm (10–14 in.) in length and 1.8–3 cm (0.75–1.25 in.) in width.

The solitary flower is borne on a pubescent peduncle which stands 15–18 cm (6–7 in.) tall. The flower is subtended by a large green bract.

The moderately keeled dorsal sepal is ovate to elliptic, yellow bordered with white, and boldly spotted centrally with raised blotches of maroon. Its lateral margins are slightly undulate and reflexed. The obtuse apex hoods the pouch aperture. The dimensions of the dorsal are 3–5 cm (1.25–2 in.) long by approximately 3 cm (1.25 in.) wide. The synsepalum is yellowish green with green venation. It measures 3.5–4.5 cm (1.3–1.75 in.) long by 1.5–2.5 cm (0.6–1 in.) wide. Both sepals are pubescent on their reverse sides.

The outspread petals are held nearly horizontally, but curve forward around the belly of the pouch. They are oblanceolate, and their margins are ciliate and undulate. Their color is rich golden yellow to ocher. The midvein of each petal and its immediate parallel veins are picked out as narrow reddish stripes. Proximally, maroon hairs adorn the petal surface. Petal dimensions are 4.5–5 cm (1.75–2 in.) long by 1.5–1.7 cm (0.75 in.) wide. The glossy pouch is golden tan with brown venation. It measures 3–3.5 cm (1.25–1.3 in.) long by approximately 2 cm (0.75 in.) wide.

FLOWERING SEASON Late spring, early summer and variable times.

Paphiopedilum fairrieanum (Lindl.) Stein   PLATES 63 & 64

Several variable flower types are known including some which have been identified as variants, although many are believed to be merely horticulturally induced cultivars. According to Cribb (1987), an albino form often called var. *album* Hort. has a prior and therefore valid appellation as var. *bohlmannianum* Matho. See Plate 64. U. C. Pradhan (1978) lists numerous varieties and forms which are possibly only cultivars, and of which the most worthy of note are var. *nigrescens*, with small flowers of the extremely dark vinicolor coloration; var. *flavum*, without purple pigment, but possessed of a yellow labellum and golden venation of the sepals and petals; and var. *giganteum*, which possesses a dorsal sepal nearly twice as large as the type. Since *P. fairrieanum* is recognized as a variable but distinctive species, most of these variant forms have been discussed without formal publication.

GEOGRAPHIC DISTRIBUTION This species has a fairly wide range in Sikkim, Bhutan and northeast India (Assam). According to Ghose (1964), most of the valleys of rivers flowing southeasterly to the plains of Assam and Bengal host colonies of *P. fairrieanum*.

HABITAT Like many other species of this section, *P. fairrieanum* clings to steep, calcareous cliffs of river valleys in bright shade of tall, herbaceous plants and a few trees. Ghose (1964) writes that plants more frequently colonize the banks with an eastern exposure and thus seldom receive any sunlight after midday. Humidity is constant and the temperatures are moderate year-round (rarely below 10° C or 50° F, and never above 24° C or 80° F), at the preferred elevations of 1,400–2,200 m (4,800–7,600 ft.). Monsoons provide heavy rainfall during summer and autumn.

DESCRIPTION The plants grow in clusters of several growths. Leaves are usually pale green, although clones bearing subdued tessellation are known. Leaves may bear minute serrations distally. Plants which produce vinicolor flowers typically bear purple spotting on the undersurfaces of the leaves.

The inflorescence bears a solitary flower; bifloral scapes are considered rare. The hirsute peduncle extends to 12–45 cm (4.75–18 in.) and is typically arching to suberect. The flower is subtended by a pubescent bract.

The dorsal sepal is white with marked vertical green and purple veins which are crisscrossed with subdued reticular venation in the same 2 colors. The apical margins undulate to form troughs to either side of the elevated midrib. Lateral margins are crisply undulate. All margins are feathered by the branching of the outermost veins. Elliptic in shape, the dorsal sepal measures 3.5–8 cm (1.3–3.2 in.) in length by 3–7 cm (1.25–2.75 in.) in width. The ovate ventral sepal is veined with green and purple and measures 2.5–3.5 cm (1–1.3 in.) long by 1.5–2.5 cm (0.6–1 in.) wide. Both sepals are pubescent upon their reverse sides.

The petals grow downward, but for the distal third of their length they curve up and back. Their orientation has been likened to that of the curved horns of the water buffalo. The petals bear parallel veins of purple and green with purple margins which are undulate and ciliolate. Petal measurements are 4–5 cm (1.5–2 in.) in length by 1–1.5 cm (0.3–0.6 in.) in width. The lip is khaki or olive green with darker venation, and it measures 3–4 cm (1.3–1.6 in.) long by 1.5–2.5 cm (0.6–1 in.) wide.

FLOWERING SEASON Late fall to mid-winter.

Paphiopedilum gratrixianum (Masters) Guill.   PLATES 65 & 66

According to Cribb (1987), *P. affine* De Wild. is a later synonym for this species, which is another member of the *P. insigne* alliance. However, *P. affine* also shows a strong affinity with *P. villosum* (Lindl.) Stein, and according to Mark (1987), is found growing sympatrically with the latter. The taxon in question is included here as *P. gratrixianum* var. *affine*.

P. *henryanum*, from southern Yunnan Province in China, is a recent discovery currently considered a species in its own right, but which may be later designated a rose-pigmented variant of this species. The glossy flower of this new taxon is distinguished by a broad cream dorsal sepal richly spotted with large blotches of mahogany, and by rosy purple petals and pouch. See its description below in alphabetic sequence.

GEOGRAPHIC DISTRIBUTION Laos and Vietnam are the host countries for this species. Var. *affine* is found in Yunnan Province, China.

HABITAT Located well inland, this species is a terrestrial. Data on temperature, elevation, rainfall, exposure, and other pertinent facts are parsimonious or unavailable.

DESCRIPTION Colonies of clustered plants produce growths with 4–7 leaves. The leaves lack tessellation but bear purple spotting beneath. They achieve lengths of up to 30 cm (12 in.) and measure 2–2.5 cm (0.75–1 in.) in width.

The solitary flower has a lacquered appearance and is held on an erect, pubescent peduncle which grows up to 25 cm (10 in.) tall. The pubescent bract is green with purple spotting.

The glossy dorsal sepal is pale green basally, white above, and bears bold purple to dark maroon spotting. Its margins are subundulate and somewhat reflexed. The dorsal measures 4.8–5.2 cm (2 in.) long by approximately 4.5 cm (1.75 in.) wide. It is ovate to subcircular. The ventral sepal is pale green, ovate to elliptic, and about half as wide as the dorsal. Both sepals bear purple pubescence on their outer surfaces.

The waxen petals are honey yellow, veined with purple and flushed with purple proximally; distally, the tips may be flushed with green. Spathulate in shape, the petals are held just below horizontal and curve forward; the margins are subundulate. Petal dimensions are 4.5–5 cm (1.75–2 in.) in length by 2–2.5 cm (0.75–1 in.) in width. The glossy pouch has an expanded orifice and a tapered apex. It is yellowish tan and measures approximately 4 cm (1.6 in.) in length.

FLOWERING SEASON Winter and spring.

Paphiopedilum henryanum Braem, sp. nov.   PLATE 67

Described in 1987, this species is included with *P. insigne* in its alliance.

GEOGRAPHIC DISTRIBUTION *P. henryanum* is found near the Vietnamese border in Yunnan Province, China.

HABITAT While very little has been learned about the habitat of this newly described species, Emerson "Doc" Charles (personal communication) describes a creek in Yunnan which hosts a population of *P. emersonii* on one bank and another of *P. henryanum* on the opposite bank. Braem (1987a) describes *P. henryanum* as a humus epiphyte.

DESCRIPTION Mature fans may possess as few as 3 leaves. Leaf length is up to 17 cm (6.75 in.).

The leaves are green and devoid of tessellation; sparse purple pigmentation occurs basally upon the lower surfaces.

The densely pilose inflorescence reaches heights of up to 16 cm (6.3 in.) and bears a solitary flower. The flower is subtended by a bract which also exhibits small amounts of purple pigmentation.

The suborbiculate dorsal sepal is creamy yellow with heavy aubergine blotching. The spots are larger basally, and attractively spaced; from about midway above the base, the spotting ends and the midvein is marked with a dark maroon stripe. Apically, the dorsal is shortly acute. Its margins are ciliate and slightly undulate; basal margins reflex. The reverse surface of the dorsal is densely pubescent, while the face is glossy and glabrous. The dorsal measures 3.4 cm (1.4 in.) in length and width. Carinate by its midvein, it is held well over the pouch. The concave, elliptic synsepalum is bicarinate and bidentate; it measures 2.5 cm (1 in.) long by 1.6 cm (0.6 in.) wide. Creamy yellow in color, the ventral sepal lacks distinct spotting, although it may exhibit inconspicuous, blurred pigmentation. Glabrous inside, it is densely pilose upon the reverse surface and bears ciliate margins.

The horizontally spreading petals are broadly spathulate and measure 3.6 cm (1.4 in.) long by 1.5 cm (0.6 in.) wide. The pale cream petal margins are both ciliate and undulate. Their flat surfaces are glabrous. The rounded petal apices curve forward moderately. Petal color is rich rose magenta, and mahogany spotting occurs over the proximal third of each petal. The glossy labellum is elongate with infolded lateral lobes. It measures up to 4.2 cm (1.6 in.) long by 2 cm (1.75 in.) wide. Pouch color is also rose magenta; the rim is slightly paler.

FLOWERING SEASON November to late winter and early spring.

Paphiopedilum hirsutissimum (Lindl. ex Hook.) Stein   PLATES 68 & 69

GEOGRAPHIC DISTRIBUTION The extreme northeastern extension of India hosts this species in the Khasia Hills and in the Naga Hills along the Indo-Burmese border. Formerly a part of Assam, this region is now Mizoram. Var. *esquirolei* (Schltr.) Cribb, comb. et stat. nov. originates in northern Thailand and in Guizhou Province, China. Var. *chiwuanum* (Tang & Wang) Cribb, comb. et stat. nov. is known only from Yunnan Province, China.

HABITAT The type grows at elevations of 700–1,200 m (2,400–4,100 ft.), while var. *esquirolei* lives at 1,200–1,800 m (4,100–6,200 ft.), and var. *chiwuanum* is found at 700 m (2,400 ft.). Growing either lithophytically or epiphytically, the type receives monsoon rains during the summer months and survives near-freezing temperatures in the winter.

CULTURAL NOTES *P. hirsutissimum* and var. *esquirolei* are grown under cool conditions, but var. *chiwuanum* should be grown at intermediate temperatures.

DESCRIPTION Long, slender, green leaves make up the clustered growths. The undersurfaces are typically spotted with purple, although var. *esquirolei* lacks this pigmentation, according to Mark (1987). Leaf dimensions are 30–45 cm (12–18 in.) long by 1.5–2 cm (0.6–0.75 in.) wide.

The peduncle is densely hirsute, up to 25 cm (10 in.) tall, and bears a solitary flower subtended by a sheath as well as a bract, both of which are pubescent.

The dorsal sepal is dark brown, margined with pale green. Ovate or elliptic, its margin exhibits some undulation with moderate lateral reflexion basally. The dorsal measures 3.8–4.5 cm (1.5–1.75 in.) long by 2.5–4 cm (1–1.75 in.) wide. The ventral sepal bears a wider green border and exhibits less lateral reflexion than the dorsal. Elliptic to lanceolate, it is smaller than the dorsal.

The petals are green, bearing purple hairs and spotting proximally; the distal portions are rich lavender purple. The upper margins are crisply undulate proximally. Held horizontally, the petal apices become supinate by a quarter spiral and tend to recurve somewhat.

The apices are also broad, spathulate and rounded. Petal length is 5.5–7 cm (2.2–2.75 in.) while the width is only 1–2 cm (0.3–0.75 in.). The well-inflated pouch is green or yellow green and minutely spotted and flushed with purple. It measures 3.5–4.5 cm (1.3–1.75 in.) in length.

Var. *esquirolei* diverges from the type primarily in its range. However, the somewhat larger flowers of this variant bear slightly shorter pubescence. Var. *chiwuanum* is notable for its much smaller flowers. There is an albinistic form which lacks purple pigmentation; in all likelihood, it should be considered a cultivar.

FLOWERING SEASON April and May.

Paphiopedilum insigne (Wall. ex Lindl.) Pfitz.   PLATES 70 & 71

Although geographically discrete, this species bears a strong resemblance to several other species in its section including *P. barbigerum*, *P. exul* and *P. gratrixianum*. Furthermore, this species is somewhat plastic with many named cultivars differing primarily in the abundance of purple or brown spotting, although the proportion of yellow to green coloration is a secondary variable. Among these, var. *sanderanum*, and var. *sanderae* possess little or none of the purple or brown pigmentation of the type. Among the more pigmented forms, var. *maulei* produces somewhat larger flowers. Perhaps best-known is *P. insigne* 'Harefield Hall,' a cultivar now known to be triploid and long recognized for its size and bold spotting. However, by far the most fascinating of all the variants of this species is *P. insigne* var. *variegatum*, the clone with variegated foliage. The leaves are striated white and green in vivid, longitudinal stripes. Never abundant, this clone is not well understood but is probably a sport or mutant. Chief among the interesting aspects of this variant is its retention of typical flowers along with the highly altered pattern of foliar pigment, which is so dramatically different from the transverse, barred variegations of tessellated leaves in this genus. Longitudinal striations in variegated leaves, while rare, are not restricted to this species, however. They occur in leaves of complex hybrids and in wild plants of *P. purpuratum* as well. See *P. purpuratum* below.

GEOGRAPHIC DISTRIBUTION This species has a limited range in northeast India in the State of Meghalaya, formerly a part of Assam, and in eastern Nepal.

HABITAT Typically rooted upon dolomitic outcrops with an eastern exposure, populations inhabit valleys near waterfalls at elevations of 1,000–1,500 m (3,400–5,100 ft.). Monsoons bring rain from May through October promoting rapid growth. Flower spike formation follows the monsoon season. The plants require bright shade. Two different leaf sizes are reported by U. C. Pradhan (1974), who states that luxuriant, long, dark green leaves characterize plants which receive seepage from the rock strata, but the individuals which inhabit drier sites are typically short-leaved and of a pale green cast.

DESCRIPTION The leaves are variable in length and width, measuring up to 35 cm (14 in.) long by 2–3 cm (0.75–1.25 in.) wide. They are untessellated green above and spotted with purple beneath.

A solitary flower is borne on an erect peduncle extending to 23 cm (9 in.) in height. The glabrous bract is green, spotted basally with purple.

The dorsal sepal is yellow or pale green, margined with white and spotted with raised maroon or brown blotches, or devoid of spotting, depending upon the variant observed. In shape, the dorsal is ovate to elliptic. Its lateral margins are undulate and slightly reflexed; the obtuse apical margin hoods the pouch orifice. The dorsal measures 4–6.5 cm (1.6–2.5 in.) long by 3–4 cm (1.25–1.5 in.) wide. The ventral sepal is similarly marked and colored except in its lack of a white margin. It is elliptic and smaller than the dorsal, measuring 4–5 cm (1.5–2 in.) long by 2–2.5 (0.75–1 in.) wide.

The glossy, spathulate petals curve toward the pouch; the superior margins are undulate, proximally. Petals are yellow green to yellow brown. Median longitudinal stripes of red or brown occur in the petals of normally pigmented forms, but they are absent from albinistic variants. Petal dimensions are 5–6.5 cm (2–2.5 in.) in length by 1–2 cm (0.3–0.75 in.) in width. The labellum is yellow or yellowish green; it may or may not bear a brownish or purple suffusion, depending upon which variant is observed. It measures 4–5 cm (1.5–2 in.) long by approximately 3 cm (0.75 in.) wide.

FLOWERING SEASON Autumn and early winter.

Paphiopedilum spiceranum (Reichb. f. ex Masters & T. Moore) Pfitz.   PLATE 72

This lovely and distinctive species is closely allied with *P. charlesworthii* (Rolfe) Pfitz., with which it grows sympatrically, and with *P. druryi.*

GEOGRAPHIC DISTRIBUTION This slipper originates in the northeast extension of India (formerly Assam) and in northwest Burma.

HABITAT *P. spiceranum* inhabits near-vertical cliffs of river gorges at lower elevations of 300–1,300 m (1,000–4,500 ft.). Plants receive daily mists as well as constant seepage from the calcareous strata of the cliffs. Sunlight filtered through tall herbs and ferns provides the ideal level of light. High summer temperatures, together with monsoon rains during June-September, create conditions which require the plants to maintain shallow roots in order to avoid stagnation and decay. Moderate temperatures prevail during the dry season in the shelter of these gorges at the elevations favored by this species.

DESCRIPTION Clustered growths cling to steep, rocky ravines; the leaves are held in a pendulous orientation. The basal margins of the leaves are undulate; purple spotting marks the undersurfaces basally.

The inflorescence bears a solitary flower, except in the case of certain clones which consistently produce bifloral scapes. In cultivation, the stalk arches and is borne at approximately 45°; upon the cliffs, the wild plant holds its flowerscape nearly perpendicular to the cliff face. The stalk extends up to 25 cm (10 in.) in length. Small green bracts subtend the flowers which are remarkably uniform in shape and color, varying from clone to clone primarily in size.

The dorsal sepal of this species is distinctive and serves as an instant means of identification. From above, the shape of the large dorsal is reminiscent of a paper funnel; both the pronounced reflexion of the basal margins and the resulting convolution are apparent from this vantage point. The dorsal is white with a broad basal suffusion of apple green, and is marked with a prominent central stripe of maroon from base to apex. Apically, the dorsal hoods the pouch aperture as a broad, dual-troughed awning, with the midvein arching between the troughs as a sharp ridge. Both surfaces of the dorsal are pubescent. Its measurements are 2.5–4.5 cm (1–1.75 in.) in length by 3.5–5 cm (1.3–2 in.) in width. In shape, the dorsal is transversely elliptic, nearly twice as broad as long. The smaller synsepalum is greenish white, ovate and pubescent upon the reverse surface. It measures 2.5–3.5 cm (1–1.3 in.) long by 1.5–2.5 cm (0.6–1 in.) wide.

The petals are yellowish green, with some faint brown suffusion. The midvein is maroon or brown; additional veins may be darkened to a variable degree. The superior petal margins are crisply undulate, while inferior margins are only slightly so. The petals are held just below horizontal and curve forward somewhat. In shape, they are linear, tapering very slightly. Petal dimensions are 3–4 cm (1.25–1.5 in.) in length and 0.5–1.5 cm (0.25–0.6 in.) across. The labellum is green, suffused with khaki or brown, and veined with brown. It measures 3.5–4.5 cm (1.3–1.75 in.) long by 2.5–3 cm (1–1.25 in.) wide.

FLOWERING SEASON Autumn through early winter.

Paphiopedilum villosum (Lindl.) Stein   PLATES 73 & 74

Also a highly variable species, *P. villosum* has 2 variants which are included here: var.

boxalli (Reichb. f.) Pfitz., and var. *annamense* Rolfe. Other variants are merely bolder or paler versions of these.

This species is also related to the *P. insigne* group, but more distantly than the inner 4 species of the alliance. A tenable hypothesis places *P. villosum* among the earliest to diverge from the group, thereby having altered to a greater degree.

GEOGRAPHIC DISTRIBUTION The species ranges from northeast India (Assam) to Moulmein in southeast Burma, down into Thailand and eastward to portions of Laos. Variant forms extend toward the east with the type being collected from India and Burma. Var. *boxalli* originates in Burma and var. *annamense* is indigenous to Laos and Vietnam (formerly called Annam).

HABITAT *P. villosum* is typically epiphytic, although it may also occur as a lithophyte or as a humus terrestrial rooting in mossy substrates upon steep slopes. It prefers montane sites at 1,100–2,000 m (3,800–6,800 ft.) in elevation and is subjected to cool temperatures in winter. Unlike the semiterrestrials found in the same region, this species does not restrict its sites to riverine valleys; however, at the higher elevations preferred there is no extended dry season nor is there a lack of humidity. Excellent air circulation prevails year-round.

DESCRIPTION This species occurs as clustered growths constituting large colonies. The leaves are 14–45 cm (5.5–18 in.) in length by 2.5–4 cm (1–1.5 in.) in width. Basally, their undersurfaces are spotted with anthocyanin.

A single flower is borne on the hirsute peduncle. Held at approximately 45° off vertical, the peduncle extends to 25 cm (10 in.) in length, although shorter flower stalks are common. The glossy flower is subtended by a large bract.

The dorsal sepal is green marginally and flushed with purple-to-brown suffusion basally. Var. *boxalli* exhibits raised purple spotting on the dorsal, while var. *annamense* lacks spotting but displays a white dorsal sepal with a basal suffusion or blotch of rich violet which may continue upward to the apex as a mid-dorsal stripe. Inferior flowers are frequently seen, having the dorsal and ventral sepals held backward at a distinct angle and giving the appearance of a broken back. In shape, the dorsal sepal is ovate to elliptic but appears narrow due to the reflexion of its lateral margins. It measures 4.5–6.5 cm (1.75–2.5 in.) long by 3–3.5 cm (1.25–1.5 in.) wide. The ovate synsepalum is green and measures 4–5 cm (1.6–2 in.) in length by 2–2.5 cm (0.75–1 in.) in width. Its orientation varies widely from close appression to the undersurface of the pouch to a backward angle which emphasizes the broken back appearance of the flower.

The spathulate petals are held horizontally and curve forward around the belly of the pouch to a variable degree. The midvein is marked with a deep red stripe. Above the midvein, the color is rich terra cotta or brownish maroon; the lower section is khaki with some degree of reddish suffusion. Purple hairs adorn the proximal petal surfaces. The upper margins exhibit a variable degree of undulation. Petal dimensions are 4.5–7 cm (2.25–2.75 in.) in length by 2.5–3 cm (1–1.25 in.) in width. The labellum is tawny, honey yellow, flushed with rose or reddish brown. It is elongate, tapers apically, and measures 4–6 cm (1.5–2.3 in.) long by 3–4 cm (1.25–1.6 in.) wide.

FLOWERING SEASON Late winter and early spring.

Section *Barbata*

This section is characterized by tessellated leaves and typically unifloral inflorescences. The petals of most of the species are verrucate (warted).

The section consists of clusters of closely allied species, much like complexes in various stages of evolutionary divergence. Until the 1980s, each group was placed in a separate section. In accordance with Atwood (1984b) and Cribb (1987), the formerly separate sections have been combined as 1 section, based on their morphological similarities in staminode, labellar side-lobes, petals, and plant habit.

Geographically this group extends over most of the range of the genus. Resegregation into several sections, based upon ecological, geographical and physiological criteria and/or other data yet to be interpreted, is likely at some time because of the large number of species incorporated and the diversity represented within this current treatment.

By consolidation of synonymous binomials under the appropriate (usually the first described) species epithet, Cribb (1987) reduces the number of species to 24, although a 25th species, *P. sangii* Braem, sp. nov., was introduced in 1987. This necessary excision of a plethora of binomials from the rolls of legitimate species is of enormous taxonomic value. Perhaps, before the turn of the century, horticulturists will accept into common usage such sweeping and beneficial revisions in nomenclature.

Synonyms and any other unsupported binomials in common use for various species are listed alphabetically and within the relevant text. The omission from this section which concerns horticulturists most gravely is *P. curtisii* (Reichb. f.) Stein, which is discussed as *P. superbiens* (Reichb. f.) Stein.

Paphiopedilum acmodontum Schoser ex M. Wood   PLATE 75

GEOGRAPHIC DISTRIBUTION Philippine in origin, this species is believed to be native to the Island of Negros and to several smaller islands in the Visayan Sea.

HABITAT Habitat information on this species is sparse. The climate is warm and humid with little seasonal variation in temperature. The rainy season is June–November. No special care is needed beyond the typical, intermediate regimen of *Paphiopedilum* culture.

DESCRIPTION The leaves are tessellated above but devoid of anthocyanin on the lower surfaces. They measure 15–25 cm (6–10 in.) long by 4 cm (1.6 in.) wide.

The erect inflorescence is pubescent and bears a solitary flower at a height of approximately 25 cm (10 in.). A moderately large bract subtends the flower.

The dorsal sepal is ovate; its acute apex slightly hoods the pouch aperture. It measures 4 cm (1.6 in.) long by 3 cm (1.2 in.) wide. The color is white flushed with pink basally. Parallel purple veins of unequal length traverse the dorsal, stopping short of the narrow margin of white. The ovate synsepalum is considerably smaller and bicarinate or nearly so. Its ground color is white, blushed with purple and veined with both purple and green.

The petals are oblanceolate to subspathulate in shape. They are held very near to horizontal and well back, with recurved, shortly acute apices. Petal margins are slightly undulate. They measure 4–4.5 cm (1.6–1.75 in.) long by approximately 1.5 cm (0.6 in.) wide. Petal color is pale greenish white basally, marked with green veins and sparse purple dots. Approximately midway of the petals' length, the spotting intensifies. Distally, purple suffusion and darker purple veins characterize the petals, while spotting is absent. The lip is olive green with a flush of bronze on the frontal surface. It measures 4 cm (1.6 in.) long by 2.3–2.5 (1 in.) wide.

FLOWERING SEASON Summer.

Paphiopedilum amabile Hallier. See *P. bullenianum* (Reichb. f.) Pfitz.

Paphiopedilum amabilis (Hallier) Merrill. See *P. bullenianum* (Reichb.f) Pfitz.

Paphiopedilum appletonianum (Gower) Rolfe   PLATES 76–78

According to Cribb (1987), this species was treated as a variant of *P. bullenianum* (Reichb. f.) Pfitz. for some time, around the turn of the century. Furthermore, *P. wolterianum* (Kraenzl.) Pfitz., considered by Fowlie (1969a) as a distinct species, is well within the normal variability of *P. appletonianum* as measured by Cribb (1987). Another binomial which may be rarely applied is *P. poyntzianum* O'Brien. It, too, is rejected by Cribb (1987) as a minor variation.

P. appletonianum is a member of an alliance of species which have traditionally been distinguished from each other largely on the basis of staminodal characteristics. Consideration must be given, however, to distribution, corroborative morphological distinctions, and to all the pertinent criteria in placing these species, variants, and superfluous binomials in their rightful alignments. Cribb's (1987) condensation of the former section *Spathopetalum* into fewer, more accurate, and more meaningful species, and Atwood's (1984b) prior assimilation of that section into section *Barbata* along with the erstwhile section *Phacopetalum* into which it grades, are both significant and germane clarifications of groupings which were, prior to the 1980s, at best cumbersome and at worst a pseudo-taxonomic hodgepodge.

During 1987 yet another binomial appeared in this assemblage—*P. hainanense* Fowlie, sp. nov.—which is well within the described variability of *P. appletonianum* (see Plate 78). It is unique in originating from Hainan Island, China. Fowlie (1987) describes subtle differences in leaf tessellation and staminode.

GEOGRAPHIC DISTRIBUTION The range of *P. appletonianum* includes parts of Thailand, Laos, Cambodia, and most recently, Hainan Island, China.

HABITAT This species is found at elevations of 600–700 m (2,000–2,400 ft.) where it grows in humus and detritus as a terrestrial.

DESCRIPTION The plant is fairly small and bears leaves 8–25 cm (3.2–10 in.) in length that are tessellated above and spotted or streaked with a variable amount of purple beneath. Fowlie (1987) reports that plants he describes as *P. hainanense* are heavily tessellated; however, divergent leaf patterns are not infrequently found among the individuals of a single colony, so this evidence must not be allowed to overturn the stability created by Cribb (1987).

The unifloral, rarely bifloral, flower stalk is quite tall and reaches a height of 20–50 cm (8–20 in.). A green bract subtends the flower.

The dorsal sepal is ovate but strongly reflexed basally, while the acute apex bends sharply forward over the labellum. White veined with dark green, the dorsal is frequently suffused overall with palest green or basally with pink. Its measurements are 2.5–4.5 cm (1–1.75 in.) long by 2–2.5 cm (0.75–1 in.) wide. The ventral sepal is elliptic to lanceolate with markings similar to those of the dorsal. It measures 2–3 cm (0.75–1.2 in.) long by 1–1.5 cm (0.3–0.6 in.) wide.

The petals are held horizontally, with crisp undulations of the proximal superior margins and a quarter volution of the apical portion. Spathulate in shape, the proximal portions are green with blackish green stripes and dark maroon spots. The distal portions expand and clear to a rich pink. Petal dimensions are 4.5–6 cm (1.75–2.4 in.) long by 1–1.9 cm (0.03–0.75 in.) wide. The labellum is elongated and tan in color flushed with pink or lavender. It measures 3.5–4.5 cm (1.3–1.75 in.) in length.

FLOWERING SEASON Mid-winter.

Paphiopedilum argus (Reichb. f.) Stein   PLATE 79

GEOGRAPHIC DISTRIBUTION This species is an endemic of Luzon, Philippines.

HABITAT *P. argus* grows in the mountains at elevations of 800–2,500 m (2,400–8,600 ft.). It prefers bright shade and roots in moss at the bases of trees or in deep humus in bamboo thickets. Cribb (1987) reports that it is only found on east- or west-facing slopes. Temperatures in summer are moderate, dropping to just above freezing during winter nights. Ample rainfall occurs year-round, with the exception of March and April, and is heaviest during the summer typhoon season. High humidity prevails at all times.

CULTURAL NOTES This species thrives well in hanging baskets. It prefers the brightest light suitable for slippers. It has a rambling root system. Slightly higher than normal levels of fertilizer are recommended. *P. argus* is not difficult to bloom, but growers who have inconsistent success with it are advised to lower its temperatures in December.

DESCRIPTION The leaves are tessellated above and purple-flushed beneath basally. They measure 10–25 cm (4–10 in.) in length by 2.5–5 cm (1–2 in.) in width.

A solitary flower is borne atop a peduncle which measures up to 45 cm (18 in.) tall. The bract is moderately large.

The ovate dorsal sepal measures 3.5–4.5 cm (1.3–1.75 in.) long by 3–4 cm (1.2–1.6 in.) wide. Its acute apex recurves slightly. The ground color of the dorsal is white adorned with green stripes of unequal length and basal purple spotting. The elliptic synsepalum is similar in length to the dorsal, but its width is only approximately 2 cm (0.75 in.). In color, it is greenish white striped with darker green.

The petals arch downward and backward and exhibit undulate, hirsute margins and a quarter-turn volution of the apical half. Petal color is white; green veins merge to maroon stripes on the distal third, where a pink blush also suffuses the apices. However, the most striking adornment is the abundance of spots and warts which frequently merge to large blotches of blackish purple and are dispersed over the entire petal surface. Petal dimensions are 4.5–6.5 cm (1.75–2.6 in.) in length and 1.5–2 cm (0.6–0.75 in.) in width. The green-veined pouch is green beneath but flushed rosy brown above, and it measures 4–5 cm (1.6–2 in.) in length.

FLOWERING SEASON Midwinter to spring.

Paphiopedilum barbatum (Lindl.) Pfitz. subsp. *lawrenceanum* (Reichb. f.) M. Wood. See *P. lawrenceanum* (Reichb. f.) Pfitz.

Paphiopedilum barbatum (Lindl.) Pfitz. subsp. *lawrenceanum* (Reichb. f.) var. *hennisianum* M. Wood. See. *P. hennisianum* (M. Wood) Fowlie.

Paphiopedilum barbatum (Lindl.) Pfitz.   PLATE 80

This species is closely related to *P. callosum* (Reichb. f.) Stein. Their geographic distribution indicates that historically the 2 species could have been more closely associated, possibly as divergent taxa of the same complex.

Cultivars or varieties included in this taxon have been variously described, even having been synonymously described as separate species. Var. *nigritum* (Reichb. f.) Pfitz. is described below.

GEOGRAPHIC DISTRIBUTION This species is found on the Malay Peninsula and on Penang Island.

HABITAT *P. barbatum* is typically lithophytic but also roots in moss and leaf mold. It grows in heavily shaded granitic valleys at elevations of 200–1,300 m (700–4,500 ft.). Rainfall is quite low during the winter and resumes again in early spring; heavy rains fall from August until November. Mists are a daily feature of the habitat and seepage provides moisture at the roots year-round. Temperatures are mild. The warmest daytime temperatures of approximately 30° C (85° F) occur in April, with night temperatures of 15° C (60° F). Drops of only a few degrees characterize the balance of the year. Light breezes prevent stagnation.

DESCRIPTION The leaves are pale green and mottled above with dark green. They measure 12.5–15 cm (5–6 in.) in length and 3.5–4 cm (1.3–1.6 in.) in width.

The inflorescence typically bears a single flower. Certain clones, usually identified as var. *biflorum*, regularly bear bifloral scapes, while an occasional bifloral display occurs at random on many individuals of this species. The peduncle reaches heights of up to 35 cm (14 in.). Small bracts sheath the ovaries. Bracts, peduncles and ovaries are finely pubescent.

The striking dorsal sepal is subcircular with an acute apex. It measures up to approximately 5 cm (2 in.) in either dimension. Upon a white ground, stripes of green arise from the base and gradually merge into purple as they meet and cross a mesial, arched, transverse streak of purple. The stripes are uneven in length and stop off to leave a wide white margin. The narrowly elliptical ventral sepal is significantly smaller and greenish white with darker green stripes shading to purple.

The spreading petals droop slightly below horizontal. Lanceolate with ciliate margins, they are maroon in color and bear blackish maroon warts along their proximal upper margin, although both margins may bear warts. Marginal undulation is exhibited by the petals to varying degrees. Petal dimensions are 5–6 cm (2–2.3 in.) in length by 1–1.5 cm (0.3–0.6 in.) in width. The pouch is rich purple frontally and pale greenish brown beneath. Its rosy purple side-lobes are richly spotted with crimson. It measures 4.5–5 cm (1.75–2 in.) long by 2–2.5 cm (0.75–1 in.) wide.

Var. *nigritum* is more richly pigmented with deep maroon purple over more of the surfaces of each segment. Its use in breeding produces the vinicolor trait in a significant percentage of the progeny.

FLOWERING SEASON Early winter and often, again, in early summer.

Paphiopedilum bougainvilleanum Fowlie   PLATE 81

Most closely allied to *P. violascens* Schltr., according to Cribb (1987), this species receives separate specific rank based both on geographic and morphological criteria. The reader is referred to Cribb's monograph for details.

GEOGRAPHIC DISTRIBUTION The Island of Bougainville, largest in the Solomons, is the home of this species.

HABITAT Granite outcrops host this endemic at elevations of 1,100–1,850 m (3,800–6,400 ft.) in moist, shady sites. The volcanic soil is fertile; rainfall and humidity are abundant, while air movement is sluggish.

DESCRIPTION The tessellations on the leaves of this species are not pronounced. Purple pigmentation of the undersurfaces is absent.

A solitary flower subtended by a bract is borne upon an erect, pubescent peduncle which may stand 10–25 cm (4–10 in.) in height.

The ovate, acute dorsal sepal is white with brilliant green stripes; the basal margins are reflexed. Its dimensions are 3.5–4 cm (1.4–1.6 in.) long and wide. The concave synsepalum is similarly colored and marked. It measures 2.5 cm (1 in.) long by 1.5–1.7 cm (0.6 in.) wide.

The oblanceolate petals are fairly broad and arch downward. Their color is white marked with green stripes that merge to form a green region proximally and change to pale pink distally. Their margins are ciliate. Petal dimensions are 4–5 cm (1.6–2 in.) in length and 2–2.5 cm (0.75–1 in.) in width. The pouch is green veined in darker green. It measures 4–5 cm (1.6–2 in.) long by 2–2.5 cm (0.75–1 in.) wide.

FLOWERING SEASON Spring.

Paphiopedilum bullenianum (Reichb. f.) Pfitz.   PLATES 82 & 83

According to Cribb (1987), binomials in use for this taxon include: *P. amabile* Hallier, *P. amabilis* (Hallier) Merrill, *P. celebesense* Fowlie & Birk, *P. johorense* Fowlie & Yap, *P. linii* Schoser, *P. robinsonii* (Ridl.) Ridley and *P. tortisepalum* Fowlie. Many of these are offered in trade, and avid collectors inadvertently invest in several plants by these names, only to discover at flowering just how minor the variations actually are. Refer to Cribb's monograph for distinguishing features among these allied entities, and for a full discussion of the group. He recognizes var. *celebesense* (Fowlie & Birk) Cribb, comb. et stat. nov. as a valid variety of *P. bullenianum*. Differences between the type and this variant are included in the text below.

The full extent of the alliance is broader than *P. bullenianum*, however, and includes *P.*

appletonianum and its associated variants and binomials as well as *P. hookerae* (Reichb. f.) Stein and its var. *volonteanum* (Sander ex Rolfe) Kerch.

GEOGRAPHIC DISTRIBUTION The type is native to Borneo, Sumatra and the Malaysian peninsula. Var. *celebesense* grows on the island of Celebes and eastward in the Moluccas.

HABITAT Inhabiting varying sites from sea level to 1,850 m (6,400 ft.), this species and its variant grow as epiphytes rooted in moss on mangrove roots, as humus-lithophytes on tree-shaded scarps, or in deep humus as terrestrials, in the shade of dense vegetation. The latter habitat at elevations of around 950 m (3,250 ft.) is the one favored by var. *celebesense*, according to Birk (1983). The region is subject to high annual rainfall and humidity.

DESCRIPTION The plant is small and bears leaves 7–15 cm (2.75–6 in.) in length with distinct tessellations above and purple mottling beneath.

The tall, pubescent peduncle supports a solitary flower, subtended by a small bract, at a height of up to 55 cm (22 in.). The flower of var. *celebesense* is somewhat paler and smaller than that of the type.

The dorsal sepal is white or very pale green, with dark green stripes. Its proximal margins are reflexed in var. *celebesense*, but the type dorsal is usually concave. In most flowers a blotch of purple marks the center of the dorsal basally; this pigmentation is more pronounced in the type than in the variant. The acute apex of the dorsal hoods the pouch orifice. Ovate in shape, the dorsal measures 2.5–3 cm (1–1.2 in.) long by 1.5–2.5 cm (0.6–1 in.) wide. The synsepalum is striped with green, lanceolate, and measures 2–2.5 cm (0.75–1 in.) long by 1–1.5 cm (0.4–0.6 in.) wide.

The petals are spathulate and held at the horizontal or just below. Green proximally, the coloring grades to purple toward the apices in the type. Var. *celebesense* has petal tips of pink or lavender. Blackish maroon spots adorn the superior proximal margins, which are crisply undulate and ciliate. Petal dimensions are 4–5 cm (1.6–2 in.) long by 1–1.5 cm (0.4–0.6 in.) wide. The pouch of the type is green at the toe grading to maroon about the rim; that of the variant is pale cream at the toe flushed with deepening brown to mahogany toward the rim. The pouch measures 3–4 cm (1.2–1.6 in.) in length.

FLOWERING SEASON Fall and winter.

Paphiopedilum burbidgei (Reichb. f) Pfitz. See *P. dayanum* (Lindl.) Stein.

Paphiopedilum callosum (Reichb. f.) Stein   PLATES 84 & 85

Cribb (1987) lists var. *sublaeve* (Reichb. f.) Cribb stat. nov. as a distinct varietal entity commenting, however, that it might be conspecific with *P. barbatum*. Atwood (1984b) suggests that *P. barbatum* and *P. callosum* form a cline. Geographically and morphologically there is no doubt that these taxa are allied. I agree with Cribb that no useful purpose will be served by combining the 2 species, and I perceive the differences as more than adequate to support the view that the taxa are indeed 2 separate species. It provides, instead, a justifiable sense of elation that the 3 entities—*P. barbatum* from the Malay Peninsula, *P. callosum* var. *sublaeve* from a region farther north, and the entity unofficially called *P. thailandense* by Fowlie (1979b) that bridges right into the range of *P. callosum*—all contribute to form a large, transitional ecocomplex, which supports the theory of the diversifications of complexes over this particular region of Asia. Perhaps the various entities will be definitively placed in their proper relationships with meaningful correlations elucidated and documented before the end of the 20th century. Their transitional similarities and differences in combination with their transitional distribution furnish adequate impetus for further comparison which will ultimately yield a logical continuum reflective of their relationships and affinities.

GEOGRAPHIC DISTRIBUTION This species has a widespread range in mainland Thailand, Cambodia and Laos. Var. *sublaeve* is found in northwest Malaya and in peninsular Thailand.

HABITAT *P. callosum* grows on the lower slopes of montane ridges at elevations of 300–1,300 m (1,000–4,500 ft.) in a region which receives monsoon rains during the autumn months, and up to 325 cm (130 in.) of rainfall per year. Mists provide plentiful moisture during drier seasons. Moderate shade is provided by stands of trees and shrubs. Temperatures are cool to mild. Soil is poor with leaf litter, sand and mosses as components of the substrate.

DESCRIPTION The leaves are tessellated above and marked to a varying degree with purple pigmentation beneath. Their dimensions are 10–20 cm (4–8 in.) in length by 3.5–5 cm (1.3–2 in.) in width.

Typically, flowers are solitary, and bifloral scapes are considered rare. The pubescent peduncle is erect and stands up to 45 cm (18 in.) in height. A small bract clasps the ovary.

The dorsal sepal is white, flushed purple basally. Veins of unequal length merge from green to purple as they extend upward; the venation traverses the dorsal to within a few millimeters of its undulate margin. A band of pink suffusion underlies the purple-veined midregion of the dorsal sepal. The dorsal is broadly ovate to subcircular, apically acute, and measures up to 6 cm (2.3 in.) in both dimensions. It is somewhat keeled by its midvein. The synsepalum is concave, elliptic to lanceolate, and acute. Its color is greenish white; olive to purple veins stripe the ventral sepal.

The petals are falcate, reflexed and subsigmoid, typically growing downward at an acute angle. They are cream to yellow green proximally, with rosy purple suffusion upon their distal thirds. Color is richer above the midvein than below. Maroon spotting and hairs adorn the superior petal margins; the region below the midvein is striped by green veins. Petal angle, markings and coloration vary to some degree in this species. The petals may be held almost vertically. Warting may be profuse, both on the body of the petal and upon the inferior margin. Rosy pigmentation may enhance more than the apical portion of the petals. Petal dimensions are 4.5–7 cm (1.75–2.75 in.) in length by approximately 1.5 cm (0.6 in.) in width. Var. *sublaeve* holds its petals more horizontally than does the typical variety.

The labellum of *P. callosum* is elongate, measuring 2.5–4.5 cm (1–1.75 in.) in length. It is green in color with mauve or rose overlaying the green frontally. The incurved side-lobes bear rosy brown dots and warts. Reticular veins of mahogany or maroon adorn the pouch.

FLOWERING SEASON February through early autumn.

Paphiopedilum ciliolare (Reichb. f.) Stein
PLATE 86

This species is closely allied to *P. superbiens* (Reichb. f.) Stein from Sumatra.

GEOGRAPHIC DISTRIBUTION This Philippine species inhabits Luzon, Dinaget, Camiguin and Mindanao.

HABITAT High humidity, heavy rainfall for much of the year, and temperatures which remain above 10°C (50°F) year-round characterize the habitats where *P. ciliolare* is found. It grows in tussocks of moss and in detritus on wooded slopes at elevations of 300–2,000 m (1,000–6,900 ft.).

DESCRIPTION Leaf length is up to 15 cm (6 in.); width is 2.5–5 cm (1–2 in.). To a marked degree, these boldly tessellated leaves resemble the foliage of *P. argus*. New growths are produced in the axils of the leaves of old growths, thereby producing clustered colonies of plants. Some purple pigmentation is present on the basal undersurfaces of the leaves.

A single large flower is borne atop an erect, pubescent peduncle. The ovary is clasped by a small bract.

The dorsal sepal is broadly ovate and apically acute. In color, it is rosy white with purple veins which fade to pale green near the white margin. The veins are unequal in length. Dimensions of the dorsal sepal are 4–6 cm (1.6–2.4 in.) in length by 3–5 cm (1.2–2 in.) in width. The synsepalum is elliptic and narrower than the dorsal; its color is white marked with green veins.

The strap-shaped petals are held well down from horizontal, arch slightly, and recurve at the apices. Upon a creamy pink ground, the veins are purple. Blackish maroon spots and warts adorn the proximal two-thirds of the petals; both superior and inferior margins bear cilia. Petal dimensions are 5–7.5 cm (2–3 in.) in length by 1.5–2 cm (0.6–0.75 in.) in width. The pubescent labellum is veined with mahogany over rich maroon brown. It measures 4.5–6 cm (1.75–2.3 in.) long by 3–3.5 cm (1.2–1.4 in.) wide.

FLOWERING SEASON Late spring to early summer.

Paphiopedilum curtisii (Reichb. f.) Stein. See *P. superbiens* (Reichb. f.) Stein.

Paphiopedilum dayanum (Lindl.) Stein   PLATES 87–89

See Cribb's (1987) monograph for details of distinctions made by him between this species and *P. petri* (Reichb. f.) Rolfe and *P. burbidgei* (Reichb. f.) Pfitz.—two entities, perhaps natural hybrids, found in the same region. Cribb indicates that *P. petri* is rightfully considered a variant of *P. dayanum*, while *P. burbidgei* is a natural hybrid of *P. dayanum* and *P. javanicum* var. *virens*. Richard Topper (personal communication) believes the 3 entities are naturally occurring forms of *P. dayanum*. Electrophoretic studies may reveal sufficient evidence to end the conjecture. I shall treat both the questionable forms as variants of *P. dayanum*. Refer to Plates 87–89 for comparisons.

GEOGRAPHIC DISTRIBUTION Sabah in northern Borneo is where this endemic species makes its home.

HABITAT *P. dayanum* roots in detritus in bamboo thickets on the forested slopes of Mt. Kinabalu at elevations of 300–1,450 m (1,000–5,000 ft.). Its range overlaps that of *P. rothschildianum* in part. Winter brings cool temperatures and heavy rains, while high temperatures and somewhat drier conditions prevail during the remainder of the year. The soil is alkaline. Both bright and dim shade are acceptable to this species.

DESCRIPTION Two vegetative forms exist in this boldly tessellated taxon. The dark green leaves are tessellated with either yellow green or bluish green; the 2 forms grow intermixed. Leaf dimensions are 15–20 cm (6–8 in.) long by 5 cm (2 in.) wide. Leaves of maturing plants are held erect, while those of flowered plants tend to become progressively more prostrate. Following flowering, the growths persist for several years and produce numerous offshoots from the axils of the leaves.

The pubescent peduncle bears a solitary flower subtended by a pubescent bract. The inflorescence measures up to 25 cm (10 in.) in height.

The ovate, acute dorsal sepal is large, white, and boldly striped with green; its margins are ciliate. It measures 5–6 cm (2–2.3 in.) in length by 2.5–3 cm (1–1.2 in.) in width. The synsepalum is similar and proportionally smaller.

The petals of *P. dayanum* lack spotting; they are rosy violet in color, veined with purple. Their margins are ciliate. In shape, the petals are oblanceolate, nearly spathulate. Petal dimensions are 7.5–8 cm (3–3.2 in.) long by 1–1.5 cm (0.3–0.6 in.) wide. They are oriented in a spreading attitude just below horizontal. The pouch of this species is rich maroon to mahogany. Narrow and long, it measures 5 cm (2 in.) in length by 2 cm (0.75 in.) in width. Its infolded side-lobes are richly spotted with maroon.

FLOWERING SEASON Often twice a year, in early summer and midwinter.

Paphiopedilum denisii Schoser. See *P. wentworthianum* Schoser & Fowlie.

Paphiopedilum fowliei Birk. See *P. hennisianum* (M. Wood) Fowlie.

Paphiopedilum hainanense Fowlie, sp. nov. See *P. appletonianum* (Gower) Rolfe.

Paphiopedilum hennisianum (M. Wood) Fowlie   PLATE 90

The taxonomic history of this species is well-documented by Cribb (1987), and the reader is referred to his monograph for details. In accordance with Cribb, *P. fowliei* (Birk) Cribb is considered as a variant of *P. hennisianum* within this text.

Morphologically, this species is allied with *P. barbatum*, *P. lawrenceanum* and *P. callosum*. Because of geographic distribution, the relationship must be considered to be of ancient vintage.

GEOGRAPHIC DISTRIBUTION The species is indigenous to the Philippine islands of Panay and Negros and the smaller islands of that group in the Visayan Sea. Var. *fowliei* is found only in remote, mountainous sections of Palawan Island.

HABITAT Occurring at elevations of 650–1,050 m (2,200–3,600 ft.), *P. hennisianum* grows as a terrestrial rooted in deep humus in bright shade of saplings and shrubs. This species is associated with calcareous rock. Monsoons bring heavy rainfall twice each year. The months of April and May are driest, but high humidity persists year-round. The temperatures are moderate to warm and range between 17°C (63°F) and 33°C (91°F).

DESCRIPTION The leaves are lightly tessellated and measure up to 18 cm (7 in.) long by 4 cm (1.6 in.) wide. The leaves of var. *fowliei* exhibit a distinct blue green coloration.

The pubescent inflorescence is single-flowered and reaches a height of up to 32 cm (13 in.). A small bract subtends the flower. The flowers of var. *fowliei* are generally smaller than those of the type.

The dorsal sepal is white and prominently striped with green. Broadly ovate and apically acute, it measures 3–4.5 cm (1.2–1.75 in.) long by 3.2–4.8 cm (1.3–2 in.) wide. The concave ventral sepal is elliptic in shape, measuring 2.3–3.4 cm (0.9–1.4 in.) long by approximately 2 cm (0.75 in.) wide. It is similar in color to the dorsal.

The recurved petals of this species bear marginal warts, more abundantly on the variant than on the type. The white petals are veined with green and suffused with rose toward the apices. Petal dimensions are 4.6–5.5 cm (1.75–2.2 in.) in length and 1–1.4 cm (0.3–0.6 in.) in width. Pouch color varies from pale chestnut brown to rich purplish mahogany. The labellum measures 3.8–4.8 cm (1.5–2 in.) in length.

FLOWERING SEASON Spring.

Paphiopedilum hookerae (Reichb. f.) Stein   PLATES 91 & 92

This slipper and its variant, var. *volonteanum* (Sander ex Rolfe) Kerch., are allies of *P. appletonianum* and *P. bullenianum*, although *P. hookerae* is distinctive with its widened petals and flatter, unstriped dorsal sepal. The recently described *P. schoseri* Braem is obviously allied with this species; I prefer to treat it as a synonym until further study indicates otherwise.

GEOGRAPHIC DISTRIBUTION This species grows in Sarawak and western Kalimantan on Borneo. Var. *volonteanum* is found in Sabah in the northern portion of the island both on the slopes of Mt. Kinabalu and at lower elevations.

HABITAT The type grows on calcareous and sandstone outcrops at elevations of 150–600 m (500–2,100 ft.). The variant inhabits a wide range of elevations of 60–2,100 m (200–7,200 ft.) on Mt. Kinabalu and in the lower surrounds. It is associated with the basic serpentine rock and soils of the area, according to Fowlie (1984c). Seepage of water keeps the roots of these slippers constantly moist. Bright shade is provided by an open canopy of trees or by shrubby undergrowth. Plants occasionally cling to mossy tree roots but are generally rooted in humus overlying the rock strata or are lithophytic upon the rocks themselves.

Winter monsoons bring heavy rainfall. Some drying usually occurs during late winter, although July and August are the only severely dry months.

DESCRIPTION *P. hookerae* is a moderately small plant, bearing leaves which measure 7.5–25 cm

(3–10 in.) in length. The leaves are boldly marked with tessellations of pale green upon a dark green ground. Fowlie (1981e) describes various leaf colorations as ecotypes, including gray green and yellow green foliar entities. He states that these leaf colors are determined by the amount of light received, but illustrates these so-called ecotypes living side by side. The leaves of the type lack purple pigmentation on the undersurfaces, while those of the variant bear anthocyanin spotting.

A solitary flower is borne atop a tall, pubescent peduncle which extends up to 50 cm (20 in.). A small bract subtends the flower.

The dorsal sepal is ovate and apically acute. Its basal margins reflex less than is the case in most of the allies of this species. In color, the dorsal is bright green with creamy white margins. It measures 3–4 cm (1.2–1.6 in.) long by 2.5–3 cm (1–1.2 in.) wide. The bidentate synsepalum is elliptic; its color is pale yellow. It measures 2–3 cm (0.75–1.2 in.) in length and approximately 1.5 cm (0.6 in.) in width.

The petals are spathulate and apically subacute. The flower of var. *volonteanum* differs from that of the type in having broader petals with obtuse apices. Held just below horizontal, the petals may recurve to a variable degree; typically, they exhibit a quarter to half turn about midlength. Petal dimensions are 4–5.5 cm (1.6–2.2 in.) long by 1.5–2.5 cm (0.6–1 in.) wide. The undulate, ciliate margins are purple in color; distally, these purple margins broaden to create a rich purple apical band. Proximally and extending as a broad midpetal streak, the petal color is green, spotted and striped with dark maroon. The labellum is greenish brown at the toe, deepening to honey brown or mahogany toward its rim. The pouch measures approximately 4 cm (1.2 in.) in length.

FLOWERING SEASON Spring.

Paphiopedilum javanicum (Reinw. ex Lindl.) Pfitz.   PLATE 93

Cribb (1987) includes both *P. virens* (Reichb. f.) Pfitz. and *P. purpurascens* Fowlie within this taxon as *P. javanicum* var. *virens*, designating *P. purpurascens* as synonymous with var. *virens*.

GEOGRAPHIC DISTRIBUTION The type ranges over Java, Bali, Flores, and possibly Sumatra; it is not abundant in any of these sites. Var. *virens* is found only in the northwest portion of Borneo.

HABITAT Var. *virens* is found on the slopes of Mt. Kinabalu in Sabah. Here it grows on rocky terrain on the steep slopes of rivers in forest shade at elevations of 900–1,650 m (3,100–5,700 ft.). It roots in detritus.

The type also occupies deeply shaded slopes where it roots in detritus overlying volcanic substrates, at elevations of 750–2,100 m (2,600–7,200 ft.).

DESCRIPTION The leaves are lightly tessellated; purple pigmentation is absent from the lower surface. Leaf dimensions are 10–25 cm (4–10 in.) long by 3.5–4 cm (1.3–1.6 in.) wide.

The erect, pubescent inflorescence stands 15–35 cm (6–14 in.) tall and bears a solitary flower.

The ovate, acute dorsal sepal is greenish white with dark green stripes. Its lateral margins are reflexed. It measures 3–4 cm (1.2–1.6 in.) long by 2.5–3 cm (1–1.2 in.) wide. The synsepalum is lanceolate and pale green; it is 2.5 cm (1 in.) long by 1.2 cm (0.5 in.) wide. Both sepals are pubescent upon their reverse surfaces.

The narrowly oblongate petals vary in their orientation from nearly horizontal to 45° below. Green in color proximally, the petal apices are flushed rosy purple. Small blackish purple spots adorn the proximal portion; the margins are ciliate. Petal dimensions are 4–5 cm (1.6–2 in.) long by up to 1.5 cm (0.6 in) wide. The labellum is green with darker green veins; a pale bronze flush occurs near the frontal rim. It measures 3.5–4 cm (1.3–1.6 in.) long by approximately 2 cm (0.75 in.) wide.

The flower of var. *virens* is, according to Cribb (1987), predominantly green in color with less spotting.

FLOWERING SEASON Intermittently, but more typically in summer.

Paphiopedilum johorense Fowlie & Yap. See *P. bullenianum* (Reichb. f.) Pfitz.

Paphiopedilum lawrenceanum (Reichb. f.) Pfitz.   PLATE 94

See Cribb's (1987) monograph for a discussion of the history and variants or cultivars of this species including inaccurately identified importations of *P. nigritum* from Borneo in the 1960s, and other taxonomic associations with *P. barbatum*.

I include the albino form, var. *hyeanum* Reichb. f., as a valid variant, based on its ability to breed true in transmitting albino coloration to its progeny.

GEOGRAPHIC DISTRIBUTION *P. lawrenceanum* is found on Borneo in Sarawak and Sabah.

HABITAT Growing on river banks at elevations of 300–500 m (1,000–1,700 ft.), this species roots in detritus and moss overlying clay and limestone.

DESCRIPTION The leaves are mottled pale yellow green and dark green above; purple pigmentation is typically absent from the lower leaf surface. Leaf dimensions are 17.5–20 cm (7–8 in.) long by 4–6.5 cm (1.6–2.3 in.) wide.

Flowers are solitary, subtended by a small bract, and borne atop a pubescent peduncle extending to 30 cm (12 in.) in height.

The dorsal sepal is broadly ovate to subcircular and apically acute; it is approximately 6 cm (2.3 in.) in both dimensions. The margins are gently undulate and often reflexed laterally. The color is greenish white with green veins basally; midway the veins blend to purple where a rosy flush paints an arch across the dorsal. The veins are unequal in length, tapering and fading to leave a broad white margin. The synsepalum is narrow and lanceolate; it measures 4 cm (1.6 in.) long by 1.5 cm (0.6 in.) wide. In color, it is a pale facsimile of the dorsal.

The slender petals are warted and ciliate on both undulate margins and dip to just below horizontal. In color, they are green, tinted rosy purple distally. Dark green veins traverse the midlines of the petals. Petal measurements are approximately 6 cm (1.3 in.) in length by 1 cm (0.3 in.) in width. The labellum is green and flushed with chestnut brown or khaki frontally. It measures 5.5–6.5 cm (2.2–2.6 in.) in length and approximately 3 cm (1.2 in.) in width.

FLOWERING SEASON Summer.

Paphiopedilum linii Schoser. See *P. bullenianum* (Reichb. f.) Pfitz.

Paphiopedilum mastersianum (Reichb. f.) Stein   PLATE 95

Most closely allied to *Paphiopedilum papuanum* (Ridl.) Ridley which is much smaller, *P. mastersianum* is large and striking in appearance. Two distinct color forms of this species are reported by Peterson (1985) who writes that copper red colonies are indigenous to Ambon while Ceram hosts colonies with maroon-colored flowers. Those colonies found on Buru are presumed to be composed of the more common copper-flowered individuals.

Richard Topper (personal communication) refers to an entity called *P. moorianum* which he considers to be no more than a distinct color form of *P. mastersianum*. Having no further information, I leave this form unexamined.

GEOGRAPHIC DISTRIBUTION This species has been collected from 3 of the Moluccan islands: Ceram, Buru and Ambon.

HABITAT Growing at elevations of 900–2,000 m (3,100–6,900 ft.), *P. mastersianum* inhabits pockets of humus on sheer scarps in moderate shade. Heavy monsoon rains occur during most of the year, while only the summer months are considered to be the dry season on these islands just south of the equator. Seepage, mists and occasional rain provide ample summer moisture. Day length and temperature vary minimally during the year.

DESCRIPTION This species bears tessellated leaves measuring 20–30 cm (10–12 in.) in length. Purple pigmentation is absent from the lower surface.

The large flower, subtended by a small bract, is borne singly atop a tall, hirsute peduncle which measures 20–37.5 cm (8–15 in.) in height.

The broadly ovate, acute dorsal sepal is apple green veined with slightly darker green; it bears a creamy white, ciliated margin. The dorsal measures 3–4 cm (1.2–1.6 in.) in length by approximately 2 cm (0.75 in.) in width. The synsepalum is yellow green and proportionally smaller in dimensions. Both sepals are pubescent upon the reverse surfaces.

Commonly the spathulate petals are copper-colored (populations from Ceram produce maroon-red petal pigments), paling proximally to yellow or yellow green below the midvein. Both the midvein and the upper margin are more or less verrucate. Proximally the petals bear scattered cilia. Petal dimensions are 4.5–5.5 cm (1.75–2.25 in.) long by 1.5–2 cm (0.6–0.75 in.) wide. Held nearly horizontally, the upper distal margin of the petal typically exhibits a wide, indented undulation. The pouch is pale chestnut brown and often speckled with small purple dots. Depending upon the clone, shadings of coppery orange or of maroon (matching the predominant petal color) suffuse the lip toward the toe. The pouch measures 4.5–5 cm (1.75–2 in.) in length.

FLOWERING SEASON Spring and early summer.

Paphiopedilum nigritum (Reichb. f.) Pfitz. See *P. barbatum* (Lindl.) Pfitz. and *P. lawrenceanum* (Reichb. f.) Pfitz.

Paphiopedilum papuanum (Ridl.) Ridley   PLATE 96

A synonym for this species is *P. zieckianum* Schoser.

GEOGRAPHIC DISTRIBUTION Papua New Guinea hosts its namesake.

HABITAT *P. papuanum* is found at 800–1,700 m (2,700–5,800 ft.) in bright shade. The substrate is fairly deep soil overlying granite outcrops. Annual rainfall of up to 300 cm (118 in.) averages close to 1 cm (0.3 in.) per day and maintains conditions of high humidity, moderate temperatures and ample moisture to roots all year.

DESCRIPTION The tessellated leaves are up to 25 cm (10 in.) in length. The lower surface is devoid of anthocyanin.

The inflorescence bears a solitary flower, subtended by a small bract, at a height of up to 30 cm (12 in.). The ovate, acute dorsal sepal is yellow or yellow green marked with purple veins and bears a white, ciliate margin. Its dimensions are 2.5 cm (1 in.) in length by 2–2.5 cm (0.75–1 in.) in width. The synsepalum is yellowish green, elliptic to lanceolate, and quite small, measuring under 2 cm (0.75 in) long by less than 1 cm (0.3 in.) wide.

The spathulate petals are held nearly horizontally. Petal color is maroon with the exception of the proximal area located below the midvein, which is yellow green and marked with narrow brown stripes and verrucae. The ciliate margins exhibit some undulation. The petals measure 4 cm (1.6 in.) long by 1.5–1.8 cm (0.6–0.75 in.) wide. The pouch is 2.5–4 cm (1–1.6 in.) long and suffused with a dull, reddish brown color.

FLOWERING SEASON Winter and early spring.

Paphiopedilum pardinum (Reichb. f.) Pfitz. See *P. venustum* (Wall.) Pfitz. ex Stein.

Paphiopedilum petri (Reichb. f.) Rolfe. See *P. dayanum* (Lindl.) Stein.

Paphiopedilum purpurascens Fowlie. See *P. javanicum* (Reinw. ex Lindl.) Pfitz.

Paphiopedilum purpuratum (Lindl.) Stein   PLATE 97

Mark (1982) discusses a variant of this species, forma *aphaca*, which lacks warts and bears a pair of lateral sepals rather than a synsepalum.

GEOGRAPHIC DISTRIBUTION This somewhat diminutive species is native to Hong Kong, to adjacent mainland China (Guangdong Province) and probably to Hainan Island.

HABITAT *P. purpuratum* grows at elevations of 30–700 m (100–2,400 ft.) where freezing temperatures may occur in conjunction with drier conditions in winter. Summer temperatures, corresponding with the rainy season, rarely exceed 27°C (80°F). Humidity averages 70–80% even during the dry season. It is likely that seepage keeps the roots moist during the winter months. Rooted in moss or detritus on steep, rocky hillsides and river gorges with north-facing slopes, these plants enjoy light shade of trees or bamboo thickets where the light intensity is approximately 700 footcandles.

DESCRIPTION Leaf color is variable from yellow green to bluish green, and the degree of tessellation also varies. According to T. C. Lee (1975), a rare sport bearing longitudinal green/white striping upon the leaves is known in this species. No anthocyanin pigment appears upon the lower leaf surfaces. Leaf dimensions are 7.5–17.5 cm (3–16 in.) in length by 2.5–4 cm (1–1.6 in.) in width.

The solitary flower is borne atop an erect, pubescent flowerscape at a height of up to 20 cm (8 in.). A small bract clasps the ovary.

The acute dorsal sepal is broadly ovate with reflexed lateral margins. It is 2.5–3 cm (1–1.25 in.) long by 2–3.4 cm (0.75–1.3 in.) wide. The ground color is white; unequal veins of purple stripe the dorsal to within 1 millimeter of the margin. The synsepalum is lanceolate and measures 2–2.5 cm (0.75–1 in.) in length by 1.5 cm (0.6 in.) in width. It is green with dark green venation.

The glossy, elliptic petals are dark maroon with the exception of a small proximal region of attachment which is greenish white. Blackish maroon spots are liberally dispersed over the proximal third of the petals; the margins are ciliate. Petal orientation is more or less horizontal with some tendency to recurve apically. Petal dimensions are 3.5–4.5 cm (1.3–1.75 in.) in length by approximately 1 cm (0.3 in.) in width. The lip is maroon to mahogany and measures 3–4 cm (1.25–1.6 in.) long by 2 cm (0.75 in.) wide.

FLOWERING SEASON Late autumn and early winter.

Paphiopedilum robinsonii (Ridl.) Ridley. See. *P. bullenianum* (Reichb. f.) Pfitz.

Paphiopedilum sangii Braem, sp. nov.   PLATE 98

Described in 1987, this new species most closely resembles *P. bougainvilleanum* and *P. violascens*. Its lobed or auricled dorsal, however, sets it quite apart from either, as do both its range and coloration.

GEOGRAPHIC DISTRIBUTION This species is native to the island of Sulawesi in the Celebes.

HABITAT As humus epiphytes, populations are found in open woods near sea level where temperatures range from intermediate to warm. Moisture is abundant throughout the year as a result of seepage.

DESCRIPTION Mature growths typically consist of 4 boldly tessellated leaves which measure up to 28 cm (11 in.) long by 5 cm (2 in.) wide.

The erect, unifloral inflorescence stands up to 25 cm (8.9 in.) in height. A bract subtends the flower.

The dorsal sepal of this flower exhibits a uniquely notched margin that disposes itself as a pair of bilaterally symmetrical lobes or earlike extensions. This unusual feature is not found uniformly on all flowers of all specimens, but is still considered common or typical. The narrowly ovate, acuminate dorsal measures 4.3 cm (1.7 in.) long by 3.3 cm (1.4 in.) wide. Its ground color is creamy yellow; a deep green basal portion extends green venation over the mesial band of the dorsal. The bifid synsepalum is yellowish green overlaid with green stripes; it measures 3.2 cm (1.4 in.) in length by 1.6 cm (0.7 in.) in width. Stiff hairs adorn both sepals.

The pendant petals bear crisp undulation along their upper margins. Petal color is purple mesially, but the margins and rounded apices are apple green. Petal measurements are 4.6 cm (1.8 in.) long by 1.4 cm (0.6 in.) wide. The pouch resembles that of *P. venustum* in color, shape and venation; somewhat greenish cream in color, it is marked with incised veins of green.

FLOWERING SEASON Not reported.

Paphiopedilum schoseri Braem. See *P. hookerae* (Reichb. f.) Stein.

Paphiopedilum sublaeve (Reichb. f.) Fowlie. See *P. callosum* (Reichb. f.) Stein

Paphiopedilum sukhakulii Schoser & Senghas   PLATE 99
Most closely allied to *Paphiopedilum wardii* Summerh., this species is outstanding and easily identifiable. Breeders have shown a great deal of interest in *P. sukhakulii* and have successfully crossed it both with other species and with complex hybrids.
GEOGRAPHIC DISTRIBUTION This species is endemic to the region around Mount Phu Luang in the province of Loei in northeast Thailand.
HABITAT *P. sukhakulii* is found rooted in loamy soil on slopes at elevations up to 1,000 m (3,400 ft.). It prefers river banks and moderate shade. At its lower elevations, it grows in proximity to colonies of *P. callosum*.
DESCRIPTION The leaves of this species are tessellated; purple pigmentation dots the bases of their undersurfaces. Leaf dimensions are up to 25 cm (10 in.) in length and 5 cm (2 in.) in width.

The erect peduncle may stand as tall as 25 cm (10 in.) or more and typically bears a solitary flower. Both bract and stalk are pubescent.

The broadly ovate dorsal sepal is white with 11–13 intensely green veins which extend to the margin, often exhibiting a dichotomy within the last millimeter. Spaced among the longer veins are 4–8 shorter veins. Sparse purple dots adorn the base of the dorsal. It is strongly conduplicate and concave; its acute apex hoods the pouch orifice to some extent. The dimensions of the dorsal sepal are approximately 4 cm (1.6 in.) in length by 3 cm (1.25 in.) in width. The synsepalum is smaller and similarly colored.

The oblongate petals are held very near the horizontal. They measure 5–6 cm (2–2.3 in.) long by 1.5–2 cm (0.6–0.75 in.) wide. Petal color is apple green; abundant maroon spots adorn the entire surface; both the superior and inferior margins are hirsute. The pouch measures 5 cm (2 in.) long by 2.5 cm (1 in.) wide. It is green beneath with a rich flush of copper or mahogany over the frontal surface. Reticulate veins of chestnut brown adorn the lip.
FLOWERING SEASON Autumn; when well-grown in spring as well.

Paphiopedilum superbiens (Reichb. f.) Stein   PLATE 100
Cribb's (1987) monograph presents a summary of the nomenclatural confusion surrounding this species and gives adequate cause for reducing *P. curtisii* (Reichb. f.) Stein, the binomial most used in horticulture, to synonymy in this case. However, the reader is referred to Vermeulen's (1981) article in *Orchid Digest* for a conflicting viewpoint on the

matter of merging the plants under 1 binomial. Geographically and morphologically, the evidence for the assimilation of *P. curtisii* into this taxon is extremely convincing.

GEOGRAPHIC DISTRIBUTION North central Sumatra is the extent of the range of this species.

HABITAT *P. superbiens* inhabits wooded slopes of the mountains near Padang at elevations of 900–1,300 m (3,100–4,500 ft.). The soil is decomposed sandstone upon which deep humus provides a rooting medium for this species. Day length and temperature vary little during the year. However, there is a dry season encompassing the northern hemisphere's summer season, June–August, and a wet season which embraces most of the balance of the year. Winter monsoons provide heavy downpours with maximum precipitation during November–January. Humidity is consistently high.

DESCRIPTION The heavily tessellated leaves bear some purple pigmentation upon their lower surfaces. Leaf dimensions are 15–25 cm (6–10 in.) in length and 4–6.5 cm (1.6–2.5 in.) in width.

The erect, pubescent inflorescence is unifloral and reaches heights of 15–25 cm (6–10 in.). A bract sheaths the base of the ovary.

The dorsal sepal is broadly ovate and apically acute. It measures 3–5.5 cm (1.2–2.25 in.) in length and breadth. It is pale greenish white both basally and apically, while its midsection is flushed with pink. Venation of the dorsal merges from green to purple and back to green; the veins are unequal in length and fade out before reaching the creamy green margin. The synsepalum is ovate to elliptic and similar in color and markings to the dorsal sepal.

The falcate petals are oblanceolate and pendulous. Proximally their color is green grading to rosy purple distally. Green veins run the length of the petals above the midvein; faint purple veins are exhibited below. Numerous purple spots are dispersed over the petal surfaces. The margins are ciliate and gently undulate; a quarter-turn spiral occurs toward the distal apices. Petal dimensions are 5–7.5 cm (2–3 in.) in length and 1.5–2 cm (0.6–0.75 in.) in width. The labellum is dark maroon to mahogany with purple-spotted, involute side-lobes; it measures 4.5–6.5 cm (1.75–2.6 in.) long by 2.5–3 cm (1–1.2 in.) wide.

FLOWERING SEASON Summer.

Paphiopedilum superbiens (Reichb. f.) Stein subsp. *ciliolare* (Reichb. f.) M. Wood. See *P. ciliolare* (Reichb. f.) Stein.

Paphiopedilum thailandense Fowlie. See *P. callosum* (Reichb. f.) Stein

Paphiopedilum tonsum (Reichb. f.) Stein   PLATE 101

GEOGRAPHIC DISTRIBUTION This species grows in north and central Sumatra sympatric with *P. victoria-regina* (Sander) M. Wood and *P. superbiens* (Reichb. f.) Stein.

HABITAT Rooted in deep humus, this slipper grows on calcareous substrate at elevations of 875–1,000 m (3,000–3,500 ft.). It receives abundant rainfall or moisture from condensation and seepage all year; high humidity is a year-round feature of the habitat. There is little variation in day length; temperatures are moderate.

DESCRIPTION The leaves of this species bear tessellations above; the lower surfaces are pigmented with anthocyanin. Leaf length is 15–20 cm (6–8 in.).

The inflorescence is pubescent and erect bearing a single flower at a height of up to 35 cm (14 in.). The flower is subtended by a small bract.

The dorsal sepal is obovate, apically acute, and measures approximately 4.5 cm (1.75 in.) in length and width. Its color is white, basally flushed with pale yellow green and mesially suffused with pink. Green veins merge into maroon stripes which extend only to the white border. The smaller, elliptic synsepalum is bicarinate; it is pale green with darker green stripes. Its measurements are 3.5 cm (1.3 in.) long by 1.5 cm (0.6 in.) wide.

The oblongate petals are held very nearly horizontally. Petal dimensions are 5–6.5 cm (2–2.6 in.) long by approximately 2 cm (0.75 in.) wide. Khaki or olive green with buff-colored apices, the petals are striped with darker green or chestnut brown and bear a sparse scattering of verrucae above the midvein. The labellum is khaki-colored with a flush of pink or chestnut brown; the veins are faintly picked out in darker brown or maroon. Labellar dimensions are 5–5.5 cm (2–2.3 in.) long by 3–3.5 cm (1.25–1.3 in.) wide.

FLOWERING SEASON Winter.

Paphiopedilum tortisepalum Fowlie. See *P. bullenianum* (Reichb. f.) Pfitz.

Paphiopedilum urbanianum Fowlie

Having no personal experience with this plant, I rely upon Fowlie's (1981d) description.

GEOGRAPHIC DISTRIBUTION Mindoro Island in the Philippines is the site of the discovery of this species.

HABITAT The species inhabits rocky soil at elevations of 450–700 m (1,500–2,500 ft.). Occasionally *P. urbanianum* grows as an epiphyte. Monsoon winds bring heavy rain and cool temperatures in summer, while dry conditions and cool night temperatures prevail for much of the winter. Early spring is the warmest time of the year, but at all times the temperatures are moderate to warm. Bright conditions prevail in winter when cloud cover permits.

DESCRIPTION The leaves are faintly tessellated above; purple pigmentation is absent from the lower surfaces. Leaf length is 12–20 cm (4.75–8 in.), while the width is 3–4 cm (1.2–1.6 in.).

The flowerscape is erect and pubescent; it bears 1 or 2 flowers at a height of 20–25 cm (8–10 in.). A large pubescent bract subtends each flower.

The dorsal sepal is at least 3 cm (1.25 in.) long and wide, broadly ovate to subcircular and apically acute. Its color is greenish white marked with 11–13 green or maroon veins of unequal length. The concave ventral sepal is ovate to elliptic, green with darker green veins, and measures 3 cm (1.25 in.) or more in length by 1.5–2 cm (0.6–0.75 in.) in width.

The petals are held at an approximate 45° angle. They are oblanceolate and measure 5–6 cm (2–2.3 in.) long by 1–2 cm (0.4–0.75 in.) wide. In color they are green with green veins proximally; the distal two-thirds are richly suffused with coppery bronze or with maroon and are veined in darker maroon. Typically, there are blackish maroon warts along the superior margin as well as upon the mesial surface of the petals. The lip color agrees with the petal color, exhibiting either copper or maroon pigmentation, with a green rim and green beneath the toe. The pouch measures 4–5 cm (0.6–1 in.) in length; the width is 1.5–2.5 cm (0.3–1 in.).

FLOWERING SEASON Winter and early spring.

Paphiopedilum venustum (Wall.) Pfitz. ex Stein   PLATES 102 & 103

U. C. Pradhan (1975) describes a number of variant flowers of this species. The variants are ecotypes found in isolated populations, exhibiting a notable range in color, size and orientation of the segments. One of the variants bears a strong resemblance to *P. wardii*, an allied species which occupies a range adjacent to that of *P. venustum*. Pradhan believes isolative inbreeding is the origin of these variants.

Another notable feature of this species is its tendency to hybridize in nature with sympatric species—*P. spiceranum* and *P. fairrieanum*, and possibly *P. wardii*.

Plate 103 illustrates an albinistic variant. According to Cribb (1987), albino plants should be designated as var. *measuresianum*; he considers these variants to be merely cultivars.

GEOGRAPHIC DISTRIBUTION This species is indigenous to northeast India, Nepal, Sikkim and Bhutan. Its distribution is wide in comparison with most *Paphiopedilum*.

HABITAT Monsoons create a hot summer season saturated with moisture, while the winter and spring are cooler and drier. This species prefers shaded river valleys where it roots in detritus at elevations of 60–1,350 m (200–4,500 ft.).

DESCRIPTION The leaves are 12.5–25 cm (5–10 in.) long by 2.5–5 cm (1–2 in.) wide. Richly tessellated light and dark green above, they are mottled with purple beneath.

Typically, a solitary flower is borne atop an erect, pubescent peduncle.

The ovate, acute dorsal sepal is white striped with dark green. It measures 3–4 cm (1.25–1.6 in.) long by 2.5–3 cm (1–1.25 in.) wide. The ventral sepal is greenish white and similar, although proportionally smaller.

The oblanceolate petals are greenish white proximally with green veins; distally the apical third is flushed purple or coppery orange and recurved. Several large blackish purple warts adorn the transitional midregion. The petals measure 4.5–5.5 cm (1.75–2.2 in.) in length by up to 1.5 cm (0.6 in.) in width; they are held in a very nearly horizontal position. The lip is yellow with some purple or copper suffusion; distinct green veins impart a puckered appearance to the pouch. Its dimensions are 3.5–4.5 cm (1.3–1.75 in.) long by 2.5–3 cm (1–1.25 in.) wide.

FLOWERING SEASON Winter.

Paphiopedilum violascens Schltr.   PLATE 104

Var. *gautierense* J. J. Smith is listed by Cribb (1987) as a synonym published subsequent to the type, rather than as a valid variant. *P. violascens* is a distinctive species neither easily misidentified nor widely variable.

GEOGRAPHIC DISTRIBUTION New Guinea and adjacent islands are the sites from which this species is reported.

HABITAT Several substrates support populations of this slipper including volcanic soils, limestone outcrops and quite acid sphagnum humus. Colonies have been found growing in the shade of a wide variety of canopies and at elevations from 200 m (700 ft.) to 1,200 m (4,000 ft.). High humidity and moderate temperatures are features of all the habitats on these islands.

DESCRIPTION The foliage of this plant is tessellated with a predominance of the pale green over the darker green. Purple spotting is not a feature of the undersurfaces. Leaf lengths vary between 7.5 cm (3 in.) and 25 cm (10 in.), while the width is 2.5–4 cm (1–1.6 in.).

The inflorescence stands 20–30 cm (8–12 in.) in height and bears a single flower which is subtended by a small bract. Both bract and stalk are pubescent.

The apically acute dorsal sepal is quite small although broadly ovate. In color, it is greenish white with vivid green stripes. A small blotch of purple extending as a purple stripe marks the midvein. Basal reflexion of the margins is not pronounced. Its dimensions are 2.5–3 cm (1–1.2 in.) long by 3 cm (1.2 in.) wide. The ovate synsepalum is green with darker green stripes. It measures 2–2.5 cm (0.75–1 in.) long by 1.5 cm (0.6 in.) wide. Both sepals are pubescent upon their outer surfaces.

The petals are distinctive and lack spotting but are suffused with a fairly uniform violet color throughout their length, except for the proximal third which is pink or white. Oblongate, the petals arch downward crescentically and bear short cilia upon their margins. Petal dimensions are 3.5–4.5 cm (1.3–1.75 in.) in length by 1.5–2 cm (0.3–0.75 in.) in width. The bulbous pouch is the most notable feature of this species. It is grooved by its veins, white near the aperture, flushed brown frontally, and green beneath. It measures 4–5 cm (1.6–2 in.) long by 2–2.5 cm (0.75–1 in) wide.

FLOWERING SEASON Spring and early summer.

Paphiopedilum virens (Reichb. f.) Pfitz. See *P. javanicum* (Reinw. ex Lindl.) Pfitz.

Paphiopedilum wardii Summerh.   PLATE 105

GEOGRAPHIC DISTRIBUTION North central Kachin State in Burma and Yunnan Province in China are the sources of this species.

HABITAT *P. wardii* grows as a lithophyte or as a terrestrial. It inhabits deep leaf litter over rocky soil on steep slopes at elevations of 1,200–1,500 m (4,100–5,100 ft.). It thrives in medium shade in its natural habitat; plants found in bright situations are usually stunted. Thien Pe (1981) reports that this orchid inhabits regions subject to flash flooding following heavy rainfall, and that plants frequently root in moss tussocks upon the stilt roots of trees. He further states that mean daily temperatures range from 10–27°C (50–80°F) with May–October providing the warmest temperatures while January is the coldest month. Annual rainfall is approximately 250 cm (100 in.). The majority of the precipitation occurs during June–September; December and January are the driest months.

DESCRIPTION The bluish green tessellated leaves are heavily pigmented with anthocyanins beneath. Leaf dimensions are 12.5–17.5 cm (5–7 in.) in length and 3.5–5.5 cm (1.3–2.25 in.) in width.

The solitary flower is borne upon an erect pubescent stalk and is subtended by a slender bract. The peduncle achieves heights of up to 20 cm (8 in.).

The dorsal sepal is ovate, acute, and measures 4–5 cm (1.6–2 in.) in length and 2–3 cm (0.75–1.25 in.) in width. It is white veined with green. The ventral sepal is similar but proportionally smaller. Both sepals are pubescent upon their outer surfaces.

The oblanceolate petals are held at a pendulous angle; their dimensions are 5–6.5 cm (2–2.5 in.) in length by 1.5–2 cm (0.6–0.75 in.) in width. Petal color is pale green marked with darker green veins and heavily spotted with maroon. Many of the flowers show a rich suffusion of maroon to chocolate brown over much of the surface of the petals. Both the superior and inferior margins are hirsute. The lip is green flushed with mahogany and finely spotted with brownish maroon.

FLOWERING SEASON Winter.

Paphiopedilum wentworthianum Schoser & Fowlie

Sympatric with *P. bougainvilleanum* Fowlie and probably allied with it and with *P. violascens* Schltr., this taxon has absorbed plants of *P. denisii* Schoser, a subsequent synonym. See Cribb's (1987) monograph for details of this species and its allies, as well as nomenclatural information.

GEOGRAPHIC DISTRIBUTION This species is native to Bougainville and Guadalcanal in the Solomons.

HABITAT *P. wentworthianum* prefers heavy shade and roots in a light, fibrous soil or in moss. It clings to steep slopes at 900–1,800 m (3,100–6,200 ft.). High humidity and ample rainfall are features of the climate, as is moderation in temperature.

DESCRIPTION The leaves are 12–25 cm (4.75–10 in.) in length. The lower surface is devoid of purple pigmentation; tessellations mark the upper surface.

A solitary flower is borne atop a tall, pubescent peduncle, at up to 35 cm (14 in.) in height. A pubescent bract subtends the flower.

The broadly ovate dorsal sepal is concave with an acute apex. It is green, margined with cream, flushed basally with dull purple, and striped with green. It measures approximately 3 cm (1.2 in.) long and 2.5–3.5 cm (1–1.3 in.) wide. The synsepalum is ovate and green in color. It measures 2–2.5 cm (0.75–1 in.) in length by 2.5 cm (1 in.) in width.

The petals are oblongate and held just below horizontal. Their lacquered sheen is reminiscent of the petals of *P. mastersianum*. Purple above and brownish maroon below, the proximal third is somewhat greenish below the midline. No spotting occurs on the petals; the superior margin is undulate, while both margins bear cilia. Petal dimensions are 4.5 cm (1.75 in.) long by 1.5–2.5 cm (0.6–1 in.) wide. The labellum is chestnut or coppery brown; it measures 4.5 cm (1.75 in.) in length.

FLOWERING SEASON Spring and early summer.

Paphiopedilum wolterianum (Kraenzl.) Pfitz. See *P. appletonianum* (Gower) Rolfe.

Paphiopedilum zieckianum Schoser. See *P. papuanum* (Ridl.) Ridley.

CHAPTER 5

The Genus *Selenipedium*

Although this unique tropical American genus consists of only 6 species, its constituents are plants of such large stature that it is difficult to credit that they are indeed slipper orchids. Despite the fact that none of its species is of horticultural value, *Selenipedium* is so poorly known that it perennially sparks interest among slipper growers. Its inclusion in this text is grounded in the natural curiosity of cypriphiles about this least known genus of slipper orchids, rather than in any relevance to its virtually non-existent merits under cultivation. Only greenhouses of commercial size are of sufficient height to accommodate several of these giants of the slipper world; the comparatively insignificant size of *Selenipedium* flowers erodes their commercial appeal.

Selenipedium is distributed over a limited area of Central and South America including Panama, northern Brazil, Guyana, Trinidad, Venezuela, Colombia and Ecuador. The generic characteristics include a branched canelike plant habit, extending up to 4–5 m (14–17 ft.) in height; adaptation to a terrestrial habitat; alternate, plicate leaves unmarked with spotting or tessellation; 3 stigmata; a trilocular ovary with axile placentation; staminodes reduced in size; and flowers which are produced in terminal racemes or panicles. Certain of these characteristics indicate the primitive status of the genus: the large, branched canes, the terrestrial habitat, the presence of 3 stigmata, the trilocular ovary and the floriferous panicles, as well as several anatomical features of a rather technical nature. Thus, *Selenipedium* is believed to be the modern relic of the phylogenetically ancestral stock of the subfamily which Atwood (1984b) calls *Protoselenipedium*.

Given the size of the vegetative portion of the plant, the size of the individual flower is disproportionately small. Any claim these species have to showiness is limited to their characteristic of producing several to many successive flowers per raceme over a brief period of time. Racemes bearing seed pods, mature flowers, and buds simultaneously, are common in this genus.

Atwood's (1984b) cladistic studies point to a relationship between *Selenipedium* and 2 multifloral *Cypripedium, C. californicum* and *C. irapeanum*. The latter is closer to *Selenipedium* in range as well as in morphological features. The reader is referred to Atwood (1984b) for details of the described relationship. Further studies, including new data from the recently described *C. dickinsonianum* and *C. subtropicum*, should provide additional clues about the early development of the subfamily as well as the relative positions of various genera, subgenera, sections and species.

Due to its unsuitability for greenhouse culture, this small genus of large plants is primarily of interest to botanists. Although the reduced threat of extinction by exploitative collectors indicates a somewhat brighter future than that of the related genera in the slipper family, the danger from clear-cutting of tropical forests continues unabated.

The genus *Selenipedium* includes the following species:

> *Selenipedium aequinoctiale* Garay
> *Selenipedium chica* Reichb. f.
> *Selenipedium isabelianum* Barb. Rodr.
> *Selenipedium palmifolium* (Lindl.) Reichb. f.
> *Selenipedium steyermarkii* Foldats
> *Selenipedium vanillocarpum* Barb. Rodr.

Species discussions follow, including data on geographic distribution and habitat as well as vegetative and floral descriptions. No flowering season is given for several of the species. While at least one species of *Selenipedium* blooms in the first 2–3 months of the year, and another is commonly called a mayflower, extrapolations from these are likely to be misleading. This is true because temperature changes are less extreme in the equatorial zone inhabited by this genus, so that actual conditions at such locations are influenced less by the solar calendar than by elevation, rainy seasons or other local variables. Thus, flowering season data is omitted where factual data is missing from the published descriptions. Cultural data is inapplicable in this genus. Common names are reported for only one species.

Selenipedium aequinoctiale Garay

GEOGRAPHIC DISTRIBUTION This species is reported from the lower slopes of mountains in Ecuador.

HABITAT Aside from its terrestrial growth habit at elevations near 1,000 m (3,400 ft.), other habitat data is unavailable.

DESCRIPTION The branched vegetative axis is suberect to arcuate and reaches heights of up to 1 m (39.3 in.). The slender stems bear lanceolate to elliptic-lanceolate leaves which are plicate, green, and measure up to 16 cm (6.3 in.) long by 3.5 cm (1.4 in.) wide. The leaves are sparsely pubescent.

The racemose inflorescences arise terminally on the branches and are arching to pendulous with short peduncles. The several flowers open in rapid succession, each subtended by a concave, ovate bract.

The elliptic, acute dorsal sepal is yellowish green and measures up to 3 cm (1.3 in.) in length by 1.8 cm (0.6 in.) in width. The synsepalum is apically bidentate, only slightly smaller than the dorsal, and similar in color. Both sepals are glabrous upon the inner surfaces and pubescent upon the reverse.

The linear-lanceolate petals are yellowish green in color. Their dimensions are up to 2.5 cm (1 in.) in length by 4 mm (0.2 in.) in width. The labellum is yellowish green with blotches of dark violet marking the lateral surfaces. It is inflated to a shallow ovoid shape; its margins are involuted. It measures up to 3 cm (1.2 in.) long by 2.5 cm (1 in.) wide.

PLATE 1. **Cypripedium acaule**, typical pink form of the Moccasin Flower. Photograph by Carlisle Leur.

PLATE 2. **Cypripedium acaule** forma **albiflorum**. Photograph by Victor Soukup.

PLATE 3. **Cypripedium arietinum**. Photograph by Victor Soukup.

PLATE 4. **Cypripedium arietinum** forma **albiflorum**. Photograph by Victor Soukup.

PLATE 5. *Cypripedium calceolus* var. *pubescens*.
Photograph by Victor Soukup.

PLATE 6. *Cypripedium calceolus* var. *parviflorum*, typical
bifloral specimen. Photograph by Carlisle Leur.

PLATE 8. *Cypripedium calceolus* var. *planipetalum*.
Photograph by Victor Soukup.

PLATE 7. *Cypripedium calceolus* var. *kentuckiense*, sometimes elevated to species rank as *Cypripedium kentuckiense*. Photograph by Carson Whitlow.

PLATE 9. *Cypripedium californicum*.
Photograph by Carlisle Leur.

PLATE 10. *Cypripedium candidum*.
Photograph by Carson Whitlow.

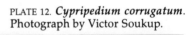

PLATE 12. *Cypripedium corrugatum*.
Photograph by Victor Soukup.

PLATE 11. *Cypripedium cordigerum*.
Photograph by Carson Whitlow.

PLATE 13. *Cypripedium fasciculatum*.
Photograph by Carlisle Leur.

PLATE 14. *Cypripedium flavum*.
Photograph by Victor Soukup.

PLATE 15. *Cypripedium formosanum*.
Photograph by Dieter Hach,
courtesy of Carson Whitlow.

PLATE 16. *Cypripedium guttatum* var. *yatabeanum*.
Photograph by Carson Whitlow.

PLATE 17. *Cypripedium henryi*.
Photograph by Carson Whitlow.

PLATE 18. *Cypripedium irapeanum*.
Photograph by Carlisle Leur.

PLATE 19. *Cypripedium japonicum*.
Photograph by Victor Soukup.

PLATE 20. *Cypripedium macranthum*.
Photograph by Victor Soukup.

PLATE 21. *Cypripedium margaritaceum.*
Photograph by Joan Davis,
courtesy of Carson Whitlow.

PLATE 22. **Cypripedium montanum.**
Photograph by Carlisle Leur.

PLATE 23. **Cypripedium passerinum.**
Photograph by Victor Soukup.

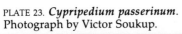

PLATE 24. **Cypripedium reginae,** typical form.
Photograph by Carson Whitlow.

PLATE 26. *Cypripedium ventricosum*, two inflorescences. Also pictured, a single flower of C. *macranthum*.
Photograph by Youri Uspensky,
courtesy of Carson Whitlow.

PLATE 25. *Cypripedium reginae* var. *albolabium*.
Photograph by Victor Soukup.

PLATE 27. *Cypripedium ventricosum* var. *album*.
Photograph by Victor Soukup.

PLATE 28. *Paphiopedilum ang thong* 'Hopson'
HCC/AOS.
Photograph courtesy of Emerson "Doc" Charles.

PLATE 29. *Paphiopedilum bellatulum* 'Casa Luna'
AM/AOS.
Photograph from the Cash-Waters collection.

PLATE 30. *Paphiopedilum concolor*.
Photograph by Emerson "Doc" Charles.

PLATE 31. *Paphiopedilum godefroyae*.
Photograph by Richard Topper.

PLATE 32. *Paphiopedilum niveum*.
Photograph from the Cash-Waters collection.

PLATE 34. *Paphiopedilum delenatii*.
Photograph from the Cash-Waters collection.

PLATE 33. *Paphiopedilum armeniacum*.
Photograph by Emerson "Doc" Charles.

PLATE 36. *Paphiopedilum malipoense*.
Photograph by Emerson "Doc" Charles.

PLATE 35. *Paphiopedilum emersonii*.
Photograph by Emerson "Doc" Charles.

PLATE 37. *Paphiopedilum micranthum* 'Jumbo Jamboree' FCC/AOS. Photograph by Emerson "Doc" Charles.

PLATE 38. *Paphiopedilum glaucophyllum* var. *moquettianum*. Photograph from the Cash-Waters collection.

PLATE 40. *Paphiopedilum primulinum*. Photograph by Emerson "Doc" Charles.

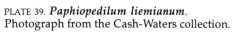

PLATE 39. *Paphiopedilum liemianum*. Photograph from the Cash-Waters collection.

PLATE 41. **Paphiopedilum victoria-mariae**.
Photograph by Richard Topper.

PLATE 42. **Paphiopedilum victoria-regina**, showing its
similarities to and differences from the smaller **P.
glaucophyllum**.
Photograph by Emerson "Doc" Charles.

PLATE 43. **Paphiopedilum adductum**.
Photograph by Richard Topper.

PLATE 44. **Paphiopedilum glanduliferum**.
Photograph by Richard Topper.

PLATE 45. *Paphiopedilum kolopakingii*.
Photograph by Richard Topper.

PLATE 46. *Paphiopedilum kolopakingii* var. *topperi*.
Photograph by Richard Topper.

PLATE 47. *Paphiopedilum philippinense*.
Photograph by Emerson "Doc" Charles.

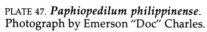

PLATE 48. *Paphiopedilum randsii* showing the cleft chin
of the labellum. Photograph by Richard Topper.

PLATE 49. ***Paphiopedilum rothschildianum*** 'Charles E'.
FCC/AOS.
Photograph courtesy of Emerson "Doc" Charles.

PLATE 50. ***Paphiopedilum sanderanum*** 'Jacob's Ladder',
illustrating both the plant habit and the unique, elongated petals of this species. Photograph by Mark
Pendleton; plant owned by Wharton Sinkler III and
grown by Orchid Zone.

PLATE 51. ***Paphiopedilum stonei*** 'Oceano' AM/AOS.
Photograph courtesy of Emerson "Doc" Charles.

PLATE 52. ***Paphiopedilum supardii***.
Photograph by Richard Topper.

PLATE 53. *Paphiopedilum haynaldianum*.
Photograph by Emerson "Doc" Charles.

PLATE 54. *Paphiopedilum haynaldianum* var. *album*
'Charles' FCC/AOS.
Photograph courtesy of Emerson "Doc" Charles.

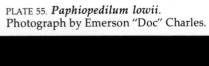

PLATE 55. *Paphiopedilum lowii*.
Photograph by Emerson "Doc" Charles.

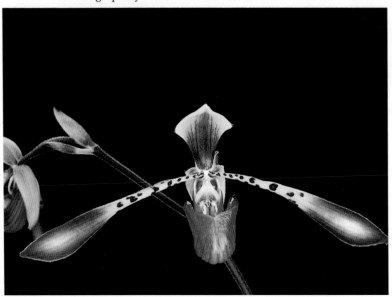

PLATE 56. *Paphiopedilum parishii*.
Photograph by Don Osborne.

PLATE 57. *Paphiopedilum parishii* var. *dianthum*.
Photograph by Richard Topper.

PLATE 58. *Paphiopedilum richardianum*.
Photograph by Richard Topper.

PLATE 59. *Paphiopedilum barbigerum*.
Photograph by Richard Topper.

PLATE 60. *Paphiopedilum charlesworthii*.
Photograph by Emerson "Doc" Charles.

PLATE 61. ***Paphiopedilum druryi*** 'Graceful' CCM/AOS. Photograph courtesy of Emerson "Doc" Charles.

PLATE 62. ***Paphiopedilum exul***. Photograph by Emerson "Doc" Charles.

PLATE 63. ***Paphiopedilum fairrieanum*** 'Betty Jo' AM/AOS. Photograph courtesy of Don Osborne.

PLATE 64. ***Paphiopedilum fairrieanum*** var. ***album*** 'Hager' FCC/AOS. Photograph courtesy of Emerson "Doc" Charles.

PLATE 65. *Paphiopedilum gratrixianum*.
Photograph by Richard Topper.

PLATE 66. *Paphiopedilum gratrixianum*, the form identified as the synonymous *P. affine*.
Photograph by Richard Topper.

PLATE 67. *Paphiopedilum henryanum*.
Photograph courtesy of Emerson "Doc" Charles.

PLATE 68. *Paphiopedilum hirsutissimum*.
Photograph by Don Osborne.

PLATE 69. *Paphiopedilum hirsutissimum* var. *esquirolei*.
Photograph by Richard Topper.

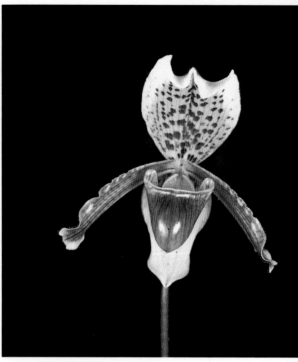

PLATE 70. *Paphiopedilum insigne*.
Photograph by Richard Topper.

PLATE 71. *Paphiopedilum insigne* var. *sanderae*.
Photograph from the Cash-Waters collection.

PLATE 72. *Paphiopedilum spiceranum* 'St. Albans'.
Photograph by Emerson "Doc" Charles.

PLATE 73. *Paphiopedilum villosum*.
Photograph by Emerson "Doc" Charles.

PLATE 74. *Paphiopedilum villosum* var. *annamense*.
Photograph by T. C. Lee,
courtesy of Emerson "Doc" Charles.

PLATE 75. *Paphiopedilum acmodontum*.
Photograph by Emerson "Doc" Charles.

PLATE 76. *Paphiopedilum appletonianum* 'Tip Top'.
Photograph courtesy of Emerson "Doc" Charles.

PLATE 77. *Paphiopedilum appletonianum* var. *alba*.
Photograph by Richard Topper.

PLATE 78. *Paphiopedilum appletonianum* var.
hainanense. Photograph by Richard Topper.

PLATE 79. *Paphiopedilum argus* 'Jalen' HCC/AOS.
Photograph courtesy of Emerson "Doc" Charles.

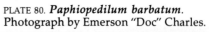

PLATE 80. *Paphiopedilum barbatum*.
Photograph by Emerson "Doc" Charles.

PLATE 81. *Paphiopedilum bougainvilleanum*.
Photograph by Richard Topper.

PLATE 82. *Paphiopedilum bullenianum*.
Photograph by Richard Topper.

PLATE 84. *Paphiopedilum callosum*.
Photograph by Emerson "Doc" Charles.

PLATE 83. *Paphiopedilum bullenianum* var. *celebesense*.
Photograph by Richard Topper.

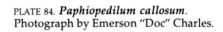

PLATE 85. *Paphiopedilum callosum* var. *sublaeve*.
Photograph by Richard Topper.

PLATE 86. *Paphiopedilum ciliolare* 'Val' AM/AOS.
Photograph courtesy of Emerson "Doc" Charles.

PLATE 87. *Paphiopedilum dayanum* 'Cerritos'.
Photograph courtesy of Emerson "Doc" Charles.

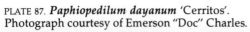

PLATE 88. *Paphiopedilum dayanum* var. *petri*, or according to some authorities, *P.* × Petri, a hybrid of *P.
dayanum*.
Photograph from the Cash-Waters collection.

PLATE 89. **Paphiopedilum dayanum** var. **burbidgei**, considered by some to be **P.** × Burbidgei, a hybrid of **P. dayanum**. Photograph by Richard Topper.

PLATE 90. **Paphiopedilum hennisianum** 'Chester Hills' CBM/AOS.
Photograph courtesy of Emerson "Doc" Charles.

PLATE 91. **Paphiopedilum hookerae**.
Photograph by Emerson "Doc" Charles.

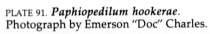

PLATE 92. **Paphiopedilum hookerae**, the form newly identified by the synonym **P. schoseri**.
Photograph by Richard Topper.

PLATE 93. ***Paphiopedilum javanicum***.
Photograph from the Cash-Waters collection.

PLATE 94. ***Paphiopedilum lawrenceanum***.
Photograph by Emerson "Doc" Charles.

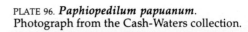

PLATE 96. ***Paphiopedilum papuanum***.
Photograph from the Cash-Waters collection.

PLATE 95. ***Paphiopedilum mastersianum***, the color form
from Ambon.
Photograph courtesy of Emerson "Doc" Charles.

PLATE 97. *Paphiopedilum purpuratum*.
Photograph by Richard Topper.

PLATE 98. *Paphiopedilum sangii*.
Photograph by Richard Topper.

PLATE 100. *Paphiopedilum superbiens*.
Photograph by Emerson "Doc" Charles.

PLATE 99. *Paphiopedilum sukhakulii*.
Photograph by Emerson "Doc" Charles.

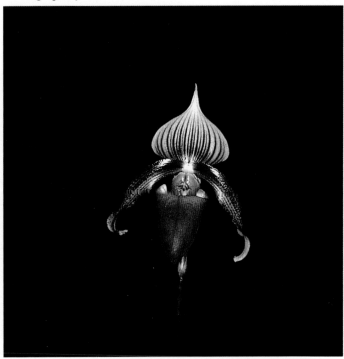

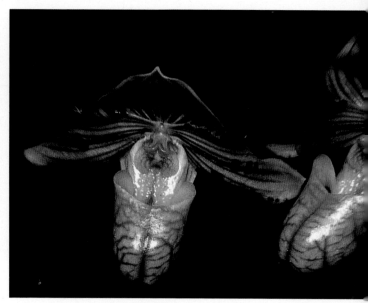

PLATE 102. *Paphiopedilum venustum*.
Photograph courtesy of Emerson "Doc" Charles.

PLATE 101. *Paphiopedilum tonsum* var. *superbum*.
Photograph by Emerson "Doc" Charles.

PLATE 104. *Paphiopedilum violascens*.
Photograph by Emerson "Doc" Charles.

PLATE 103. *Paphiopedilum venustum* var. *album*
'Winfield' AM/AOS.
Photograph courtesy of Emerson "Doc" Charles.

PLATE 105. **Paphiopedilum wardii**, Chinese form.
Photograph by Richard Topper.

PLATE 106. *Selenipedium chica*, side view showing a
number of buds in the paniculate inflorescence.
Photograph by Kerry Dressler,
courtesy of Robert Dressler.

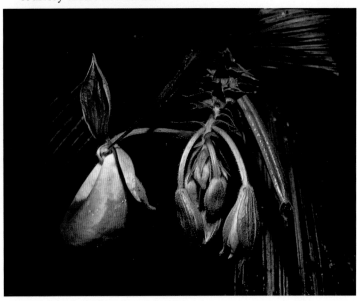

PLATE 107. *Selenipedium chica*, front view.
Photograph by Kerry Dressler,
courtesy of Robert Dressler.

PLATE 108. *Selenipedium palmifolium*.
Photograph by Lubbert Westra,
courtesy of Robert Dressler.

PLATE 109. *Phragmipedium besseae*, Peruvian form. Photograph by Frank Stermitz.

PLATE 110. *Phragmipedium besseae*, Ecuadoran form. Photograph by Frank Stermitz.

PLATE 111. *Phragmipedium schlimii*. Photograph by Louis Hegedus.

PLATE 112. *Phragmipedium lindleyanum*. Photograph by Louis Hegedus.

PLATE 114. *Phragmipedium sargentianum*.
Photograph by Frank Stermitz.

PLATE 113. *Phragmipedium lindleyanum* var. *kaieteurum*,
also described as *P. kaieteurum*.
Photograph by Frank Stermitz.

PLATE 115. *Phragmipedium caudatum* 'Stumpfle'.
Photograph by Frank Stermitz.

PLATE 116. *Phragmipedium lindenii*.
Photograph by Frank Stermitz.

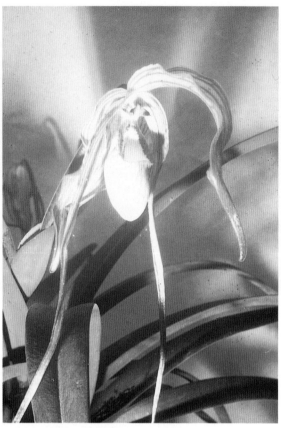

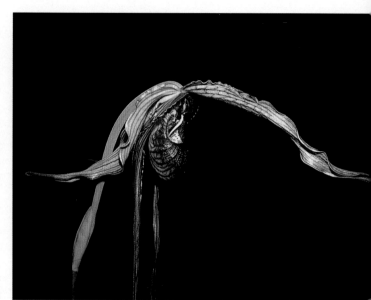

PLATE 118. *Phragmipedium warscewiczianum*.
Photograph by Frank Stermitz.

PLATE 117. *Phragmipedium wallisii*.
Photograph from the Cash-Waters collection.

PLATE 119. *Phragmipedium caricinum*.
Photograph by Frank Stermitz.

PLATE 120. *Phragmipedium klotzcheanum*, showing the
narrow, sedgelike leaf. Photograph by Louis Hegedus.

PLATE 121. *Phragmipedium pearcei*.
Photograph by Frank Stermitz.

PLATE 122. *Phragmipedium pearcei* var. *ecuadorense*, also
described as *P. ecuadorense*.
Photograph by Frank Stermitz.

PLATE 123. *Phragmipedium boissieranum*.
Photograph by Frank Stermitz.

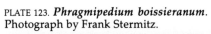

PLATE 124. *Phragmipedium boissieranum* var. *czerwiakowianum*, also described as *P. czerwiakowianum*.
Photograph by Frank Stermitz.

PLATE 125. *Phragmipedium boissieranum* var. *reticulatum*, also described as *P. reticulatum*.
Photograph by Frank Stermitz.

PLATE 126. *Phragmipedium longifolium*.
Photograph by Frank Stermitz.

PLATE 127. *Phragmipedium longifolium* var. *hartwegii*, also described as *P. hartwegii*.
Photograph by Frank Stermitz.

PLATE 128. *Phragmipedium longifolium* var. *roezlii*, also described as *P. roezlii*. Photograph by Frank Stermitz.

PLATE 129. **Phragmipedium vittatum**.
Photograph by Louis Hegedus.

PLATE 130. Phragmipaphium Hanes Magic 'Bion'
AD/AOS. **Phragmipedium** Albopurpureum ×
Paphiopedilum stonei.
Photograph courtesy of Emerson "Doc" Charles.

PLATE 131. **Paphiopedilum** Harrisianum 'G. S. Ball'. **P.
barbatum** × **P. villosum**. Photograph by John Hanes.

PLATE 132. **Phragmipedium** Sedenii. **P. schlimii** × **P.
longifolium** var. **hartwegii**.
Photograph by Frank Stermitz.

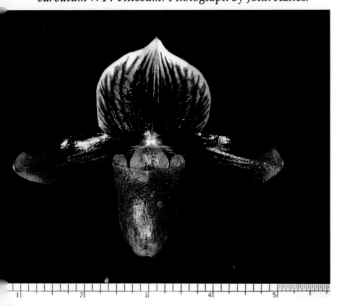

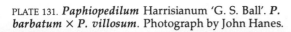

PLATE 134. *Phragmipedium* Calurum. *P. longifolium* × *P. Sedenii*. Photograph by Frank Stermitz.

PLATE 133. *Paphiopedilum* Leeanum. *P. insigne* × *P. spiceranum*.
Photograph from the Cash-Waters collection.

PLATE 135. *Phragmipedium* Grande. *P. caudatum* × *P. longifolium* var. *hartwegii*.
Photograph by Frank Stermitz.

PLATE 136. *Phragmipedium* Schroderae. *P. caudatum* × *P. Sedenii*. Photograph by Louis Hegedus.

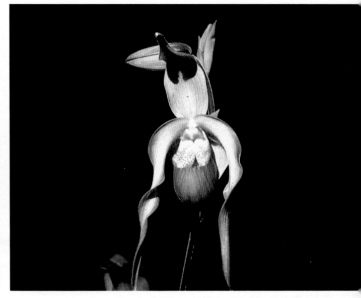

PLATE 137. **Phragmipedium** Stenophyllum. **P. caricinum × P. schlimii**. Photograph by Frank Stermitz.

PLATE 138. **Phragmipedium schlimii × sargentianum**. Photograph by Frank Stermitz.

PLATE 139. **Phragmipedium schlimii × boissieranum** var. **czerwiakowianum**. Photograph by Louis Hegedus.

PLATE 140. **Cypripedium** Genesis 'Unique'. **C. calceolus** var. **pubescens × C. reginae**. Photograph by Carson Whitlow.

PLATE 141. **Cypripedium** Promises 'Prodigious'. **C. formosanum** × **C. acaule**. Photograph by Tom Hillson, courtesy of Carson Whitlow.

PLATE 142. Believed to be **Cypripedium (corrugatum × flavum) × corrugatum**, and borne out by electrophoretic studies, the parentage of this **Cypripedium** is otherwise unconfirmed. Note the excellent distribution of color and broad, flat segments. This hybrid and some of its siblings are currently producing pods with several species of native American **Cypripedium**, according to Carson Whitlow (personal communication), who photographed this specimen.

PLATE 143. **Paphiopedilum** Maudiae 'The Queen' AM/AOS. **P. callosum** var. **sanderae** × **P. lawrenceanum** var. **hyeanum**. Photograph courtesy of John Hanes.

PLATE 144. **Paphiopedilum** Goultenianum Album 'Doug'. **P. callosum** var. **sanderae** × **P. curtisii (superbiens)** var. **sanderae**. Photograph by John Hanes.

PLATE 145. *Paphiopedilum* Alma Gevaert 'Bob'. *P. lawrenceanum* var. *hyeanum* × *P*. Maudiae. Photograph by John Hanes.

PLATE 146. *Paphiopedilum* Emerald. *P. curtisii (superbiens)* var. *sanderae* × *P*. Maudiae. Photograph from the Cash-Waters collection.

PLATE 147. Specimen plant of *Paphiopedilum* Clair de Lune 'Edgard van Belle' CCM/AOS. *P*. Emerald × *P* Alma Gevaert. Photograph courtesy of John Hanes.

PLATE 148. *Paphiopedilum* Faire-Maud 'Zinfandel' HCC/AOS. *P*. Maudiae 'Blackrock' × *P. fairrieanum* 'Red'. Photograph by John Hanes.

PLATE 149. *Paphiopedilum* Makulii 'Alba'. *P.* Maudiae × *P. sukhakulii* var. *album*. Photograph by John Hanes.

PLATE 150. *Paphiopedilum* Maudiae coloratum 'Bertch's' HCC/AOS. *P. callosum* × *P. lawrenceanum*. Photograph courtesy of John Hanes.

PLATE 151. *Paphiopedilum* Emerald 'Winesap'. *P.* Maudiae 'Ebony Queen' × *P. curtisii (superbiens)* 'Black Monarch'. Photograph by John Hanes.

PLATE 152. *Paphiopedilum* Gwenpur. *P.* Gwen Hannen × *P.* Purity. Photograph by John Hanes.

PLATE 153. *Paphiopedilum* Gowerianum 'Mrs. Leonard Dixon'. *P. curtisii (supérbiens)* var. *sanderae* × *P. lawrenceanum* var. *hyeanum*.
Photograph by John Hanes.

PLATE 154. *Paphiopedilum* Delrosi. *P. delenatii* × *P. rothschildianum*.
Photograph by Emerson "Doc" Charles.

PLATE 155. *Paphiopedilum* Neptune 'Mars' AM/AOS. *P. Io 'Grande'* × *P. rothschildianum*.
Photograph courtesy of Emerson "Doc" Charles.

PLATE 156. *Paphiopedilum* Iantha Stage 'Malvern' AM/AOS. *P. sukhakulii* × *P. rothschildianum*.
Photograph courtesy of Emerson "Doc" Charles.

PLATE 157. *Paphiopedilum* Vanguard 'Knob Creek'
AM/AOS. *P. glaucophyllum* × *P. rothschildianum*.
Photograph courtesy of Don Osborne.

PLATE 158. *Paphiopedilum* Olivia. *P. tonsum* × *P. niveum*.
Photograph by Don Osborne.

PLATE 159. *Paphiopedilum* Madame Martinet. *P. callosum*
var. *sanderae* × *P. delenatii*.
Photograph by Emerson "Doc" Charles.

PLATE 160. *Paphiopedilum* Vanda M. Pearman. *P.
delenatii* × *P. bellatulum*.
Photograph by Emerson "Doc" Charles.

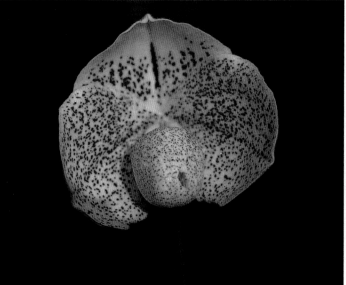

PLATE 161. **Paphiopedilum** Psyche 'Sweet Thoughts'. **P. bellatulum** × **P. niveum**. Photograph by John Hanes.

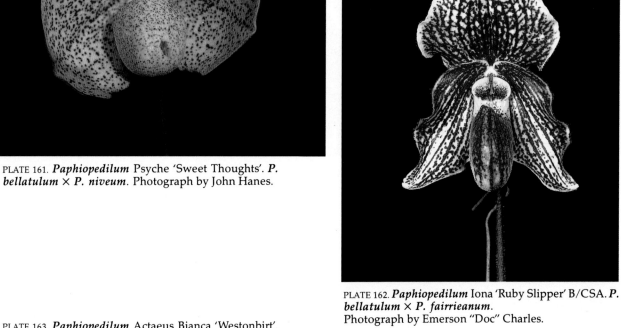

PLATE 162. **Paphiopedilum** Iona 'Ruby Slipper' B/CSA. **P. bellatulum** × **P. fairrieanum**. Photograph by Emerson "Doc" Charles.

PLATE 163. **Paphiopedilum** Actaeus Bianca 'Westonbirt'. **P. insigne** var. **sanderae** × **P.** Leeanum 'Prospero'. Photograph courtesy of John Hanes.

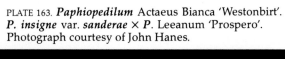

PLATE 164. **Paphiopedilum** Papa Rohl 'Prodigal' AM/AOS. **P. sukhakulii** × **P. fairrieanum**. Photograph by Emerson "Doc" Charles.

PLATE 165. **Paphiopedilum** Colorkulii 'Golden Jamboree'. **P. concolor × P. sukhakulii**. Photograph courtesy of Emerson "Doc" Charles.

PLATE 166. **Paphiopedilum** Nisqually 'Bertha Burroughs' AM/AOS. **P. appletonianum × P. sukhakulii**. Photograph courtesy of Emerson "Doc" Charles.

PLATE 167. **Paphiopedilum** Papyrus. **P. charlesworthii ×** **P**. Earl of Tankerville. Photograph by John Hanes.

PLATE 168. **Paphiopedilum** Leyburnense 'Magnificum', also named **P**. Mrs. Haywood. **P. charlesworthii × P**. T. B. Haywood. Photograph by W. W. Wilson.

PLATE 169. *Paphiopedilum* Daphne 'Penn Valley' AM/AOS. *P. exul* × *P. charlesworthii*. Photograph courtesy of W. W. Wilson.

PLATE 170. *Paphiopedilum* Woodrose 'Echo' AM/AOS. *P. charlesworthii* × *P*. Normandy. Photograph by Emerson "Doc" Charles.

PLATE 171. *Paphiopedilum* Christopher 'Grand Duke Nicholas' FCC/RHS. *P.* Actaeus 'F. H. Cann' × *P.* Leeanum 'Corona'. Photograph by W. W. Wilson.

PLATE 172. *Paphiopedilum* Chrysostum FCC/RHS. *P.* Christopher × *P.* Pyramus. Photograph by W. W. Wilson.

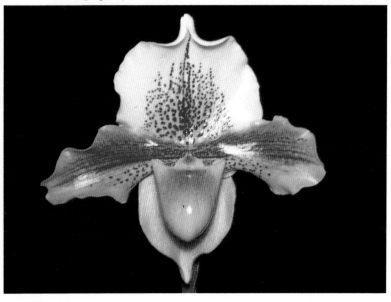

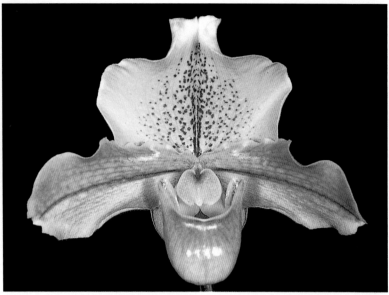

PLATE 173. ***Paphiopedilum*** Gwen Hannen 'Viridiflora'
AM/RHS. *P.* Christopher × *P.* Florence Spencer.
Photograph by W. W. Wilson.

PLATE 174. ***Paphiopedilum*** Chardmoore 'Mrs. Cowburn'.
P. Christopher 'Grand Duke Nicholas' × *P.* Lena.
Photograph by John Hanes.

PLATE 175. ***Paphiopedilum*** Perseus FCC/RHS. *P.*
Alcibiades × *P.* Lady Dillon.
Photograph by W. W. Wilson.

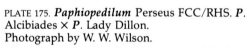

PLATE 176. ***Paphiopedilum*** Cardinal Mercier AM/RHS. *P.*
Lathamianum × ? Photograph by W. W. Wilson.

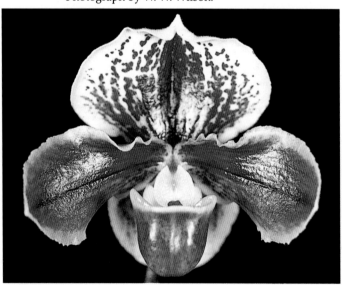

PLATE 177. *Paphiopedilum* Atlantis 'The Cardinal'. *P.* Chloris × *P.* Cardinal Mercier. Photograph by W. W. Wilson.

PLATE 178. *Paphiopedilum* F. C. Puddle 'Supurbum'. *P.* Actaeus × *P.* Astarte. Photograph by John Hanes.

PLATE 179. *Paphiopedilum* Freckles 'Pinkie'. *P.* F. C. Puddle × *P.* Burleigh Mohur. Photograph by John Hanes.

PLATE 180. *Paphiopedilum* Dimity 'Alexandra' AM/RHS. *P.* F. C. Puddle × *P.* Gorse. Photograph by Emerson "Doc" Charles.

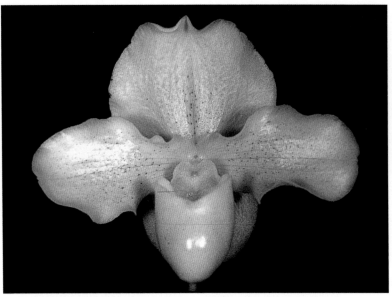

PLATE 181. ***Paphiopedilum*** Huddle 'Penn Valley' AM/AOS. ***P***. F. C. Puddle × ***P***. Hellas. Photograph courtesy of W. W. Wilson.

PLATE 182. ***Paphiopedilum*** Susan Tucker 'Sylvia'. ***P***. F. C. Puddle × ***P***. Shalimar. Photograph by Emerson "Doc" Charles.

PLATE 183. ***Paphiopedilum*** Banchory. ***P***. Dickler × ***P***. Grace Darling. Photograph by John Hanes.

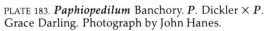

PLATE 184. ***Paphiopedilum*** Gertrude West 'Langley' AM/RHS. ***P***. Lady Phulmoni × ***P***. Robert Paterson. Photograph by W. W. Wilson.

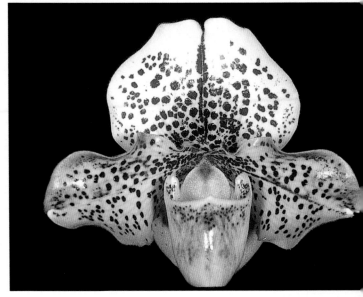

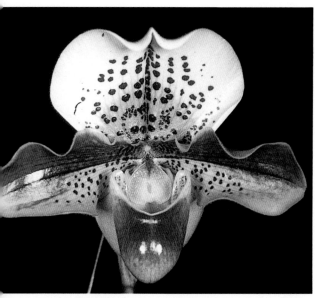

PLATE 185. *Paphiopedilum* Maori 'Oaklands' BA/OSSC. *P*. Jura × *P*. Thisbe-Beckton. Photograph by W. W. Wilson.

PLATE 186. *Paphiopedilum* Mildred Hunter, clones 'LaFayette' and 'Ileana'. *P*. Atlantis × *P*. Everest. Photograph by Emerson "Doc" Charles.

PLATE 188. *Paphiopedilum* Dusty Miller 'Mary' AM/AOS. *P*. F. C. Puddle × *P*. Chardmoore. Photograph by Emerson "Doc" Charles.

PLATE 187. *Paphiopedilum* Aladin 'Penn Valley' AM/AOS. *P. delenatii* × *P*. Atlantis. Photograph by W. W. Wilson.

PLATE 189. *Paphiopedilum* Miller's Daughter 'Prudence'
HCC/AOS. *P.* Chantal × *P.* Dusty Miller.
Photograph by Emerson "Doc" Charles.

PLATE 190. *Paphiopedilum* Dusky Maiden 'Minnehaha'
HCC/AOS. *P.* Sophomore × *P.* Susan Tucker.
Photograph by John Hanes.

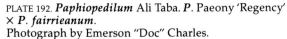

PLATE 192. *Paphiopedilum* Ali Taba. *P.* Paeony 'Regency'
× *P. fairrieanum*.
Photograph by Emerson "Doc" Charles.

PLATE 191. *Paphiopedilum* Sophomore 'Redskin', *P.
fairrieanum* var. *album*, and *P. fairrieanum* 'Princess'.
The influence of the species on *P.* Sophomore (*P.
fairrieanum* × *P.* Chardmoore) is readily seen.
Photograph by Emerson "Doc" Charles.

PLATE 193. ***Paphiopedilum*** Winston Churchill 'Indomitable' FCC/AOS, among the most prolific and reliable parents of all time, producing offspring with spotted dorsals and superb form. ***P***. Eridge × ***P***. Hampden. Photograph by W. W. Wilson.

PLATE 194. ***Paphiopedilum*** Winston Churchill 'Redoubtable' FCC/AOS, with its flare dorsal, is as impressive in every way as its sibling. Photograph by W. W. Wilson.

PLATE 196. ***Paphiopedilum*** Crazy Horse 'February' FCC/AOS. ***P***. Winston Churchill × ***P***. Hellas. Photograph by W. W. Wilson.

PLATE 195. ***Paphiopedilum*** Sioux 'Bozo' AM/AOS. ***P***. Winston Churchill × ***P***. Gigi. Photograph by W. W. Wilson.

PLATE 198. **Paphiopedilum** Amber Gold 'A'. **P**. Agnes de Burc × **P**. Winston Churchill. Photograph by John Hanes.

PLATE 197. **Paphiopedilum** Keyeshill 'Leah'. **P**. Winston Churchill 'Indomitable' × Carl Keyes 'Misfire'. Photograph by John Hanes.

PLATE 200. **Paphiopedilum** Winchilla 'Penn Valley' AM/AOS. **P**. Orchilla × **P**. Winston Churchill. Photograph by W. W. Wilson.

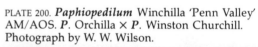

PLATE 199. **Paphiopedilum** Duncan York AQ/AOS, a selection of first-bloomed seedlings awarded as a group. **P**. Winston Churchill × **P**. Black Thorpe. Photograph by John Hanes.

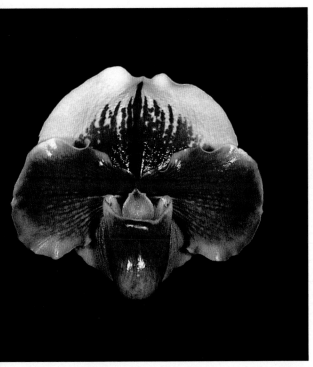

PLATE 201. ***Paphiopedilum*** Uncas 'January' AM/AOS. *P.* Winston Churchill × *P.* Mildred Hunter. Photograph by W. W. Wilson.

PLATE 202. ***Paphiopedilum*** Hellas 'Westonbirt'. *P.* Desdemona × *P.* Tania. Photograph by Emerson "Doc" Charles.

PLATE 203. ***Paphiopedilum*** Ogallala 'June' AM/AOS. *P.* Hellas × *P.* Inca. Photograph by W. W. Wilson.

PLATE 204. ***Paphiopedilum*** Paeony 'Regency' AM/RHS. *P.* Noble × *P.* Belisaire. Photograph by John Hanes.

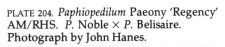

PLATE 205. *Paphiopedilum* Orchilla 'Chilton' FCC/AOS. *P.* Paeony × *P.* Redstart. Photograph by John Hanes.

PLATE 206. *Paphiopedilum* Tama 'Nittany' AM/AOS. *P.* Hellas × *P.* Paeony. Photograph by W. W. Wilson.

PLATE 207. *Paphiopedilum* Burpham 'Penn Valley' AM/AOS. *P.* Finetta × *P.* Winston Churchill. Photograph by Edward Waxman, courtesy of W. W. Wilson.

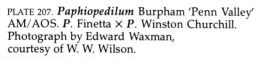

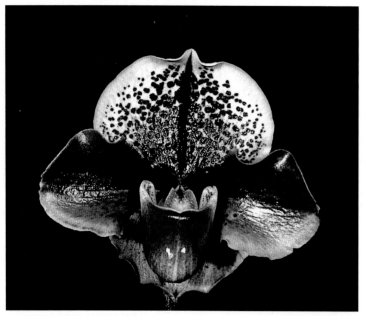

PLATE 208. *Paphiopedilum* Fairhunter 'Jennifer'. *P. fairrieanum* × *P.* Mildred Hunter. Photograph by Emerson "Doc" Charles.

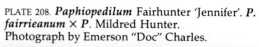

PLATE 209. *Paphiopedilum* Memoria Percy Bannerman. *P.* Evanhurst × *P. niveum*. Photograph by John Hanes.

PLATE 210. *Paphiopedilum* Pink Fantasy 'Bion'. *P.* Lelantis × *P.* Mem. Percy Bannerman. Photograph by John Hanes.

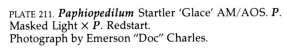

PLATE 211. *Paphiopedilum* Startler 'Glace' AM/AOS. *P.* Masked Light × *P.* Redstart. Photograph by Emerson "Doc" Charles.

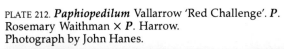

PLATE 212. *Paphiopedilum* Vallarrow 'Red Challenge'. *P.* Rosemary Waithman × *P.* Harrow. Photograph by John Hanes.

PLATE 213. ***Paphiopedilum*** Valwin 'Triumph' AM/AOS. *P.* Vallarrow × *P.* Winston Churchill. Photograph by John Hanes.

PLATE 214. ***Paphiopedilum*** Gigi 'Malibu' AM/AOS. *P.* Sheba × *P.* Momag. Photograph by John Hanes.

PLATE 215. ***Paphiopedilum*** Halo 'St. Clayton' AM/AOS. *P.* La Honda × *P.* Littledean. Photograph by John Hanes.

PLATE 216. ***Paphiopedilum*** Pittsburg 'St. John' HCC/AOS. *P.* Pittlands × *P.* Gurkley. Photograph by John Hanes.

PLATE 217. ***Paphiopedilum*** Shapely 'Geisha' HCC/AOS.
P. Pittsburg × ***P***. Diversion. Photograph by John Hanes.

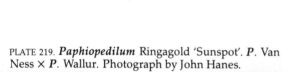

PLATE 219. ***Paphiopedilum*** Ringagold 'Sunspot'. ***P***. Van Ness × ***P***. Wallur. Photograph by John Hanes.

PLATE 218. ***Paphiopedilum*** Van Ness 'Lillian' AM/AOS. ***P***. Golden Diana × ***P***. Burleigh Mohur. Photograph by John Hanes.

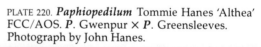

PLATE 220. ***Paphiopedilum*** Tommie Hanes 'Althea' FCC/AOS. ***P***. Gwenpur × ***P***. Greensleeves. Photograph by John Hanes.

PLATE 221. *Paphiopedilum* Sheila Hanes 'Clear Green'. *P.* Caddiana × *P.* Agnes de Burc. Photograph by John Hanes.

PLATE 222. *Paphiopedilum* Reezy 'Princess' HCC/AOS. *P.* Agnes de Burc × *P.* Denehurst. Photograph by John Hanes.

PLATE 223. *Paphiopedilum* Betty Bracey 'Springtime' AM/AOS. *P.* Gwenpur 'Symmetry' × *P.* Actaeus Bianca. Photograph by John Hanes.

PLATE 224. *Paphiopedilum* Meadowsweet 'Purity' AM/RHS. *P.* Chilton × *P.* F. C. Puddle. Photograph by John Hanes.

PLATE 225. *Paphiopedilum* Blanche Sawyer 'Snowman' AM/AOS. *P.* F. C. Puddle × *P.* Gwen Hannen. Photograph by John Hanes.

Selenipedium chica Reichb. f.   PLATES 106 & 107

GEOGRAPHIC DISTRIBUTION This species is endemic in Panama.

HABITAT *S. chica* is a terrestrial found at approximately 8° N of the equator. Panama has a fairly warm climate year-round with temperatures influenced more by elevation than by calendar; lowland temperatures average around 27°C (80°F). Humidity and rainfall are rather high, with approximately 325 cm (130 in.) of rainfall annually. Air circulation is excellent throughout the year. *S. chica* is found at 60–90 m (200–300 ft.) in the foothills northeast of Panama City and in riverine valleys of the Canal Zone.

DESCRIPTION The erect, leafy stems of this, the largest terrestrial orchid in the New World, are reported to reach a height of up to 5 m (over 16 ft.), although Robert Dressler (personal communication) states that the plants he has seen in Panama were only about 2.15 m (7 ft.) tall. The leaves measure 15–30 cm (6–12 in.) in length by 1.5–5 cm (0.6–2 in.) in width. They are lanceolate to elliptic-lanceolate; their lower surfaces are sparsely pubescent.

The many-flowered inflorescence is a terminal panicle of small slipper flowers. Each branch of the panicle as well as each flower is subtended by a bract. All portions of the flowerscape are densely pubescent. Opening in rapid succession, the flowers are quickly deciduate unless fertilized.

The overall size of the individual flower rarely exceeds 5 cm (2 in.). Sepals, petals and lip are pale pink to greenish dun in color with orange suffusion about the lip and a deep purple blotch marking the involute margins. The sepals are ovate to ovate-lanceolate and rather flat. They measure approximately 2 cm (0.75 in.) long by 1 cm (0.3 in.) wide. The synsepalum is bidentate, apically. Both sepals bear pubescence basally upon the reverse surfaces.

The petals are linear and measure up to 2 cm (0.75 in.) in length by approximately 2 mm (less than 0.1 in.) in width. The bedpan-shaped lip is simple, with involute margins. Labellar dimensions are 2–3 cm (0.75–1.2 in.) long by 1–1.8 cm (0.3–0.6 in.) wide.

Selenipedium isabelianum Barb. Rodr.

GEOGRAPHIC DISTRIBUTION The province of Para, Brazil hosts this species.

HABITAT Damp woods.

DESCRIPTION This species is small to moderate in height, ranging from 50 cm (20 in.) to 2 m (6.5 ft.). The short, woody rhizome produces 1–2 aerial stems every 1–2 years which are sub-erect, branched distally. The branches are slender; the bases of the erect leaves sheath the stems. Deep green in color, the leaves are oblong-lanceolate and acuminate. They bear short, sparse pubescence on the lower surfaces; the pubescence creates a slightly paler green color below. Strongly plicate, the lower surface of the leaves is ribbed by the prominent venation. Foliar dimensions are 17–22 cm (6.75–7.6 in.) long by 5–6 cm (2–2.3 in.) wide.

The flowers are borne in unbranched, terminal racemes. The short pedicels are pubescent. The broadly lanceolate bracts are erect and open, even reflexed. They measure up to 1.2 cm (0.5 in.) long, only about one-fourth as long as the ovaries. Apically, the bracts are acuminate; each bears short, dense pubescence upon its outer surface.

The pale yellow sepals are subequal in size, glabrous upon the front, inner surface, and pubescent upon the reverse. The dorsal sepal is both acute and reflexed apically. Sepal shape is oblongate-lanceolate. The concave ventral sepal is slightly wider and apically bidentate. Sepal dimensions are 1.2 cm (0.5 in.) long by 0.3–0.4 cm (0.25 in.) wide.

The yellowish, linear petals taper to an acute apex and are held flat or somewhat reflexed. They measure 1.5 cm (0.6 in.) in length. Short hairs emerge from the surface of the petals near the labellum; the balance of the petal surface is glabrous. The pale yellow labellum is marked laterally with golden orange spots. Dorsiventrally flattened, it is slightly blunted or even indented at the toe; its aperture is rounded. Except for a ladder of internal pollinator hairs, the pouch is glabrous. It measures 1.5 cm (0.6 in.) long by 1 cm (0.4 in.) wide. The staminode is narrowly spathulate arching out and downward; it incompletely covers the anthers and the 3 large stigmata. The capsule, measuring 4–5 cm (1.5–2 in.) long, is aromatic.

Selenipedium palmifolium (Lindl.) Reichb. f. PLATE 108

GEOGRAPHIC DISTRIBUTION This species has been reported from Trinidad, Venezuela, Guyana and Brazil.

HABITAT Habitat information is limited to the fact of its terrestrial existence in a tropical climate.

DESCRIPTION This relatively small species ranges from 50 cm (20 in.) to 2 m (6.5 ft.) in height. The aerial stems arise from a strong subterranean rhizome. Deep green lanceolate leaves are arranged alternately along the aerial stems.

The terminal raceme bears a succession of 40–50 flowers which are relatively large for the genus. Bracts subtend each flower.

The maroon-suffused dorsal sepal is broadly ovate. The synsepalum is similar, although apically bidentate and smaller. Both sepals are pubescent upon their reverse sides.

The petals are linear and acute; in color, they are similar to the sepals. The petals arch forward following the curve of the belly of the pouch. The lemon yellow to cinnabar red pouch is broad and shallow; the inner surface, where the margins infold, is marked with a blackish purple blotch.

Selenipedium steyermarkii Foldats

GEOGRAPHIC DISTRIBUTION The range of this species is restricted to the southeastern part of Venezuela, and perhaps in neighboring Guyana.

HABITAT This species prefers a loose, sandy, acid soil. It grows in fairly shady locations where it blends with the grassy foliage it so closely resembles. It is found at elevations of 1,100–1,700 m (3,800–5,800 ft.) on densely forested slopes. The early months of the year are rather dry; a cloud-forest climate with abundant rain and mist prevails for most of the rest of the year.

DESCRIPTION Aerial stems of 1–4 m (3.25–13 ft.) in height are common. Stem height appears to be a variable of the habitat; the taller stems are found where populations are surrounded by tall vegetation. Dunsterville (1971) postulates that aerial stems reach heights necessary to raise the inflorescence above the surrounding vegetation. Lanceolate leaves of 15–30 cm (6–12 in.) are arranged alternately along the aerial stems. The surfaces of both stems and leaves are pubescent.

The inflorescence emerges from the base of the terminal leaf of a mature stem. Green, pubescent and pendulous, it produces a succession of flowers each of which is subtended by a bract.

The dorsal sepal is ovate and acute; the color of the segments ranges from white blushed with pink to a dull, pastel reddish brown in hue. The similarly colored ventral sepal is bidentate apically.

The linear to linear-lanceolate petals are narrow and outspread; their color is paler and suffused with green. They measure up to 2.5 cm (1 in.) in length by only a few millimeters in width. The labellum of this species is cream-colored apically with pink or peach at the rim of the aperture. Deep rose spots mark the infolded side-lobes. Labellar dimensions are 2.5–3 cm (1–1.2 in.) in length by 2.5 cm (1 in.) in width.

The Dunstervilles (1980) punningly referred to *S. steyermarkii* as a commodious orchid, because of the bowl-shape of the lip, and the dorsal sepal which flaps down over the pouch of older flowers after the fashion of a commode lid. The apparent result of this closing of the flower is to prevent insects from entering the pouch, but it has not yet been documented that this closing occurs after pollination, nor that it is any more than a maturation feature of these flowers. Investigation into this question is needed.

Selenipedium vanillocarpum Barb. Rodr.

GEOGRAPHIC DISTRIBUTION This species comes from Brazil.

HABITAT Wooded areas.

DESCRIPTION The woody rhizome bears 1–4 erect to arching, terete stems which are sheathed by the bases of plicate leaves arising at short internodes so that they are spaced only 3–6 cm (0.75–1.5 in.) apart. Sparse glandular hairs occur upon the surface of the upper reaches of these branches, although the epidermis is glabrous basally.

The oblongate, acuminate leaves are held erect to spreading. Their venation stands out as 5 prominent ribs upon the sparsely pubescent lower surfaces. The upper surfaces of the leaves are glabrous. Leaf dimensions are 20–23 cm (8–9 in.) long by 5–6 cm (2–2.3 in.) wide.

The inflorescence is a simple, terminal raceme extending 5–7 cm (2–2.75 in.) and bearing 1 or 2 flowers. The densely pubescent peduncles recurve. The open, erect bracts are lanceolate and sharply acuminate. They measure 4–5 cm (up to 2 in.) in length, which is only one-third the length of the ovaries.

The dorsal sepal is erect, concave, oblongate and apically acute. It bears pubescence upon its reverse surface, as does the ventral sepal which is similar but slightly larger and bifid apically. The dimensions of the small dorsal sepal are 0.2–0.3 cm (0.15 in.) long by 0.1 cm (less than 0.1 in.) wide. The ventral sepal measures 1.6 cm (0.6 in.) by 0.3 cm (0.15 in).

The linear, basally attenuate, acute petals are ciliate and measure 1.5 cm (0.6 in.) long by 0.3 cm (0.1 in.) wide, with pilose apices. The veined, lilac pouch is elongate-obovate with infolded sidelobes; hooded by the dorsal sepal and longer than the ventral sepal, it measures 3–5 cm (1.25–2 in.) in length. The aperture is oblong. Barbosa Rodrigues (1937) appended a comment in French to the Latin description disclaiming knowledge of flower color for any of the segments other than the pouch, since he used a dried specimen for his description.

The capsule is arched, 3-sided (3-cornered) and covered with glandular hairs. It measures up to 35 cm (12 in.) in length at maturity. The species epithet *vanillocarpum* refers to the resemblance of the fruit to the *Vanilla* pod or bean.

FLOWERING SEASON May.

COMMON NAMES *Flor de maio*, or Mayflower, as a common name reflects the flowering season of this species. A second common name, *Baunilha*, translates from the Portuguese as Vanilla.

CHAPTER 6

The Genus *Phragmipedium*

Phragmipedium is a genus restricted to the tropics of Central and South America. Species of this genus most closely resemble *Paphiopedilum* in general appearance, including the conduplicate leaves and, superficially, the flowerscape and flowers. However, *Phragmipedium* differs from *Paphiopedilum* in several respects. Generally, the *Phragmipedium* plant habit is more grasslike with larger, more linear-lanceolate leaves held nearly erect. No tessellations mark the leaves and their color is most often bright green, although 1 section of the genus bears darker green, sedgelike leaves. The flowerscape is conspicuously jointed, typically tall, multiflowered, and in some species, branched. Frequently, a bracted node bisects the lower section of the stalk. The bracts, whether cauline or floral, are conspicuous. The flowers are borne successively with the exception of those of the section *Phragmipedium* in which 2 or more flowers open simultaneously. Perianths typically fall from the ovary while the segments appear fresh.

Less apparent differences also serve to distinguish *Phragmipedium* from *Paphiopedilum*. A trilocular ovary and axile placentation characterize the former, in contrast to the unilocular ovary with parietal placentation found in the latter. Significant differences exist between the chromosomes of the 2 genera, possibly accounting for the dearth of intergeneric hybrids. The base genome for *Phragmipedium* is probably 2n = 20, in contrast to a base genome of 2n = 26, for a typical species of *Paphiopedilum*. Furthermore, the chromosomes of *Phragmipedium* are significantly smaller than those of *Paphiopedilum*. Other more qualitative chromosomal differences are currently under investigation.

The tropical American *Phragmipedium* appear to occupy similar niches to those of the Asian *Paphiopedilum*. Both are tropical genera frequently found clinging with strong roots to steep cliffs in shaded, moist situations. Species of both survive flash-flooding down the ravines which they inhabit. Their habitats are also similar in that they provide seepage, high humidity and copious precipitation. Both genera avoid infection from fungal and bacterial organisms by clinging tenaciously to trees or near-vertical scarps where they enjoy perfect drainage. Terrestrial, lithophytic and epiphytic forms are found in both genera.

While the habitats of the 2 genera are more similar than different, the differences are not insignificant. The major difference, reflected in their culture as well, lies in the adaptation of *Phragmipedium* to a more acid pH than that preferred by the genus *Paphiopedilum*. Most species of the former prefer acid substrate and acid water, at a pH as low as 5–6, although few are considered to be at severe risk from water at a neutral 7. Dr. Louis Hegedus (personal communication) reports that when the pH of his municipal water supply was raised without notice, an entire year's production of *Phragmipedium* seedlings already in community pots died very quickly. He further notes that while the mature plants survived, they exhibited leaftip browning, only producing unmarked leaves after the pH of the water was readjusted with small quantities of acid. *Phragmipedium* culture differs further from that of *Paphiopedilum* in that, while as a general rule, the former may be grown at intermediate temperatures under the same potting and watering regimens as the latter, the culture of *Phragmipedium* exhibits these 3 important modifications: 1) no calcium carbonate is incorporated into the potting medium; 2) a slightly higher level of nutrients is provided; and 3) maintenance of medium-to-high light intensity is required. Low light intensity tends to inhibit flowering in most species. Hybrid plants exhibit remarkable vigor, providing abundant reward for very little effort on the part of the grower.

Garay (1979) organizes the genus into 5 sections consistent with the alliances observed by Pfitzer in 1903, although only 3 of Pfitzer's section names are retained. I follow Garay's sectional organization here. However, I am unable to concur with the large number of species he recognizes. His list of species is inflated primarily by minor differences in staminodal traits and through the influence of Reichenbach's view of the genus. I choose, instead, to regroup several of the taxa listed by him through subordination to variant rank. This is the "lumper's" approach to species, based upon intergradations observable between the most extreme forms, in which I concur with Dr. Louis S. Hegedus (personal communication) and others. From this perspective, the concept of variable species appears not only more reflective of the natural character of these slippers but also more indicative of the need for further study of their genetic and ecological characters to reveal the essential criteria upon which to unite or divide these slippers at species rank. These investigations began in the early 1980s with the work of Wimber (1983), and Stermitz (1980), Stermitz et al. (1981, 1983), and Stermitz and Hegedus (1984), which provided much needed insights into the genus and generally supported the case for subordination of several taxa as variants of fewer species.

The "splitter's" approach to taxonomy has created a wealth of species names merely reflecting the outdated Linnaean idea of the immutable type, but doing very little to illustrate the actual fluidity of evolutionary variance in this genus or to clarify taxonomic confusion.

I shall arbitrarily use the species name of the oldest known member of the group if possible (in some cases, 2 or more binomials date from the same year), thus reducing subsequently described taxa to the rank of variant. This approach is in accord with the *International Code of Botanical Nomenclature*. The probability that, in certain instances, the first-described taxon is an evolutionarily derived taxon rather than the stock from which related variants have evolved is obviously a matter of concern. It is, however, one which can be addressed only when more data is gathered and published from which sound conclusions can be drawn.

As I have redrawn the boundaries in this genus, the variants listed (with the exception of var. *albiflorum* of *P. schlimii*) are the same as those named by Garay (1979) at species rank. For instance, *P. lindleyanum* var. *kaieteurum* here is equivalent to Garay's *P. kaieteurum*. The taxa here have also been increased by the inclusion of *P. besseae* which was discovered since

Garay's revision of the genus in 1979. The clusters of variable species in the genus *Phragmipedium* are capable of illustrating alliances or relationships, thus more closely agreeing with the principles of population genetics. Measured morphological differences among closely related taxa in this genus are astonishingly slight, even obscure in several cases, while consisting only of intergradations in others. Therefore, rather than dealing with 22 discrete species, I shall attempt to create order among only 14 species and their variants.

The sections and the included species and variants of the genus *Phragmipedium* are:

Section *Micropetalum*
    P. *besseae* Dodson & Kuhn
    P. *schlimii* (Lindl. & Reichb. f.) Rolfe
        var. *albiflorum* Linden

Section Platypetalum
    P. *lindleyanum* (Schomb. ex Lindl.) Rolfe
        var. *kaieteurum* (N. E. Br.) Reichb. f. ex Pfitz.
    P. *sargentianum* (Rolfe) Rolfe

Section *Phragmipedium*
    P. *caudatum* (Lindl.) Rolfe
    P. *lindenii* (Lindl.) Dressler & N. Wms.
        Syn. *Uropedium lindenii* Lindl.
    P. *wallisii* (Reichb. f.) Garay
    P. *warscewiczianum* (Reichb. f.) Garay

Section *Himantopetalum*
    P. *caricinum* (Lindl. & Paxt.) Rolfe
    P. *klotzscheanum* (Reichb. f.) Rolfe
    P. *pearcei* (Reichb. f.) Rauh & Senghas
        var. *ecuadorense* Garay

Section *Lorifolia*
    P. *boissieranum* (Reichb. f.) Rolfe
        var. *czerwiakowianum* Reichb. f.
        var. *reticulatum* Reichb. f.
    P. *longifolium* (Reichb. f. & Warsc.) Rolfe
        var. *dariense* Reichb. f.
        var. *hartwegii* Reichb. f.
        var. *hincksianum* Reichb. f.
        var. *roezlii* Reichb. f.
    P. *vittatum* (Vell.) Rolfe

With regard to natural hybrids and natural pollination, once more the blank wall of ignorance is the major problem. If careful investigation is begun before the wild populations disappear, much may be learned about relationships of *Phragmipedium*, particularly with regard to the *P. longifolium* complex. These investigations are gravely needed, and haste is perhaps even more urgent in light of the inadequacy of conservation measures on behalf of this genus.

The imperative for conservation must be stressed once again, and in the most emphatic terms. Reports of clear-cutting of tropical forests in Central and South America are appalling to conservationists everywhere, but they arouse acute concerns among orchid conservationists.

In the following pages, species of *Phragmipedium* are described in some detail in the order given above. Cultural notes are not incorporated unless particular requirements pertain. Furthermore, descriptions of individual species or complexes included in this chapter do not include information on flowering season, as the tropical American *Phragmipedium* tend toward an extended flowering interval on a rather erratic schedule. Not only may most of the species initiate bloom at any time over a 6–9 month interval, continuing in flower for several months, but flowering schedules tend to shift gradually, following importation to northern hemisphere greenhouses. Therefore, data on flowering seasons would be more misleading than informative. Discussions of species do not include common names because none are in use by horticulturists.

Section *Micropetalum*

This section of 2 species is characterized by colorful overlapping sepals and petals, which, while they are not large segments, do impart roundness to the flowers. Both *P. schlimii*, the pink or rose species, and *P. besseae*, a recently discovered cinnabar red species, are variable in their color intensity. Particularly in *P. schlimii*, the clones with the richest hues are found less commonly than are the forms which exhibit paler, white-marbled segments. The 2 species included in this section are desirable, as are hybrids made from *P. schlimii*. To date, no hybrids of *P. besseae* have flowered, although unflowered seedlings are available, and anticipation is keen.

Phragmipedium besseae Dodson & Kuhn   PLATES 109 & 110

The discovery and publication of a new species of *Phragmipedium* in 1981 was a spectacular event both from the standpoint of the event itself and the unparalleled beauty of the new orchid. It is a source of amazement that an orchid of such vivid color should have escaped detection for so many years.

Hegedus and Stermitz (1986) report an extended blooming season from May through October on a rescued and revitalized plant from the original collection. Although they further report self-sterility and failure to set hybrid pods using the pollen of this particular clone of *P. besseae*, there are seedlings in flask at this writing. Anticipation runs high among orchidists at the prospects awaiting.

GEOGRAPHIC DISTRIBUTION This species is native to Peru and Ecuador. There is a distinctive difference in the petals of the specimens from the 2 populations, so that collections from each locale are readily recognizable. See Plates 109 and 110 and the description below.

HABITAT Living as a lithophyte on granite or as a terrestrial in gritty soil, *P. besseae* grows at 1,100 m (3,800 ft.) in the eastern foothills of the Andes in north central Peru. It receives semi-shade from shrubby growth and evergreens. Temperatures in the region are subtropical. Annual precipitation is rather high; seepage supplies moisture to the roots during dry periods. No details of the Ecuadoran habitat have been forthcoming.

DESCRIPTION: The dark green leaves are subsucculent, and measure up to 22 cm (8.6 in.) in length by 4 cm (1.6 in.) in width.

The erect, pubescent inflorescence bears 1–6 flowers in succession. The flowers consist of concolor segments of striking cinnabar red; pubescence occurs on all segments. Overall measurements of the flower are 6 cm (2.3 in.) wide by 5 cm (2 in.) vertically.

The dorsal sepal is ovate, apically obtuse, and slightly concave. Its base is fused with the base of the synsepalum. The dorsal measures approximately 2.5 cm (1 in.) in length by 1.5 cm (0.6 in.) in width. The broader synsepalum is bidentate and bicarinate; it, too, is slightly concave.

The flat petals are held horizontally. Ovate with obtuse or acute apices, they measure 3 cm (1.2 in.) long by 2 cm (0.75 in.) wide. They overlap the sepals, giving roundness to the flower shape. The color is arranged in stripes of pale and deep cinnabar. There is a distinct difference in the petals of populations from Peru and those of Ecuadoran natives. Peruvian plants have much wider petals for an overall appearance of a rounder, fuller flower. Conversely, the Ecuadoran flower is more star-shaped with slender, pointed segments. In both cases, the lip is ovoid with a pointed toe. Striping of varying intensity also marks the lip. The very small labellar orifice is subrectangular and marked with deep red spots upon the involute margins. The pouch exhibits translucent fenestrae; these windows permit light to illuminate the bowl of the labellum, in much the same way as is true of *Cypripedium irapeanum* from Mexico. Such parallelism between divergent groups of the subfamily is always of interest to botanists.

Phragmipedium schlimii (Lindl. & Reichb. f.) Rolfe   PLATE 111

Phragmipedium schlimii has several unusual reproductive features including its large genome (2n = 30), a tendency toward autogamy (self-fertility), self-sterility, and in some undesirable clones, cleistogamy (self-fertilization within a closed bud). Cleistogamous clones are, of course, horticulturally worthless. If possible, *P. schlimii* should be purchased while in flower. This facilitates selection of forms with excellent color and averts the purchase of cleistogamous specimens. Self-fertility and self-sterility occur quite commonly within this species in flowers which open normally. The cause and effect involved has yet to be elucidated.

On the other hand, fertile clones of *P. schlimii* are valued for their remarkable fecundity; many worthy selfings and hybrids have been produced from this species. However, because it is an evolutionary dead end for the species, the frequency of self-fertility is a major negative feature.

Atwood (1984b) and Wimber (1983) among others have studied the chromosomes of this species and given the genome as 2n = 30. Atwood illustrates the peculiarly squared shape of these chromosomes; the centromeres are obscure, as are the arms themselves, leaving the investigator stymied in his efforts to compare them with the chromosomes of other species in the genus. Thus, this species, which possesses the largest number of chromosomes in the genus, gives little indication as to how the additional chromosomes originated.

GEOGRAPHIC DISTRIBUTION *P. schlimii* is native to Colombia.

HABITAT Steep slopes on both the eastern and western flanks of the Andean Cordillera at elevations near 1,300 m (4,500 ft.).

DESCRIPTION: The leaves are bright green, measuring 23–30 cm (9–12 in.) in length by 2.5–5 cm (1–2 in.) in width.

The jointed, pubescent inflorescence reaches heights of up to 30 cm (12 in.) or more; it typically produces secondary branches. A bract subtends each of the 2–6 flowers. The pubescent flowers, which are borne successively, are pale to rich pink, measuring up to 5 cm (2 in.). Var. *albiflorum* is virtually pure white. Veitch (1889), reports that var. *albiflorum* originates on the western slopes of the Cordillera, while the colored forms are collected from the eastern slopes. Because the intensity of color is such a highly variable characteristic, the actual veracity of 2 distinct taxa is highly questionable. It is more likely that intergrading forms exist broadening the species description to include a color range from deep lavender pink through pearl white.

The keeled dorsal sepal is ovate to subcircular and concave. Its acute apex hoods the pouch orifice to some degree. Typically flushed with a rather uniform pink color throughout, it measures approximately 1.5–2 cm (0.6–0.75 in.) in either dimension. The ventral sepal is similar, although somewhat larger and more broadly ovate. Proximally, the ventral sepal is flushed with green; pink suffuses the distal portion in many clones, while the typical synsepalum is greenish white.

The petals are ovate, overlapping the sepals to create a pleasantly rounded flower. Proximally, rose spotting adorns the petals, while typically the entire petal is suffused to some degree with pink or rose. Petal dimensions are 2–2.5 cm (0.75–1 in.) in length by up to 2 cm (0.75 in.) in width. The labellum is spheroid to ellipsoid, densely mottled with rose over a white or pink ground in the typical flower. The infolded margins are heavily spotted with rose or maroon about the near-circular aperture. The staminode is a beautiful feature of this slipper; it is rich golden yellow centrally, bearing a white margin and a large butterfly-shaped blotch of maroon basally.

There is a strong but superficial resemblance between this flower and that of *Paphiopedilum delenatii*, a resemblance which must be viewed as no more than a striking example of convergent evolution.

Section *Platypetalum*

Platypetalum, the flat-petalled *Phragmipedium*, is a section comprised of 2 species and 1 variant, which bear narrow spathulate petals that are approximately twice as long as the sepals although only about half as wide.

Phragmipedium lindleyanum (Schomb. ex Lindl.) Rolfe   PLATES 112 & 113

This species and var. *kaieteurum* (N. E. Br.) Reichb. f. ex Pfitz. are sympatric taxa. Garay (1979) states that they are divisible on the criteria of staminodal differences, leaf color and shape, and flower color. Because of intergrading forms with an overlapping range, it appears logical to subordinate the more recent taxon as a variant. The leaves of *P. lindleyanum* are longer and margined with yellow, while those of var. *kaieteurum* are solid green and shorter; both are strap-shaped. However, habitat differences, particularly in light intensity, produce substantial differences in leaf length and color. The differences in flower color are quite subtle. A small degree of intensity marks the difference between maroon petal margins or rosy margins; this variance, together with the presence or absence of a bronze cast to the labellum and some variability in quantity and intensity of spotting, are well within the parameters of variation found within a species. Similarly, staminodal variations consist of subtle differences in shape, and do not exceed ordinary levels of variability within a species. See plates 112 and 113 for comparisons.

The scantiness of the morphological differences, coupled with the evidence provided by the work of Stermitz, et al. (1981), which showed identical alkaloids in these variants (with a significantly different result for *P. sargentianum*), provides sufficient grounds for reducing *P. kaieteurum* to varietal status within *P. lindleyanum*, while maintaining *P. sargentianum* as a separate species.

GEOGRAPHIC DISTRIBUTION Both species and variant are indigenous to Guyana and have been reported from neighboring Venezuela as well.

HABITAT Found at 3,000 m (10,300 ft.), on eastward-facing, rocky cliffs in the Kanuku Mountains, the most vigorous colonies of this species inhabit detritus-filled clefts of tree roots, where they receive semishade. Cool breezes maintain constant air circulation. Full sun is received until about 10 A.M.; 60% shade prevails during the balance of the day. Seepage trickling down granite scarps provides constant moisture to the roots. Mats of filamentous algae grow in profusion amidst the seepage channels; amine solutions and other algal metabolites percolating into the seepage flow provide a source of nitrogen-enriched nutrients. Both the humus and the water supply are quite acid. A few plants are found growing epiphytically alongside streams which flood during the July–September rainy season.

It is important to note that colonies of less robust plants often grow nearby in a somewhat less hospitable habitat. These shorter-leaved plants, growing in full sun, bear smaller flowers.

Temperatures range from 26° C (78° F) during the day to 18° C (66° F) at night. Dense mists occur during late evening and early morning.

DESCRIPTION: Leaves of this species reach lengths of 45–60 cm (18–24 in.) and widths of 7.5 cm (3 in.). The leaves may be uniform rich green or bordered with yellow green, depending upon the variant observed.

The erect, pubescent inflorescence is branched and reaches heights of up to 1 m (39.3 in.). A succession of up to 30 flowers, each subtended by a bract, is borne over an extended flowering period. The flowers appear rather small for the height of the inflorescence. Overall flower measurements rarely exceed 7 cm (2.75 in.).

The dorsal sepal is green and typically veined with rose. Ovate to elliptic in shape and apically acute, it measures 4 cm (1.6 in.) long by 1.8 cm (0.75 in.) wide. The apical margin curls forward to a variable degree. The synsepalum is similarly colored; its dimensions are 3 cm (1.2 in.) in length by 2.5 cm (1 in.) in width. The outer surfaces of both sepals bear pubescence, while the entire flower bears very little pubescence upon the open faces of the segments.

The linear-lanceolate, arcuate petals are bluntly rounded apically; both the superior and inferior margins are undulate and hirsute. The petals may exhibit some twisting. The ground color is pale green proximally; reddish veins and margins blend distally to form a rosy or maroon apical flush, depending upon the variant. The pouch is elongate and roundly inflated at the toe, with a circular aperture. The toe of the pouch tends to be not only glabrous but to bear a high sheen. Pouch color ranges from green flushed with bronze in var. *kaieteurum* to golden yellow veined with amber in the type. Maroon spotting adorns the pale infolded side-lobes of both variants.

Phragmipedium sargentianum (Rolfe) Rolfe
PLATE 114

GEOGRAPHIC DISTRIBUTION The Pernambuco district of Brazil hosts this species.

HABITAT Growing in streamside peat bogs on the slopes of the Organ Mountains, this species inhabits a region approximately 10° south of the equator. Elevations of 850–950 m (2,800–3,200 ft.) suffice to moderate temperatures to the 20–30° C (68–85° F) range. Afternoon shade is provided by deciduous forests and shrubs on the preferred east-facing slopes. Rainfall in the area is moderate; however, seepage, mists and dew provide abundant water to colonies of this species. The water of the streams is quite acid, as is the humus in which *P. sargentianum* roots. Air movement is excellent. De Ghillany (1972) reports wild specimens in bud and flower in July and August.

DESCRIPTION: The green leaves are margined with yellow; they reach lengths of 20–45 cm (8–18 in.) and widths of 5–7.5 cm (2–3 in.).

The erect inflorescence extends to 1.3 m (50 in.) or more and bears 2–5 small flowers in succession. Each flower is subtended by a bract.

The concave dorsal sepal measures 3 cm (1.2 in.) long by 1.5 cm (0.6 in.) wide. Elliptic-lanceolate in shape, its apex is obtuse; the apical margin is involute. The ground color of the dorsal is pale cream green, heavily veined with maroon. The synsepalum is similar in color; it is broadly ovate to subcircular in shape and measures 2.8 cm (1 in.) long by 2.5 cm (1 in.) wide.

The petals are slender with bluntly rounded apices. The margins are undulate and shortly hirsute. Proximally and mesially, the ground color is cream green; the margins and distal half are veined and suffused with maroon. The petals are held at approximately 45° off horizontal; they measure 5 cm (2 in.) long by 1 cm (0.3 in.) wide. The labellum is buff-colored, veined with red and densely spotted with red over the infolded side-lobes. It is elongate, up to 3.5 cm (1.3 in.) long, with a subrectancular orifice.

Section *Phragmipedium*

Flowers produced by the 4 species in this section are characterized by extremely elongated petals which continue their elongation for several days past full anthesis. The second unique feature of this section is the concurrent anthesis of 2–4 flowers per scape. The petals may serve as a ramp for pollinators, but no supporting evidence for this function is available. The petals of *Paphiopedilum sanderanum*, which elongate to a similar degree, are considered an example of parallel evolution.

Garay (1979) makes an excellent case on geographic criteria for maintaining the 4 discrete species he recognizes in this section. The karyotypic data indicates that the genome of this section is 2n = 28; however, these studies have revealed no basis for determination of species rank for the taxa studied. The results of studies by Stermitz et al. (1981), employing techniques of thin-layer chromatography and spectroscopy of the alkaloid content of these taxa, are inconclusive and show 1 factor where *P. wallisii* and *P. lindenii* are indeed closely related as Garay indicates. However, data on 1 clone of *P. caudatum* is suspect by the investigators, while the remaining data shows a shared lack of alkaloids in both *P. caudatum* and *P. warscewiczianum*. Until more data is produced, the grounds for establishing 2 complexes are no more conclusive than those for recognizing 4 species. There is little evidence to support the former position that all 4 taxa in this section are variants of a single species, *P. caudatum*. Therefore, Garay's recognition of 4 separate species, based largely upon the discrete geographic ranges of the 4 taxa, is the logical conclusion at this time with respect to this section, although nearer affinities appear to exist between pairs of these species. That is, *P. caudatum* and *P. warscewiczianum* have more morphological and physiological characteristics in common, as *P. lindenii* and *P. wallisii* likewise have with each other. Certainly the section is a well-defined one with a high degree of similarity and unity among the 4 member species.

Habitat information and cultural notes given for *P. caudatum* apply as well to all 4 species in this section.

Phragmipedium caudatum (Lindl.) Rolfe   PLATE 115

GEOGRAPHIC DISTRIBUTION The range of this species is limited to localized sites in Ecuador, Peru, and possibly Colombia.

HABITAT This species is typically lithophytic on granite cliffs where it roots in mosses associated with seepage channels at elevations of 2,000–3,000 m (6,900–10,300 ft.). It receives bright shade to full sun and tolerates bright light very well. It prefers north- and east-facing exposures, where light is at a maximum below the equator.

The warm, rainy season extends from November through April with daytime temperatures up to 22° C (80° F), while nighttime temperatures descend to around 13° C (55° F). Winter is drier and cooler extending from May through October with temperatures dropping to 5–7° C (40–45° F) at night. Relative humidity exceeds 50% at all times.

Amine solutions, resulting from the metabolism of algae associated with sedge plants situated higher up on the cliffs, provide nitrogen-rich nutrition as a constituent of the seepage water.

Fowlie (1972) reports that the species flowers in April and May, in the wild, and that it may produce a second season of bloom in October. Following importation into Northern Hemisphere greenhouses, however, the flowering schedules may alter or not.

CULTURAL NOTES *P. caudatum* thrives in a wooden or wire mesh basket hanging in bright light. Hanging not only encourages flowering, but serves to maximize elongation of the petals as well, for it has been observed that petal elongation ceases once the petal tip makes contact with any surface such as foliage or a bench top. Manipulation of petals to prevent contact with obstructive surfaces during the days immediately following anthesis insures maximum elongation and symmetry of the petals.

DESCRIPTION The large, green leaves achieve lengths of 60–90 cm (24–36 in.) and are held semierect.

The inflorescence is glabrous and bright green extending to nearly 1 m (approx. 40 in.) in height. Pedicels of individual flowers reach lengths of up to 15 cm (6 in.) or more. The 2–4 long-lasting flowers open within a few days of each other. This species is spectacular despite the muted colors of its perianth.

The dorsal sepal is cream-colored and exhibits reticulate venation varying from rich maroon through buff to green. Lanceolate and acute, it measures up to 20 cm (7 in.) in length, by 2.5–3 cm (1–1.2 in.) in width. It droops far forward over the pouch aperture, extending well down in front of and below the entire pouch. Its margins are undulate and involute apically. The ventral sepal is similar, although nearly one and one-half times as large as the dorsal.

The elongate petals of *P. caudatum* are the unique features of the entire section, the tails which inspired its specific epithet. At anthesis, the petals are already up to 15 cm (6 in.) in length. Over the succeeding 4–10 days, elongation continues so that lengths of up to 75 cm (30 in.) are typically reached providing growth is unimpeded. Petal width is less than 2.5 cm (1 in.) proximally; the elongate linear tails are ribbonlike, only a few millimeters in width. Proximally the margins are crisply undulate, while the color is similar to that of the dorsal; distally the extended ribbons are deep rose to magenta in color. The pouch is elongate and roundly inflated at the toe; its aperture is sub-triangular. Measuring up to 6 cm (2.3 in.) or more in length, the buff-colored pouch is suffused and veined with chestnut brown. The rim of the aperture is richly colored with maroon and contrasts vividly with the infolded side-lobes of ivory white.

Phragmipedium lindenii (Lindl.) Dressler & N. Wms. PLATE 116

This peloric species with 3 petals and no pouch makes a distinctive departure in form from the pouched flower typical of the subfamily. In 1846 Lindley created a separate genus for it naming it *Uropedium lindenii*. In the years following Lindley's description, it was reclassified as a variant of *Phragmipedium caudatum*. However, this unique, peloric taxon, so divergent from the typical 2 petals and a lip of the subfamily, was scrutinized carefully by Garay (1979), who pointed out that while populations of *P. lindenii* produce the occasional anomalous, normally pouched flower, they never interphase in habitat with populations of other taxa in this section. Furthermore, the anomalous, normal flower is in all morphological features identical to *P. wallisii* (also formerly identified as a variant of *P. caudatum*, but having its own discrete geographic range as well as certain morphological distinctions from that latter taxon which are discussed below). The results of investigations of the alkaloid content of taxa in this section performed by Stermitz et al. (1981) correlate *P. lindenii* with *P. wallisii* and further substantiate the assumption that *P. lindenii* is discrete from *P. caudatum* which is believed deficient in alkaloids. Presently, the data appears insufficient to warrant merging *P. lindenii* into *P. wallisii* given the counter evidence of the mutual exclusivity of populations of the 2 taxa. Therefore, species rank for this taxon is currently the correct rationale.

GEOGRAPHIC DISTRIBUTION *P. lindenii* has been reported throughout Venezuela, Colombia and Ecuador.

HABITAT The habitats of the 4 taxa in section *Phragmipedium* are rather similar. Elevations vary within a species as within the section. See habitat information under *P. caudatum*, as well as the cultural notes for that species.

DESCRIPTION The large green leaves of this species measure up to 50 cm (20 in.) in length.

The erect inflorescence bears 2–4 flowers simultaneously and extends to 1 m (39.3 in.) in height. Pubescence is lacking on the peduncle and pedicels. The pale flowers are buff to yellow green in color.

The dorsal sepal hoods the exposed column. Typically in *P. lindenii* and *P. wallisii*, it does not obscure the entire frontal aspect of the flower as it does in *P. caudatum* and *P. warscewiczianum*, extending only about half as long as the dorsals of the latter 2 species. The dorsal measures 7.5–10 cm (3–4 in.) or more in length. Its cream ground color is marked with reticulate venation in amber or green. The proximal margins exhibit undulations; apically the margins are involute. The synsepalum is quite similar, although somewhat larger.

This species demonstrates peloria in its possession of 3 petals as opposed to 2 petals and a pouch. All 3 petals elongate in the same way. The peloric reversion of the pouch to expression as a petal is an anomaly which is observed occasionally among complex *Paphiopedilum* hybrids and more rarely in species of *Paphiopedilum* and *Cypripedium*.

The winglike staminode and the column which is partially hidden behind the staminode both stand free from the otherwise flat-to-concave proximal perianth, giving this member of the Cypripedioideae a most uncharacteristic appearance. This species bears 3 fertile anthers rather than the 2 typical of the subfamily. The third fertile anther is located beneath the column. Along with its staminode as a sterile anther, the anther count rises to 4 in number—an extremely rare occurrence among monocotyledonous species. Four anthers and 3 stigmata may be found also in *Cypripedium reginae*; this condition is anomalous and worthy of the attention of phylogenists. Although more an example of parallel evolution than evidence of kinship, this staminate condition, along with the presence of 3 stigmata in these 2 disparate taxa, is of phylogenetic import in that these features may be considered both primitive and tenaciously transitional in structures that are typically quite conservatively stable in the more modern majority of the Cypripedioideae. Furthermore, in association with the peloric petal condition, the primitive column underscores the close relationship of petals to stamens as well as a similar behavioral affinity between stamens and stigmata. Induction of such anomalous flower parts is obviously originated early in the formative stages of the bud, during differentiation of meristem cells, probably by a single initiator.

The 3 pendulous, ribbonlike petals reach a length of up to 1 m (39.3 in.) if permitted to elongate free of impediment. The width proximally is 2 cm (0.75 in.), while the elongate portions are no more than a few millimeters in width. Petal color is pale green proximally; veins of maroon coalesce to produce rosy maroon tails, distally. Proximal margins are undulate.

Phragmipedium wallisii (Reichb. f.) Garay   PLATE 117

GEOGRAPHIC DISTRIBUTION This species is known from a small strip of southern Ecuador along Rio Zamora.

HABITAT *P. wallisii* is a terrestrial. Refer to habitat and culture notes in the discussion of *P. caudatum*.

DESCRIPTION Morphologically the difference between *P. wallisii* and *P. lindenii* is that of a pouch or a petal. See the description of *P. lindenii*, above.

The leaves measure up to 50 cm (20 in) long by 3.5 cm (1.3 in.) wide. The erect scape produces 2–3 simultaneous flowers of creamy green and buff coloration.

The lanceolate dorsal sepal is apically acute with undulate margins. It curves forward deeply over the pouch without completely obscuring a frontal view. It measures 10–11 cm (4–4.3 in.) long by 2 cm (0.75 in.) wide. The apically acuminate ventral sepal is broadly lanceolate, measures up to 10 cm (4 in.) long and 3.5 cm (1.2 in.) wide, and has undulate margins.

Basally the petals measure up to 1.5 cm (0.6 in.) wide; they immediately taper to a slender, pubescent filament which extends with undulations for up to 50 cm (20 in.). *P. wallisii* with its normal flower possesses the lateral 2 of the long ribbonlike petals and a pouch. The pouch is creamy white at the toe, flushed with yellow toward the rim, and striped with tan. The yellow color persists inside the pouch rim as a narrow border that is subtended by chestnut or maroon spotting. Below this border the side-lobes are ivory white. The pouch may be up to 5 cm (2 in.) long.

Phragmipedium warscewiczianum (Reichb. f.) Garay   PLATE 118

GEOGRAPHIC DISTRIBUTION Colombia and parts of Central America host this species.

HABITAT This species has been collected from 1,200 m (4,100 ft.) on granite cliff faces. See *P. caudatum* for further habitat information as well as cultural notes.

DESCRIPTION The leaves are large and dark green. They measure 50–60 cm (20–24 in.) in length.

The erect inflorescence bears 2–4 flowers simultaneously at a height of up to 1 m (39.3 in.). The inflorescence is glabrous throughout.

The lanceolate dorsal sepal is buff to greenish yellow. Its margins are undulate and apically involute. Distally the dorsal droops forward so that it not only hoods the pouch but obscures a frontal view of the flower. It measures 5–6 cm (2–2.3 in.) in length and approximately 2 cm (1.75 in.) in width. The ventral sepal is similar although broader.

If unimpeded, the petals continue to elongate for up to 7 days after full anthesis, extending up to 90 cm (36 in.). Proximally the petal width is approximately 1.5 cm (0.6 in.). It tapers to a very narrow ribbon beyond the proximal 7.5 cm (3 in.). The petals are similar in color to the sepals with maroon veins proximally, while the color suffusing the tails deepens from rose to maroon distally. The pouch is elongate, inflated, and slightly pointed at the toe. It measures approximately 5 cm (2 in.) long. Its color is shell pink to buff yellow with faint chestnut stripes and a yellow border around the aperture. The yellow border continues just inside the rim, but stops off sharply with a line of vivid maroon dots. The involute side-lobes below the dots are ivory white.

Uropedium lindenii Lindl. See *P. lindenii* (Lindl.) Dressler & N. Wms.

Section *Himantopetalum*

Both the remaining sections of the genus *Phragmipedium* require further study and clarification as to how the evolutionary process might have produced the existing taxa.

The characteristics of section *Himantopetalum* are: 1) petals 2–3 times longer than sepals; and 2) an entire margin on the pouch orifice. (Section *Lorifolia* is distinguished from this group by the pair of horns which protrude on the lateral rims of the pouch orifice.) This section is also distinguished by sedgelike leaves.

Among the species within section *Himantopetalum*, there are clear distinguishing features. *Phragmipedium klotzscheanum* bears pubescence upon scape and ovary, but none on its petals. The other 2 species have glabrous scapes and ovaries with pubescent petals. *P. caricinum* is distinguished from the other 2 species by the length of its dorsal sepal which exceeds that of the synsepalum. While both *P. pearcei* and its variant *ecuadorense* possess ventral sepals longer than their dorsals and similar coloration, they are distinguished from each other largely by the degree of undulation and twisting of their petals. The petals of *P. pearcei* exhibit crisply undulate margins and 3 or more full helices, while the petals of var. *ecuadorense* display both qualities to a lesser degree. The staminodes of these 2 variants vary both in shape and in the amount and distribution of ciliation. However, not only are the morphological differences between these latter 2 taxa rather small, but their geographic distribution is similar. If the 2 are sympatric, intergrading forms should exist; also the degree of divergence should be biochemically measurable. Stermitz et al. (1981) showed that, while *P. pearcei* contains a high alkaloid content, var. *ecuadorense* is negative for alkaloids, thus upholding physiological grounds for separating them at equal species rank. However, physiological/biochemical evidence for separating var. *ecuadorense* from *P. pearcei* at full species rank is effectively counterbalanced by the intermediate forms which link the extremes to each other. These intergrading forms appear to have an intermediate geographic range which corresponds to and correlates their morphological range, according to Dr. Louis Hegedus (personal communication).

Karyotypic studies of the species of this section show 20 or 22 chromosomes as the diploid genome. Since different clones identified as each of these same variants exhibited both genomes, the karyotypic evidence is less useful than it may be after study of larger samples.

Phragmipedium caricinum (Lindl. & Paxt.) Rolfe   PLATE 119
GEOGRAPHIC DISTRIBUTION This species is native to Bolivia and Peru.
HABITAT A montane species of the Andean highlands, its habitat is poorly documented.
DESCRIPTION The linear leaves are dark green and sedgelike (*Carex*, a genus of sedges, provides the root for the species epithet, *caricinum*). The leaves measure 30–45 cm (12–18 in.) long by only 1–1.5 cm (0.3–0.6 in.) wide.

The inflorescence achieves heights of 30 cm (12 in.) or more; 3–6 flowers are borne successively over an extended period of time. Overall flower measurements rarely exceed 7 cm (2.75 in.) vertically.

The dorsal sepal typically recurves its lateral margins. It is obovate-lanceolate and acute. Its length is 3–4 cm (1.2–1.6 in.), while its width is 2 cm (0.75 in.). The ground color is pale tan to yellow green. Faint stripes of maroon and a rosy maroon suffusion of the distal portion are reported, although apple green venation is more typical. The synsepalum is somewhat broader and shorter than the dorsal, but similar in color.

The pendulous, ribbonlike petals are tan with maroon stripes; the distal portions are suffused with maroon. The petals are typically twisted through 3 full spirals. Petal length, as in all species except those in section *Phragmipedium*, is fully developed at anthesis and measures approximately 8–9 cm (3.2–3.5 in.). The labellum is yellow green with amber venation and flushing near the rim. The ivory side-lobes are bordered with yellow and spotted with maroon.

Phragmipedium klotzscheanum (Reichb. f.) Rolfe   PLATE 120
GEOGRAPHIC DISTRIBUTION Guyana and Venezuela are the host countries for this species.
HABITAT Known from the Roraimo and Pakaraimo mountains, this species is found at elevations of 300–1,000 m (1,000–3,400 ft.) along river valleys. Colonies receive full sun to semishade and prefer an eastern exposure. Constant moisture is supplied by spray from waterfalls, mists and the riparian habitat which is typical of this species. Because of its preference for streambank habitats, this species is periodically submerged by intervals of flash flooding. The roots anchor in loose, gravelly sands and trap detritus borne along by

stream currents. Temperatures reach highs of 32° C (90° F) during the daytime, falling to 18° C (65° F) overnight. Constant air movement is a feature of the habitat.

DESCRIPTION The slender, sedgelike leaves are dark green in color and measure 30–37.5 cm (12–15 in.) in length.

The erect inflorescence is pubescent. It bears 2–6 successive flowers at a height of up to 60 cm (24 in.).

The lanceolate dorsal sepal measures 5 cm (2 in.) in length by up to 2 cm (0.75 in.) in width. It is rather flat and leans forward over the pouch. Its ground color of pale greenish tan is overlaid with stripes of maroon. The ovate ventral sepal is similar in ground color but only faintly striped with maroon. It measures 4 cm (1.6 in.) in length by 2.5 cm (1 in.) in width.

The pendulous, linear petals reach lengths of 10 cm (4 in.) or more. They are typically twisted through 2 full spirals. In color and markings, they are similar to the dorsal sepal. The elongate pouch is roundly inflated at the toe. Rich yellow in color, the margins of the orifice are spotted with maroon. The side-lobes are ivory white within.

Phragmipedium pearcei (Reichb. f.) Rauh & Senghas   PLATES 121 & 122

Intermediate forms exist which closely link the variant extremes—the apparently divergent taxa which were identified as separate species by Garay (1978, 1979). Therefore, in light of these intermediate forms, it seems best to include var. *ecuadorense* Garay within *Phragmipedium pearcei*. Dr. Louis S. Hegedus (personal communication) reports that there is also an atypical large-flowered clone, heavily marked with dark red pigmentation, which is currently identified as *P. pearcei*.

GEOGRAPHIC DISTRIBUTION These slippers come from Ecuador and Peru.

HABITAT This terrestrial species has been collected from imprecise localities growing on vertical cliffs over water. Var. *ecuadorense* is frequently epiphytic.

DESCRIPTION *P. pearcei* achieves heights of up to 25 cm (10 in.) and bears arching leaves. Var. *ecuadorense* stands up to 45 cm (18 in.). The erect inflorescence bears 2–4 large showy flowers in succession, each of which is subtended by a bract.

The ovate dorsal sepal is acuminate apically. Green veins line the white ground; the margins are typically flushed pink in the type. The dorsal measures 3.5 cm (1.3 in.) long by 1 cm (0.3 in.) wide. The synsepalum is ovate and apically obtuse, measuring 3.4 cm (1.3 in.) long by 2.4 cm (1 in.) wide. It is similar in color to the dorsal. The pink flushing of the type is absent from the sepals of var. *ecuadorense*, although intermediate color forms link the 2 variants.

The broadly linear petals bear a thickened apex. Pubescence is restricted to the region proximal to the column and to the margins and apices. Petal color is greenish yellow proximally, while the margins become flushed with purple distally. The petals measure 6 cm (2.5 in.) long by 0.8 cm (0.3 in.) wide. Both variants hold the petals in a pendent attitude; marginal crisping is prominent in the type. The unique petal apices of var. *ecuadorense* are usually bilobed. The ovoid labellum is elongate, although rounded at the toe, and measures up to 3 cm (1.2 in.) long.

Section *Lorifolia*

This section is characterized by the horns which adorn the lateral margins of the pouch orifice.

Phragmipedium boissieranum (Reichb. f.) Rolfe   PLATES 123–125

Within this species I include as variants 2 taxa which Garay (1979) identifies as separate species. The work of Stermitz et al. (1981) supports the separation of *P. czerwiakowianum*

(Reichb. f.) Rolfe at species rank on biochemical evidence. However, these 3 taxa which I group together in *P. boissieranum* are all Peruvian and differ only slightly in morphological details. The available criteria for distinction include incomplete data on alkaloid content and minor differences in staminode shape. Therefore, *P. boissieranum* includes var. *czerwiakowianum* Reichb. f. and var. *reticulatum* Reichb. f.

GEOGRAPHIC DISTRIBUTION All 3 variants of this species are native to Peru; var. *reticulatum* also extends into Ecuador.

HABITAT Found in the Huanoco District of the Peruvian Andes, this montane species is epiphytic and prefers much the same sort of habitat as *P. caudatum*.

DESCRIPTION The large, green leaves reach lengths of 60–65 cm (24–26 in.). The erect inflorescence achieves heights of 60–80 cm (24–32 in.), bearing 2–8 flowers successively.

The lanceolate to oblong-elliptic dorsal sepal has crisply undulate margins; pale green, it is veined in dark green. The length of the dorsal is 5–6.5 cm (2–2.6 in.), while the width rarely exceeds 1.5 cm (0.6 in.). The obovate synsepalum is more than twice as broad and measures up to 6.5 cm (2.6 in.) in length by 4–4.5 cm (1.6–1.75 in.) in width. It is similar in color to the dorsal. The margins of the ventral sepal are crispate and recurved. Degree of marginal undulation is one of the variable features of the included taxa.

The linear petals range from outspread just below horizontal to pendulous; both superior and inferior margins are crisply undulate in var. *boissieranum* and less so in the other 2 variants. The petals twist through 2 full spirals, extending to 9–13 cm (3.5–5 in.) or more in length; in color, they resemble the sepals. The pouch is elongate with lateral horns on the margin of the aperture. Its venation creates shallow grooves, particularly the midfrontal vein. The pouch is greenish brown with darker green venation; within the pouch, the involute side-lobes are greenish white, with some greenish brown spotting.

Phragmipedium longifolium (Reichb. f. & Warsc.) Rolfe   PLATES 126–128

This species is widely distributed and highly variable. I include several varieties within the species. While the evidence is somewhat inconclusive, there are grounds for placing them as variant forms of *P. longifolium* rather than at species rank as Garay (1979) contends. The geographic and morphological ranges are linked by intermediate and transitional forms, lending weight to the idea of a single, highly variable species. Veitch (1889) wrote that the early imports bearing the varietal names are virtually indistinguishable from each other, except for minor differences in color intensity and slight vegetative variations.

Veitch included the unusual entity, which Garay (1979) calls *P. dariense* and I designate as var. *dariense* Reichb. f., as a part of this species. Veitch appears to have been familiar with the Seeman drawing (see Garay 1979) of a similar plant from the Isthmus of Darien and referred to Seeman's collection within the historical discussion of *P. longifolium*. The Seeman drawing illustrates a flower with a most unusual pouch; not only are there deeply incised auricles unlike any others in the genus, but the pouch aperture is so elongated as to diminish the toe to a very small portion of the entire pouch. Without any data other than the line drawing and Veitch's comment about Seeman's collection of *P. longifolium*, there is little evidence to support firm taxonomic conclusions with respect to this taxon. However, one is almost forced to conclude either that Seeman's draftsmanship was inadequate or that he drew an anomalous flower.

Among the other varieties included within *P. longifolium* are var. *hartwegii* Reichb. f.; var. *hincksianum* Reichb. f. and var. *roezlii* Reichb. f.

GEOGRAPHIC DISTRIBUTION *P. longifolium* is found in Costa Rica, Panama, Colombia and Ecuador; var. *dariense* is from Panama; var. *hartwegii* is native to Ecuador and Panama; var. *hincksianum* is reported from Costa Rica and Panama; var. *roezlii* is found in Costa Rica, Panama and Colombia.

HABITAT All the taxa inhabit hilly terrain bordering rivers and prefer elevations of 500–2,300 m (1,700–7,900 ft.). They live in semishade upon granite scarps, overhanging rivers. The roots take purchase in mosses where they collect detritus. Seepage provides constant moisture to the roots.

In the Choco, the northern coastal region of Colombia, *P. longifolium* is found growing on rocks just above the high tide mark where it is often bathed with salt spray and subjected to bright, reflected light.

DESCRIPTION The plant habit is rather variable depending upon the habitat and range. Leaf length varies from 45–90 cm (18–36 in.); width varies from 1.5 cm (0.6 in.) to 4 cm (1.3 in.), depending upon the variety. Varieties may have light or dark green leaves. Var. *hartwegii* is the largest of the variants.

The scape of the type, according to Veitch (1889), is purplish and pubescent, while that of var. *hartwegii* is green. Erect and jointed, the scape bears 6–10 flowers or more and attains heights of 60–90 cm (24–36 in.). The flowers are generally greenish with rose or maroon suffusion upon the petals.

The lanceolate dorsal sepal measures 5 cm (2 in.) in length by up to 2 cm (0.75 in.) in width. The ground color is pale cream to white, suffused with palest green and pink, and faintly veined with rose. The margins are subundulate and may reflex slightly. The broadly obovate synsepalum measures 3–5 cm (1.2–2 in.) long by 3–3.5 cm (1.2–1.8 in.) wide. It is concave and colored similarly to the dorsal.

The linear petals are slightly twisted; their superior margins are undulate. Spreading to subpendent, the petals are usually held at about 45° below horizontal. In color, they resemble the sepals, although the margins are deeply veined and flushed with rose or magenta. Petal length is 6–7.5 cm (2.3–3 in.). The lip is elongate and roundly inflated with a slightly pointed toe; prominent auricles occur anterior to the infolded side-lobes. Pouch color is pale green faintly flushed with chestnut or rose.

Phragmipedium vittatum (Vell.) Rolfe   PLATE 129

GEOGRAPHIC DISTRIBUTION This species inhabits the Central Planalto (high plateau) region of Brazil.

HABITAT Abundant moisture is available in the streamside bogs favored by this species. Growing in semishade along wide river valleys at an elevation of 1,050 m (3,600 ft.), *P. vittatum* is found beneath stunted trees amidst grassy growth where its roots are anchored in rich, fibrous humus.

DESCRIPTION The linear leaves are margined with yellow. They reach lengths of 25–30 cm (10–12 in.).

The sparsely pubescent inflorescence reaches a height of approximately 30 cm (12 in.) and bears 1–4 flowers. The stalk is heavily sheathed.

The dorsal sepal is greenish white with pale rose and green venation. Lanceolate in shape, it measures up to 4 cm (2.6 in.) in length by 1.5 cm (0.6 in.) in width. Typically, it recurves at the apex. The ovate, concave synsepalum is also pale green; it measures 3 cm (1.2 in.) long by 2 cm (0.75 in.) wide.

The linear petals are pale green in color proximally and mesially with margins and veins of maroon coalescing to reddish aubergine over the apical two-thirds. The superior margins are rather crispate, while the inferior margins are subundulate; the petals are deflexed to at least 45° below horizontal and moderately twisted. Petal length is 5–7.5 cm (2–3 in.). The pouch is elongate and cylindrically inflated. Pale green in color, it is lightly flushed and veined with chestnut brown; the pouch rim is bordered in pale yellow and spotted inside with rosy purple.

This species is not only irregular in its flowering but infrequent as well, according to Dr. Louis Hegedus (personal communication).

Hybrid *Phragmipedium* are discussed in Chapter 7. However, it is worthwhile to comment here upon the paucity of hybrids available from this genus. With the advent of *Phragmipedium besseae* hybrids, perhaps possibilities will be explored in this charming genus to a greater extent than previously. Neglect of the hybrid potential of *Phragmipedium* is a human limitation which deserves correction. It is still unclear whether intrinsic capabilities for complex *Phragmipedium* hybrids exist, although discovery of such capabilities would provide a significant boost to hybridization.

CHAPTER 7

Hybridization of Slippers

Hybridization in the slipper orchids is a study in contrasts. More crosses have been made in the genus *Paphiopedilum* than in any other orchid genus; hybridization in the genus *Phragmipedium* has proceeded at a sedate pace, however, while registered artificial hybrids in the genus *Cypripedium* have only appeared within this decade, and none have been reported in the genus *Selenipedium*. Perhaps the fact which is least characteristic of the orchid family is the dearth of proven intergeneric hybrids within the subfamily Cypripedioideae.

The purpose of this chapter is to treat selected aspects of hybridization presenting:

1. An overview of breeding in the subfamily with an introduction to the methods used by breeders.
2. A survey of the history of slipper breeding, including species and hybrids pivotal to successful breeding, a treatment of both novelty and complex hybrids, and a look at the trends of the past and present as well as the potentials still untapped, particularly in the genus *Paphiopedilum*.
3. An examination of selected topics pertinent to genetics, technical aspects and problems peculiar to *Paphiopedilum* hybridization.

While there is a wealth of information which is broadly useful to the cypriphile, it is beyond the scope of a single chapter to provide the particulars which would serve as a manual for would-be breeders. Therefore, information on flasking of seeds and other technical matters is restricted to generalizations founded on basic principles. Provision of complete and detailed pedigrees of other than representative hybrids is not only impracticable but may be derived by the interested reader who possesses the patience to work through *Sander's List of Orchid Hybrids*.

INTRODUCTION TO BREEDING

The following summary of activities and events in hybridization relates primarily to the genus *Paphiopedilum*—the dominant area of interest to date in slipper hybridization.

Hybridization is an extended process. It begins even before pollination with the critical selection of the 2 parents. (This most critical aspect of breeding is explored in some depth in the succeeding pages.) Following pollination, months elapse before the seeds mature, and 4–10 years, or even more, are required to reach first blooming of individual siblings.

Pollination is discussed from the natural standpoint in Chapter 1. Pollination by hand involves removal of the pouch for easy access to the column; transfer of pollen from an anther of 1 parent to the stigma of the second parent, most often with the aid of a toothpick; and careful labeling of the pod-parent with parental names and the date of pollination. Pollen may be gathered and stored under refrigeration for several months for use in cross-seasonal pollination.

The relatively long interval between pollination and fertilization in the slipper orchids is required for the growth of the pollen tubes through the stigma and style and downward into the inferior ovary. This interval may last only a week or so in *Cypripedium* and *Phragmipedium* or more than a month in *Paphiopedilum*. During this time, and at an increased rate after the pollen tubes have delivered sperm to the egg cells in the ovules, the ovary expands. Meanwhile, the perianth deteriorates rapidly after pollination, dropping off entirely in *Paphiopedilum* and *Phragmipedium*. Several months are required for maturation of the fertilized ovules to form seeds, during which time the expanding ovary is termed a pod or capsule.

The pod is typically gathered before it is completely desiccated—just as it turns from green to brown—so as to prevent the loss of the minute seeds through its drying and increasingly brittle, dehiscent walls. However, green-pod harvesting is preferred by some hybridists who sow seeds prior to their synthesis of auxins which delay germination. The seeds may be briefly refrigerated for storage, although immediate sowing is preferable, as germination rates are believed to be greater.

Seeds may be sown symbiotically, which requires infecting the embryo with beneficial mycorrhizal fungi, or asymbiotically, which involves providing nutrients to the embryo artificially through sterile culture media. As orchid seeds lack stored food reserves, the nutrients required for initial growth are derived from an external source. In nature, fungi supply the nutrients. Once they have invaded the embryo, the fungi benefit from the shelter of plant tissue, while providing the germinating embryo with surplus nutrients. The number of surviving offspring derived from the asymbiotic method so far exceeds the crop resulting from symbiotic culture that asymbiotic culture has been adopted almost universally among amateurs and commercial growers alike.

If symbiotic seed propagation is undertaken, seeds are sown on sphagnum moss-covered potting medium at the base of strong adult plants that must be symbionts. Due to the wide-spread preference for asymbiotic methods of culture among commercial suppliers of plants, the only means of being certain of the presence of mycorrhizal fungi in a prospective surrogate mother plant is to utilize plants collected from the wild. Growers should feel free to inquire of their suppliers whether plants are symbionts or free of mycorrhizae.

Asymbiotic sowing and replating is a methodical process requiring sterile technique as well as a steady hand for uniform spreading of the fine seeds. It must be carried out within sterile transfer chambers accessed by rubber glove-sealed apertures. Attention to sterile technique is imperative to the success of asymbiotic culture of seedlings, as the nutrients which support the life of the dependent orchid seedlings make equally suitable nourishment for lethal fungus microorganisms, the spores of which are abundant not only on virtually every surface but in the dust in the air as well. Furthermore, selection of the nutrient medium, incorporating optimal levels of the most efficacious biochemicals such as nicotinic acid (niacin) and other growth regulators, requires not only considerable knowledge of plant physiology but also careful experimentation. Pertinent articles appear frequently in the publications of orchid societies, and the equipment and materials are relatively inexpensive, so asymbiotic culture is no longer restricted to laboratories, although many amateurs send their pods away for this service.

Within the sterile transfer chamber the seeds to be cultured are disinfected in a weak solution of calcium or sodium hypochlorite. Next they are introduced to flasks containing sterile culture medium which has typically been adjusted to a pH acid enough to offset and nearly neutralize the alkalinity of the calcium hypochlorite disinfectant. The sowing process is called plating; it requires skill at uniform spreading of the seeds over the surface of the medium so that optimum room is allowed for growth of the maximum number of protocorms. This skill comes with practice.

After plating the flasks are stoppered with sterile cotton to filter out potential colonizing spores and are loosely sealed with aluminum foil or parafilm to conserve moisture. The flasks are then usually stored at optimum temperature and light conditions in growth chambers, although seedlings may be successfully germinated and grown in flasks placed on greenhouse benches, providing the temperature remains near 22° C (72° F) and low-to-intermediate light is available for at least 8–9 hours per day.

In either symbiotic or asymbiotic propagation, germination involves imbibition of water for a variable period of time, followed by swelling and rupture of the testae (seed coats), and emergence of the embryos. Soaking seeds prior to sowing facilitates germination when they have been held in storage. Germination may take months or even years. The time elapsing before it is complete for all the viable seeds of a particular flasking varies with environmental conditions, with the cross, and even among seeds of the same pod. Frequently, greening protocorms are seen in the same flask with newly-germinated seeds and those yet to sprout, reflecting this variability.

The minute seeds contain colorless, microscopic embryos. As germination proceeds, rapid mitosis (cell division) ensues, enlarging the embryos. Subsequently, differentiation is initiated. In this process the embryo, composed of meristem (undifferentiated bud tissues capable of mitosis and subsequent specialization to produce mature epidermis, mesophyll and components of the vascular system), enlarges further at the same time that maturation occurs; these changes include both growth and development and mark the embryo's progress to the protocorm stage. Orchid seedlings are uncharacteristic of the greater plant kingdom, however, in that chlorophyll production is delayed for several weeks or months even though growth and maturation proceed. The sugars, amino acids and other organic molecules required to support this dependent phase of growth (that period from germination to greening of protocorms) must either be incorporated in the asymbiotic medium or supplied by symbiotic, mycorrhizal fungi from the mother plant, if orchid seedlings are to survive.

At the protocorm stage, seedlings are composed of rapidly proliferating tissue which is, as yet, only marginally differentiated; thus, protocorm-stage seedlings become crowded and typically require replating if asymbiotically grown. This procedure is usually delayed until the onset of the greening period, although all the seedlings will not have developed to the same stage simultaneously. Replating is a painstaking process which again requires scrupulously sterile technique. During the crowding of the protocorm stage, symbiotically cultivated seedlings experience the thinning effects of natural selection.

Shortly after chlorophyll appears, the apex of each seedling exhibits its budlike characteristics so that within a few weeks the rudimentary first leaf is visible. Once greening occurs, seedlings are able to photosynthesize their own organic molecules and to progress similarly to ordinary seedlings that require soluble mineral elements or fertilizers in their medium. Thus, replating logically occurs at the time of protocorm greening so that a medium more suited to the needs of independent plantlets may be provided. Growers who are confident of their sterile technique replate the greened individuals as each group reaches this stage, leaving dependent seedlings behind with more space for further development in the original flask. This selectivity means opening the flask several times before all the seedlings are replated; the risk of contamination by pathogenic fungi is increased with each access.

Following placement in the second flask, the plantlets are typically allowed to grow until they reach the top of the flask. The time elapsing in the second flask varies, depending upon methods and nutrients as well as the physiological characteristics of the grex. One approach, the 3-flask method, involves replating horizontally, in which case the leaves have only limited room in which to grow, so plantlets will be replated once more to a third, upright flask, to bring them along to a size suitable for planting in community trays or pots. Some growers, on the other hand, reflask directly into an upright flask. Thus, when this 2-flask method is used, seedlings must be spaced more sparsely to prevent crowding. However the breeder handles reflasking, the nutrients required for green growth differ from those provided for the early, dependent stages prior to greening, so different media are used. Agar formulas incorporating mineral nutrients and a lowered concentration of carbohydrates and amino acids are used at this stage.

Typically, young seedlings should be large enough to be separated from the mother plant or removed from the final flask and planted into community pots or trays, within 2 years of pollination. (Plantlets are capable of this transition when they possess 2–3 leaves, the largest of which is at least 10 cm (4 in.) long.) A potting medium similar to that used for mature plants is provided. The major differences in community pot media are that small-particle substrate is incorporated to support seedling roots, and fertilizer levels are reduced. Fertilization of seedlings is carried out by watering with dilute applications of a complete, high-nitrogen fertilizer at frequent intervals. Seedlings are permitted to remain in compots or community trays until crowding dictates the need to repot individually.

Much variation in the rate of maturation is to be expected. The most precocious seedlings typically flower within 4–5 years after pollination (about 2–3 years after independent establishment), while the slowest individuals may require up to 10 years or more to bloom. First flowering is fairly indicative of the quality of flower to be expected throughout the plant's life.

Unflowered plantlets are marketable in the flask stage, and many flasks are sold to be potted in community pots by the purchaser. Such speculative purchases are among the least expensive means of expanding a collection. However, since the number of plantlets per flask is often excessive for hobby growers, flask purchases are typically restricted to commercial houses or to societies or groups of hobbyists. Once seedlings have flowered, the cost of select seedlings rises based upon the quality of the flower. Very fine siblings sell at a premium price, if they are not reserved by the breeder as future stud plants. Inferior siblings are culled. Purchase of flasks involves the risk that some or all of the seedlings will be inferior in nearly every cross. However, the possibility of acquiring a bonanza is a tremendous lure. Hobby growers are able to enjoy the speculative purchase of just a few unflowered seedlings from trays or compots. The anticipation and the gambler's instinct are a large part of the appeal of this aspect of growing.

An interesting generalization is that the largest populations of seedlings are to be expected from asymbiotically reared crosses of species. Species selfings and primary crosses generate more prolific capsules than do crosses of greater extraction (more than 4 generations). Much information has been amassed about the incompatibilities which reduce fecundity as breeding becomes more complex, but a great deal more remains to be discovered before the means to control or overcome the various forms of diminished fertility become commonplace. See "Genetics and Other Technical Aspects of Slipper Breeding" later in this chapter for more details of genetic and technical difficulties relative to fecundity.

The naive often view hybridizing as a scientific, highly technical procedure. In reality, most of the widely acclaimed successful hybrids were and are produced out of subjective, intuitive judgments as to the parents selected, or even, though rarely, by random pairings between plants flowering coincidentally. Thus, successful breeding of slippers, although increasingly oriented toward the genetically enlightened, scientific end of the spectrum, remains more an art than a science. Crosses are never made only because the purely scientific data indicate that success is likely; the subjective aspect of the expectation of improved form, color or some other desirable feature of the proposed hybrid is always paramount in the breeder's intent.

While Dominy's pioneer crosses occurred contemporaneously with the abortive debut of Mendel's laws of heredity, the foundations of slipper breeding predated the rediscovery and recognition of the significance of the Mendelian science of genetics in 1900. So, while a de facto competence in genetics is in no way a guarantee of success, it is, nonetheless, safe to predict that the future of *Paphiopedilum* breeding will wed the science of genetics to the art of successful selection of parents for even greater percentages of successful crosses. It is increasingly difficult to succeed on intuition alone given the large numbers of species and hybrids currently available for use as parents in the genus *Paphiopedilum*, particularly in light of the number of infertile hybrids among them.

At present, the major contribution by the science of genetics to breeding practices is largely restricted to providing clues to the failure of a particular cross or to the fruitlessness of pursuing certain avenues in breeding which, in light of current technical limitations, should be avoided. In short, genetics makes a far greater impact negatively than positively. Only in the rare breeding establishment is the selection of parents a decision based on formulated genetic principles, and even in those instances, the elements of experience coupled with subjective judgment take precedence over other guidelines. Experience and an intuition for genetic concepts such as dominance and recessiveness have been the fountainheads of most of the noteworthy hybrid slippers both in the past and yet today.

Because of the immense variability observed in slipper orchids, it would be the height of folly to assume that science will quantify hybridization or exert a major degree of exactitude upon it in the immediate future. The variability possible among the individuals of a single species introduces a great degree of randomness within the hybrid progeny sired out of that species. The random variations are not merely doubled by the crossing of 2 variable species, but rather increase geometrically. If one considers a modern complex hybrid with its scores of assorted parents, grandparents and great-grandparents, and the subtle variations which might have resulted had only 4 or 5 of those predecessors been selected from different clones of a particular species or hybrid, the odds for variance reach astronomical proportions. See the discussion of polygenic inheritance in "Genetics and Other Technical Aspects of Slipper Breeding" for an example of the capacity for variation in a single trait of *Paphiopedilum*.

The registration of hybrids is performed meticulously and with a remarkably high degree of accuracy. Unfortunately, only the grex names are normally registered. That is, *Paphiopedilum* Winston Churchill, for example, is listed as a cross first in the registry, then as a parent, but there is no indication of which sibling from the Winston Churchill cross or grex is the actual parent of any particular hybrid bred from it. Yet, breeders are quick to point out that, because of the immense variability inherent in this group of plants, the outcome of a cross is greatly influenced by the particular clone selected as a parent. The ramifications of the use of several named clones of *P.* Winston Churchill are discussed in "Complex Hybrids of *Paphiopedilum*" later in this chapter.

It is perhaps necessary to clarify some terms, at this point, lest confusion arise. All the seedlings which come from a single seed pod are siblings, the common progeny of 1 cross, commonly called a grex. In the case of orchids, a grex is also, quite unlike the typical flowering plant, the progeny of only 2 parents. This is true, whether pollination is natural or artificial, because orchid pollen is transferred as a mass, a pollinium, from 1 anther to 1 stigma, in contrast to the dusty, individual grains which are transferred from scores of anthers to many stigmata, as is typical of other plant families. As a consequence, while orchid siblings can and do exhibit remarkable variance from each other, they all bear the same grex name (e.g. *P.* Winston Churchill) and share the identical pair of parents, (which in the case of *P.* Winston Churchill are *P.* Eridge × *P.* Hampden). Therefore, each significant sibling from a grex is given its own clonal name to assist in distinguishing it from another with that same grex name. A clonal name is a sibling name, of course, but, because any sibling is destined to be vegetatively reproduced over the years through divisions, then a clone of identical plants bearing the same genetic content and the same sibling or clonal name comes into existence. Thus, *P.* Winston Churchill 'Indomitable' is a distinct hybrid clone with its own sired line of offspring; these hybrids are rather easily distinguished from sibling *P.* Winston Churchill 'Redoubtable' and its particular scions. Further, clonal names of orchids are set apart by enclosing them in single quotation marks. Thus, *P.* Winston Churchill 'Indomitable' and Winston Churchill 'Redoubtable' are 2 important, awarded clones consisting of many divisions each which grew from 2 individual filial seedlings out of the same original grex. The 2 sibling clones, and indeed the offspring sired by them, are readily distinguishable by the markings of their dorsal sepals. See "Complex Hybrids of *Paphiopedilum*" later in this chapter for particulars. See also Plates 193 and 194. The fact that clonal names are omitted from the registry of hybrids is therefore exposed as a weakness of the registration system; the interested breeder or grower is less well-informed than would be the case with more detailed registration.

The term "cultivar," which may indicate any individual altered in any way by man's intervention—from a greenhouse-induced alteration in a species to an artificial hybrid grex name to a sibling or clonal name—is so inexact in orchid usage that its use within these pages is limited.

By definition, vegetative reproduction is the only source of additional plants with the same genetic composition and the same clonal name. It involves taking cuttings or divisions of the nonfloral, that is, nonsexual, organs of a plant. Division of growths is currently the only reliable means of vegetatively propagating slipper orchids. However, other orchid genera lend themselves well to meristemming—a method of proliferating many undifferentiated cells through tissue culture, after which each cell is grown to maturity (in the same way embryos are cultivated) to yield plants which are genetically identical clones of the original plant.

To have an exact replica of any excellent plant, sexual reproduction must be avoided so as to circumvent genetic recombination. Thus, even if *P.* Hellas 'Westonbirt', for example, is selfed (pollen placed on the stigma of the same flower or another flower of the same plant or clone), the progeny will possess randomly recombined alleles, and must, therefore, be treated as a new grex. No single seedling of the new, selfed grex can correctly be named *P.* Hellas 'Westonbirt', since no individual can be proved to be genetically identical to clone 'Westonbirt', although certainly all are *P.* Hellas (F2). Use of a clonal name must be restricted to the vegetative reproductions of a single seedling plant. It is equally important that 2 growers not give different clonal names to divisions of the same plant.

However, in the case of species, varietal names appended to the species epithet reflect a very different situation. A variety, e. g. *P. insigne* var. *sanderae*, is properly considered a naturally occurring, variant subpopulation of a species (in this example, an albino form of *P. insigne*). Only vegetative or clonal divisions of a single specimen of such a variety are sure to have precisely identical genetic properties. Therefore, a name such as *P. insigne* var. *sanderae* 'Sundance' identifies all the vegetative propagations of 1 individual of such a natural variant subpopulation. This is also another example of the conventional usage of a clonal name, (always enclosed in single quotation marks), in this case for clones of a particular individual variant form of a species. Thus, clonal names are not reserved just for distinguishing between hybrid siblings. The use of a clonal name is both proper and helpful in keeping track of the vegetative offshoots of any orchid plant, whether it be species/variant or hybrid.

With terminology defined, and clarification of the use of single quotation marks around clonal names identified as the convention for naming all vegetatively reproduced clones of a distinctive, individual orchid, the original point which must be reiterated is that the hybrid registry is less precisely informative than it might have been had clonal names identified specific parents (as opposed to anonymous or unspecified individuals from an entire grex) over the years. Should a breeder wish to remake a certain cross, the registry information alone will not enable him to do so, since a number of aunts and uncles might be used in place of the actual parents originally selected. The outcome of a remake is vastly changed through such deliberate substitutions. However, it is worthy of note that because of the immensity of the variations possible in the assortments of genetic combinations, even when breeding with aunts and uncles, the probability of obtaining some quite similar offspring remains. What is certain to differ are the ratios of siblings exhibiting various traits in the offspring of 2 such similar but not precisely identical crosses.

This lack of specificity of parentage permeates the entire hybrid registry, involves almost every cross and proliferates geometrically. It is unfortunate that, while the mechanism to enhance the precision of registry information exists, such information is currently available only from the registrants. However, this shortcoming is often less detrimental than might be inferred. Frequently, hybridizers remake earlier hybrids precisely to supplant a prior parent with what is believed to be a superior and distinctive clone. It should be pointed out, however, that this intention is certainly more common in remakes of early primary and novelty crosses than in rebreeding complicated lineages. The latter is virtually unheard of because of the scores of years required to accomplish such a task.

Due to the typical reproductive characteristic of orchids in incorporating many to virtually all the possible random assortments of alleles of 2 parents within the progeny of 1 grex, not only are the possible random outcomes of each pairing immense, but the widely different outcomes possible from very similar pairings are only marginally comprehensible. This characteristic reproductive strategy of orchids is an outgrowth of 2 unusual factors: 1) the production of massive pollinia which are transported whole as opposed to dusty pollen grains dispersed from many anthers to a number of stigmata as in virtually all other plant families; and 2) the unusually large number of ovules typically contained in each ovary. These factors enable orchids to thoroughly exploit the enormous number of possible random combinations of alleles. In orchids as a group, the possibility of seeds numbering in excess of 100,000 per capsule is not uncommon. In slipper orchids, however, such fecundity is rarely if ever observed. A major morphological difference in slipper orchids likely accounts for part of this shortfall; the slipper group is distinguished from the mainstream of orchids by its possession of 2 fertile anthers, as opposed to only 1. Thus, while a slipper seed capsule has only 2 parents, as is typical of orchids, each slipper flower is atypically capable of pollinating 2 other flowers. It is probable that the number of male gametes per pollen mass is fewer in slippers than in orchids which produce only 1 pollinium, and therefore, that slippers also lack the capacity to produce the vast numbers of ovules/seeds typical of the balance of the orchid family. The probability that inhibiting chemicals are present in slipper orchids must be investigated also, in an effort to unravel the mysterious causes of their restricted fecundity. More will be said about problems of infertility and reduced fertility growing out of highly extracted breeding in the discussion of genetics and technical aspects of complex *Paphiopedilum* hybrids at the end of this chapter.

Reading through *Sanders' Complete List of Orchid Hybrids* (the earliest registry volume complete through January 1, 1946), the names of frequently used early parents leap out again and again from the pages, leading to the immediate but false assumption that the reader is fully familiar with the orchids identified by those names. In actuality, the degree of genotypic and phenotypic diversity between 2 clones of a primary hybrid such as *P.* Leeanum, for example, is often quite astonishing. Parenthetic comments included in the older lists continually remind the reader of the existence of clones, and of the quite different outcomes resulting from use of one or the other. There is, in fact, abundant evidence as to the futility of attempting to confine the exuberant variability of orchids within the expected simplification of or restriction by scientific laws.

It is interesting, however, to read through the tables of hybrids because of the perspective gained as to the importance of various pivotal parents. *P.* Actaeus, for example, was used as a parent of 85 different crosses in the first, inclusive, standardized list released by Sander in 1947, while *P.* Cardinal Mercier was incorporated into over 100 different hybrids, and *P.* Leeanum sired an impressive 134 crosses. *P.* Christopher, *P.* Chrysostum, *P.* Gwen Hannen, *P.* Grace Darling, *P.* Harrisianum, *P.* Hera, and *P.* Lady Dillon are among some of the most-used hybrid parents in the early lists. One has only to look at the pedigrees of modern hybrids such as *P.* Tommie Hanes (refer to Table 11) to see the preponderance of certain of these parents and to grasp the integral and axiomatic influence exerted by them.

However, the laws of genetics presently serve as little more than useful guidelines. Most breeders thrive on the challenge and suspense of the multiplicity of unknown, although somewhat predictable, variables at play and would become bored with hybridizing, should it degenerate into dial-a-grex simplicity. While *Paphiopedilum* breeding may be inexact or even haphazard, adjectives such as prosaic or predictable can never be invoked.

Before turning to the mainstream of the very successful lines of hybridization being carried on, it is well to deal with the topic of wide hybrids in slippers as an important aspect of this overview. Because of the discrepancy in chromosome size, as well as temporal, mechanical, physiological and other incompatibilities between *Paphiopedilum* and *Phragmipedium*, it is not surprising that successful intergeneric hybridization between 2 genera so deceptively similar in appearance remains tantalizingly beyond the grasp of hybridizers. It is necessary to reiterate the observation made in Chapter 1 that, although a great many intergeneric crosses have been attempted, and although a few putative vegetative progeny have been grown, the evidence for indisputable intergenerics is extremely limited. That is to say, the floral evidence is insufficient or entirely lacking depending upon the cross.

The Wimber and Hanes (1985) account of Phragmipaphium Hanes' Magic 'Bion' (Plate 130) provides insights into the single intergeneric cross which has flowered and been accepted by qualified AOS judges as exhibiting a sufficient number of traits of both genera to be recognized as an intergeneric hybrid. The flowered plant received an AD-AM/AOS in 1985. The parents used in the cross are *Paphiopedilum stonei* 'Bion' and *Phragmipedium* Albopurpureum (*Phragmipedium schlimii* × *Phragmipedium* Dominianum). Chromosomal studies, however, reveal only the 26 large chromosomes of the *Paphiopedilum* pod-parent present in the cells of the awarded offspring, according to Wimber and Hanes (1985). This plant, while by no means an undisputed intergeneric hybrid, is unique in this field and deserving of the further study undertaken by Dr. Wimber. According to Wimber and Hanes (1985), the flower of Phragmipaphium Hanes' Magic is undoubtedly more than a parthenogenetic *P. stonei* (Plate 51). Yet, they can offer no clear explanation for the slight influence of *Phragmipedium* Albopurpureum manifested in this cross nor for the absence of *Phragmipedium* chromosomes in microscopic preparations of tissues. These ambiguous conclusions of 2 well-recognized experts, one a qualified scientist and the other an experienced breeder, serve to emphasize the tremendous perplexities and difficulties yet to be overcome in this line of breeding.

More than a century has elapsed since the first hybrid slippers appeared, and for much of that time, the dream of an intergeneric hybrid has motivated breeders to persevere in attempting such crosses. Bigeneric crosses in orchid subfamilies other than the Cypripedioideae were made by Dominy and others within the first decades of orchid hybridization. In the vandaceous and oncidiaceous groups, intergenerics incorporating fractions of the genomes of numerous species of as many as 4 or more genera all within 1 grex, are readily produced, as is also true in *Cattleya*-type wide hybrids. While much delayed, the slipper world is on the threshold of such an achievement, although it is by no means certain to occur through the ordinary sexual avenue of gametic fusion. The development of reliable hybrids between *Paphiopedilum* and *Phragmipedium* appears to depend upon a breakthrough in tissue culture of slipper orchids—a breakthrough which will revolutionize slipper culture at several levels and permit successful somatic cell fusion, among other aims. More information about tissue culture, meristem cloning and somatic cell fusion is to be found in "Genetics and Other Technical Aspects of Slipper Breeding" later in this chapter.

Wide hybrids in the Cypripedioideae are not, however, limited to crosses between *Paphiopedilum* and *Phragmipedium*. Carson E. Whitlow (personal communication) has young seedlings in flask resulting from crosses of *Cypripedium reginae* with both *Phragmipedium caudatum* and *Phragmipedium sargentianum*. He reports seeds from a *Cypripedium* pod which are significantly larger than typical *Cypripedium* seeds, as well as young seedlings which differ both in appearance and in response to cultural parameters from the *Cypripedium* seedlings which he has grown previously. Because both these genera complete fertilization after pollination more rapidly than *Paphiopedilum*, he anticipates that there are further compatibilities between them which have facilitated successful intergeneric slipper hybridization.

PRIMARY AND NOVELTY HYBRIDS

The epic of slipper hybridization begins in the 1860s, when Dominy, a grower for Veitch's Royal Exotic Nursery in Chelsea, England, created the first hybrid *Paphiopedilum*. His cross of *Paphiopedilum villosum* × *Paphiopedilum barbatum* yielded viable seeds which grew into mature plants. When the first hybrid plants flowered in 1866, the cross was named appropriately, *Paphiopedilum* Harrisianum (Plate 131), in honor of Dr. Harris who initially encouraged Dominy to undertake orchid hybridizing.

It is an interesting coincidence that the debut of *P.* Harrisianum occurred in the same year as the original, but obscure, publication of Mendel's laws of heredity. The time was ripe in the scientific and horticultural worlds alike, for major developments in previously undreamed of frontiers. Plant hybridization and the field of genetics both experienced erratic progress in their early years, and it is useful to recall that, particularly in orchid hybridization, early records of parentage were kept more widely and with greater care than occurred in the breeding of most other plant families. This single, fortuitous factor has influenced and facilitated subsequent progress in orchid breeding immeasurably. Certainly, many early crosses were made without the benefit of records for posterity, but many of those same crosses were duplicated by other hybridizers who did record parentage, so that relatively little of the early history of slipper hybridization has been lost.

This first hybrid, *Paphiopedilum* Harrisianum, was and still is a vigorous, floriferous plant. Selected clones such as 'Superbum' and the tetraploid 'G. S. Ball' remain prized plants today, more than 120 years after the beginnings of the arts, skills and lore of hybridization and even after the production of literally thousands of newer hybrids.

Dominy registered 2 more crosses in 1870: *Paphiopedilum barbatum* × *Paphiopedilum fairrieanum* produced *Paphiopedilum* Vexillarium, while the cross *Phragmipedium caricinum* × *Phragmipedium caudatum* produced the first hybrid *Phragmipedium*, registered as *Phragmipedium* Dominianum.

In 1874 Seden, also a grower for Veitch, produced a second *Phragmipedium* hybrid which he registered as *Phragmipedium* Sedenii (Plate 132), a cross of *Phragmipedium schlimii* × *Phragmipedium longifolium*. Thus, in the first decade of slipper breeding, it is significant that work in the genus *Phragmipedium* kept pace with that in the genus *Paphiopedilum*. However, in view of the tremendously broader selection of *Paphiopedilum* species with which to experiment, it is not surprising that hybridization of *Paphiopedilum* soon outstripped work with *Phragmipedium*. Furthermore, several decades later breeders became so entranced with the unusual progression evidenced in *Paphiopedilum* breeding that all but the most persistent came to ignore *Phragmipedium* altogether.

During those pioneer decades, while only a few of the progeny survived, and some of these were inferior to their parents, it is certain that many of the offspring were vigorous, attractive and desirable. Moreover, many demonstrated their promise as parents as well. Early hybridizers were caught up in the idea that the possibilities were infinite. Today, this same optimism prevails, although tempered by experience. The perennial truth is that the number of possible, successful crosses is somewhat less than infinite, circumscribed as it is by limitations both genetic and aesthetic, and that barriers to some pairings remain insurmountable until certain manipulative techniques are successfully brought to bear upon various problems in slipper breeding, regardless of how desirable the crosses appear to be.

It is worthy of note that both the conduplicate-leaved slipper genera were erroneously called *Cypripedium*, not only during those pioneer years, but in general usage for over a century after the first importations of tropical slippers. Gradually, the early growers acknowledged the differences between Old World and New World slippers, so a second erroneous genus name, *Selenipedium*, came into limited use for *Phragmipedium* species and hybrids in the latter years of the 19th century. Thus, the registrations of the first 94 years of hybrids were uniformly made under the generic names *Cypripedium* and *Selenipedium*, although the hybrids registered belonged to neither genus. Invariably, the early *Cypripedium* were actually *Paphiopedilum*, while the early *Selenipedium* were all *Phragmipedium*. Horticulturists, in their excitement over the explosion in breeding, had no time for dull, musty works in taxonomy, so they virtually ignored questions of nomenclature. Thus, while the genera *Phragmipedium* and *Paphiopedilum* were established in the botanical community as early as 1886, the final acceptance of the correct generic nomenclature in this otherwise well-studied, widely grown group was not widespread among horticulturists or breeders until the 1960s.

Further difficulties with the early practices of naming and registration of hybrids are described by Rodney Wilcox Jones in his prefatory notes to *Sanders' Complete List of Orchid Hybrids* (1947). Commenting on registries issued prior to that monumental edition, he mentions the 1901 publication of *Sander's Orchid Guide* specifically, relating that even so early there were over 1,000 so-called Cypripedium hybrids listed, although in actual fact, a vast amount of duplication occurred prior to concerted efforts to standardize registration. A case in point is the cross of Cypripedium *spiceranum* × C. Hyeanum, which was registered under 10 names. The correct number of individual slipper crosses in existence in 1901 was nearer to half the number listed.

The monumental task of standardizing the registration of hybrids required years, during which the number of new hybrids continued to skyrocket. However, since the earliest days at Veitch's establishment, records on orchids had been kept with a diligence that was unequalled in other groups of plants, so at last Sander's efforts produced as nearly perfect a list as could be compiled. Over the years, the registry begun by Sander has been continued by the Royal Horticultural Society through maintenance with supplementary publications.

Hybridization swept the orchid world. Fascination with this aspect of slipper culture was so inordinately compelling that interest in slipper species faded almost entirely. In the Foreword to *Sanders' Complete List of Orchid Hybrids* (1947), Jeremiah Colman not only concluded that traffic in species had become an unprofitable venture, but he referred to those growers who continued to "treasure fine species" as "mid-Victorian anachronisms, to be tolerated but not emulated." The fact is that such growers were viewed as both eccentric and reactionarily unenlightened for a century. In the same vein, James Veitch (1889) had previously concluded, "It may be safely affirmed that no greater triumph has been achieved in modern times by the gardeners' art than the production of the hybrid Cypripedes." As late as the 1960s, it was difficult to find growers who cared to give bench space to species and novelty crosses. The hybrid slipper was the unchallenged monarch of the slipper world for the century prior to the renaissance of appreciation of species and novelty hybrids in the past 2 or 3 decades.

To illustrate the degree of enthusiasm for this new branch of slipper culture, Veitch (1889) further commented,

> So generally is muling among Cypripedes now practised [sic], not only in Great Britain, but also on the Continent of Europe, and in the United States of America, that there is scarcely an orchid collection of note in which a batch of seedlings may not be found; such at least may be said to be the general rule but there are many prominent exceptions; it has thence resulted that the actual number of hybrid Cypripedes has become practically indefinite.

Vast quantities of new information proliferated so rapidly that it is incredible to find so much remaining on record of those early experiments. Certainly, today's breeders and slipper enthusiasts owe Veitch, Sander and many others a great debt of gratitude for both the preservation of records and on-the-scene observations of events and their implications in the burgeoning field of orchid hybridization.

Announcing the production of *Phragmipedium* Sedenii, Veitch (1889) discussed the quality known as hybrid vigor; the hybrid was significantly more robust than its sickly parent, *Phragmipedium schlimii*, and rather more vigorous than its easily cultivated parent, *Phragmipedium longifolium*. However, it is well to remember that, with the primitive methods of culture available at that time, only the most vigorous progeny of any grex survived the dependent phase following germination. Thus, while postgermination success was a hit-or-miss proposition, once seedlings of *Phragmipedium* Sedenii established themselves the survivors demonstrated incredible vitality. Wider observation confirmed the generality that hybrids exhibit exceptional vigor. Early plant breeders in the agricultural arena capitalized on this feature in the breeding of corn and other grains, later broadening their work to include a whole spectrum of cultivated plants.

As the number of new hybrids mushroomed, several further observations emerged, of which some were more accurate and far-sighted than others. It was noted by Veitch (1889) that variation of offspring was manifested differently in hybrids of Eucypripedium (*Paphiopedilum*), depending upon which species was the pod-parent and which was the pollen-parent. By contrast, in the genus *Phragmipedium*, which he called *Selenipedium*, he stated that the offspring varied considerably less with regard to which parent served as donor and which as receptor of pollen. Today, it is widely recognized that the maternal parent typically exerts the preponderant influence over the grex, because of the role of the DNA contained in color plastids within egg cells, structures not present in sperm gametes. Unfortunately, while the convention exists to name the pod-parent first when recording the parents of a hybrid, it is certain that this convention has not always been scrupulously observed, so that it is frequently impossible to determine which parent was the pod-parent.

Although from our perspective his concern appears extreme, Veitch (1889) was also alert to the possibility of the development of detrimental trends in hybridization when he pointed out the need for a careful "PROCESS OF SELECTION" (the upper case is Veitch's) in those post-Darwinian years. He recommended that the hybrid progeny not be allowed to become "very numerous" nor to achieve a "very mixed character." He was greatly concerned that only *"improved"* (Veitch's italics) progeny be fostered. How amazed Veitch would be today at the quality of the prolific and complex hybrids available to be grown, used as parents, studied and enjoyed. Yet, the entire course of hybridization would have varied considerably had not culling of inferior plants been one of the major tenets to which breeders subscribed early.

Veitch was also concerned about the naming of hybrids. He deplored the early habit of naming hybrids with "the pseudo-latin names so much in vogue" as well as the alarming trend of naming sibling offspring from the same grex by different names. The use of clonal or sibling names, in single quotation marks appended to grex names, would later partially resolve this early source of confusion, although the convention is a departure from that used in the case of hybrids in all other plant genera. Veitch and other cypriphiles of the time, notably including Reichenbach, were equally gravely concerned over the number of early hybrids of unrecorded parentage. Fortunately, while it was impossible to prevent the making of such hybrids, Sander later agreed to restrict their registration, so that today there are relatively few gaps in the pedigrees of most of our favorite hybrids.

Unfortunately, however, there were unscrupulous hybridizers along the way who deliberately registered hybrids under the wrong parentage in order to gain some momentary and usually illusory advantage over their competitors. Such a shortsighted and neurotic practice has been deplored by responsible horticulturists throughout the history of slipper, and indeed all plant breeding, both on principle and occasionally with dismay in the course of a breeding program. Modern breeders understand how little advantage such dishonesty provides, as well as the great value of preserving accurate records of hybrid lines. Unfortunately, inadvertent inaccuracies have also played a part in the confusion of hybrid lines, and worse, such errors persist indefinitely.

A rather prophetic and useful effort undertaken by Veitch (although not in the way intended) was his attempt to classify hybrids. His classification scheme, while pseudo-scientific, naive, and ultimately completely futile per se, yet revealed an inspired insight into the qualities of the early hybrids, the dominant traits of which were destined to establish trends and to eventually result in the round-flowered, glossy, complex hybrids of modern times. For details the reader is referred to the "Proposed Classification of Cypripedium Hybrids," *Manual of Orchidaceous Plants* (Veitch 1889). What is of interest today begins with his separation of the Eucypripedium (*Paphiopedilum*) hybrids from the *Selenipedium* (*Phragmipedium*) hybrids. Thus far, his scheme is sound, even if the nomenclature is not. Of further interest is that within the Eucypripedium section, he identified 8 distinct groups of *Paphiopedilum* hybrids (as well as a ninth small miscellany which he could not place in any of the 8 groups). The Harrisianum group is an example in point. Veitch described it as descended from *Paphiopedilum villosum*, large-flowered with glossy segments, a broad dorsal, and concave, spathulate petals. Stripped of particulars of color and measurement, this depiction is a remarkably accurate description of modern complex hybrids. The significance of this example is that it illustrates, several decades in advance, not only the influence which *Paphiopedilum villosum* was destined to exert on modern hybrids but also the uncannily insightful gift of prophecy possessed by the early pioneers who lacked today's advantage of hindsight. Veitch's Ashburtoniae group similarly illustrates the potential influence of *Paphiopedilum insigne*. A third group, the Leeanum (*insigne* × *spiceranum*) group, is less prophetically described, although it was to exert a powerful influence in hybridizing over subsequent decades (Plate 133). The influence of other species and/or alliances given a place in Veitch's attempt to classify hybrids has proved less prophetically documented, although the fact is that in today's modern hybrids the influence of species other than *Paphiopedilum insigne*, *P. spiceranum* and *P. villosum* remains less pronounced in the majority of cases. Veitch's classification scheme, for all its naiveté, is a valid example of the early, intuitive comprehension of the potentials in the genus *Paphiopedilum* by the pioneers in hybridization.

Thus, as early as 1889, many of the future trends characteristic of complex hybrids as yet unmade were already emerging embryonically. Around the turn of the century orchid judges, breeders and growers gradually developed a consensual image of the ideal hybrid *Paphiopedilum*. The desirable characteristics included a round shape with overlapping segments, heavy substance and large size. In addition, breeders undertook to improve clarity of color as well as color options, efforts which continue to bear fruit in these latter decades of the 20th century. Today's breeders, either studiously or out of the intuitive understanding borne of experience, routinely resort to the principles of dominance and recessiveness in altering and improving *Paphiopedilum*. For more information on dominance and recessiveness, see "Genetics and Other Technical Aspects of Slipper Breeding" later in this chapter.

However, hybridization in *Phragmipedium* has lagged behind, failing to move beyond the level achieved in the 19th century (primary crosses, rarely of more than 2–3 generations), while hybridization of true *Cypripedium* has been generally ignored until this decade. Introductions of new species of *Paphiopedilum* created a renewed interest in species and primary hybrids of that genus beginning in the late 1960s.

Listings of some of the important primary hybrids of all 3 cultivated genera, but particularly of *Paphiopedilum*, are useful. To separate and distinguish among the quantities of hybrids, some are historically significant, others are pivotal in the development of complex hybrids, while a third group, novelty hybrids, falls into neither category but is currently the most popular group for purely aesthetic reasons. The complex hybrids with their lengthy history and lineages are discussed later in this chapter.

Phragmipedium Hybrids

Important *Phragmipedium* hybrids include, of course, the pioneers—*Phragmipedium* Dominianum and *P.* Sedenii. The former retained the long, ribbonlike petals of *Phragmipedium caudatum* while receiving some greenish coloration from *P. caricinum*. All considered, it was more important as a milestone than as an aesthetic improvement upon either of the natural species. On the other hand, *P.* Sedenii was an improvement on both its parents; its shape is intermediate between that of *P. schlimii* and *P. longifolium* rather than totally dominated by the rounder form of *P. schlimii*, while its color is a subtle rose pink derived from both parents, fortunately influenced more by the rosy *P. schlimii*. Its improved vigor and size over *P. schlimii* are its primary merits.

Veitch (1889) also classified his Selenipedium (*Phragmipedium*) hybrids into 2 groups: the Dominianum group and the Sedenii group. The former group has the tailed *Phragmipedium* in the parentage throughout with the resultant long-petalled appearance. The Sedenii group has *P. schlimii* in its parentage throughout and is comprised of delicately rosy pink hybrids frequently exhibiting shortened petals. The pubescence of the flowers of *P. schlimii* appears to be uniformly recessive in its progeny.

In the genus *Phragmipedium*, however, Veitch's classification scheme bears a less-prophetic value than it had for the hybrid *Paphiopedilum*. The dominance of *P. schlimii* for pink color is little noted in his account; the hybrid vigor imparted to *P. schlimii* progeny is better documented. His proposed dominance of the long-petalled parents was perhaps overstated. Furthermore, the genus *Phragmipedium* has yet to reveal major trends or potential for development of outstanding size, shapes or other features comparable to those which were capitalized upon early in the development of complex hybrids of *Paphiopedilum*.

Worthy hybrids in these groups as well as crosses from outside either group are available. Although some are direct vegetative descendants of the original progeny while others are more recent remakes or new combinations, it is not always possible to determine the provenance of a particular clone. Regardless of provenance, certain crosses merit inclusion in this account.

P. Ainsworthii is a synonym for *P.* Calurum (Plate 134); this hybrid resulted from a backcross of Sedenii on *P. longifolium* which differs but little from *P.* Sedenii. It is unfortunate that both names for the same cross have persisted even until today.

P. Albopurpureum is an interesting and beautiful hybrid of *P. schlimii* × *P.* Dominianum (*caudatum* × *caricinum*). It, therefore, is allied with both Veitch's groups, combining elongate, twisted, pendulous petals with the rosy coloration of *P. schlimii*. Produced by Seden and described by Reichenbach in 1877, it is both vigorous and desirable. The question of its contribution to Phragmipaphium Hanes' Magic lends further fascination to this hybrid.

P. Grande (*caudatum* × *longifolium*) and *P.* Nitidissimum (*warscewiczianum* × Conchiferum *caricinum* × *longifolium*) are long-petalled crosses (Plate 135). Both are predominantly yellow to beige of sepal, maroon brown upon the elongate petals, and pink or brown of pouch with coloration varying with the particular clone of either grex. Both are spectacular for their size when in flower.

P. Schroderae (Plate 136) is a favorite of the initiated. A hybrid of *P. caudatum* × *P.* Sedenii, it bears moderately elongate petals on its 3–5 flowers per scape. The pink color trait of *P. schlimii* dominates, while the 12.5–15 cm (5–6 in.) petals owe their intermediate length more to polygenic inheritance than to simple dominance. For details of polygenic inheritance, refer to "Genetics and Other Technical Aspects of Slipper Breeding" later in this chapter.

P. Stenophyllum (Plate 137) is an interesting hybrid of *P. schlimii* × *P. caricinum*. Rose pink color predominates with some green venation. The petal length is approximately twice as long as that of *P. schlimii*, as Reichenbach described this hybrid in 1876. In 1978 Stermitz et al. (1983) remade the cross, but the petals of the progeny approximated the length of those of *P. caricinum*, although they were wider, while the coloration remained in the pink range true to *P. schlimii* dominance. (The flower illustrated in Plate 137 is from the 1978 cross.) It cannot be determined now, however, whether the differences observed are because of using different clones as parents or whether these differences are owing simply to the variability observable among a greater population of surviving siblings.

Numerous *Phragmipedium* hybrids are being made today. See Plates 138 and 139 for examples of variations in form and color being bred in this area. Several of recent vintage

Table 2. Awarded *Phragmipedium* hybrids of the 1980s.

Name/Parentage	Clone	Description
P. Ainsworthii (*P.* Calurum) Sedenii × *longifolium*	'Sicily'	Compact flower; rose/white, green-veined segments
P. Albopurpureum *schlimii* × Dominianum	'Sir Arthur'	Long rose maroon petals; peach to rose pouch
P. Cardinale Sedenii × *schlimii*	'Birchwood'	Compact pink
P. Carol Kanzer *pearcei* × *schlimii*	'Pheasant Hill' 'Doris Dukes'	Compact; white, rose segments, veined green
P. Court Jester *caudatum* × *boissieranum*	'Comedy King' 'Anna' 'Merlin' 'King's Pleasure' 'The Clown'	Medium to long petals; buff, green segments
P. Dominianum *caudatum* × *caricinum*	'Bob Mc' 'Gloria Anne'	Long yellow to pink petals; yellow green lip
P. Giganteum *caudatum* × Grande	'Harold' 'Eureka' 'Crownpoint'	Similar to Grande
P. Grande *caudatum* × *longifolium*	'Kensington' 'Jean' 'Old's Variety' 'Bertsch' 'Maybrook' 'Red Beard' 'Betty Hamric' 'Stephenson' 'Elwood' 'Ray' 'Honey'	Largest-flowered hybrid; long petals; cream, yellow-green, tan segments
P. Nitidissimum *warscewiczianum* × Conchiferum	'Gleneyrie' 'Rayber' 'Neville' 'Mt. Whitehorse'	Long petals; yellow to ocher or chestnut segments
P. Schroderae *caudatum* × Sedenii	'Fort Caroline' 'J & M' 'La Regia' 'Clyde' 'Enchanted Garden' 'Jessie' 'Claire' 'Bolin' 'Coos Bay' 'Monroe' 'Orchidcrest'	Medium to long petals; white to rose segments, veined green
P. Sedenii *schlimii* × *longifolium*	'Tallahassee' 'Edie' 'Penn Valley' 'Quail Hollow' 'Shirley' 'Achterhof' 'Kathy'	Compact pink
P. Sorcerer's Apprentice *longifolium* × *sargentianum*	'Mickey's Magic'	Medium petals; bronze to maroon, veined green
P. Stenophyllum *schlimii* × *caricinum*	'Orchid Loft'	Rose white segments, veined green

along with many of the perennial favorites have received awards in the past 2 decades. A representative selection of awarded *Phragmipedium* hybrids is found in Table 2.

Hybrids made from the recently introduced *P. besseae* should stimulate wider interest in hybridizing in this genus. Seedlings are currently priced at a premium rate. Substantial uncertainty exists as to aesthetic value or vigor, although the cinnabar red segments promise new avenues of progress in both form and color. Thus, while the verdict is not in on this line of breeding, anticipation is keen. If *P. besseae* shares with *P. schlimii* the characteristic of color dominance in crosses, then some very fine progeny are on the near horizon. It is remotely possible that crosses between these 2 species may result in the emergence of trends toward hybrid *Phragmipedium* which share with complex *Paphiopedilum* hybrids the potential to echo the amazing scope of alteration beyond species which developed early in the genus *Paphiopedilum*.

Cypripedium Hybrids

The first well-documented artificial hybrids of *Cypripedium* were only made, grown, flowered, registered, photographed and discussed in the past decade by Whitlow (1988a). Numerous references to artificial hybrids of *Cypripedium* occur in the literature of the late 19th century, but these hybrids were neither entered into the registry nor widely disseminated. Having remained obscure, these hybrids are omitted from this text, although I am curious as to the possibility that a few may still persist in English gardens.

As in any pioneer field, Whitlow's account is replete with a variety of difficulties, including high mortality rates at virtually every stage of *Cypripedium* hybridization. His first hybrid was *C.* Genesis (*pubescens* × *reginae*), while his second, *C.* Promises (*formosanum* × *acaule*), is both more beautiful and more interesting, uniting the genome of an Asian species with that of a North American species. See Plates 140–142 for illustrations of these hybrids as well as a putative cross of *C.* (*corrugatum* × *flavum*) × *corrugatum*. This latter hybrid, although of uncertain parentage, has been subjected to electrophoretic studies which bear out the assumptions made about its lineage.

Of the 3, the unnamed hybrid shows the greatest aesthetic promise. The qualities to which I call your attention are color and shape; there is an excellent distribution of color over the attractively broad, flat segments. Whitlow (personal communication) is employing this Asian hybrid and some of its siblings in further breeding with native American *Cypripedium*.

Although neither named hybrid appears to be a significant improvement upon its parent species, the breakthrough in asymbiotic culture of *Cypripedium* is an extremely important part of this work. Culture of *Cypripedium* from seeds was a rare accomplishment prior to the past 2 decades. Through the efforts of Whitlow and others, the way is opened not only to exploration of hybridization utilizing a wide spectrum of species, but to the means of conserving endangered, wild species through selfing as well.

This branch of slipper hybridization deserves expanded effort. The influence of many more species as well as many more survivors per grex is yet to be tested. So, while the initial results have been relatively muted in color and subdued in overall appearance, they are merely a promise of great things to come. Whitlow is to be congratulated for his landmark achievement in an area too long neglected. Slipper growers are rightfully enthusiastic over the exciting prospects in this field.

Whitlow (personal communication) states his current aims in breeding as oriented toward ease of culture, a necessary preliminary step if this group of hybrids is to enjoy wide popularity.

Primary *Paphiopedilum* Hybrids

The account of *Paphiopedilum* hybridization is virtually synonymous with the history of slipper breeding, representing more than 90% of the work done in the entire subfamily. However, the dichotomy between primary/novelty breeding and breeding for complex, round hybrids necessitates an explanatory word here. The course of *Paphiopedilum* hybridization through its development to the current impressive array of modern, round hybrids will be discussed separately later in this chapter. But of course, both the early primary crosses and the more recent rage for primary/novelty creations are of interest. We shall see how both the beginning and the ending of the story—thus far—of hybridization are dominated by primary/novelty crosses.

While the list of primary/novelty hybrids of *Paphiopedilum* is tediously long, particular examples, illustrative of the extensive breeding history of this group, are so impressive as to compel careful scrutiny.

P. Maudiae, a primary hybrid made by Charlesworth in 1900, (and remade countless times since) originated as a cross of the albino forms of 2 species: *P. callosum* var. *sanderae* × *P. lawrenceanum* var. *hyeanum*. The result was a fine, large flower of exquisite icy white/green-striped color, with much the same shape as the *P. lawrenceanum* parent, borne on a long, straight stalk emerging from tessellated, green-and-white foliage. This primary cross and related hybrids of similar appearance (bred from closely related species, nearly all of which are from section *Barbata*) remain greatly prized and in heavy demand, having maintained a place among the most highly awarded slippers of the past decades. The reader is referred to Plates 143–151. Included in the Maudiae-type hybrids are not only the green-flowered original group, but also the coloratum group exhibiting pink and green coloring (due, in most cases, to having been bred from the normal color forms of the species rather than from albinistic forms), and the vinicolor, or deep burgundy hybrids (bred from heavily pigmented variants of the same group of species).

Although their popularity declined slightly in the 1940s and 1950s, renewed interest in these and other hybrids bred from the *Barbata* section has gripped the slipper world since the late 1960s. It is no exaggeration to characterize *P.* Maudiae as the single slipper orchid which epitomizes the genus *Paphiopedilum*, species and hybrids alike. It appeals equally to the novice and the connoisseur. Numerous awards to the collective group of Maudiae-type hybrids attest to its merits on the judging tables.

The original *P.* Maudiae bears tessellated leaves and a large flower very like its parents both in shape and in its green-and-white striping; the intrinsic beauty of green-and-white, tessellated leaves surmounted by spectacular green-and-white flowers on tall scapes is awe-inspiring. Several exceptionally large clones are known to be tetraploids. The perfection of color and symmetry of these clones is enhanced by the increased overall size induced by tetraploidy without detriment to proportion or balance of segments. The Maudiae-type hybrids are not only the most desirable *Paphiopedilum* for the cut-flower trade, but the high-quality, awarded clones command high prices as well. Demand for these slippers perennially exceeds supply, due not only to aesthetic reasons, but also to their ease of culture and reliable blooming, often more than once a year. All these factors contribute to making this category of hybrids uniquely desirable.

Not only have Maudiae-type hybrids been appreciated for most of a century, but breeders have developed many variations upon the theme. In the green/white group, the crossing of albino forms of *P. callosum* × *P. curtisii* (synonymous with *P. superbiens*) yielded *P.* Goultenianum in 1894 preceding Maudiae. When Maudiae was backcrossed to *P. lawrenceanum* var. *hyeanum*, *P.* Alma Gevaert, an even larger, though quite similar, hybrid resulted in 1911. *P.* Emerald made its debut in 1920 from a cross of Maudiae with the albino

P. curtisii parent. When *P.* Emerald was bred to *P.* Alma Gevaert, the enormous *P.* Clair de Lune was created in 1927. The similarities among *P.* Maudiae, *P.* Goultenianum, *P.* Emerald, *P.* Alma Gevaert and *P.* Clair de Lune are readily apparent. Subtle differences in size and the angles at which petals are held reflect to the discerning eye the presence of particular parents like *P. suberbiens* or *P. callosum* in the parentage. Many hobbyists content themselves with only the flower-size criterion when distinguishing among this closely related group, preferring the largest flower obtainable regardless of other factors.

Other early crosses in this category include *P.* Faire-Maud, originally made by G. F. Moore in 1909. This cross is predominately a coloratum type, whether using a pigmented clone of *P. fairrieanum* or its *album* variant as a parent. The coloratum group of hybrids exhibits reddish pigmentation in the pouch as well as in the striping of petals and sepals. Coloratum progeny result from Maudiae-type breeding incorporating the normally pigmented variants of the typical *Barbata* species rather than the albinistic forms, or in some instances, from crosses utilizing even the albinistic forms of both *P. fairrieanum* and *P. sukhakulii*, neither of which tends to breed more than a small percentage of its progeny in the green/white color range.

For some years preceding the renewed interest in species and novelties, coloratum hybrids were of little import to orchid fanciers. The perennial fascination exerted by Maudiae-type hybrids has depended traditionally upon the icy green/white coloration, abetted by their vigor, ease of culture, rapid production and maturation of growths, all of which result in frequent flowering after 5–6 growths have developed.

While Maudiae-type hybrids are not integral in the breeding of most complex hybrids, the popularity of the albinistic clones rarely exhibited so much as a small decline even during the years when species and novelties were virtually ignored. Resurgence of interest in novelty crosses during the past 2 decades has increased the value of coloratum clones, along with that of all novelty hybrids. Currently, Maudiae-type breeding has extended into speculative crosses with a variety of species, novelty hybrids, and even complex, round hybrids. In fact, since the novelty look has become the most popular avenue in *Paphiopedilum* breeding, supplanting the 6–7 decades of devotion to ever-larger, ever-rounder complex hybrids, there has been a veritable explosion of experimental breeding with Maudiae and her ilk.

Maudiae crosses including 2 other albinistic forms have produced *P.* Faire-Maud (Maudiae × *fairrieanum* 'album') and *P.* Makulii (Maudiae × *sukhakulii* 'Paleface'), with a limited yield of green/white clones. Although neither of these albinistic variant parents is a true albino, a small percentage of the progeny of each grex, devoid of red and brown pigmentation, is highly prized. The unique petals of *P. fairrieanum* tend to give quite a twist to the petals of *P.* Faire-Maud, while the broad, horizontal, spotted petals of *P. sukhakulii* come through in *P.* Makulii progeny as well. *P.* Makulii breaks multiple growths, providing spectacular and continuous flowering. Punsters and etymologists are sure to be gratified by the name *P.* Makulii. Obviously, it is something of a hybrid of the names of its parents, while the Latin term *maculae* meaning "spots," describes the densely spotted petals of most of the progeny.

The story of the *P.* Maudiae group is incomplete without mention of the vinicolor branch of this line of breeding. The vinicolor end of the spectrum is not new to Maudiae-type enthusiasts, although recent work with an outstanding selection of species vinicolors (variants with exceptionally dark burgundy pigmentation of the flowers) has broadened the scope of this noteworthy group. Since the debut of the very first *Paphiopedilum* hybrid, *P.* Harrisianum, dark burgundy hybrids have been made from members of section *Barbata*. During the 1970s and 1980s, the darkest forms of several species of the section, denoted as vinicolors, have been employed as parents of strikingly dark vinicolor hybrids which have earned numerous awards. Remakes of many of the *Barbata* section hybrids, using darker- or larger-flowered parents, have produced improved, award-quality progeny which have been well-received by cypriphiles.

P. Harrisianum × *callosum* yielded the very dark, maroon to mahogany P. Ledouxiae back in 1891. This hybrid remains available and in demand today. Work with the Maudiae group in the past 2 or 3 decades incorporated 2 noteworthy vinicolor clones, *P. callosum* 'Jac' and *P. callosum* 'Sparkling Burgundy', recipients of AM/AOS and FCC/AOS respectively, to yield hybrids of deepest near-black burgundy, for example, P. Maudiae 'Ebony Queen.' The tendency of the vinicolors to produce small flowers pointed up the necessity for breeding for both size and dark color. Breeding with coloratum parents or to species such as *P. superbiens* (*P. curtisii*) and *P. lawrenceanum* were 2 successful avenues which increased size in the vinicolor group. Deeply pigmented clones of *P. sukhakulii* and *P. fairrieanum* and their darkest progeny have augmented the vinicolor end of the spectrum and added their own charming attributes.

This entire group of orchids has received its fair share of admiration and awards, during its development over 9 decades of gracing orchid benches. Never allow P. Maudiae and related hybrids to be dismissed as unimportant, merely for their minimal participation in the mainstream of complex hybridization; this group of hybrids unquestionably maintains its unique, perennial appeal.

Lest the emphasis on how little Maudiae-types have contributed to the lineages of complex hybrids create misapprehensions, it is imperative to mention a couple of avenues of extracted breeding which include such primaries in their pedigrees. Among yellow/green hybrids such as P. Tommie Hanes and P. Betty Bracey, P. Maudiae shows up as the grandparent of P. Gwenpur (Gwen Hannen × Purity) through its parentage of P. Purity (Plate 152). In the backgrounds of several red and spotted red hybrids, another Maudiae-type, P. Gowerianum (Plate 153), enters the lineage as a parent of P. Farnley (Harri-leeanum × Gowerianum). P. Farnmoore (Farnley × Chardmoore), made in 1946, sired such outstanding crosses as P. Black Moore (× Black Thorpe), P. Mooreheart (× Greatheart), P. Sea Cliff (× Littledean), P. Mendocino (× Margaret), P. Milmoore (× Mildred Hunter) and P. Pacific Ocean (× Langley Pride). All of these Maudiae-influenced complex hybrids include important awarded clones which continue to contribute to current breeding programs. More will be said of certain of these individuals in the latter portion of this section devoted to complex *Paphiopedilum* hybrids.

The multiflowered novelty hybrids are another departure in *Paphiopedilum* breeding which have contributed much in aesthetic value, although having no bearing upon the mainstream of complex hybrids. No species has surpassed *P. rothschildianum* in producing exquisitely beautiful, awarded, multifloral progeny. The reader is referred to Plates 154–157. P. A. de Lairesse is a spectacular novelty hybrid made by Sander dating from 1895. Resulting from a cross of *P. rothschildianum* × *P. curtisii* (now known as *P. superbiens*), its elongate, tapering petals and rich pigmentation, so reminiscent of *P. rothschildianum*, make it a striking multiflowered primary. *P. rothschildianum* has produced other, similar, lovely primary hybrids, including P. W. R. Lee (*rothschildianum* × *superbiens*) in 1894 (which, of course, differs but little from P. A. de Lairesse), P. Callo-rothschildianum (*callosum* × *rothschildianum*) registered in 1897, P. Shillianum (Gowerianum × *rothschildianum*) registered in 1899, P. Rolfei (*bellatulum* × *rothschildianum*) from 1901, and both P. St. Swithin (*philippinense* × *rothschildianum*) and P. Transvaal (*chamberlainianum* × *rothschildianum*) also from 1901. (Within this text and others, *P. chamberlainianum* is a synonym for *P. victoria–regina*.)

One cross was registered each decade for the next 2 decades using *P. rothschildianum*: P. Franconia (*callosum* var. *sanderae* × *rothschildianum*) in 1911 and P. Vanguard (*glaucophyllum* × *rothschildianum*) in 1921. The ever-popular P. Delrosi (*delenatii* × *rothschildianum*) was registered in 1961 (Plate 154). While all of these hybrids inherited to some degree the slow maturation of growths characteristic of *P. rothschildianum*, their popularity sustains a high demand for these and related hybrids.

  P. rothschildianum hybrids are rather easy to identify by the typical petal influence so characteristic of that parent. However, when *P. rothschildianum* is crossed onto species of subgenus *Brachypetalum*, as in the cases of *P.* Rolfei and *P.* Delrosi, the broad *Brachypetalum* petals exert a strong influence over the lanceolate petals of *P. rothschildianum*. In any case, all *P. rothschildianum* progeny are so distinctive that novice growers quickly come to recognize both their names and photographs. When seen in life, the flowers of this group are electrifying, consistently measuring up to all expectations. The reader is referred to Plate 49, *P. rothschildianum*, for visual comparisons of the species with illustrations of its progeny.

  P. Julius (*lowii* × *rothschildianum*), made in the 1970s, is a much-awarded cross which carries 3 or more large flowers per scape, demonstrating the possibilities open to breeders in crosses of *Pardalopetalum* species with those in section *Coryopedilum*. *P.* Julius has been among the most frequently awarded *Paphiopedilum* hybrids for most of the 1980s.

  Cochlopetalum and *Pardalopetalum* species have generated interesting multiflowered novelty hybrids, although they are perhaps less-frequently awarded than crosses with species of section *Coryopedilum*. *P.* Jogjae, a cross of *P. glaucophyllum* with *P. praestans* (synonymous with *glanduliferum*) is a popular novelty cross which is multifloral from both parents, as a pairing of a *Cochlopetalum* species with a *Coryopedilum* species. Unfortunately, some of the progeny have received from the *Cochlopetalum* parent the successive-blossoming trait without the extended production typical of that section, producing only 2–4 flowers, 1 at a time. The best clones of the cross bear either numerous, successive flowers on extended scapes or open 3–4 flowers simultaneously.

  The *Brachypetalum* subgenus has contributed less toward roundness of flowers and petal-width of complex hybrids than was expected, although its species have been integral in the development of the white and pink complex hybrids. It is too soon to determine the long-term influence of the newer members comprising the *Parvisepalum* section of subgenus *Brachypetalum* upon breeding of *Paphiopedilum*, although much work is underway. Species such as *P. armeniacum*, *P. emersonii* and *P. micranthum* are being used in speculative crosses. Emerson W. "Doc" Charles (personal communication) reports that a cross currently in flask is a whimsical wordplay upon his name; *P. emersonii* × *P. charlesworthii* is certain to be registered as *P.* Emerson Charles. The clonal name given to the first awarded seedling is equally likely to be 'Doc'. While speculative, such a cross will perhaps reveal some of the potential of the new section. The possible presence of a green-suppressor gene in *P. emersonii* is an unknown factor, so the khaki-colored petals and pouch of *P. charlesworthii* may be detrimental in this cross. Only time will tell whether the results of such a pairing lead to fine progeny or are merely informative about breeding strategies to be avoided. Moreover, comparable speculative crosses must be made in diverse directions before full information is at hand. The possibilities must be broadly explored. Breeding of *Parvisepalum* species with complex hybrids of the major color categories, multifloral species, other *Brachypetalum*, and *Barbata* species and various novelties is required to fully elucidate the capabilities of the genomes of these recently introduced species.

  The novelty crosses incorporating section *Brachypetalum* species and *P. delenatii* are surely among the most beautiful and highly awarded of the novelty group. The lovely *P.* Olivia (Plate 158), a pink hybrid of *P. tonsum* × *P. niveum* made by Oakes Ames in 1898, illustrates the capacity of *P. niveum* to suppress green pigmentation such as is preponderant in *P. tonsum*. *P.* Madame Martinet (*callosum* var. *sanderae* × *delenatii*), *P.* Colorkulii (*concolor* × *sukhakulii*), *P.* Delrosi (*delenatii* × *rothschildianum*), *P.* Vanda M. Pearman (*delenatii* × *bellatulum*), and *P.* Psyche (*bellatulum* × *niveum*) are excellent primaries illustrating the possibilities inherent in novelty *Brachypetalum* breeding. The reader is referred to Plates 154 and 159–161.

The use of *P. delenatii* as a parent has failed in large part to produce the hoped-for break-throughs in breeding of complex pink hybrids, although it has generated some exquisite novelties. Of these, *P.* Vanda M. Pearman (Plate 160) is distinguished more by the enormous numbers of awards it has merited than as a stud plant. For some years it held the record, numbering more than 50, for awards to a primary hybrid, although a remake of *P.* Iona (*bellatulum* × *fairrieanum*), a cross originally made in 1913, has recently challenged and surpassed the former record. These spectacular new clones of *P.* Iona (Plate 162) have been bred using high quality, awarded clones of the species as parents.

Certain primary hybrids are of pivotal historical significance for their influence in the breeding of complex hybrids. A cross of *P. insigne* × *P. spiceranum* was registered in 1884 as *P.* Leeanum (Plate 133). While not a tremendous improvement upon either parent, neither is it without merit. Its major fascination lies, however, in its early contribution to the backgrounds of virtually all the complex hybrids in existence. The spotting of the dorsal sepal of *P. insigne* persists many generations later in many of the complex hybrids, although recent trends show some diminution of the popularity of spotted hybrids. *P. spiceranum* exerts a strong influence on flare-dorsal coloration and the excellent, wide dorsals of complex hybrids. The width of the *P. spiceranum* dorsal has been a dominant and valuable trait for breeders of most of the round hybrids. Tracing ancestry of various popular, modern hybrids illustrates just how consistently *P.* Leeanum, its parents and its progeny have figured in pedigrees. See Tables 6–13 for verification of the importance of *P.* Leeanum, its parents, and comparable early hybrids to the history of *Paphiopedilum* breeding.

Another hybrid which has had a marked influence upon modern hybrids is *P.* Nitens, an 1877 cross of *P. insigne* × *P. villosum*. In the case of this hybrid, the tendency toward spotted dorsals is rather similar to that shown in *P.* Leeanum. The *P. villosum* influence produces excellent substance in the progeny. *P. insigne* (Plate 70), spotted dorsal notwithstanding, has surely had a greater influence on modern, round hybrids than any other species. In the literature, it is not uncommon to find complex hybrids referred to as *insigne*–type hybrids. Its variant, *P. insigne* var. *sanderae* (Plate 71), has had an equally pivotal influence on hybrids with unspotted dorsals, as well as in the breeding of yellow/greens, whites and pinks.

No discussion of pivotal primaries having a major influence upon later complex hybrids would be complete without reference to *P.* Actaeus (*insigne* × Leeanum), made by Veitch in 1895. See Plate 163. A step beyond the species and the primary *P.* Leeanum, it was a parent of *P.* Christopher, *P.* F. C. Puddle, *P.* Purity, *P.* Graceful, *P.* Moonlight and *P.* Anita, among others. This hybrid along with its offspring had a vast influence upon modern hybrids, figuring prominently and repeatedly in the lineages of today's leading complex hybrids.

P. Winnieanum (*druryi* × *villosum*), an old cross rarely seen today, is found in the background of great hybrids such as *P.* Hellas, *P.* Tommie Hanes and others. Lost to cultivation for many years, *P. druryi* (Plate 61) has been employed in many new crosses in the past 2 decades since its rediscovery by Mammen and Mammen. Most of these new hybrids are primary crosses, although crosses with *P.* Freckles and *P.* Hellas may yield some fine progeny. The contribution made by this relative of *P. insigne* and *P. spiceranum* remains marginal to moderate.

P. Papa Rohl (*sukhakulii* × *fairrieanum*) exemplifies primary crosses in which progeny show an improvement over both the parents. The reader is referred to Plate 164. Clones of this novelty hybrid which retain the unusual shape of either parent are considered less worthy. The rationale is that the shapes and color patterns of the species are already manifest attributes of the genus, and that the breeding of minor changes is a goalless, if not an outrightly deleterious, path. However, well-known clones of *P.* Papa Rohl not only exhibit

excellent proportions of segments and an interesting striped pattern to the spotting, but outstanding size and coloring as well. *P. fairrieanum* exerts its influence for red coloring even
more effectively, however, in its infusion into complex reds and pinks. It has the added
advantage, in this latter avenue, of increasing scape length. More attention is devoted to the
influence of *P. fairrieanum* on complex hybrids in the latter portion of this section.

    P. sukhakulii has also produced a number of outstanding primaries and novelties. Its
offspring are desirable for several important reasons: vigorous growth and the probability of
2 or more flowerings per year; strong, tall scapes; and distinctively spotted petals.
P. Colorkulii (Plate 165) shows *Brachypetalum* influence combined with the unique characteristics of *P. sukhakulii*. An unusual departure using *P. sukhakulii* onto *P appletonianum* (a
species rarely used in breeding) created *P.* Nisqually (Plate 166).

    P. charlesworthii has made a smaller contribution overall to *Paphiopedilum* breeding than
was expected. Its excellent, broad pink dorsal has been used to advantage when bred onto
complex hybrids, although the resultant shortening of the stalk has discouraged extensive
experimentation. Some representative early hybrids include *P.* Rachel (*charlesworthii* ×
curtisii) registered in 1900, and *P.* Papyrus (*charlesworthii* × Earl of Tankerville) registered in
1923 (Plate 167). The latter is of some significance in complex breeding lines.
P. Leyburnense (Plate 168), often called *P.* Mrs. Haywood, is a beautiful cross registered perhaps incorrectly as *P. charlesworthii* × *P.* T. B. Haywood (*druryi* × *superbiens*). Made in 1905,
this lovely pink hybrid is treasured by discerning growers today. Breeding with
P. charlesworthii continued for several decades into the 20th century without further notable
success, because of the tendency of the narrow, khaki-colored petals of *P. charlesworthii* to
dominate in its progeny. Two other early primary crosses awarded in the 1970s are *P.* Jessie
(*P. charlesworthii* × *P. fairrieanum*) and *P.* Daphne (*P. exul* × *P. charlesworthii*) (Plate 169).
P. Rosita is another older, but very attractive, lavender rose primary cross of *P. callosum* ×
P. charlesworthii. Finally, *P.* Woodrose (*charlesworthii* × Normandy) (Plate 170) is an outstanding example of the crossing of this species onto a complex hybrid in 1978 to yield excellent, award-quality progeny of the complex type. Although *P. charlesworthii* possesses excellent potential as a parent, successful breeding programs depend upon researched or intuitive selection of the appropriate mates which will release that potential while suppressing its
unfortunate petals. Results may be somewhat unpredictable, according to van Ede (1978),
depending upon the loci of alleles for the presence of anthocyanins and for chloroplasts.
That is, the control of each type of flower pigment requires a particular suppressor gene at
the appropriate locus in the chromosomes of the mate. Identification of mates which are
capable of the desired control has been only partially successful. Certain of the species in the
Brachypetalum section, primarily *P. niveum*, are known to possess a gene which suppresses or
inhibits green in flowers. Control of anthocyanins as well as green pigment to develop clear
whites and pinks appears to be possible when parents are selected in keeping with the most
recent discoveries about dominance and recessiveness in pigmentation. Bertsch
(1981a,b,c,d) deals with these topics in some detail.

    One of the highly awarded hybrids of the mid–1980s is *P.* Watercolor Artist (*masters-
ianum* × Virginia Moffett). This hybrid caught the attention of judges over and over, although
it rarely achieved high scores. Two seldom-used species show their merits in this hybrid. In
effect, the flower is a larger, broader-petalled *P. mastersianum*. Color modifications are due to
the influence of the primary hybrid parent *P.* Virginia Moffett (*callosum* × *acmodontum*).
P. acmodontum is perhaps a contributor to the petal width as well as the color. *P. mastersianum*
was also crossed onto *P. lawrenceanum* to produce *P.* William Matthews, a prolific hybrid with
large, glossy flowers of tremendous substance on very long scapes. With *P.* Supersuk (*P. sukhakulii* × *P.* William Matthews) a spectacular hybrid was made. Not only is this hybrid among
the largest of the novelties, but its vigor, stance, keeping-quality and color carry on the best

attributes of its parents as well. Future breeding with *P. mastersianum* and its offspring is anticipated as much potential remains to be released.

Hybrids of *P. henryanum*, a recently discovered species from Yunnan Province in China, are eagerly awaited. Resembling an early complex hybrid in its similarity to *P. insigne*, it has the additional advantages of wider petals and a rounder shape than is found in related species. Its rosy coloration indicates that its impact on complex breeding may be outstanding. It will be equally interesting to see the results of novelty crosses of this new species.

In summary, according to Dopp (1984), over a period of about a year in the early 1980s, the ratio of awards given to species, primaries and the novelty progeny of crosses between complex hybrids and species or novelties to the awards given to the round hybrids was approximately 2 to 1. This trend continues unabated. No longer are devotees of the species and their unique qualities considered anachronistic. The piquancy of variety wields an irresistible attraction for today's cypriphiles, while the species and novelty hybrids may be seen to have at last achieved the attention and acclaim they so richly deserve.

COMPLEX HYBRIDS OF *PAPHIOPEDILUM*

The history of the mainstream of *Paphiopedilum* hybridization is one of serendipity, a hit-or-miss, trial-and-error narrative of the heartbreak or elation associated with dead ends or breakthroughs. It is a complex account of the interaction between man and the slipper orchids, of the malleability and intractability of both the breeders and the intricate genomes of these plants whether species or hybrids.

The myriad complexities barring thorough understanding of the genetics of primary hybrids multiply exponentially once hybrid offspring are outcrossed to new species, backcrossed on parent species, or crossed with each other for up to 12 or more generations. Only patient pursuit of a particular trait's appearance and augmentation throughout complex pedigrees rewards the breeder with fresh vision for future work.

A historical view of hybridizing begins in 1866, with the initial feverish work in primary crosses, followed by more extensive breeding between the progeny of those hybrids. During the last 3 decades of the 19th century, approximately 475 *Paphiopedilum* hybrids and 36 *Phragmipedium* hybrids were registered. The turn of the century marked the introduction of directed purpose into *Paphiopedilum* breeding, coupled with far more extensive breeding beyond the primary level. Deterministic hybridization paid off with improvements in size, form, color and substance. In 1902, the introduction of *P.* Christopher, hailed as the first of a new trend in large-flowered hybrids, heralded a series of marvelous breakthroughs. The parentage of *P.* Christopher is shown in Table 3, page 178.

In 1914, *P.* Christopher was remade by G. F. Moore using particular clones of *P.* Actaeus ('F. H. Cann') and Leeanum ('Corona'), so it is not always possible to determine which of these 2 crosses produced the particular clones of *P.* Christopher used in various steps in subsequent hybrids, nor is it clear how exclusively the select, 1914 aneuploid clone 'Grand Duke Nicholas' was used. It is, however, currently believed that 'Grand Duke Nicholas' was the significant clone in most instances in extracted pedigrees containing multiple infusions of *P.* Christopher. Aneuploidy, the possession of a fraction of a whole genome, is manifested in this clone as the possession of 27 chromosomes—1 more than the 26 chromosomes characteristic of a normal diploid.

This incredibly simple pedigree reveals that *P.* Christopher received all its genetic input from only 2 species, although probably more than 1 variant of *P. insigne* was involved as well as the different clones of *P.* Leeanum and *P.* Actaeus which were incorporated into the 2 crosses. See Plates 71, 72, 133, 163 and 171, illustrating the 2 species, the 2 primary hybrids and *P.* Christopher 'Grand Duke Nicholas'. Breeders of that time, lacking the hindsight with which we are blessed, found themselves confronted by a breakthrough which failed to point clearly in any single direction. In fact, *P.* Christopher raised more questions than it answered, and most of them would be answered only in part even after intensive, time-consuming experimentation. Among those questions, the following were some of the more crucial and urgent:

1. Could either of the parent species be the sole source of this hybrid's unprecedented size, and if so, which one?
2. Might the size increase be duplicated in other lines using ordinary breeding, or was *P.* Christopher a marvelous sport?
3. If indeed a sport, could it be induced to pass its heritage along to future generations?

At that point in the development of slipper breeding, any understanding of Mendel's laws was largely confined to the ivied halls of academia and botanical institutes, so few clues existed as to how best to proceed. (In fact, it would be primarily extrapolations from Mendel's original work which would only later apply to the more complex genetics of slippers.) Hybridizers settled, through necessity, for a series of stabs in the dark. Although subsequent advances in size did occur, the answers to some of these questions remain not only incompletely formulated but poorly documented. So, while the positive results of subsequent breeding are clear, a thorough understanding of how the successes occurred is elusive. Aneuploidy is known to affect size. Today, enlightened speculation is possible, while conclusive proof, requiring documentation which is long-lost, remains beyond our reach. Since aneuploidy possibly had no bearing on the less-pronounced increase in size of many of the siblings of the 1902 *P.* Christopher cross, the mystery has never been completely cleared up. More will be said about aneuploidy in "Genetics and Other Technical Aspects of Slipper Breeding" later in this chapter.

With the present level of knowledge, experiments in breeding such as those carried out with *P.* Christopher yield information about dominance and recessiveness, linkages, loci of particular traits and other genetic particulars. However, without specific knowledge, in many cases, about which clones of parents were used in breeding with particular clones of *P.* Christopher, and lacking the opportunity to survey the ranges of traits appearing in those Roaring Twenties progeny, much valuable information about past breeding remains permanently inaccessible.

Nonetheless, hybridization was given a marvelous boost as a result of this important milestone. Breeding with *P.* Christopher proceeded immediately. Karasawa and Kimura (1973) wrote that this hybrid, especially the clone 'Grand Duke Nicholas', revolutionized *Paphiopedilum* breeding. G. F. Moore, who registered the improved *P.* Christopher of 1914, used the 'Grand Duke Nicholas' clone as a parent to produce, among others, *P.* Chrysostum (*P.* Christopher × *P.* Pyramus) and *P.* Gwen Hannen (*P.* Christopher × *P.* Florence Spencer) which were registered in 1922, and *P.* Chardmoore (*P.* Christopher × *P.* Lena) in 1927. See Plates 172–174. These progeny of *P.* Christopher are excellent and frequently-used parents, possessed of high fertility and the ability to pass along dominant size and, in some cases, substance to their progeny. Refer to pedigrees of modern hybrids in this section such as *P.* Tommie Hanes from 1967 (Table 11), or *P.* Sheila Hanes, 1972 (Table 12), to see the great frequency with which *P.* Christopher and its progeny were used, and the resulting concentration of its influence in individual lineages.

The marvelous size of *P.* Christopher is dominant in its offspring while color may be varied by selection of its mate (predominantly only when the mate is the pod-parent; that is, when *P.* Christopher is the male or pollen-parent). Although good whites, yellows and greens predominate, excellent reds and spotted progeny have also descended from these early crosses. Many of the initial progeny, however, were open flowers of poor shape. Only through careful selection of mates was improvement in form achieved in *P*. Christopher's significant grandchildren.

Among the most compelling and ultimately beneficial aspects of these *P*. Christopher progeny as a group are their excellent size, their recessiveness for shape and their superior fecundity. The progress so evident today, which would come about through the influence of this parent, could only be guessed at during the 1920s and 1930s.

However, as pointed out by Karasawa and Kimura (1973), *P*. Finetta (*P*. Chrysostum × *P*. Christopher 'Grand Duke Nicholas') registered in 1930, was an experiment in line-breeding with *P*. Christopher which produced what was at that time "the most successful stud plant in Japan." They report that *P*. Finetta AM/JOS is an aneuploid with 27 chromosomes, as is its famed parent, which has been widely used in Japan as a parent because of its high fertility (particularly as a pollen-parent), good form and size, and long scape. Progeny such as *P*. Sasa (*P*. Glosan × *P*. Finetta in 1963) and *P*. Aiko Yamamoto (*P*. Yumedono × *P*. Finetta) illustrate the tendency of *P*. Finetta to influence form positively, and to produce award-winning clones. This influence is not limited to yellow hybrids, but depending upon the pod-parent selected, good red, white and spotted offspring are produced which typically exhibit great vigor.

Subsequent to the flurry of intensive breeding stimulated by *P*. Christopher, *P*. Perseus (Plate 175) exemplified yet another of the desirable goals of slipper hybridization in 1917. Excellent form, consisting of overlapping segments and proportions which lent roundness to the shape, was the hallmark of this hybrid. However, as we shall see, this step was not to provide a major breakthrough nor to influence future lines as did *P*. Christopher.

Like *P*. Christopher, *P*. Perseus is strongly influenced by *P*. *insigne*. However, in this cross, the heavy infusion of *P*. *villosum* (*P*. *boxalli* is a variant of *P*. *villosum*) produced quite different genotypic and phenotypic conditions. The pedigree of *P*. Perseus is given in Table 4, page 178.

Although *P*. Perseus was widely used in subsequent breeding, its progeny have proved to be of little value. No significant lines of breeding emerged out of this avenue. Instead, breeders found improved shape could be selected from the progeny of a number of crosses of diverse origin. Thus, *P*. Perseus is better remembered as an early indicator of an innate capacity for roundness within *Paphiopedilum* than as a significant stud plant. A number of more recent hybrids, including *P*. Hellas 'Westonbirt', several clones of *P*. Winston Churchill and others are recognized as parents dominant for form, however.

The interval between the two world wars produced the most rapid and significant advances in *Paphiopedilum* hybridizing in the entire history of the endeavor. Routine judging sponsored by the Royal Horticultural Society in England, the American Orchid Society in the USA, and under similar auspices in other countries provided the impetus to weed out inferior individuals and work for higher quality in hybrids. Improved complex hybrids in the yellow and green trends emerged from the potential demonstrated by *P*. Christopher during the interval between the world wars.

Stimulated by this enormous activity in breeding, the George Moore Medal was established in 1926, becoming the most highly prized award for excellence in *Paphiopedilum* circles. For a unique perspective on the progress in *Paphiopedilum* hybridization over the past 60 years, the list of George Moore Medal recipients is required reading. The reflected glory which devolves upon the registrants of medal-winning hybrids has assured the commercial success of several orchid houses, as this honor is bestowed only upon the most outstanding of the hundreds of slippers awarded during routine judgings in a year. Unfortunately, a great many of the medal-winning slippers over the years have failed to prove themselves as parents.

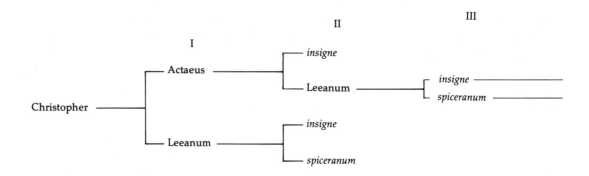

Table 3. Pedigree of *Paphiopedilum* Christopher.

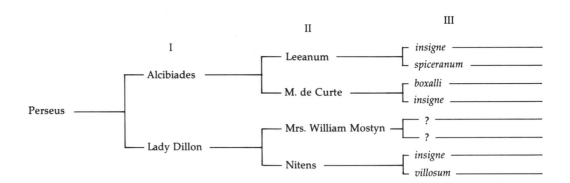

Table 4. Pedigree of *Paphiopedilum* Perseus.

To resume the chronology of important hybrids, another breakthrough occurred in 1921 when *P.* Cardinal Mercier (Plate 176) was introduced. Its background is questionable. It may be a clone of *P. Lathamianum* (*spiceranum* × *villosum*), or a hybrid from it, in which case the name of the second parent is lost. This hybrid introduced 2 new features into the narrative. The first example of excellent red color in *Paphiopedilum* breeding, it is also the ideal example of a hybrid which, although inferior in shape, was heavily used in breeding for its color dominance. E. C. Wilcox (1971), Peter Black (1973) and breeders in general concur that *P.* Cardinal Mercier is not only the significant breakthrough in reds, but is present in the background of many of the high quality, modern, red hybrids. So important was this hybrid that *P.* Cardinal Mercier was the single *Paphiopedilum* hybrid mentioned by name (1947) in Fred K. Sander's prefatory words to *Sanders' Complete List of Orchid Hybrids*. This landmark hybrid is found in the backgrounds of such noteworthy parents as *P.* Atlantis (× *P.* Chloris) (Plate 177), *P.* Blagrose (× *P.* Eurybiades) and others.

Thus, *P.* Cardinal Mercier illustrates that to be valuable a hybrid need not be worthy of award. The converse is also true in that award-winning hybrids are not necessarily excellent parents. Perhaps the most daunting aspect of hybridization is this divergence between what you see (phenotype) and what you get (genotype). Therefore, it is necessary to specify whether a particular hybrid is an award-quality plant, a good parent or both. The excellent parent must not only possess desirable genes at critical loci, but it must also be fecund. All too often the qualities which determine excellence as a parent are invisible, that is, they do not manifest themselves in the phenotype at all. It is, therefore, all the more amazing that early breeders made the remarkable strides for which they are so justly famous.

The progress of hybridization gathered further momentum during the period between the two world wars due to Knudson's (1922) pioneering work on culture media which permitted the bypassing of symbiotic mycorrhizae in seedling culture. Inert agar, incorporating nutrients and carefully sterilized, was found to be capable of successfully supporting both germination and growth of embryonic orchid seedlings through the early dependent phase of their development, and with nutrient modifications, even to the stage of transplanting into community flats. Knudson's formula, and others derived subsequently, revolutionized the breeding of orchids, speeding the process and tremendously increasing the yield of successful seedlings per pod. The significance of an improved survival rate among progeny, regardless of quality, lies in the better grasp by breeders of the ratios of various traits in each assortment, providing improved guidelines for subsequent crosses.

But as a consequence, the necessity for weeding out inferior plants reached immense proportions. As the number of surviving plantlets per grex increased dramatically, breeders saw a tremendous amount of greenhouse space taken over by seedlings, many of which were of poor quality. Weeding out involved both discarding sickly individuals and culling the numerous healthy plants producing inferior flowers. Even with the improved ability to grow from seeds, however, many crosses made today produce sparsely filled pods that yield only 25–200 offspring. All too frequently, the degree of fecundity of parents is still a limiting factor in hybridization. (See "Genetics and Other Technical Aspects of Slipper Breeding" later in this chapter.)

Thus, despite Knudson's impressive contribution and that of his successors, breeders were destined to confront even more difficulties. Particular problems, apparently inherent in the genus and persistent yet today, include both reduced fecundity and a lower germination rate relative to other orchid genera. Extensive breeding, yielding ever more complex pedigrees, generated particular problems. By the decades of the 1920s and 1930s, several pitfalls had surfaced with sufficient regularity that they were identified as more than mere flukes. The problems, in their simplest definitions, were:

1. Increasingly pervasive sterility among some of the most desirable plants available for stud.
2. A growing number of brownish or khaki-colored hybrids (variously termed "muddy monsters," "toads," and "bulldogs").
3. And most discouraging of all, a veritable epidemic of deformities among complex hybrids.

The understanding necessary to cope with these problems was slower to coalesce than might be the case in today's milieu of slipper growers and hybridizers who count among their ranks a growing number of qualified scientists. With training and experience based in such disciplines as molecular biology, genetics, physiology and biochemistry, these individuals are able to immediately put the best of modern scientific thinking and techniques to work on hybridization problems, through a network of colleagues and research facilities.

The problem of deformity yielded to intuitive solutions such as culling deformed plants and recording and publishing crosses which produced a high percentage of deformed progeny. The problem, while not eliminated, was largely brought under control through avoidance.

By way of explaining the nature of the remaining problems and the available solutions to them, it is also necessary to explore the practices which created the difficulties. See "Genetics and Other Technical Aspects of Slipper Breeding" later in this chapter for a discussion of polyploidy and its implications in breeding, especially as it relates to lowered fecundity amounting to functional sterility. Experimentation together with careful study of larger percentages of progeny per grex cleared the way for better understanding of dominant/recessive influences in color, so gradually much of the unattractive coloring was eliminated.

The decades between the world wars also introduced the potential for good whites, although form and size lagged behind color in this line of breeding. The landmark debut of *P. F. C. Puddle* in 1932 was the major breakthrough in good white hybrids. It remains an excellent and reliable stud plant both in terms of the quality and the quantity of its progeny, as it continues to sire good whites and pinks after nearly 7 decades of use. Its influence was destined to equal and even exceed in importance that of the breeder for whom it was named. In 1933, the George Moore Medal was awarded to *P. F. C. Puddle 'Bodnant'*. A look at its heritage (Table 5) shows the influence of *P. insigne* var. *sanderae* as well as a solid injection of *Brachypetalum* influence, through *P. bellatulum* and *P. niveum*. Plate 178 illustrates *P. F. C. Puddle 'Superbum'*.

F. C. Puddle (1947), the breeder, pointed out that the backbone of good, white hybrid stock comes from *P. niveum* crossed with a particular clone of *P. insigne*. The *P. insigne* parent which best suppresses pigmentation in white hybrids is always var. *sanderae*. Other forms of this species, albinistic or colored, produce predominantly pigmented progeny.

Subsequent progress in white breeding lines was to include some interesting developments. When *P. F. C. Puddle* was crossed with the yellow *P. Doris Black* (*P. Florence Spencer* × *P. Golden Wren*), the product, *P. Vestalia*, was an excellent grex of all white progeny. *P. Snow Bunting* (*P. Florence Spencer* × *P. F. C. Puddle*) was equally successful. These 2 crosses of *P. F. C. Puddle* with yellow parents produced large, white flowers of good form on tall scapes. *P. F. C. Puddle* has been used in countless crosses, a few of which are so outstanding they cannot be omitted from this account. *P. Dimity* (× *P. Gorse*), *P. Dusty Miller* (× *P. Chardmoore*), *P. Freckles* (× *P. Burleigh Mohur*), *P. Heartsease* (× *P. Minster Lovell*), *P. Huddle* (× *P. Hellas*), *P. Lohengrin* (× *P. Golden Beauty*), *P. Meadowsweet* (× *P. Chilton*), *P. Rosepoint* (× *P. Nowara*), *P. Silvara* (× *P. Sungrove*), *P. Susan Tucker* (× *P. Shalimar*), and *P. Whitemoor* (× *P. Dervish*) make up an impressive, though incomplete, list of awarded slippers, all sired by *P. F. C. Puddle*, although not all of these are useful as

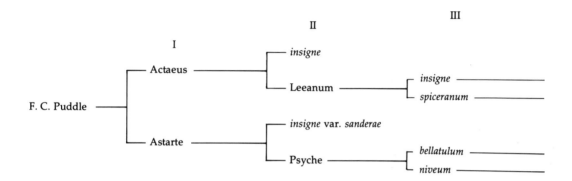

Table 5. Pedigree of *Paphiopedilum* F. C. Puddle.

parents. (See Plates 179–182, 188, and 224.)

Puddle (1947) wrote that his success in white breeding depended so heavily upon his choice of yellow parents that he had begun to breed his own yellows for use as stud plants. He also cautioned that, as breeding lines became ever more complex, the yellow pigment would require repeated suppression by reinfusions of the genomes of parents such as *P. F. C. Puddle*, at intervals. An especially rewarding outcome of Puddle's line of breeding was the combination of summer- and winter-flowering stock which produced a line of hybrids that flower throughout the year.

Among other promising hybrids up through the 1930s, there are several reliable stud plants still in use today and noteworthy as major contributors to today's modern hybrids. *P. Agnes de Burc, P. Anita, P. Atlantis, P. Balaclava, P. Banchory, P. Blagrose, P. Chardmoore 'Mrs. Cowburn', P. Diana Broughton, P. Doris Black, P. Gertrude West, P. Gold Luna, P. Gold Mohur, P. Golden Beauty, P. Golden Wren, P. Grace Darling, P. Graceful, P. Great Mogul, P. Grey Friar, P. Gwen Hannen, P. J. M. Black, P. Lady Mona, P. Maori, P. Mildred Hunter, P. Momag, P. Rosemary Waithman, P. Rosy Dawn,* and *P. W. N. Evans* make up a partial list of these pivotal hybrid parents whose names recur frequently, tracing the ancestry of today's award-winning round hybrids. See Plates 173, 174, 177, 183–186.

Slowly in this intricate story, several constants emerge:
1. Breeders strive for improved shape (roundness), size, color and substance.
2. Hybrids are subjected to a special and consistent scrutiny (centrally by a panel of judges in England, or against an established point-score system applied by qualified judges in the geographically far-flung United States) as a means of maintaining quality and improving breeding.
3. There are 2 categories of worthy hybrid plants—the excellent, award-quality hybrid and the proven stud plant—each with its own distinct characteristics, although these need not be mutually exclusive.

These constants apply, however, primarily to the complex hybrids. Novelty hybrids, particularly those incorporating the multiflowered *Pardalopetalum, Coryopedilum* and *Cochlopetalum* species, are not judged on the same criteria, nor is their breeding carried out with either the same goals or difficulties which remain constraints in complex hybridization. While color, substance and size remain important criteria in novelty breeding, obviously form is modified by the narrow- and often long-petalled species influence. Selection of parents involves fewer preconceived goals; infertility rarely strikes. In short, creativity in primary and novelty breeding is less circumscribed, but more speculative or openly experimental. Therefore, in the 1970s, separate judging criteria for novelty *Paphiopedilum* hybrids were established by the American Orchid Society.

Within the complex hybrids it is necessary to delve further into the divergence between the useful parent and the award-quality offspring being pursued. The successful breeder possesses the experience to select 1 less-than-perfect parent for its fecundity and its desirable characteristics to be crossed with a carefully selected second parent having the complementary desirable traits. The expertise of the breeder resides in his ability to discern prolific parents possessing dominant alleles for good qualities in spite of that parent's outward appearance. Dominance and recessiveness deserve more attention in the narrative of hybridization. "Genetics and Other Technical Aspects of Slipper Breeding" later in this chapter is devoted in part to this topic.

Reduced fertility due to an increase in production of triploid (3n) progeny became a significant impediment in the 1940s and 1950s; details of this particular aspect of the problem are also discussed in the final section of this chapter.

The appearance of *P. Hellas* in 1940 was a major stride in *Paphiopedilum* hybridization. While *P. Hellas 'Westonbirt'* is an awarded clone and is considered to have good form, its substance is poor by today's standards. The major contribution of *P*. Hellas 'Westonbirt' has proved to be its capacity to breed improved progeny. *P*. Hellas 'Westonbirt' offspring have better substance, improved form, and a variety of color possibilities largely controlled by the coloration of the mate.

During the 1950s, as *P*. Winston Churchill and other superb hybrids began to make their appearance, breeders' appetites were whetted for an excellently formed red hybrid of good color. Offspring of *P*. Winston Churchill and other contemporary successes were to fulfil those dreams. Yet, in fact, during the early 1950s, breeders would have been forced to admit that they were far from satisfied with the overall status of hybrids. At that time, the hybrids with the finest form were the yellows and greens, although these typically lacked substance. Good red color was rarely found in well-formed flowers, and whites tended to fall short on form, substance and size. During the 1960s, many of these problems yielded to long years of intensive breeding, so that much progress was made. And, while the 1970s were to open the floodgates to a renewed interest in species and novelty crosses, steady improvement continued among the round, complex hybrids.

One of the most interesting aspects of the entire story of hybridization is the unpredictability of cypriphiles' tastes in orchids. The buying public, influenced by preferences of the judges, creates trends during which a certain type of slipper is in or out of vogue for a time. The near-total decline of interest in species which prevailed for an entire century after the beginnings of hybridization is the prime example of the impact of trends and preferences upon the slipper world. Emerson "Doc" Charles (personal communication) illustrated the degree of whimsy in this aspect of hybridization when he observed that in the past decade a group of slippers, formerly considered undesirable as "dirty browns" has become a marketable category since being given the appellations "porcelains" and "autumn tones," although undoubtedly much improvement in color clarity has occurred along the way as well. Furthermore, while the spotted hybrids fell out of favor during the 1960s and 1970s, renewed interest in this group has recently occurred as a result of breeding for larger spots with greater contrast. The complex hybrids as a whole, while not in disfavor, have continued to rank a poor second in popularity to novelty crosses since the early 1970s. Expression of preferences, including initiation of certain vogues or trends in slipper popularity, is one of the more human aspects of the entire narrative of hybridization.

An interesting trend which never quite caught on was the development of dwarf clones. These are often called "pygmy paphs" as they range in size from teacup-size specimens to individuals just on the small side of normal. Smaller individuals were known from England as early the 1920s and 1930s, and, according to Fordyce (1976) miniaturization is said to have been actively pursued by the Japanese at one time. Plants which qualify for inclusion should be hybrids, but although often of dwarf species extraction, not the dwarf species themselves. Furthermore, a plant must not be deemed a pygmy based only on its first bloom, but should demonstrate its pygmy status for several years before inclusion in this group. Ideally, both foliage and flower are diminutive. Several of the hybrids discussed in this chapter have contributed clones to the pygmy paph category, including *P*. All Taba, *P*. Vexillarium, *P*. Psyche, *P*. Vanda M. Pearman, *P*. Madame Martinet, and *P*. Leyburnense. See Plates 159–161, 168 and 192.

A number of growers and breeders worked on developing this tangent in *Paphiopedilum* hybridization particularly in the 1960s and 1970s, but the public response was minimal. This is unfortunate, as the same standards of excellence (with the exception of the size criterion) might have been applied equally well to produce very high quality miniature hybrids of every color category. However, as long as a challenge exists, there is reason to expect that it will eventually be met by the dedicated breeders who walk among their *Paphiopedilum* benches with toothpicks in hand, ever ready to pollinate.

As an outgrowth of the reawakened interest in species and primary hybrids, the 1970s produced numerous speculative crosses of great worth pairing species with complex hybrids. Several of these have been noted elsewhere in this chapter as meritorious hybrids. This avenue of breeding has made a noteworthy contribution in the production of fine, complex, pink hybrids. The use of *P. fairrieanum* for its red influence in such speculative hybrids particularly deserves comment. In such hybrids, the form is frequently though not always modified toward the unusual species forms. Among the various crosses of *P. fairrieanum* with *insigne*-type hybrids, the following are exemplary: *P.* Sophomore (× *P.* Chardmoore), *P.* Plumfairie (× *P.* Plumly), *P.* Oto (× *P.* Winston Churchill), *P.* Fair Yerba (× *P.* Yerba Buena), *P.* Fairhunter (× *P.* Mildred Hunter) and *P.* Ali Taba (× *P.* Paeony). See Plates 159–161, 168 and 192. Subsequent breeding with these hybrids has produced *P. fairrieanum* grandchildren of enormous worth; *P.* Dusky Maiden is one such hybrid which is discussed below.

Species other than *P. fairrieanum* that are being successfully incorporated into crosses with complex hybrids include *P. bellatulum*, *P. callosum*, *P. charlesworthii*, *P. concolor*, *P. delenatii*, *P. glaucophyllum*, *P. hirsutissimum*, *P. mastersianum*, *P. niveum*, *P. primulinum*, *P. rothschildianum*, *P. sukhakulii*, *P. tonsum*, *P. venustum* and *P. villosum*. From these and other speculative crosses, several outstanding new looks are destined to appear, as this is the material from which new trends emerge. Many of these crosses are just coming into first flower, so descriptions and illustrations of their true scope are unavailable. This, however, is a group worthy of attention, with the potential for award-winning clones. Readers may consult orchid society bulletins to keep up with the latest registrations.

While it is clear that each of the modern, round hybrids represents a continuous line of breeding which can be traced (barring errors, inadvertent or deliberate) back to its origins, an exhaustive effort to do so for the thousands of hybrids now available would require vast amounts of time and space. Moreover, such an endeavor would not only be tedious and confusing, but pointless. Pedigrees of representative examples of the major trends in modern hybrids are illustrative of the whole of hybridizing. Thus, a reconstruction of the background and pedigrees of only a few, selected, modern hybrids provides a reliable prospectus of and insight into more than a century of *Paphiopedilum* breeding. Always bear in mind, of course, the importance of those pivotal species and early hybrids discussed in the preceding pages.

Most complex hybrids fall into one of the following categories: green (with or without spotting); yellow (with or without spotting); bronze, brown or orange (autumn colors or porcelains); maroon-spotted or -flushed (flare-dorsals); cream, white and/or pink. While the individual hybrids in any color class were developed in unique linear steps, the overall percentage of infusion of various clones of species and their variants, such as *Paphiopedilum spiceranum*, *P. insigne* and *P. villosum*, is often remarkably similar throughout all lines of breeding. Through the serendipitous and/or calculated use of the genomes of these species parents, and certain albinistic forms of them, together with judicious or accidental admixtures of genomes from other species (such as *P. fairrieanum*, *P. bellatulum* and *P. niveum*) or hybrids (including *P.* Christopher, *P.* Cardinal Mercier, *P.* F. C. Puddle, *P.* Chardmoore and their like), the trends were established and developed. Exploration along these lines continues, with unabated enthusiasm. Furthermore, several excellent parents, such as *P.* Hellas 'Westonbirt' and clones of *P.* Winston Churchill, are producing worthy progeny in more than 1 color line of the large, round, complex hybrids.

The trend toward pink-flowered hybrids was a refreshing innovation that matured during the past two decades and has the potential to produce lavender, peach and coral hybrids. Not only has this trend produced aesthetically pleasing flowers, but it has broadened the appeal of slippers to include orchidists who were hitherto unimpressed with complex hybrids as a whole.

Several approaches have yielded beautiful pink hybrids. The obvious approach was, of course, through use of *P. delenatii* as a parent. Unfortunately, in the genus *Paphiopedilum* the most obvious approach is rarely the most successful. A number of exquisite novelty crosses in pink and rose have resulted from the use of *P. delenatii*, including *P.* Vanda M. Pearman (× *P. bellatulum*) and *P.* Madame Martinet (× *P. callosum*). Incorporation of this species has not, however, produced a wide range of round, complex hybrids. Lack of fecundity of *P. delenatii* offspring is the major obstacle to success with this approach, as it blocks pursuit of a necessary sequence of crosses designed to enhance desirable traits. *P.* Aladin (*P.* Atlantis × *P. delenatii*), made in 1936, produced a small grex of almost 100% pink progeny, but its grandchildren and great-grandchildren are few in number (see Plate 187). *P.* Lady Clunas (*P.* Gertrude West × *P. delenatii*) in 1945 was a qualified success in the use of *P. delenatii* to create complex pink hybrids; it opens its flowers with heavy khaki overtones, showing pinker hues as the flowers mature. While 1 of the 3 surviving clones displays an interesting lavender pink color, the smallness of the grex is a drawback. More recently in 1980, *P.* Alix de Valec (*P. delenatii* × *P.* Calvi) is an example of a somewhat successful pink hybrid in this category. Ultimately, breeding from these 3 semicomplex hybrids of *P. delenatii* promises to be difficult as none of them is likely to be a prolific parent until improved technology intervenes.

A second and more successful avenue in pink breeding involves the mating of complex *insigne*-type hybrids with species of the *Brachypetalum* section to produce some exceptional pink-flowered complex hybrids. Among them, *P.* Solitaire (*P.* Gorse × *P. niveum*), *P.* Campion (*P.* Lucid × *P. niveum*) and *P.* Caprice (*P.* Chardmoore × *P. bellatulum*) are promising progeny. A major limitation in this line of breeding has been the shortness of scapes. Another difficulty arises with the tendency of certain albinistic forms in the lineage to induce purple spotting rather than pink suffusion. Bertsch (1981c) provides an excellent summary of the difficulties and the alternatives in this line of breeding.

A third approach to pink breeding, according to Bertsch (1981b), involves the crossing of *P.* F. C. Puddle onto almost any fertile complex hybrid. Oddly enough, good breeders in porcelains (including khaki greens and browns), flare-dorsals (red or maroon), yellow/greens to tans, and white/pink complex hybrids are grandparents of today's leading pink hybrids emerging from this line of breeding. An example of a Puddle grandchild illustrating this approach is *P.* Miller's Daughter, a highly awarded George Moore Medal winner. Its parents are *P.* Chantal and *P.* Dusty Miller. *P.* Dusty Miller (see Plate 188) resulted from *P.* F. C. Puddle × *P.* Chardmoore, an open, *insigne*-type flower. While neither the white *P.* F. C. Puddle nor the buff-colored *P.* Chardmoore has overlapping segments, a few of the several hundred *P.* Dusty Miller siblings are quite round, marvelously improved over their parents. Bertsch (1981b) points out that *P.* F. C. Puddle rarely produces a grex of several hundred progeny, while *P.* Chardmoore often yields numerous "truly ugly" progeny with lax, open flowers. The fecundity of *P.* Chardmoore and the potential for whites and pinks from *P.* F. C. Puddle produced only a few fine offspring in the *P.* Dusty Miller grex, a cross which spread its first flowering out over approximately 20 years. As a stud plant, *P.* Dusty Miller is not noted for fecundity; however, its few progeny have been excellent. The *P.* Miller's Daughter (Plate 189) grex produced a high percentage of plants which received the AM/AOS; furthermore, awarded progeny of *P.* Dusty Miller include *P.* Rosy Prospect (× *P.* Amanda) and *P.* Show Boat (× *P.* Botan).

The grex out of which the celebrated *P.* Miller's Daughter sprang consisted, according to Bertsch (1981b), of only 49 flowered seedlings, of which about 30 were of excellent quality, although only 1 showed significant pink blushing over its white background. *P.* Miller's Daughter has, therefore, an albino/green parent in *P.* Chantal, and a blush parent in *P.* Dusty Miller. Bertsch further points out that *P.* Miller's Daughter has a lineage composed of 11 generations, and while determination of the mathematical proportions of the species infused into this genealogy is easily done, the actual allelic ratios which were incorporated into each of the clones used at each generation is purely speculative. Thus, although Bertsch (1981b) provides a table showing proportions of each of 7 species participating in the 11-generation pedigree, there is no way of determining the genotypic ratios of alleles of any single parent in this tortuous pedigree. Therefore, as Bertsch points out, such a table is no more than a surface indication of the intricate genetic complexity involved.

It must be borne in mind that any offspring receives 50% of its inheritance from each parent, that the percentage is halved again for each prior generation in the lineage, and that the particular 50:50 ratio inherited at any step is not only random, but may involve many genotypic factors which have no phenotypic manifestations at all. The pedigree of *P.* Miller's Daughter is shown in Table 6, pages 192–193.

According to Bertsch (1981c), one of the most important species in producing pink hybrids is *P. fairrieanum*. *P.* Dusky Maiden (*P.* Sophomore × *P.* Susan Tucker) produced 100% pink offspring with excellent tall scapes. The reader is referred to Plates 191 and 192; compare *P.* Sophomore with its remarkable offspring, *P.* Dusky Maiden, as well as with specimens of *P. fairrieanum*. In background, *P.* Dusky Maiden is similar to *P.* Miller's Daughter, but with 2 significant differences: the pedigree is shorter and the infusion of *P. fairrieanum* into the lineage appears to be the source of both the increased pinkness and the longer scapes of this grex over those of *P.* Miller's Daughter. The pedigree of *P.* Dusky Maiden is shown in Table 7, page 194.

Breeding with species and novelties has infused interesting new characteristics into several complex hybrid trends. *P.* Ali Taba (*P.* Paeony 'Regency' × *P. fairrieanum*) is an example in which 25% of the progeny were excellent round hybrids, while 75% were novelty types that more closely resemble the *P. fairrieanum* parent, according to Emerson "Doc" Charles (personal communication). Many crosses are coming to the awards tables today out of recent work infusing the vinicolor species and novelties into complex red hybrids. This approach to breeding is not only providing award-quality progeny but is having a pronounced effect on the red and pink hybrids which will sire future generations. Breeding with *P. charlesworthii, mastersianum, wentworthianum* and others has also infused novel possibilities into old, established breeding lines.

Opinions abound as to which of the complex hybrids is most representative of the other, established color trends in modern hybrids. However, choosing from among the wealth of available candidates is not completely arbitrary. The following selections qualify as representative hybrids based on their 2 most important criteria: they have been selected for their prowess both on the awards tables and as stud plants—their beautiful phenotypes as well as their fruitful genotypes. In an account such as this, I prefer to select as representatives those somewhat older hybrids which are proven parents and dominators of trends rather than the latest progeny out of the ultimate generations. The newcomers to the awards tables of the past 2 or 3 years are as yet unproven as breeding stock. Thus, while their importance as potential innovators cannot be denied, their place in this narrative is to underscore the important contributions to the larger perspective that has been made by their parents and grandparents.

P. Winston Churchill is possibly the best known and most prolific of the spotted/flare-dorsal, red trend in *Paphiopedilum* hybrids. Made and registered by Stuart Low, this hybrid dates from 1951. It is found in the background of a preponderance of the complex red hybrids being awarded today. Several excellent clones of this hybrid are recognized as superior stud plants deserving of recognition, including 'Redoubtable' AM-FCC/AOS with a typical flare-dorsal, 'Indomitable' AM/AOS, which is densely marked on its dorsal with maroon black spotting, 'Invicta' AM/RHS, 'Kingston' AM/AOS, and 'British Enterprise' AM/AOS. All received their awards between 1951 and 1961. *P.* Winston Churchill reproduces not only prolifically but reliably; its progeny carry dominant form as well as good color to new levels as their many awards attest. Various clones have spawned their own lines of breeding when used with carefully selected mates. Thus, some of the finer spotted hybrids owe their quality to the 'Indomitable' clone, while excellent flare-dorsal reds continue to be sired by the clone named 'Redoubtable'. The pedigree for *P.* Winston Churchill is shown in Table 8, page 195. The reader is also referred to Plates 193–201, 207 and 213.

Some of the widely acclaimed progeny of *P.* Winston Churchill awarded in the mid–1980s include *P.* Sioux (× *P.* Gigi), *P.* Crazy Horse (× *P.* Hellas), *P.* Keyeshill (× *P.* Carl Keyes), *P.* Burpham (× *P.* Finesse), *P.* Sitting Bull (× *P.* Great Mogul), *P.* Great Pacific (× *P.* Pacific Ocean), *P.* Amber Gold (× *P.* Agnes de Burc), *P.* Monongahela (× *P.* Megantic), *P.* Frank Pearce (× *P.* Paeony), *P.* Duncan York (× *P.* Black Thorpe), *P.* Algonquin (× *P.* Redezelle), *P.* Winchilla (× *P.* Orchilla), *P.* Uncas (× *P.* Mildred Hunter), and *P.* Personality (× *P.* Blendia), to name just a few. Included in the list are many fine spotted hybrids of a wide variety of colors and several great red hybrids.

P. Winston Churchill grandchildren and great-grandchildren are also gracing the awards tables, now. *P.* Adwin (*P.* Winlantis × *P.* Advancement) and *P.* Alseid (*P.* Hunston × *P.* Yeat's Country) are but 2 examples of the many acclaimed extractions from this marvelous hybrid.

P. Hellas 'Westonbirt' (Plate 202) is an interesting study in contrasts. Its progeny typically surpass it in size and form, while color varies depending upon the plant to which it is bred. The progeny include exemplary reds, yellows, autumn colors and spotted hybrids. A cross with *P.* Freckles yielded *P.* Via Otai, a grex of some spectacular whites with fine overall mahogany spotting. However, when *P.* Hellas 'Westonbirt' is selfed, the F2 *P.* Hellas progeny show improved form. Interest in breeding with *P.* Hellas has not declined over the years; although this fine cross was registered in 1940 and was then acclaimed both for its aesthetic merit and as a stud plant, it continues to be pivotal in breeding today.

Paul Phillips (1982), the noted English hybridizer, describes the use of *P.* Hellas 'Westonbirt' with *P. wentworthianum* to produce *P.* Solamba. While by no means the only instance of crossing *P.* Hellas with a species, this particular grex is worthy of comment due to the excellent length of scape and outstanding size and form of the flower. Substance is also exceptional for a Hellas-bred flower, according to Phillips. The color description of *P.* Solamba is, perhaps, the most appealing feature; Phillips calls it "burnished gold" or "red-bronze." More than 90% of the progeny exhibit tessellated foliage, so that the overall visual impact of color is dazzling. The *P.* Hellas pedigree is shown in Table 9, page 196.

An abridged list of the recently awarded hybrids of *P.* Hellas includes *P.* Tama (× *P.* Paeony), the highly-awarded *P.* Ogallala (× *P.* Inca), *P.* Huddle (× *P.* F. C. Puddle), *P.* Essyline (× *P.* Sandra Mary), *P.* Chief Eagle (× *P.* Burleigh Mohur), *P.* George Hughes (× *P.* Halo), *P.* Claio Javier (× *P.* Van Ness), and *P.* Helgi (× *P.* Gigi). See Plates 181, 196, 203 and 206.

No account of hybridization would be complete without mention of the excellent and prolific *P.* Paeony used widely in breeding both in England and the United States. Perhaps most notable for its dominant form, its use as a parent has not been seriously impaired by its short scape or its bland color. Several clones are considered excellent parents, including 'Regency', 'Debonaire', 'Grandmaster', 'Rufus' and an F2 *P.* Paeony (*P.* Paeony 'Regency' × *P.* Paeony 'Rufus') with the clonal name 'Mulberry'. *P.* Paeony's parentage is given in Table 10, page 197. The reader is also referred to Plates 192 and 204–206.

A sample of the awarded progeny of *P.* Paeony includes: *P.* Orchilla (× *P.* Redstart), *P.* Ali Taba (× *P. fairrieanum*), *P.* Tama (× *P.* Hellas), *P.* JoAnn Bachner (× *P.* Vallarrow),

P. Universal Mandate (×*P.* Gwenpur), *P.* Frank Pearce (×*P.* Winston Churchill), *P.* Amanda (×*P.* Radley), *P.* Glowyn (×*P.* Culmo), *P.* Tomahawk (×*P.* Meridian Glory), *P.* Coffee Creek (×*P.* California Queen), *P.* Lyric (×*P.* Lucid), *P.* Commando (×*P.* Sparsholt), *P.* Rosewood (×*P.* Gitano) and *P.* Red Rounder (×*P.* Jubilee).

The preceding hybrids, *P.* Winston Churchill, *P.* Hellas and *P.* Paeony, are parents of excellent spotted and red progeny. At this point, it is necessary to deal separately with these 2 groups, listing and discussing additional excellent breeders in each group. Among spotted hybrids, *P.* Burpham 'Penn Valley' FCC/AOS (Plate 207) is a superb clone of the cross of *P.* Finesse × *P.* Winston Churchill. Among the awarded hybrids bred from *P.* Burpham are *P.* Arapaho (×*P.* Great Mogul), *P.* Pima (×*P.* Redezelle), *P.* Santee (×*P.* Olympic Forest) and *P.* Tree of Legend (× *P.* Winston Churchill). As noted previously, the clone of *P.* Winston Churchill most used to sire spotted progeny is 'Indomitable'.

Another fine spotted hybrid is *P.* Cadence (*P.* Allure ×*P.* Paeony). An excellent parent, it has produced a number of awarded progeny. *P.* Mildred Hunter (*P.* Atlantis ×*P.* Everest) is a fertile spotted parent yielding progeny which often flower twice a year. *P.* Mildred Hunter is useful in breeding both red and spotted offspring, including *P.* Milmoore (× *P.* Farnmoore), *P.* Pinkridge (×*P.* Mojave), *P.* Fairhunter (×*fairrieanum*), and *P.* Uncas (×*P.* Winston Churchill). All those named have several awarded clones. The reader is referred to Plates 186, 201 and 208.

P. Olympic Forest 'Penn Valley' AM/AOS (*P.* Menthule × *P.* Milmoore) is one of the finest parents of spotted hybrids. It passes on such important traits as excellent shape and its long scape. Among the awarded progeny of *P.* Olympic Forest are *P.* Chippewa (× *P.* Sedgewick), *P.* Dakota (× *P.* Milionette), *P.* Erie (× *P.* Jim Dandy), and *P.* Santee (× *P.* Burpham).

P. Memoria Percy Bannerman (*P.* Evanhurst ×*P. niveum*) is another versatile parent. As 1 parent of *P.* Pink Fantasy (× *P.* Lelantis), this slipper has sired an outstanding pink hybrid with superior substance, form and color purity. Others of its offspring include *P.* Silver Anniversary (× *P.* Chardmoore), *P.* Fair Banner (× *P. fairrieanum*), *P.* Pink Glory (× *P.* Lohengrin), and *P.* Ann Ashley (× *P.* Susan Tucker). See Plates 209 and 210.

A number of important red hybrids are also excellent parents. In distinguishing reds from spotted hybrids, there is, of course, some overlap; however, several reds are quite distinctive and worthy of inclusion. *P.* Keyeshill 'Potentate' AM/AOS (*P.* Carl Keyes × *P.* Winston Churchill) is deepest burgundy with a wide white margin upon the dorsal and narrow white margins highlighting the petals (Plate 197). It owes its excellent shape and color to the careful selection of outstanding parents.

The important F2 *P.* Paeony 'Mulberry' has the qualities breeders seek in a red parent; excellent dark reds are typical of its progeny. *P.* Queenanna (*P.* Loganna × F2 *P.* Paeony 'Mulberry') exemplifies many of the traits which clustered positively in the selfing of *P.* Paeony and were subsequently passed along to progeny: long scape, clear color in deepest red, excellent form and fecundity in its own right.

P. Startler 'Glace' AM/AOS (*P.* Masked Light × *P.* Redstart) is an outstanding red flower. No white areas interrupt the even pigmentation of the flower, although the redness fades to a deep, terra cotta orange along lower petal margins and over the basal portion of the pouch. Its stunning color is passed along to its progeny, as exemplified by *P.* Startan Ruby (× *P.* Botan). See Plate 211.

P. Vallarrow 'Chilton' AM/AOS (*P.* Rosemary Waithman ×*P.* Harrow) is another outstanding red hybrid deemed reliable for passing its color on to its progeny. The red hue is truer and less wine-colored than in some slippers, and maintains its integrity right to the base of the pouch. Good, flat form, superior color, exceptionally long scapes and vigor are the attributes of *P.* Vallarrow progeny, such as *P.* Telesis (×*P.* Progress), *P.* Valwin (×*P.* Winston

Churchill), and *P.* Wendarrow (× *P.* Wendbourn), all of which have received awards. See Plates 212 and 213.

Autumn tones or porcelains, the hybrids producing flowers of unusual, intermediate hues, are among the most interesting of the complex, *insigne*-type hybrids. Their insertion here is appropriate because they are intermediate between the red groups and the yellows and greens yet to be described. Furthermore, their parentage typically includes plants from each group. There is no standard description for this category. Colors range from delicate apricot through dusky, twilight tints to brassy greens and bronzes, green/burgundy two-tones, and burnished red-golds and oranges. This is the group of surprisingly spicy colors, delightful variety, and superb serendipity in breeding.

In the pastel apricot to tangerine tints, *P.* Gigi 'Malibu' AM/AOS (*P.* Sheba × *P.* Momag) vies with *P.* Hellas 'Westonbirt' FCC/RHS, AM/AOS. Both are superior stud plants, fecund and capable of transmitting their best traits at an enhanced level. Some of the awarded progeny of *P.* Gigi are *P.* Sioux (× *P.* Winston Churchill), *P.* Frostlight (× *P.* Stoke Poges) and *P.* Via Luna (× *P.* Harbur). The reader is referred to Plates 195 and 214.

P. Halo 'Fall Tones' HCC/AOS (*P.* La Honda × *P.* Littledean) is a two-tone flower. The proximal portion of the dorsal, the upper halves of the petals, and the pouch are pastel terra cotta, while the ventral sepal, the dorsal margins and the lower halves of the petals are rich green. Moreover, *P.* Halo yields progeny in typical green/yellow colors as well as orange-yellow and terra cotta tones (Plate 215). Another two-tone of stunning color is *P.* Pittsburg 'Futura' AM/AOS (*P.* Pittlands × *P.* Gurkley). The petals are arrestingly divided down the midvein into apple green below and deep mahogany above. The ventral sepal and dorsal margin repeat the apple green, while deep mahogany brushstrokes mark the basal portion of the dorsal. The pouch is buff-colored. As a parent, *P.* Pittsburg transmits a range of autumn colors, including brown, orange, green, yellow, and combinations of those colors. Among the awarded progeny of *P.* Pittsburg are *P.* Frosty Jones (× *P.* Wallur), *P.* Scatter Creek (× *P.* London Wall), and *P.* Shapely (× *P.* Diversion). *P.* Shapely × *P.* Lacrescent produced *P.* Painted Desert. Recent *P.* Shapely progeny include *P.* Jessamine Bell (× *P.* Helladero) and *P.* Forestville (× *P.* Hellas). See Plates 216 and 217.

P. Van Ness is versatile, not only producing yellow/green hybrids of good quality, but in autumn tones it transmits to its progeny two-toned petals, a preponderance of orange coloration, and excellent form. Awarded progeny of *P.* Van Ness include *P.* Green Gold (× *P.* Divisidero), *P.* Green Mint (× *P.* Gwenpur), *P.* Kenpride (× *P.* Maginot) and *P.* Ringagold (× *P.* Wallur). See Plates 218 and 219. Further extractions from these autumn-tone parents promise to lead to new color combinations of unimagined beauty.

Representing excellence in form and color in green hybrids, *P.* Tommie Hanes is an excellent hybrid; its pedigree is shown in Table 11, pages 198–199. Plate 220 illustrates this hybrid. A sampling of the progeny of *P.* Tommie Hanes includes *P.* Agincourt (× *P.* Van Ness), *P.* Lime Finch (× *P.* Denehurst) and *P.* Althea (× *P.* Yerba Buena).

P. Sheila Hanes (Plate 221) is perhaps as valuable in the green/yellow color trend as *P.* Tommie Hanes. The clones 'Chantry', 'Eleanor', 'Martha', and 'Theresa' were distinguished with the award of AM/AOS. *P.* Sheila Hanes produces capsules full of seeds and transmits to its progeny excellent color and substance. Its pedigree is shown in Table 12, pages 200–201. *P.* Sheila Hanes progeny include *P.* Trail of Tears (× *P.* Hellas), *P.* Drifting Sand (× *P.* Bantry Bay), *P.* Norwood's Creek (× *P.* Scatter Creek), *P.* Sunlit Meadows (× *P. primulinum*) and *P.* Sea Nymph (× *P.* Mudcreek).

Another important parent of yellow/green progeny is *P.* Agnes de Burc 'Green Gold' (*P.* Dickler × *P.* Gwen Hannen). Significant as one of the parents of *P.* Sheila Hanes, it also sired *P.* Amber Gold (× *P.* Winston Churchill), the 'Wallingford' clone of which received the HCC/AOS. Crossed with *P.* Meadow Lark, *P.* Agnes de Burc sired *P.* Green Meadows 'Bob'

HCC/AOS. *P*. Reezy (*P*. Agnes de Burc × *P*. Denehurst) with clones 'Irene' and 'Martha' both HCC/AOS, as well as 'Tenran' AM/AOS, is an excellent grex. See Plates 198 and 222.

P. Yerba Buena is a large-flowered yellow/green with excellent, white-margined dorsal sepals. It breeds readily and has produced such outstanding award-winners as *P*. Kay Rinaman (× *P*. Diversion) and *P*. White Alary (× *P. bellatulum*).

P. Betty Bracey 'Springtime' AM/AOS-RHS, S/CSA and 'Limelight' AM/AOS resulted from a cross of *P*. Gwenpur × *P*. Actaeus 'Bianca'. This cross of early parents was made in 1956. It reliably passes on good form and color to its progeny. See Plate 223.

Another fine green is *P*. Divisidero 'Val' HCC/AOS-ODC. Its vigorous green progeny include the awarded *P*. Engraved (× *P*. Wallur) and *P*. Stefanie Pitts (× *P*. Kay Rinaman).

P. Wallur (*P*. London Wall × *P*. Bromohur) passes on good form to its yellow and green progeny. Some of its awarded offspring include *P*. Engraved (× *P*. Divisidero), *P*. Frosty Jones (× *P*. Pittsburg), and *P*. Ringagold (× *P*. Van Ness) (Plate 219).

P. Golden Diana (*P*. Dianalus × *P*. Golden Hind), which often flowers twice a year, is the parent of several well-known, awarded yellow offspring. Its highly awarded progeny include *P*. Caddiana (× *P*. Cadina), *P*. Golden Acres (× *P*. McLaren Park), *P*. King of Sweden (× *P*. Denehurst) and *P*. Van Ness (× *P*. Burleigh Mohur). Although featured as a grandparent of *P*. Sheila Hanes, *P*. Golden Diana is not considered obsolete as a parent even today.

Excellent green/yellow parents of noted fecundity also include *P*. Kay Rinaman (*P*. Yerba Buena × *P*. Diversion) and *P*. Malibu (*P*. Ruskington × *P*. Bettina).

Selection of a single representative white hybrid is a formidable task. Improved whites began to emerge in the late 1950s with *P*. Meadowsweet. This development further stimulated hybridizers to strive for white hybrids with texture, size and form equal to any complex hybrid. *P*. Meadowsweet (*P*. Chilton × *P*. F. C. Puddle) was such an improvement over the open white flowers preceding it that it was acclaimed both for its form and its pristine white color which was virtually unspotted by the persistent maroon stippling so commonly seen at that time. Registered in 1956, the 'Purity' clone (Plate 224) of this lovely white slipper received the George Moore Medal in 1957. However, not only were its grex and similar ones quite small, but progeny of *P*. Meadowsweet have been few or obscure. Unlike *P*. Florence Spencer, *P*. F. C. Puddle, *P*. Hellas and other prolific breeders, it is conspicuously infrequent or absent from the registry of hybrids.

P. Miller's Daughter is very fine, but the shorter scapes of this hybrid are considered a drawback in comparison to *P*. Blanche Sawyer 'Snowman' (Plate 225). The latter exhibits excellent form and is probably one of the finer recent white hybrids available, currently proving its prowess as a parent. The pedigree for *P*. Blanche Sawyer is given in Table 13, page 202.

Progeny of *P*. Blanche Sawyer include *P*. Winter Scene (× *P*. Gwenpur), *P*. Jamboree Gem (× *P*. Lohengrin), and *P*. White China (× *P*. Susan Tucker).

P. F. C. Puddle is, of course, the pivotal white parent (Plate 178). This slipper has probably sired more fine, awarded offspring than any other white hybrid.

No summary of important white hybrids is complete without mention of *P*. Freckles (Plate 179); this slipper is a versatile parent, useful to sire either white or pink progeny. Examples of its awarded progeny include *P*. Tomas Garcia (× *P*. Inca) and *P*. Via Ojai (× *P*. Hellas).

P. Puddleham (*P*. F. C. Puddle × *P*. Golden Diana) and *P*. Susan Tucker (*P*. Shalimar × *P*. F. C. Puddle) (Plate 182), 2 other excellent white parents, are both noted for their fecundity. Size and shape of progeny sired by both these hybrids may safely be expected to be fine, when the mates are selected according to tried principles of inheritance.

In summary, a few clear trends have swept the world of hybrid slippers. The early days of crossing species merely to determine their capacity to interbreed gave way rapidly to a determined campaign to develop fine, round, complex hybrids in the genus *Paphiopedilum*, an endeavor which continues unabated today. Although the effort to breed superlative complex hybrids virtually eclipsed the worth of species and simple hybrids for a century, the rediscovery of the elemental beauty of species has awakened a richer awareness among connoisseurs of slippers. It is readily apparent that, whatever the current vogue in slippers, breeders and growers have been vigilant and ruthless in pursuit of quality. Inferior size, poor texture, muddy color, lax form and questionable vigor have been consistently culled out of collections and selected against in breeding programs.

Today's preference for species and novelties over complex hybrids is difficult to characterize; as a merely faddish response, it is singularly long-lived. Perhaps it is a response to the pleasures of variety. Hovering over current breeding programs is a profound challenge to the validity of pursuing only the ever-larger, round *Paphiopedilum* hybrid.

Certainly the present offers the fullest information and understanding ever available to breeders. Relevant knowledge has mushroomed as experience has plodded along on its steady course. Yet, paralleling this fantastic proliferation of information, certain questions persist unanswered. Pursuit of the perfect flower races neck-and-neck with pursuit of the unexplained. The slipper world has met challenge after challenge, yet slipper fanciers need not fear a world devoid of challenges for many years to come.

The future holds much promise. Breeders and growers are pursuing several avenues of progress, including broadening of petals, flattening of sepals and petals, better control of color (especially in the ventral sepal), and improvement in the length and sturdiness of stalks of complex hybrids. A refreshing breeze of change is blowing through the narrowly fixed ideas of the past as well. The enterprising crossing of established hybrids back onto species and novelties is opening new possibilities for innovative hybridization. After all, what comes next, after achieving such an absolute as roundness? In time, perhaps the chasm separating complex and novelty hybrids will be bridged with numerous and worthy intermediate forms. The realization of that goal will only serve to inspire pursuit of new ambitions and vistas. Once accomplished, the elusive breakthroughs in intergeneric hybrids, improved fertility, meristem clones, control of ploidy and other scientific feats will also infuse fresh life into breeding programs. Certainly the combination of retrospection with innovation will continue to generate progress.

An adventurous prognostication of the future in *Paphiopedilum* breeding includes many fascinating fantasies (a few of which are already somewhat less than fantastic): flowers with flat segments rather than concave sepals and petals; elongated spikes of flowers; new shapes, including triangles and diamonds; fringed or ruffled margins or even double flowers with petalloid staminodes; aesthetic alterations in shape, size and color of foliage; mutant (natural or induced) alleles for color in ranges of violet and lavender-blue; development of a larger, round, unstained white; and significant overall size modifications, including the true dwarf or pygmy paph as well as the gigantic. The realization of some of these fantasies is already at the threshold. Many growers are frustrated with the sameness of still more round hybrids, regardless of how much expertise goes into their production. New directions are beckoning.

Impetus in hybridization in the other cultivated genera (*Cypripedium* and *Phragmipedium*) of the subfamily is building along with overall interest in these plants. Much remains to be done; the future promises new ground to break, new directions to take, new horizons to unfold and explore in both the scientific and the intuitive aspects of hybridization. Whatever the new directions, the same critical culling of unworthy plants and the same questing for quality and improvement of hybrids must continue to guide the steps of breeders. The lure of the unknown and the conquest of the next frontier beckon as tantalizingly today as when Dominy first beheld *Paphiopedilum* Harrisianum.

192

Chapter 7

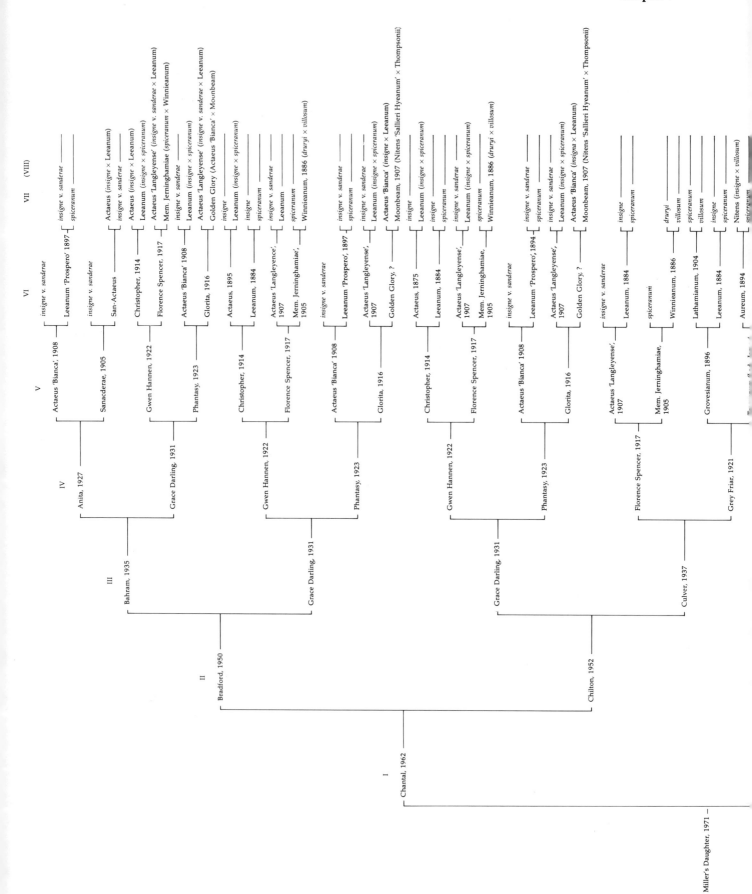

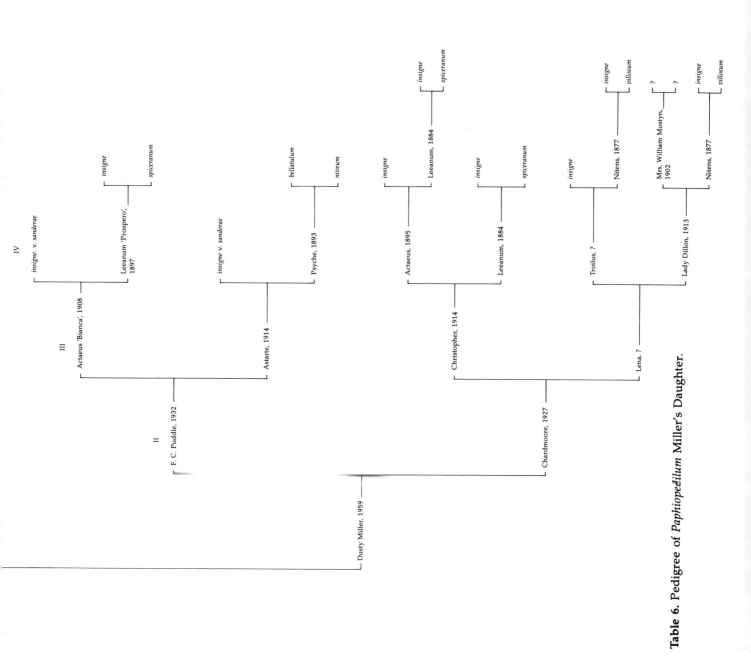

Table 6. Pedigree of *Paphiopedilum* Miller's Daughter.

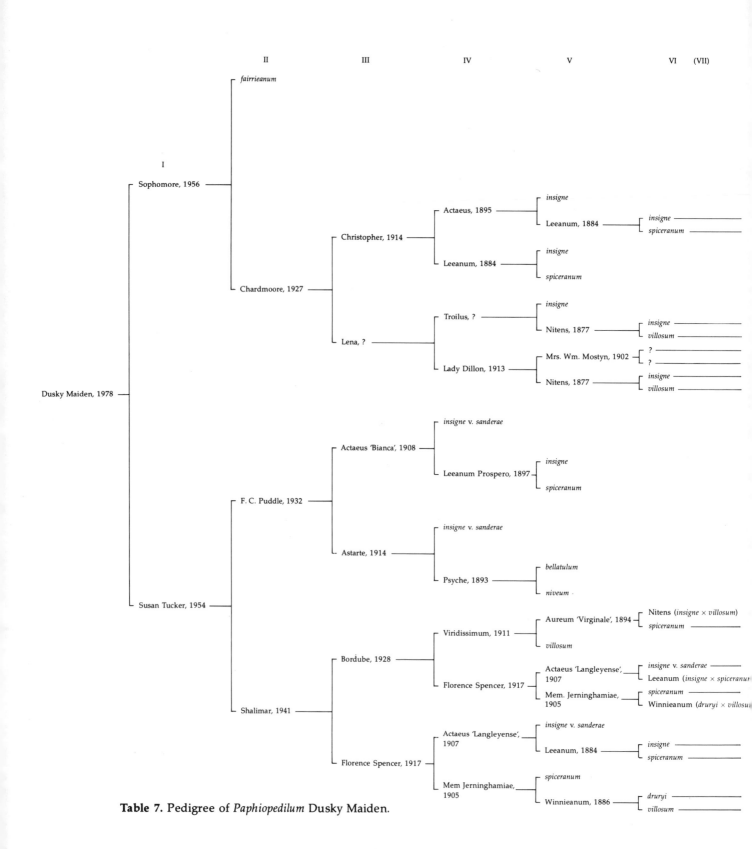

Table 7. Pedigree of *Paphiopedilum* Dusky Maiden.

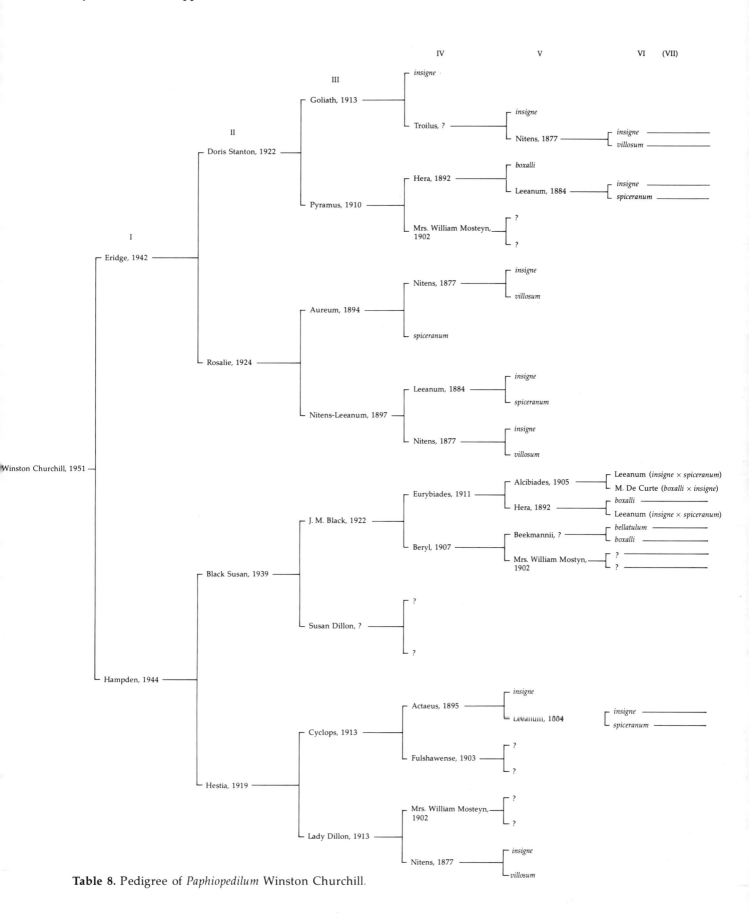

Table 8. Pedigree of *Paphiopedilum* Winston Churchill.

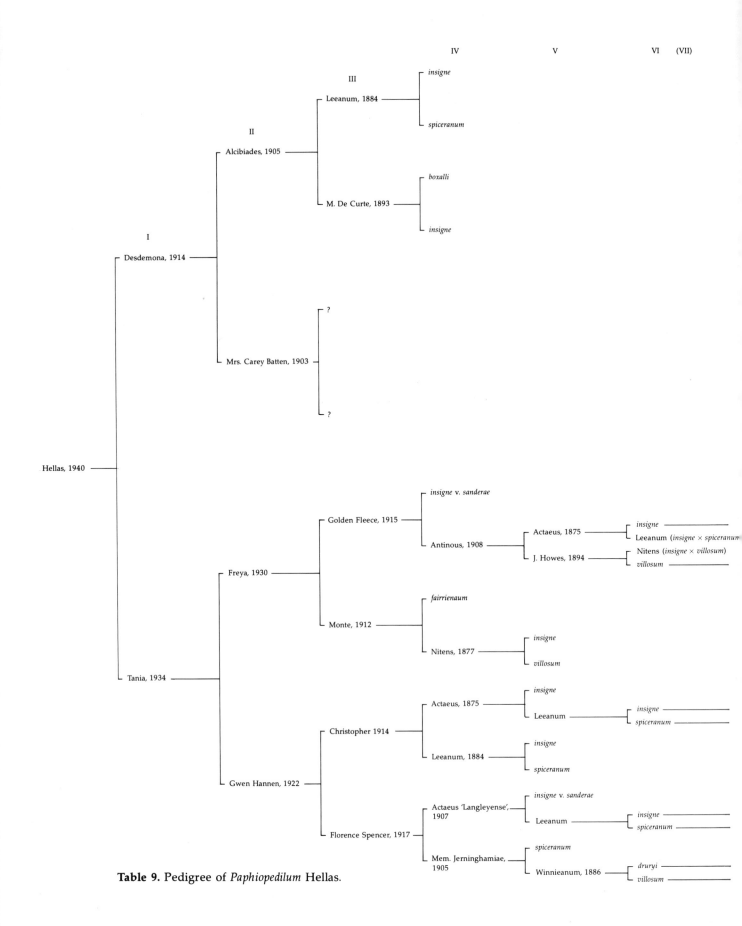

Table 9. Pedigree of *Paphiopedilum* Hellas.

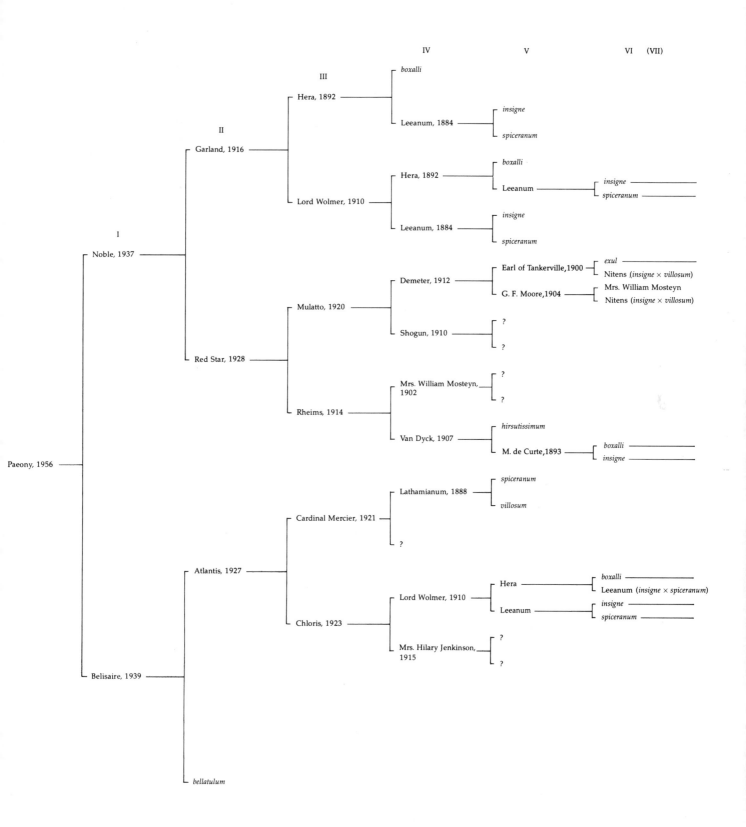

Table 10. Pedigree of *Paphiopedilum* Paeony.

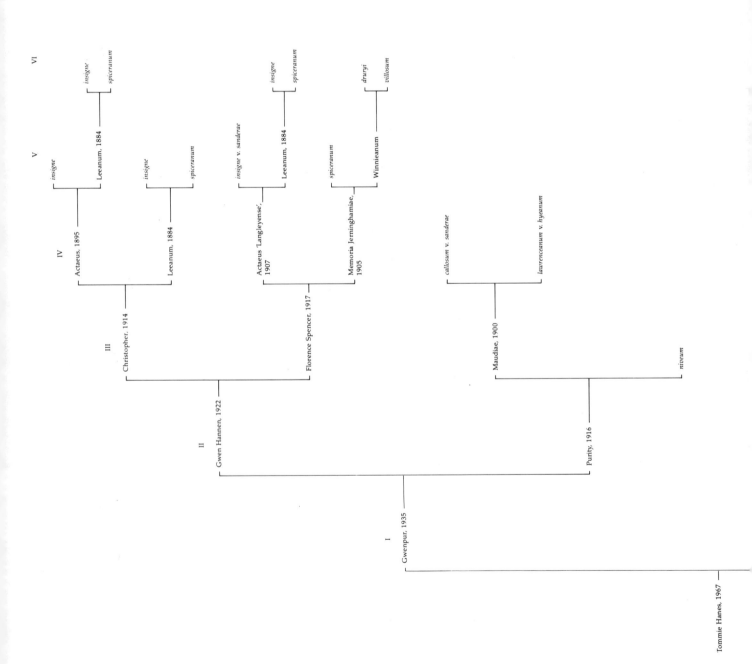

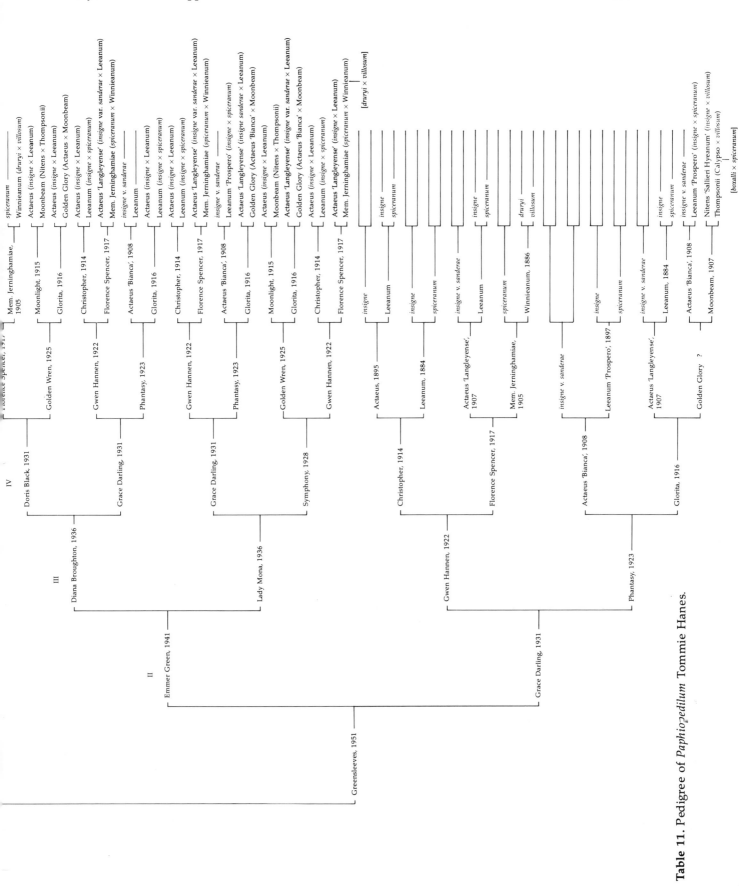

Table 11. Pedigree of *Paphiopedilum* Tommie Hanes.

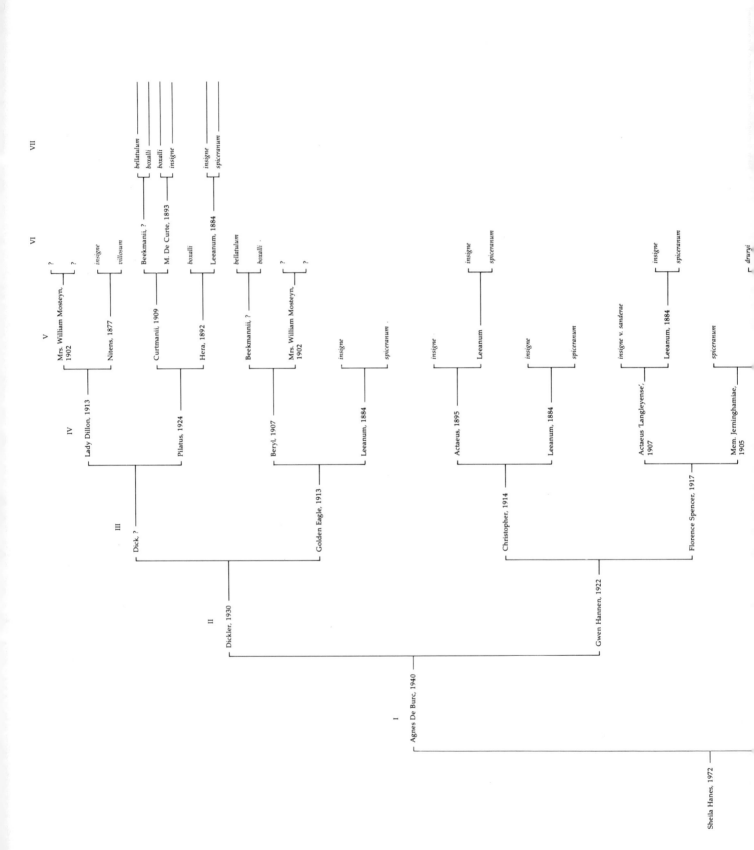

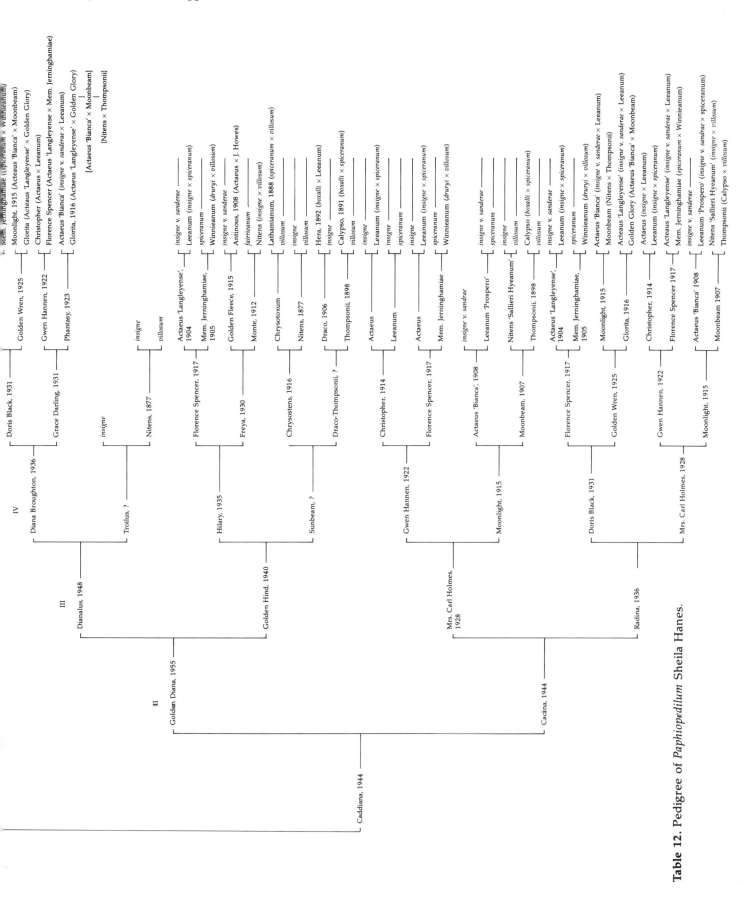

Table 12. Pedigree of *Paphiopedilum* Sheila Hanes.

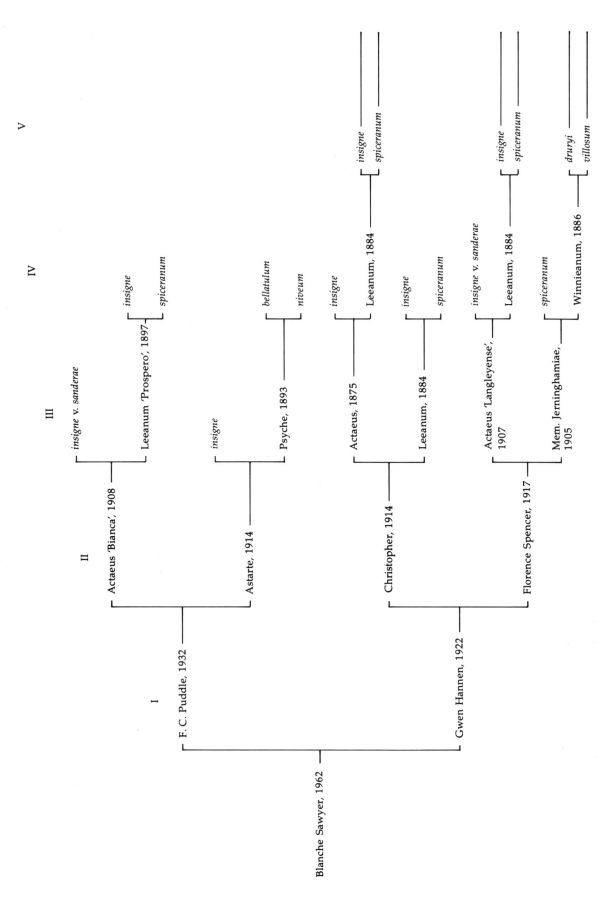

Table 13. Pedigree of *Paphiopedilum* Blanche Sawyer.

GENETICS AND OTHER TECHNICAL ASPECTS OF SLIPPER BREEDING

A number of difficulties alluded to in previous pages have impeded the progress of slipper hybridization throughout its history. This section explains the nature of certain of these problems, illustrating solutions which have already been found and setting forth factors standing in the way of successful resolution of persistent problems.

From the beginning breeders have plied their trade on intuition, often lacking a clear method or a firm foundation of knowledge. In spite of the amount of information that has been amassed and the expertise gained in the sixscore years of hybridizing, breeders find themselves still thwarted by difficulties which have yet to be surmounted. Over the years certain problems were solved, only to be supplanted by new challenges, new needs for information. Much experimentation has been carried out and years of time and effort invested to bring us to today's level of awareness. Yet, at times, breeders feel themselves to be still at the beginning.

The earliest dilemma facing breeders of slippers was their ignorance of the genetics of this group, further compounded by the constraints of symbiotic culture, the only method of culture available in the 19th century. As we have seen, careful record-keeping enabled later breeders to profit from the work of the pioneers as genetics gradually emerged both as a science and as a practical source of guidance for hybridizers. The utilization of methods of asymbiotic culture since the 1920s has further implemented successful breeding. Knudson's formula for nourishing dependent orchid seedlings was the stride which revolutionized orchid hybridization across the board and enabled breeders to gain a fuller understanding of the vastness of genetic possibilities within *Paphiopedilum* through study of both the positive and the negative features of a far wider spectrum of surviving progeny from each grex.

Science played its most spectacularly significant role in hybridization to date through the development of asymbiotic techniques of germination and seedling culture. Primitive methods of seedling culture required that the seeds be sown at the base of established slippers so beneficial mycorrhizal fungi could infect the offspring and thus provide the seedlings with the nutrition necessary for survival until they matured sufficiently to develop chlorophyll and synthesize their own nutrients. These primitive methods severely limited the scope of variables which were available for study in survivors of any grex. Further, given the lack of control in such methods, disaster struck with predictable frequency as the moisture necessary to promote both germination and the subsequent symbiotic linkage with the beneficial fungus also promoted attacks by lethal fungi upon seedlings as well as their surrogate parents.

Cytological investigation revealed the characteristic absence of stored food in the minute orchid seeds, the delay in chlorophyll production and establishment of photosynthetic pathways, and the function of mycorrhizae in providing food to the embryonic plantlets during this critical period of dependence. Thus, asymbiotic culture techniques were developed to provide for these special characteristics, and because these techniques were successful, they were widely adopted. Agar culture media were developed containing the organic nutrients which must otherwise be supplied by the mycorrhizae until weeks later when the burgeoning plantlets routinely synthesize for themselves. Sterile techniques (avoiding exposure to infectious decay-causing organisms) for introduction of seeds to a sterilized medium produced remarkable successes for the pioneers in this improved cultural procedure. As this technique matured through extensive experimentation, the incorporation of growth-regulating hormones in the medium produced improved results. Only then, when the wider scope of variance among a larger percentage of the siblings of a particular grex could be viewed and assessed, were breeders able to make still greater intuitive leaps in their understanding of practical genetics in this group.

Several additional observations about asymbiotic culture must be made. The first is that, although it was originally believed that the symbiosis between orchid and mycorrhizal fungus was obligatory, experience amply demonstrated that such is not the case. Plants which have been supported beyond the dependent stage thrive equally well with or without symbiotic fungi. The second observation is that seedling growth is more rapid under asymbiotic conditions because the supply of sugars and other nutrients to the young plantlets is more uniform, promoting maximum growth throughout the dependent interval, while none of the nutrients must be shared with a symbiont. The third observation is that not all hybridizers take advantage of asymbiotic culture. Many amateurs with their initial crosses, as well as a few commercial breeders (at least as recently as the late 1970s), sow seeds on the substrate of several mother plants. The wide prevalence of asymbiotic culture does not represent the total dismissal of symbiotic methods even today, although it does present important problems in the acquisition of sufficient numbers of symbiont mother plants to serve as hosts for grexes of numerous seeds.

Regarding genetics and its impact on plant breeding in general, it should be noted that Mendel's selection of peas as the subject of his pioneer investigations was a fortuitous choice. Dominance and recessiveness of the traits he selected for study in peas are of the simple type; that is, they are governed by a single pair of alleles. Had Mendel selected different plants from among a vast array of other genera for his studies, his results might easily have been far less definitive or even have led to erroneous conclusions, but as fortune would have it, Mendel dealt with a simple and straightforward pattern of inheritance. Not only do peas exhibit simple dominance, with each of the traits studied controlled by a single pair of alleles, but because each of the traits Mendel studied in peas is located on a separate chromosome, he was able to visualize segregation as well as dominance and other mechanisms at work. Thus he was able to unearth the fundamentals of inheritance through carefully researched and documented monohybrid (one variable trait) and dihybrid (two variable traits) crosses exhibiting clear ratios of small numbers. The familiar Mendelian ratio for an F2 generation in a monohybrid cross is 1:2:1, for instance. This ratio indicates that for every 4 offspring, 1 will carry purebred dominant alleles, 2 will be heterozygous with a dominant allele paired with a recessive allele (phenotypically, or apparently, dominant), and 1 will be homozygous recessive, with a pair of recessive alleles.

In the case of *Paphiopedilum* and many other genera of flowering plants, however, inheritance is governed by somewhat more complex linkages of genetic factors. The desired traits for color, for instance, may not be dominant first of all, so that homozygous (purebred) recessive parents must be used in such cases to produce a desired trait in the offspring. Where a parent possesses a dominant desirable trait, unless that trait is homozygous dominant, some percentage of the offspring will be less than desirable. Furthermore, the dominance or recessiveness of that trait in the second parent further alters the expected ratio of desirable progeny of the grex.

Nor is segregation simple in *Paphiopedilum*, because the allele for a desirable trait may lie on the same chromosome as another allele for an undesirable trait. Thus, with certain exceptions which are discussed below, the offspring must receive both the deleterious and the desired alleles, all on the same chromosomal unit. For example, had *P.* Cardinal Mercier's genes for red color been located on the same chromosome bearing the genes for its open form, virtually all the offspring which received good color from that parent would have displayed its poor shape as well, and today *P.* Cardinal Mercier would be among the forgotten hybrids of the past. Notable exceptions to this generality occur due to the occurrence of centric fission and other examples of chromosomal fracture. Not uncommonly, chromosomes break into 2 fragments, thus changing the (n) value as well as the (2n) and that of other ploidies. *Cochlopetalum* species are a case in point, with (2n = 26), the typical diploid number in the genus *Paphiopedilum*, modified to (2n = 30, 32, 34 and 36). Therefore, not only might a chromosome carrying 2 key traits be naturally broken, but the means to artificially sever such chromosomes, once loci are identified, are already within the scope of man's technology, even if not yet widely successful among slipper orchids. Genetic mapping to identify loci is a major need in slipper research. Artificial fragmentation of chromosomes is a technique which needs further refinement as well. Currently, should the 2 alleles which require severance lie adjacent on a chromosome, such a separation into 2 fragments at the appropriate site would tax the limits of the available technology.

Finally, there are traits which are not determined by simple dominance factors. These traits are inherited through a complex assortment of genes, so are governed by the laws of polygenic inheritance in which several pairs of alleles cooperate to determine a trait such as size or color. Depending upon the combined influence of the several randomly assorted dominant and recessive genes on several chromosomes dictating the expression of a trait, each offspring may display a degree of influence from the parents over a rather wide range. Thus, a grex of siblings exhibits the entire range of degrees of inheritance, and this range is expressed as numerical ratios more complex than simple 1:2:1 ratios. F2 ratios on the order of 1:6:15:20:15:6:1 are typical. Actual phenotypic variations of even greater scope, due both to environmental factors and the unequal influences among the pairs of alleles, create a subtle gradient of variance.

For example, let us examine a hypothetical case such as scape height, as shown in Table 14, pages 213–214. Instead of a single pair of alleles, there may be 3 pairs for the trait. All 6 genes in a purebred dominant individual are therefore alleles for maximum height, while a purebred recessive individual possesses all 6 alleles for minimum scape height. Three intrinsic variables influence the height of a flower stalk: the mean number of cells in the vertical column, the degree of elongation of those cells, and the thickness of the intercellular facing walls. Of these 3, the first 2 have the greatest effect.

Let "A" represent the maximum number of cells as the first allele, and "a" the recessive minimum-cell-number allele. Let "B" represent maximum elongation while "b" is the recessive least-elongation allele. Let "C" stand for maximum intercellular cell wall thickness with "c" representing the recessive minimum. A plant which is AABBCC has the tallest scapes. As a parent, it provides only dominant, scape-lengthening alleles in the gametes (sex cells—egg or sperm) it supplies to the cross. Conversely, a recessive plant, aabbcc, possesses the shortest scapes, and its potential in breeding will be to shorten the scape length of all its progeny. An F1 cross between 2 such homozygous or purebred individuals generates heterozygous AaBbCc offspring, all of which produce flowerscapes of intermediate height. The true scope of variability only begins to show up in F2 progeny generated from a cross of 2 of the heterozygous individuals of the F1 generation, where all possible (in this case, 7) genotypic height classes appear, as well as many more intermediate forms which are phenotypically possible. Table 14 shows the allelic combinations in these 7 categories and the internal variations each contains. The 7 categories are characterized thus:

1. All 6 of the alleles (3 paired sets, each set composed of 1 allele from each parent) of 1/64th of the individuals of a grex are dominant and produce maximum scape height.

2. When 5 dominant alleles are linked to 1 recessive, 6/64ths of the grex with this random assortment of alleles bear slightly shorter scapes. Some further variation results within this height category as well, because Cc has a lesser impact on overall height than Aa or Bb. Thus, scapes of AABBcC or AABBCc offspring (the first receiving its recessive allele from the female or pod-parent, the latter so influenced

by the pollen-parent) will appear to the unaided eye to be as tall as purebred dominants, while any of the 4 other combinations (aABBCC or AABbCC, for example) produce visibly shorter scapes as their alleles affect more gross characters in the overall influence on scape height.

3. A successively shorter height category results when 4 dominant and 2 recessive alleles combine in 15/64ths of the grex. The inequality of the influence of the Cc allele continues to create a range of variation within this category with overlap into adjacent categories. The overlap may be illustrated thus: a member of this category with AABBcc will bear scapes virtually as tall as the purebred dominant or as the tallest of the second category, while a genotype such as aABBCc will behave as the shortest individuals of the second category. Only aaBBCC or other combinations where both recessives are located in the first 2 variables accurately reflect the true nature of this third category. In other words, only in this latter case do genotype and phenotype agree.

4. The ratio 20/64ths of the grex represents the fraction of those offspring possessing 3 dominant and 3 recessive alleles. The variability and overlap resulting from the unequal influence on height of the 3 variable polygene factors are the greatest in this height category. Thus, many of the progeny falling into this genotypic height class possess phenotypic resemblances to individuals in all but class 1 and class 7.

5. For 2 dominants and 4 recessives the ratio returns to 15/64ths of the grex, leading, however, to further loss of dominance and overall reduction of scape height. The phenotypic overlap behaves as that of class 3, but on the short side of the spectrum.

6. The sixth height class, also a 6/64ths fraction, is composed of all the progeny bearing 1 dominant allele and 5 recessives. Obviously, the individuals in this class possessing a C allele as their sole dominant will produce scapes virtually as short as those in the 7th class, while others will appear the same as certain members of the preceding class in their phenotypic manifestations.

7. Progeny which receive 6 recessive alleles make up 1/64th of the grex. These bear the shortest inflorescences of all, and as was true of the homozygous purebreds of class 1, are likewise in complete agreement in their genotype and phenotype.

Thus, although the grex consists of 7 describable height classes, the appearance of the individual flowerscapes of a grex of these progeny in flower exhibits a fairly wide range of gradual variations in height. Because of the much smaller influence of Cc, it is certain that some members of the more recessive categories will possess taller scapes than some progeny in the more dominant categories and vice versa.

A specific example of such a phenotype which does not visibly reflect genotype is a 4 dominant:2 recessive such as aAbBCC, compared to a 3:3 AABbcc. The proportion of A and B factors in the second instance is greater than that in the less recessive first instance. However, since factors Aa and Bb have far greater influence on the length of a scape, such an apparent contradiction is actually true in a number of cases.

Our hypothetical example clearly shows that polygenic inheritance is the mechanism through which certain particular attributes of offspring appear to be a blend of parental traits, and that it is the source of those numerous, small degrees of intermediate variation unaccounted for in Mendel's results with peas. In some complex instances, there are as many as 5–6 pairs of alleles associated in the polygenic determination of traits. The larger the number of paired alleles involved, the greater the number of variant categories observed, both genotypically and phenotypically, and the more extensive the numerical ratios become. This illustration of how blending can appear to occur, while in fact the entire potential for variability remains intact and vigorous within a gene pool of a natural population and emerges unabated at each successive generation, is important historically. This is the precise clarification which escaped Darwin, persisting for him as a paradoxical enigma in his evaluation of the inheritance of variability and its interaction with natural selection.

All these variable factors are, of course, further influenced by environmental factors, just as scape height is affected by nutrient and water availability, light intensity and growth-regulating substances in a fluidly interactive but controlled way. Hence, the intergradations visible within a grex are made even more subtle through variations in the adequacy of the supply of environmental necessities.

Breeding thus remains a matter of trying the best parents at hand, and seeing what results are achieved. There is, as yet, no way of looking into the chromosomes of *Paphiopedilum* with anything like a clear gene map, although development of such mapping techniques is underway in some areas of genetic research. Celebrated projects in human genetic research employing the latest techniques in genetic mapping to support anticipated genetic engineering are aimed at modification of deleterious genes affecting the health of millions of people. Improved techniques and insights gained from this research will proliferate into plant hybridization work and inexorably advance the scientific progress in *Paphiopedilum* hybridization. For the present, even a complete *Paphiopedilum* gene map would fall short of solving all the problems due to the shortfall in technological advancement.

Several factors forestall or obstruct the successful exploitation of certain avenues worthy of pursuit:

1. The presence of deleterious genes on the same chromosome as desired traits, and the adjunct limitations of the technology to deal with such combinations.
2. Genetically controlled physical limitations on pollen tube growth, infertility due to differences in ploidy, and related genetic problems, many of which depend upon reliably successful tissue culture technology for resolution.
3. The extended time required for the breeding out of a wealth of less desirable polygenic factors. Literally thousands of generations would be required to completely eliminate a single deleterious recessive gene. Under observable conditions, such a gene would likely reemerge countless times as a new mutation even should such a far-fetched program be instituted.

Much new ground remains to be broken in this fascinating branch of slipper culture; not only do major frontiers exist in hybridization within the genus *Paphiopedilum*, but within the other genera and in wide hybrids as well. Bioengineering technology will be required to overcome some or all of the above-mentioned impediments, implementing recombinations of DNA (genetic material).

A difficulty frequently encountered in *Paphiopedilum* breeding is the reduced fecundity of many otherwise promising, potential parents. While presumably not all the causative factors have yet been discovered, several sources of infertility or reduced fertility are known. Solutions to some of these problems remain tantalizingly out of reach, awaiting greater success with tissue culture techniques in the slipper orchids. In fact, the problems currently thwarting progress in slipper hybridization are so thoroughly intertwined with the difficulties in successful tissue culture of slippers that the 2 overlap considerably.

In the past 3 decades, however, breeders as a whole have benefited from the marvelous strides in understanding the molecular, genetic and physiological factors which limit fertility as well as from the technology of tissue culture which may soon be useful in overcoming certain sterility problems in slippers. Additional information is currently more readily available to facilitate breeding in lines which obviate deformities and muddying of color, as well as on various means of producing desired color. As patterns of linkage and of known dominance and recessiveness emerge, a fundamental understanding of genetics becomes more widespread among breeders.

Let us examine a specific cause of infertility, the progress made to date in dealing with it, and the limitations still to be overcome. Breeders in the 1930s and 1940s attempted to improve quality by pairing excellent, small-flowered hybrids with others noted for their large flowers. The results were often frustrating. All too frequently, the progeny from such crosses showed great promise, only to be virtually sterile, thus effectively blocking a desirable avenue of breeding. Science revealed the reason for this category of sterility: the ploidy of many of these sterile offspring was odd-numbered, for example, triploid (3n) or pentaploid (5n).

In effect, such an individual is unable to complete meiotic or reduction division, that is, to divide its chromosomal complement into even halves during the process of forming gametes which, in the subsequent fertilization (gametic fusion), reinstate the necessary complement of chromosomes found in the parents. What had occurred without the knowledge of the breeder, in the simplest triploid instance, was that the small-flowered parents were normal diploids (2n), so that their haploid (n) gametes (egg or sperm) contributed 1 full complement or genome (n) of the 2 chromosomal complements to be found in a diploid (2n) individual. However, the large-flowered parents owed their unusual size to the doubling of all their chromosomal units; that is, these individuals were tetraploids (4n). Therefore, when the normal diploid parent contributed 1 chromosomal complement (n, one-half of 2n) in its gamete, and when at fertilization that gamete fused with another gamete containing 1 chromosomal complement of a tetraploid parent (2n, one-half of 4n), the resultant ploidy of the offspring was triploid (3n)—3 genomes, indivisible by 2 for meiosis—and so, sterile or incapable of normally producing the subsequent generation's gametes. At this writing, triploids (3n), pentaploids (5n), and all ploidies of odd numbers are virtually sterile, only occasionally producing a rare, few viable gametes.

By the 1950s, breeders were learning to avoid production of triploids in order to prevent thwarting their own lines of breeding, although the occasional deliberately made triploid or pentaploid continues to be produced to generate award-winning plants. The prospect of successful mastery of tissue culture techniques for slipper orchids in the near future will facilitate the doubling of ploidies so that triploids can be changed to hexaploids (6n) which are readily fertile, and pentaploids and other odd-numbered ploidies can also be doubled, resulting in fertile individuals with even-numbered ploidies in each case.

An explanatory word about polyploidy and its occurrence must be interjected at this point. Polyploidy, the possession of additional whole genomes above the normal diploid (2n) paired set of chromosomes, is a rather frequent, natural phenomenon in plants. Naturally-occurring tetraploidy (4n) has been so commonly reported in plants from the tundra regions around the Arctic Circle (about 75% of such flora) that it is considered more the rule than the exception among cold-adapted species. Desert flora of Africa also follow this pattern, leading to the inference that tolerance of environmental extremes is enhanced by tetraploidy and by polyploidy in general. Natural tetraploids occur, although less frequently, among most flowering plant families the world over. Polyploids typically grow more slowly, achieve larger size, exhibit greater vigor and adaptability, and are usually composed of cells of greater volume than their diploid counterparts. For this reason, polyploids are in great demand by hybridizers and horticulturists in every area of plant science and culture. Breeding programs in all branches of horticulture and agriculture are taking advantage of both natural and artificially induced polyploidy to increase production of crop plants, whether snapdragons or grain.

Polyploidy is of 2 types. An allopolyploid possesses multiple genomes of chromosomes which are dissimilar; that is to say, allopolyploidy is the precise term applied to poly-ploid individuals which are hybrids. An autopolyploid, on the other hand, contains multiple genomes all of which are similar, that is, of the same species. Thus, a polyploid clone of a species is precisely termed an autopolyploid. Doubling of chromosomes in these natural instances might involve failure to segregate chromosomes during the mitotic division of vegetative cells of a developing embryo, or a failure to segregate during meiosis. Within slipper orchids, examples of allopolyploidy far outnumber those of autopolyploidy.

The ability to artificially induce polyploidy is revolutionizing plant science as well as every aspect of the commercial plant arena. The implications of polyploidy for meeting the challenge of feeding the world's mushrooming population are not lost on agronomists.

Induced polyploidy is almost always accomplished during tissue culture through treat-ment of individual meristematic cells (actively dividing cells of meristem or bud tissue) with mitotic poisons which act to interrupt the orderly process of mitosis (cell division), resulting in retention of doubled sets of chromosomes in 1 cell rather than allowing completion of the process to segregate the sets into 2 new cells. Once induced and the treated cell grown to a mature plant, this condition is fully inheritable in succeeding generations. Full control of the inductive process producing polyploids is not yet possible in the slipper orchids. The progress made in other genera of orchids and in other families of flowering plants has greatly exceeded that which is currently possible in the slipper genera. Abundant success with these techniques awaits improved results in tissue culture of slippers, so the intricacies of poly-ploidy and its problems and solutions become interwoven with problems of tissue culture technology.

Improved understanding has yet to reveal a practical solution to many of the sterility problems in the slipper orchids. The commonest solution in other orchid taxa, the aforemen-tioned treatment of somatic cells during tissue culture with colchicine, podophyllin, radia-tion or other mitotic poisons, resulting in a doubling of the sets of chromosomes (the ploidy) of the orchid, remains only marginally successful in slippers. Although such technology is still in its infancy with slipper orchids, the American Orchid Society has invested in research projects designed to implement progress in techniques of tissue culture which will also facilitate meristematic reproduction. To date, the results are encouraging, but the quantity of resulting plantlets remains negligible in Cypripedioideae.

Once the technology of tissue culture in slippers reaches the level of success common in other orchid subfamilies, the ability to double the ploidy, eliminating a major cause of infertility, should be realized, along with the ability to clonally reproduce existing slippers in quantity by meristemming. The achievement of these goals will not only revolutionize hybridization with the most far-flung ramifications to date, but the availability of inexpen-sive clones of awarded plants will radically alter the future economics of breeding and com-mercial sales.

Although doubling of ploidy of triploids (3n), pentaploids (5n) and the other odd-numbered ploidies will readily remedy those related sterility problems, once technology in slippers is improved, further difficulties exist which require additional research. Aneuploids, for instance, may require sophisticated techniques of genetic engineering. While by no means always sterile, aneuploids possess a fraction of a whole genome such as (2n + 1) or (4n − 2). Routine doubling of the genomes of such plants often produces sur-prising and not always positive results.

Where infertility results from the incompatibility of dissimilar chromosomes, as is the case in intergeneric hybrids, doubling the ploidy is required for the F2 generation, but tissue culture techniques involving somatic cell fusions remain the first frontier to conquer if the F1 generations are to succeed.

Sterility is often a mechanical problem. Pollen tubes may be too short or too large in diameter to successfully facilitate karyogamy (fusion of sex cell nuclei, the integral activity in fertilization). Somatic cell fusion would also readily circumvent such incompatibilities once basic success with tissue culture becomes a reality. Many are the difficulties and slender are the avenues of success prior to breakthroughs in tissue culture technology.

Presently, success with tissue culture in slipper orchids is the major factor limiting several avenues of progress, the sole development on which hinges realization of many of the important goals of hybridizers. However, this success is destined to open a Pandora's box as well, as has already occurred in other genera, drastically changing the economics of slipper culture. Instability and upheaval await commercial houses as abundant, inexpensive, clonally reproduced species and hybrids come to market. Among all the ramifications of tissue culture success, one finds an assortment of positive features mixed with a dreaded shift in the market structure.

And, finally, there are particular infertility problems which have yet to be fathomed. For instance, precisely why so many of the progeny of *Paphiopedilum delenatii* in particular are so reluctant to set capsules, or why the number of viable seeds in the few crosses which actually succeed is so small, remain shrouded in mystery, although the presence of several types of inhibitors has been postulated in this species and others. Only when each individual problem area throughout this sizable genus is defined will precise measures to solve such problems be developed. Months or even years of research must be invested before success is achieved with some of the promising crosses which hybridizers have long desired to create.

Tissue culture, per se, is a technique which has been successfully used with most orchid genera. It involves the excision of a bud from a desirable mature plant, careful trimming away of all but a core of immature cells (meristem tissue), and pureeing of the meristem to separate it into as many single cells as possible. All these activities must be handled under sterile conditions, just as is the case in asymbiotic seed culture. The excised meristem is treated with fungicide, pulverized in a sterile blender, and the cells introduced to sterile medium.

In the case of tissue culture, however, the nutrient medium is a liquid broth; cells are suspended in the broth and agitated, using a mechanical shaker, for an extended period of time, up to 5–6 months or more. During this time, although cell divisions occur, the agitation prevents clumping of newly divided cells, so that multicellular protocorms are not formed. Instead, numerous single cells are proliferated. Use of growth chambers is virtually mandatory for this process in order to maintain optimum conditions. Once the proliferation of single cells reaches a given density, the cells are transferred to flasks of solid agar, a plating process similar to that used for sowing seeds in asymbiotic culture. Each cell continues to divide, but now actual growth occurs to form an aggregate of cells. Shortly, protocorms develop, and the rest of the growth process is identical to the development of asymbiotic seedlings. This particular technique is, however, strictly a means of vegetative reproduction. All the cells are exactly alike, and since no fusions occur, genetic recombinations are not possible. In this way, a population of clones is produced as growth progresses. Currently, this technique is relatively unsuccessful in slipper orchids, as has been noted several times.

Through this technique, many possibilities arise. The clonal reproduction of an awarded plant, yielding several thousand plantlets from the tissue of 1 bud, facilitates the production of inexpensive stock from plants of excellent quality in just a few years, whereas scores of years are required to achieve so many normal divisions. This capability in orchids other than the slippers has severely altered the economics of commercial production of orchids. Although valuable plants are available at a fraction of their former cost and the supply of desirable plants is vast, to date supply rarely exceeds demand, so that while the source of income has shifted, most commercial houses are prospering rather than losing money. Profit from selling thousands of less expensive clones exceeds that of selling 1–2 divisions at astronomical prices. However, at the time this technology first made its impact on the orchid market, during the 1960s, great uncertainty created an upheaval. Commercial growers were unsure of the buyers' reception of meristemmed plants as well as of the ultimate quality of plants created by this innovative process. Some growers hesitated to deal in such plants, and of these, some saw their businesses fail.

Tissue culture may also permit direct fusion of somatic (vegetative as opposed to gametic) cells, as has been successfully accomplished in some other genera, for quasi-sexual hybridization of hitherto inconceivable scope, permitting creation of wide hybrids of 2–3 genera. In the single-cell stage of cultured tissue, several interesting options are available. It is possible, for example, to effect somatic cell fusion of the cells of 2 plants, such as species of 2 genera, in instances where normal sex cell fusion is difficult or impossible. This artificial fusion, carried out under a microscope with the aid of micromanipulation instruments, bears some similarity to sexual reproduction, but with certain significant differences:

1. First of all, the term "somatic cell fusion" may be misleading. Rather than 2 cells being forced to merge much like 2 soap bubbles coalescing, the procedure actually involves extraction of the nucleus of 1 cell with a micropipette, and the insertion of that nucleus into the receptor cell. It is a very intricate process, subject to failures of all kinds, notably cases of cells simply imploding so that the entire process must be repeated. Nor is there any guarantee that the nuclei which are successfully induced to share the same cell will actually fuse, although they frequently do so.
2. The nuclei which fuse, behaving as quasi-gametes, are not reduced by half their chromosomal content as are sex cells. Thus, polyploidy is automatic in such fusions.
3. Because the quasi-gametes need not be particularly compatible, fusions occur which would never occur in nature, although when this happens the resultant artificial F1 hybrid is not necessarily fertile, or useful for future breeding purposes without further manipulation.

If such methods and manipulations seem futuristic, do not be misled. Not only are these and similar techniques being used with some measure of success in many genera, but far more sophisticated bioengineering techniques, enabling scientists to excise whole chromosomes, sever chromosomes, or to insert or delete particular genes as desired, are becoming commonplace in bacterial research and a few other areas. Research into designing desirable genes that are presently nonexistent is underway. The means to duplicate such feats in slipper orchids is certain to be found.

Culture of meristem tissue is a common reality for much of the orchid world. It is typically employed for the purpose of clonal reproduction, although as we have seen, far more esoteric uses can be made of it. While only limited success has been reported in tissue culture of slippers to date, there is no reason to doubt that these difficulties will be resolved. The future holds vast promise for an abundance of slippers which are the results of laboratory-manipulated wonders at cellular and subcellular levels.

Ultimately, however, we must remember our humanity amid the wealth of scientific bonanzas and the resultant conflicting aims presenting themselves. The creation of beauty remains, as always, an art. We must maintain harmony between the artistic and the scientific aspects of our own natures, even as we explore the technological possibilities in breeding new slippers. It is imperative to recall and emphasize as well the balance between our heritage and our posterity, while at the same time safeguarding our somewhat precarious equilibrium between technological progress and preservation of the natural world. However great our progress to date, the challenges we face are more daunting than at any prior period. Having been successfully guided by intuitive and artistic drives to this point, it would be a tragedy if the austere world of science assumed mastery of future developments in slippers. Fortunately, no such occurrence is likely, as slipper fanciers are a notoriously independent and determined lot. The future triumphs of slipper breeding are sure to continue to wed the breeder's art with the scientist's technology to the abiding delight of growers. Unfortunately, the enigmatic and highly technical aspects of hybridizing, along with the expense of technical equipment, may conspire to put many of these projected capabilities beyond the scope of the hobbyist. These restrictions are likely to proliferate rapidly while specialization increases, creating an ever-widening technological gap between the hobbyist and the scientist, with the commercial breeder of slippers serving as the bridge between diverse worlds.

Table 14. Ratios of siblings with 64 possible allelic combinations in a hypothetical case of the effect of polygenic inheritance on peduncle height.

Genotypic (allelic) combinations	Fraction of grex	Scape height
6 dominant alleles AABBCC	1/64	Tallest scape
5 dominant, 1 recessive aABBCC AaBBCC AAbBCC AABbCC AABBcC AABBCc	6/64	The first 4 genotypes are shorter; the latter 2 are nearly as tall as the pure dominant above, because the influence of Cc is negligible.
4 dominant, 2 recessive aaBBCC AAbbCC AABBcc aAbBCC aABbCC AabBCC AaBbCC AAbBcC AAbBCc AABbcC AABbCc aABBcC aABBCc AaBBcC AaBBCc	15/64	Wide variability exists in this category due to the inequality of the influence of Cc. Significant overlap with adjacent classes occurs as well.
3 dominant, 3 recessive aabBCC aaBbCC aaBBcC aaBBCc AabbCC AaBbCc AabBCc AaBbcC AaBBcc AabBcC AAbbcC AABbcc AAbBcc AAbbCc aAbBcC	20/64	This fraction of the grex shows the greatest degree of variability: AABbcc has the same phenotype as a 4:2 dominant individual such as AABbCc; numerous examples of overlap with the adjacent categories exist.

Assume 3 hypothetical allelic pairs influencing scape height:
1. Aa—number of cells in vertical column (phenotypic effect would be visible, in the possible range of several centimeters in overall length).
2. Bb—extent of elongation of each cell (overall effect visible, as in the case of Aa).
3. Cc—thickness of end cell walls (overall effect restricted to a few millimeters in length and poorly visible to the unaided eye).

F1 Generation:
A homozygous dominant individual, AABBCC—tall scapes—is crossed with a homozygous recessive individual, aabbcc—short scapes—to yield the F1 Generation—all heterozygous hybrids with the genotype AaBbCc and bearing intermediate scapes of about the same height.

F2 Generation, as represented above:
Crossing any 2 heterozygous AaBbCc individuals produces the F2 generation, having the illustrated genotypic 1:6:15:20:15:6:1 ratio for every 64 offspring. Phenotypic variations create further intergradations in scape height.

Table 14. Ratios of siblings with 64 possible allelic combinations in a hypothetical case of the effect of polygenic inheritance on peduncle height.

Genotypic (allelic) combinations	Fraction of grex	Scape height
aAbbCC		
aABbcC		
aABbCc		
aAbBCc		
aABBcc		
2 dominant, 4 recessive	15/64	This category shows a comparable degree of variability with the 15/64 group above, but toward the recessive end of the spectrum.
AAbbcc		
aaBBcc		
aabbCC		
AaBbcc		
AabBcc		
aABBcc		
aAbBcc		
aaBbCc		
aaBbCc		
aabBCc		
aabBcC		
AabbCc		
AabbcC		
aAbbCc		
aAbbcC		
1 dominant, 5 recessive	6/64	The scapes of the latter 2 examples in this category are virtually as short as the purebred recessive.
Aabbcc		
aAbbcc		
aaBbcc		
aabBcc		
aabbCc		
aabbcC		
6 recessive alleles	1/64	Offspring with shortest scapes.
aabbcc		

Bibliography

Arango, Alvaro, Alberto Echavarria, and Oscar Robledo. 1970. El genero *Phragmipedium*, Rolfe. *Orquideologia* 5:97–103.

Arditti, Joseph, Allison Oliva, and Justine D. Michaud. 1985. Practical germination of North American and related orchids—3. *Amer. Orch. Soc. Bul.* 54:859–866.

Armstrong, Sarah. 1975. An account of *Paphiopedilum godefroyae* from *L'Orchidophile* 1883. Trans./Repr. *Orch. Dig.* 39:29–30.

Arnold, R. E. 1933. *Cypripedium cordigerum. Orch. Rev.* 41:54.

Asher, James H., Jr. 1980a. Part I: A checklist for the genus *Paphiopedilum* for 1980–1981. *Orch. Dig.* 44:175–178.

_____. 1980b. Part II: A checklist for the genus *Paphiopedilum* for 1980–81. *Orch. Dig.* 44:213–228.

_____. 1981a. Part III: A checklist for the genus *Paphiopedilum* for 1980–81. *Orch. Dig.* 45:15–17.

_____. 1981b. Part IV: A checklist for the genus *Paphiopedilum* for 1980–81. *Orch. Dig.* 45:57–62.

_____. 1981c. Notes on the genus *Paphiopedilum* I. *Paphiopedilum glanduliferum* (Blume) Pfitzer and *Paphiopedilum praestans* (Rchb. f.) Pfitzer. *Orch. Dig.* 45:150–157.

_____. 1985. A contribution to the study of *Paphiopedilum*, subgenus *Cochlopetalum*, with an enumeration of the species within the subgenus, and a discussion of some modern techniques to evaluate and define species concepts. *Orch. Dig.* 49:15–22.

_____. 1988. Notes on the genus *Paphiopedilum* II. *Orch. Dig.* 52:209–216.

Asher, James H., Jr. and John H. Beaman. 1988. *Paphiopedilum richardianum* Asher & Beaman: A discussion about its relationship to other members of the section *Pardalopetalum. Orch. Dig.* 52:119–125.

Atwood, John T., Jr. 1984a. In defense of *Cypripedium kentuckiense* C. F. Reed. *Amer. Orch. Soc. Bul.* 53:835–841.

_____ . 1984b. The relationships of the slipper orchids (subfamily Cypripedioideae). *Selbyana* 7:129–247.

_____ . 1985a. The *Cypripedium calceolus* L. complex in North America, 106–110. *Proceedings*: *The Eleventh World Orchid Conference*. International Press Co. (Pte.) Ltd., Singapore.

_____ . 1985b. The range of *Cypripedium kentuckiense*. *Amer. Orch. Soc. Bul.* 54:1197–1199.

_____ . 1985c. Pollination of *Paphiopedilum rothschildianum*: Brood-site deception. *NGR* Spring 1985:247–254.

Ayensu, Edward S. 1975. Endangered and threatened orchids of the United States. *Amer. Orch. Soc. Bul.* 44:384–394.

Bechtel, Paul G. 1983. Cultural challenges: *Paphiopedilum rothschildianum* and its hybrids (A guide to success with temperamental orchids). *Orch. Dig.* 47:164–169.

Bertsch, Walter. 1981a. The new pink paphiopedilums—part 2. *Amer. Orch. Soc. Bul.* 50:132–138. Reprinted from *Proc. 1980 New Zealand International Orchid Conference*.

_____ . 1981b. The new pink paphiopedilums—part 3. *Amer. Orch. Soc. Bul.* 50:267–274.

_____ . 1981c. The new pink paphiopedilums—part 4. *Amer. Orch. Soc. Bul.* 50:394–398.

_____ . 1981d. The new pink paphiopedilums—part 5. *Amer. Orch. Soc. Bul.* 50:553–559.

_____ . 1981e. Use and misuse of variety and cultivar names in orchids. *Amer. Orch. Soc. Bul.* 50:811–823.

Birk, Lance A. 1981. *Paphiopedilum fowliei* Birk, sp. nov. *Orch. Dig.* 45:63–65.

_____ . 1983. *The* Paphiopedilum *growers' manual*. Lance Birk, Santa Barbara, CA.

Black, Peter. 1973. Milestones in the breeding of paphiopedilums over the last hundred years. Paphiopedilum *World* 3:77–79. Reprinted from *Orch. Rev.* Jan. 1969.

Braem, Guido J. 1987a. *Paphiopedilum henryanum* Braem, sp. nov. *Schlecteriana* 1:3–6.

_____ . 1987b. *Paphiopedilum*. Brucke-Verlag Kurt Schmersow, Hildescheim, Germany.

Castano, Guillermo R. 1974. *Cypripedium irapeanum*. Paphiopedilum *World* Oct. 1974:69–70.

Charles, Emerson. 1972. The Orchid Digest guide on the culture of orchids: II. Paphiopedilums. *Orch. Dig.* 36:17–20.

_____ . 1975. *Paphiopedilum* popularity—there are many reasons. *Amer. Orch. Soc. Bul.* 44:960–966.

Chen, S. C. 1983. New taxa of Orchidaceae from China. *Acta Phytotaxonomica Sinica* 21 (3):343–344.

_____ . 1985. *Cypripedium wumengense* and its allies. *Acta Phytotaxonomica Sinica* 23 (5):369–375.

Chen, S. C. and K. Y. Lang. 1986. *Cypripedium subtropicum*, a new species related to *Selenipedium*. *Acta Phytotaxonomica Sinica* 24 (4):317–322.

Chen, S. C. and F. Y. Liu. 1982. Notes on some species of *Paphiopedilum* from Yunnan. *Acta Bot. Yunnanica* 4:163–167.

Chen, S. C. and Z. H. Tsi. 1984. On *Paphiopedilum malipoense* sp. nov., an intermediate form between *Paphiopedilum* and *Cypripedium*, with a discussion on the origin of the genus. *Acta Phytotaxonomica Sinica* 22 (2):119–124.

Coleman, R. A. 1988. The orchids of Yosemite National Park. *Amer. Orch. Soc. Bul.* 57:609–623.

Collenette, Sheila. 1975. In search of cypripediums. *Orch. Dig.* 39:154–159. Reprinted from *Orch. Rev.*

Comber, J. B. 1972. A habitat note on *Paphiopedilum chamberlainianum* and *Phalaenopsis sumatrana*. *Orch. Dig.* 36:25.

Condon, Stan. 1974. Modern paphiopedilums. Paphiopedilum *World* 4:5–8.

Correll, D. S. 1950. *Native orchids of North America*. Chronica Botanica, Waltham, MA.

Craig, Jack E. 1972. Japan's four native cypripediums. *Amer. Orch. Soc. Bul.* 41:13–17.

Cribb, Phillip. 1987. *The genus* Paphiopedilum. Timber Press, Portland, OR.

Darnell, A. W. 1930. *Orchids for the outdoor garden.* Reprint 1976. Dover Publications, New York.

Day, Clark, Jr. 1974. *Paphiopedilum roebelinii*—one of the real charmers. *Amer. Orch. Soc. Bul.* 43:288–289.

———. 1975. *Paphiopedilum fairieanum* [sic] and the red influence. *Amer. Orch. Soc. Bul.* 44:971–973.

de Ghillany, Barao Anton. 1972. In Search of the elusive *Phragmipedium sargentianum* in Brazil. *Orch. Dig.* 35:111–115.

Dickinson, Stirling. 1967. My life and near death with *Cypripedium irapeanum. Amer. Orch. Soc. Bul.* 36:376–380.

Dirks, Dorothea. 1981. An early report on *Cypripedium montanum* by Lewis and Clark. *Orch. Dig.* 45:34–35.

Dodson, Calaway H. and Robert J. Gillespie. 1967. *The biology of the orchids.* Mid-America Orchid Congress, Nashville, TN.

Dodson, Calaway H., and Janet Kuhn. 1981. *Phragmipedium besseae*—A new species from Peru. *Amer. Orch. Soc. Bul.* 50:1308–1310.

Dopp, Alan C. 1984. Standards in judging paphiopedilums. *Amer. Orch. Soc. Awards Quart.* 15:161–164.

Dressler, R. D. 1981. *The orchids: natural history and classification.* Harvard University Press, Cambridge, MA.

Dunsterville, G. C. K. 1970a. *Phragmipedium lindleyanum* (Schomb.) Rolfe. *Orch. Dig.* 34:110–112.

———. 1970b. *Phragmipedium klotzscheanum* (Rchb. f. ex Schomb.) Rolfe. *Orch. Dig.* 34:188–189.

———. 1971. *Selenipedium steyermarkii* Foldats. *Orch. Dig.* 35:51–53.

———. 1980. Orchids of Venezuela: new names for old. *Amer. Orch. Soc. Bul.* 49:223–227.

Dunsterville, G. C. K. and E. Dunsterville. 1980. Orchids of Venezuela: *Selenipedium steyermarkii*—A "commodious" orchid. *Amer. Orch. Soc. Bul.* 49:1225–1229.

———. 1982. Hunting *Phragmipedium klotzscheanum*—An agony in eight fits. *Amer. Orch. Soc. Bul.* 51:709–712.

Ewacha, Joan. 1985. Vanishing cypripediums. *Amer. Orch. Soc. Bul.* 54:1194–1196.

Fitch, Charles Marden. 1982. *Paphiopedilum* paradise by the sea. *Amer. Orch. Soc. Bul.* 51:377–380.

Fordyce, Frank. 1976. Pygmy paphs. *Amer. Orch. Soc. Bul.* 45:576–585.

Fowlie, J. A. 1966. An annotated checklist of the species of *Paphiopedilum*, 1966. *Orch. Dig.* 30:307–313.

———. 1968. A new species of *Paphiopedilum* from the island of Bougainville. *Orch. Dig.* 32:283–284.

———. 1969a. Some notes on *Paphiopedilum appletonianum* and its natural hybrid, *P. siamense. Orch. Dig.* 33:49–50.

———. 1969b. A fascinating new species of slipper orchid of the section *Coryopedilum* from Mindanao: *Paphiopedilum randsii. Orch. Dig.* 33:321–322.

———. 1970. Some notes on *Paphiopedilum chamberlainianum* (O'Brien) Pfitz. *Orch. Dig.* 34:105–107.

———. 1972. In search of *Phragmipedium caudatum. Orch. Dig.* 36:47–48.

———. 1973a. Notes on two new color varieties of *Paphiopedilum chamberlainianum* of the *primulinum* form. *Orch. Dig.* 37:102–105.

———. 1973b. With Ghillany in Brazil: Part V. *Orch. Dig.* 37:110–114.

———. 1973c. Malaya revisited: Part II. *Orch. Dig.* 37:190–194.

_____ . 1973d. Malaya revisited: Part III. *Orch. Dig.* 37:230–234.

_____ . 1974a. Malaya revisited: Part IV. *Orch. Dig.* 38:90–94.

_____ . 1974b. A clarification of *Paphiopedilum virens* (Rchb. f.) Pfitz. including the description of a new species, *Paphiopedilum purpurascens* Fowl. *Orch. Dig.* 38:153–157.

_____ . 1974c. Malaya revisited: Part V. *Orch. Dig.* 38:186–190.

_____ . 1975a. *Paphiopedilum godefroyae*, the ladyslipper species of the Birdsnest Islands, and its confusion in modern times as *Paphiopedilum ang thong. Orch. Dig.* 39:27–28.

_____ . 1975b. Malaya revisited: Part VI. *Orch. Dig.* 39:32–37.

_____ . 1975c. Malaya revisited: Part VII. *Orch. Dig.* 39:110–118.

_____ . 1975d. *Paphiopedilum volonteanum* (Sander) Pfitz. *Orch. Dig.* 39:170.

_____ . 1975e. A historical note on *Paphiopedilum stonei* var. *platytaenium. Orch. Dig.* 39:228–229.

_____ . 1976. Malaya revisited: Part VIII. *Orch. Dig.* 40:146–150.

_____ . 1977a. Malaya revisited: Part X. *Orch. Dig.* 41:31–37.

_____ . 1977b. Two recently described species of Philippine *Paphiopedila, Paphiopedilum acmodontum* Schoser ex Wood and *Paphiopedilum hennisianum* (Wood) Fowl. *Orch. Dig.* 41:60–61.

_____ . 1977c. Malaya revisited: Part XI. *Orch. Dig.* 41:112–118.

_____ . 1977d. Malaya revisited: Part XII. *Orch. Dig.* 41:190–197.

_____ . 1978. Malaya revisited: Part XIII. *Orch. Dig.* 42:72–76.

_____ . 1979a. A brief history of the entanglements surrounding *Paph.* Jogjae and *Paph. yapianum* and some comparative illustrations and proposed solutions. *Orch. Dig.* 43:23–25.

_____ . 1979b. Malaya revisited: Part XIV. *Orch. Dig.* 43:219–224.

_____ . 1980a. *Paphiopedilum elliottianum* refound in the Philippines with some thoughts on the distribution of members of the section *Coryopedilum. Orch. Dig.* 44:70–76.

_____ . 1980b. Malaya revisited: Part XVI. *Orch. Dig.* 44:97–101.

_____ . 1980c. Malaya revisited: Part XVII. *Orch. Dig.* 44:133–135.

_____ . 1981a. *Paphiopedilum volonteanum* (Sander) Pfitz. 1890. *Orch. Dig.* 45:18–26.

_____ . 1981b. Speciation amongst the Orchidaceae as a function of climate change and topophysiography. *Orch. Dig.* 45:45–49.

_____ . 1981c. Malaya revisited: Part XVIII. *Orch. Dig.* 45:85–92.

_____ . 1981d. A new *Paphiopedilum* species from Mindoro Island in the Philippines, *Paphiopedilum urbanianum* Fowl. *Orch. Dig.* 45:131–134.

_____ . 1981e. Malaya revisited: Part XIX. *Orch. Dig.* 45:165–169.

_____ . 1981f. Malaya revisited: Part XX. *Orch. Dig.* 45:231–237.

_____ . 1982. Notes on the habitat and ecological relationships of *Cypripedium californicum* A. Gray and *Darlingtonia californica. Orch. Dig.* 46:165–170.

_____ . 1983a. Malaya revisited: Part XXII. *Orch. Dig.* 47:4–9.

_____ . 1983b. The search for *Cypripedium passerinum* Richardson in the Yukon. *Orch. Dig.* 47:19–22.

_____ . 1983c. Malaya revisited: Part XXIV. *Orch. Dig.* 47:175–182.

_____ . 1984a. The quest for *Cypripedium formosanum* Hay. in Formosa (Taiwan). *Orch. Dig.* 48:5–10.

_____ . 1984b. A new species of *Paphiopedilum* from Central Kalimantan, *Paphiopedilum kolopakingii* Fowl. sp. nov. *Orch. Dig.* 48:41–42.

_____ . 1984c. Malaya revisited: Part XXV. *Orch. Dig.* 48:59–66.

_____ . 1984d. Malaya revisited: Part XXVI. *Orch. Dig.* 48:168–174.

_____ . 1985a. Malaya revisited: Part XXVII. *Orch. Dig.* 49:48–52.

_____ . 1985b. Malaya revisited: Part XXVIII. *Orch. Dig.* 49:84–90.

_____ . 1985c. Malaya revisited: Part XXIX. *Orch. Dig.* 49:124–129.

_____ . 1985d. A new species of *Spathopetalum* from central Sumatra, *Paphiopedilum tortipetalum* Fowl. *Orch. Dig.* 49:153–156.

_____ . 1985e. Malaya revisited: Part XXX. *Orch. Dig.* 49:164–169.

_____ . 1985f. Malaya revisited: Part XXXI. *Orch. Dig.* 49:205–210.

_____ . 1986. Malaya revisited: Part XXXIII. *Orch. Dig.* 50:156–162.

_____ . 1987. *Paphiopedilum hainanense* Fowl., sp. nov. *Orch. Dig.* 51:69–70.

_____ . 1988. *Cypripedium fasciculatum* on serpentine landslides of northwestern California. *Orch. Dig.* 52:136–139.

Frosch, Werner. 1986. Asymbiotic propagation of *Cypripedium reginae*. *Amer. Orch. Soc. Bul.* 55:14–15.

Gann, William. 1977. *Cypripedium irapeanum* Llave & Lexarza. *Orch. Dig.* 41:209–210.

Garay, Leslie A. 1978. Orchidaceae. *Flora of Ecuador* 9:12–24.

_____ . 1979. The genus *Phragmipedium*. *Orch. Dig.* 43:133–148.

Gee, Ruth. 1978. Growing paphiopedilums in the Southwest. *Amer. Orch. Soc. Bul.* 47:300–305.

Ghose, B. N. 1964a. *Cypripedium fairieanum* [sic]. *Amer. Orch. Soc. Bul.* 33:844–846.

_____ . 1964b. Orchids of India: *Paphiopedilum fairrieanum*. *Amer. Orch. Soc. Bul.* 33:844–846.

_____ . 1968. *Beautiful Indian orchids*. G. Ghose, Darjeeling, India.

_____ . 1970. Asiatic paphiopedilums. *Amer. Orch. Soc. Bul.* 39:143–146.

Gorinsky, Peter. 1972. Habitat notes from a collection in Guyana of *Phragmipedium klotzcheanum*. *Orch. Dig.* 36:151–154.

_____ . 1973. Habitat Notes from a collection in Guyana of *Phragmipedium lindleyanum*. *Orch. Dig.* 37:47–51.

Griesbach, R. J. 1985. Polyploidy in orchid improvement. *Amer. Orch. Soc. Bul.* 54:1445–1451.

Griesbach, R. J. and J. H. Asher, Jr. 1982. Orchids of the Boundary Waters Canoe area of Northern Minnesota. *Orch. Dig.* 46:215–228.

Gripp, Paul. 1972. Novelty *Paphiopedilum* judging. *Orch. Dig.* 36:80–82.

Hagsater, Eric. 1971. *Cypripedium irapeanum*. *Orchidea* 15:5–7.

_____ . 1984. *Cypripedium dickinsonianum* Hagsater. *Orchidea* 28:206–212.

Han, Saw. 1972. The Burmese *Paphiopedilum*. *Paphiopedilum World* 2:53–55.

Head, Cordelia. 1985. Hand pollination of *Cypripedium acaule*. *Amer. Orch. Soc. Bul.* 54:540–542.

Hegedus, Louis S. and Frank R. Stermitz. 1986. Further facts on *Phragmipedium besseae*. *Amer. Orch. Soc. Bul.* 55:367–370.

Hindley, Kirk. 1980. The association of ladyslipper orchids and insectivorous plants: part III. *Orch. Dig.* 44:232–235.

Holman, Ralph T., William P. Cunningham, and Elizabth S. Swanson. 1981. A closer look at the glandular hairs on the ovaries of cypripediums. *Amer. Orch. Soc. Bul.* 50:683–687.

Hurlburt, Paul R. 1972. Bog-trotting for orchids in Vermont. *Amer. Orch. Soc. Bul.* 41:428–434.

Jahn, Siegfried. 1984. Observations on the natural habitat of *Paphiopedilum victoria-mariae*. *Orch. Dig.* 48:138. Reprinted from *Die Orchidee*.

Karasawa, Kohji and Motoo Kimura. 1973. *Paphiopedilum* Finetta AM/JOS—the most successful stud plant in Japan. *Paphiopedilum World* 3:75–76.

Karasawa, K. and K. Saito. 1982. A revision of the genus *Paphiopedilum* (Orchidaceae). *Bul. Hiroshima Bot. Gard.* 5:1–69.

Kennedy, George C. 1979. *Paphiopedilum gardineri* (Guillem.) Pfitz. *Orch. Dig.* 43:114–116.

Knudson, L. 1922. Non-symbiotic germination of orchid seeds. *Bot. Gaz.* 73:1–25.

Koopowitz, Harold and Phillip Cribb. 1986. *Paphiopedilum emersonii*—a remarkable new slipper from China. *Orch. Dig.* 52:134–135. Reprinted from *Orchid Advocate*.

Koopowitz, Harold and Norito Hasegawa. 1983. What is a vinicolor *Paphiopedilum*? *Amer. Orch. Soc. Bul.* 54:1428–1430.

_____ . 1984. The Status of *Paphiopedilum armeniacum* Chen & Liu. *Orch. Dig.* 48:95–98.

_____ . 1986. The new *Parvisepalum* paphiopedilums. *Amer. Orch. Soc. Bul.* 55:684–690.

_____ . 1987. The new Maudiae paphiopedilums. *Orch. Dig.* 51:4–9.

_____ . 1988. One man and his orchid: Emerson "Doc" Charles and *Paphiopedilum emersonii. Orch. Dig.* 52:131–133.

Lancaster, Roy. 1982. Five orchids of Yunnan. *Garden: J. Royal Hort. Soc.* 109:425–430.

Lee, T. C. 1975. *Paphiopedilum purpuratum* (Lindl.) Pfitz. *Orch. Dig.* 39:192–196.

Lee, Toh Ming. 1972. *Paphiopedilum barbatum* and its original habitat. *Orch. Dig.* 36:143–145.

Liem, Khe Wie. 1973. The dreamlike reality of discovering the new yellow *Paphiopedilum. Orch. Dig.* 37:106.

Linnaeus, Carolus. 1753. *Species Plantarum.* Impensis Laurentii Salvi, Stockholm.

Mammen, Verghese and Jo Mammen. 1974. Rediscovering *Paphiopedilum druryi* in southern India. *Orch. Dig.* 38:31–36.

Manuel, Pat K. 1972. Collecting paphiopedilums in southeast Asia. *Orch. Dig.* 36:63–65.

Mark, Fred. 1982. A note of discovery: *Paphiopedilum purpuratum* forma *aphaca* 'Mark'. *Orch. Dig.* 46:235–236.

_____ . 1987. A preliminary introduction to and cultivation of the chinese slipper orchids, genus *Paphiopedilum. Orch. Dig.* 51:63–82.

Matsui, Michizo and Tatsuo Niizuma. 1975. Japanese wild orchids. *Amer. Orch. Soc. Bul.* 44:768–778.

Mattes, Paul. 1982. A discovery trip to the Philippines with notes on the habitat of *Paphiopedilum fowlei* on Palawan Island. *Orch. Dig.* 46:4–10.

_____ . 1985 In search of the *Paphiopedilum* species of Pulau Tioman, western Malaysia. Trans. by George Stelzner. *Orch. Dig.* 49:233–236.

Mellichamp, T. Lawrence. 1979. The occurrence of ladyslipper orchids and insectivorous plants: Part I. *Orch. Dig.* 43:108–113.

Moore, Paul B. 1969. The "now" trend in *Paphiopedilum. Amer. Orch. Soc. Bul.* 38:45–48.

_____ . 1973. Where are we today in *Paphiopedilum* hybridizing? *Amer. Orch. Soc. Bul.* 42:964–968.

Moore, R. E. 1980. Orchids of the Shan states. *Orch. Dig.* 44:124–129. Reprinted from *Orch. Rev.*

Muick, Franz. 1978. Propagation of *Cypripedium* species from seeds. *Amer. Orch. Soc. Bul.* 47:306–308.

Nash, Ned. 1981a. The Maudiae-type paphiopedilums—Part 1. *Amer. Orch. Soc. Bul.* 50:677–682.

_____ . 1981b. The Maudiae-type paphiopedilums—Part 2—reds and other colors. *Amer. Orch. Soc. Bul.* 50:925–931.

Ohwi, Jisaburo. 1965. *Flora of Japan.* Smithsonian Institution, Washington, D.C.

Olver, Susanne. 1981. Growing *Cypripedium reginae* in controlled environment chambers. *Amer. Orch. Soc. Bul.* 50:1091–1092.

Ossian, Clair R. 1983. Orchids of Alaska: The slipper orchids—*Cypripedium* and *Calypso. Orch. Dig.* 47:151–158.

Parshul, I. M. 1976. *Paphiopedilum curtisii. Amer. Orch. Soc. Bul.* 45:1095.

Patrick, Maribeth. 1981. Wyoming native orchids. *Amer. Orch. Soc. Bul.* 50:151–152.

Pempahishey, Karma T. 1974. Orchid eaters of "Shangri-la." *Amer. Orch. Soc. Bul.* 43:716–725.

_____ . 1976. *Paphiopedilum druryi* revisited. *Amer. Orch. Soc. Bul.* 45:431–433.

Peterson, Kenneth E. 1985. *Paphiopedilum mastersianum*—Past, present, and future. *Amer. Orch. Soc. Bul.* 54:398–402.

Phillips, Paul. 1982. Paphiopedilum Hellas 'Westonbirt'—New light from an old hybrid. *Amer. Orch. Soc. Bul.* 51:34–36.

Powers, Maurice. 1977. An amateur's selection of primary hybrid paphiopedilums. *Orch. Dig.* 41:215–217.

Pradhan, Ganesh Mani. 1972a. *Paphiopedilum fairieanum* [sic]. Paphiopedilum *World* 2:12–14.

———. 1972b. Cultural notes on *Paphiopedilum spicerianum* [sic]. *Orch. Dig.* 36:27–30.

———. 1972c. *Paphiopedilum hirsutissimum.* Paphiopedilum *World* 2:84–85.

———. 1972d. Cultural notes on *Paphiopedilum villosum. Orch. Dig.* 36:147–149.

———. 1973. An orchid happening: A lesson from nature on growing *Paphiopedilum venustum* from seed. *Orch. Dig.* 37:27–30.

———. 1974. *Paphiopedilum venustum. Orch. Dig.* 38:195–198.

———. 1975. *Paphiopedilum spicerianum* [sic]. *Amer. Orch. Soc. Bul.* 44:877–879.

———. 1978. *Paphiopedilum fairieanum* [sic]. *Orch. Dig.* 42:151–158.

Pradhan, Udai C. 1971. Beautiful orchid species—2: *Paphiopedilum spicerianum* [sic]. *Amer. Orch. Soc. Bul.* 40:9–11.

———. 1974. A survey: *Paphiopedilum insigne* (Wall.) Pfitz. *Orch. Dig.* 38:222–225.

———. 1975. *Paphiopedilum venustum* (Wall.) Pfitz. *Orch. Dig.* 39:204–209.

———. 1986. The Himalayan cypripediums. *Orch. Dig.* 50:85–89.

Price, Grace Romero. 1973. A review of the Philippine species of *Paphiopedilum. Orch. Dig.* 37:120–125.

Puddle, F. C. 1947. The development of white hybrid cypripediums. Paphiopedilum *World* 4:76–78. Reprinted from *Orch. Rev.* 1974.

Radcliffe, Edna. 1967. A further note on *Paphiopedilum (Cypripedium)* Meadowsweet. *Amer. Orch. Soc Bul.* 36:493–494.

Ramsey, Edith C. 1967. Our experience with *Cypripedium irapeanum. Amer. Orch. Soc. Bul.* 36:787–789.

Rands, Ray J. 1975. Phragmipediums—and their future. *Amer. Orch. Soc. Bul.* 44:235–238.

Rathbun, William B. 1973. A national orchid bog? *Amer. Orch. Soc. Bul.* 42:687–691.

Reynolds, Calvin F. 1976. Growing "lady's-slippers" in a wildgarden. *Amer. Orch. Soc. Bul.* 45:480–483.

Rodrigues, Barbosa. 1937. *Selenipedium vanillocarpum* Barb. Rodr. *Rodriguesia*: Vol. II, No. 8:39–40. Revista do Instituto de Biologia Vegetal, Jardim Botanico do Rio de Janeiro e Estacao Biologica do Itatiaya, Brazil.

Rolfe, R. A. 1896. The *Cypripedium* group. *Orch. Rev.* 4: 327–334, 363–367.

Rowland, Patricia and Lee Rowland. 1978. Welcome to the small world of pygmy paphs. *Amer. Orch. Soc. Bul.* 47:999–1003.

Sanders' complete list of orchid hybrids. 1947. Gibbs & Banforth. St. Albans, Great Britain.

Sander's one-table list of orchid hybrids 1946–1960. 1961. David Sander's Orchids, East Grinstead, Sussex, England.

Sander's list of orchid hybrids: addendum 1961–1970. 1971. The Royal Horticultural Society, London.

Sander's list of orchid hybrids: 5-year addendum 1981–1985. 1987. The Royal Horticultural Society, London.

Schaffer, Norwood K. 1975. *Paphiopedilum hookerae,* a Bornean rarity with a note on a new collection. *Orch. Dig.* 39:164–169.

———. 1977. *Paphiopedilum superbiens*: a lost species. *Orch. Dig.* 41:44–51.

Schaffer, Norwood K. and Peter Taylor. 1975. *Paphiopedilum stonei*: a noble species. *Orch. Dig.* 39:223–227.

Schelpe, E. A. 1981. Observations on the subgenus *Anotopedilum* of *Paphiopedilum. Amer. Orch. Soc. Bul.* 50:954–958.

Schoser, Gustav. 1967. *Paphiopedilum linii*—A recent introduction. *Amer. Orch. Soc. Bul.* 36:1083–1086.

———. 1975. *Paphiopedilum wentworthianum* and *P. bougainvilleanum*—Reintroduction from the island of Bougainville. Trans./ Repr. *Orch. Dig.* 39:15–19.

———. 1981. Cultural suggestions for the paphiopedilums—Orchids for every admirer. *Orch. Dig.* 45:185–189. Trans. from *Palmengarten Bul.*

Schrenk, W. Juergen. 1981. Rare orchids in Western Europe—1—Vanishing beauties and inconspicuous ducklings. *Amer. Orch. Soc. Bul.* 50:1185–1189.

Shechter, Yaakov. 1973a. Basic genetics, its history and significance in plant breeding. Paphiopedilum *World* 3:4–7.

———. 1973b. Mendelian genetics: Monohybrid inheritance and the principles of segregation. Paphiopedilum *World* 3:32–36.

———. 1973c. Genetics for *Paphiopedilum* breeders: The dihybrid cross and modifications of Mendelian ratios. Paphiopedilum *World* 3:47–53.

Sheviak, Charles J. 1974. Some aspects of the ecology of Illinois orchids. *Amer. Orch. Soc. Bul.* 43:192–203.

Slyusarenko, Alexandr G. 1981. *Cypripedium* L.—The lady's-slippers. *Amer. Orch. Soc. Bul.* 50:776–780.

Stapf, O. 1927. *Cypripedium manchuricum virescens. Bot. Mag.* 152: Tab. 9117.

Stermitz, Frank R. 1980. Orchids from Iquitos to Cuzco to Tingo Maria, Peru. *Amer. Orch. Soc. Bul.* 49:1361–1367.

Stermitz, Frank R., Nancy H. Fink, and Louis S. Hegedus. 1981. A comparison of alkaloid content in some *Phragmipedium* species. *Amer. Orch. Soc. Bul.* 50:1346–1352.

Stermitz, Frank R., Louis S. Hegedus, and Lee Richard. 1983. A remake (?) of *Phragmipedium* Stenophyllum—Some comments on the *Himantopetalum* section of *Phragmipedium. Amer. Orch. Soc. Bul.* 52:1040–1045.

Stermitz, Frank R. and Louis S. Hegedus. 1984. *Phragmipedium* hybrids from the *Platypetalum* section. *Amer. Orch. Soc. Bul.* 53:600–603.

Steyermark, Julian, G. C. K. Dunsterville, and E. Dunsterville. 1970. Finding *Phragmipedium caudatum. Amer. Orch. Soc. Bul.* 39:484–491.

Stone, Paul G. 1972. A very special *Paphiopedilum. Amer. Orch. Soc. Bul.* 41:1068–1073.

Tang, T. and F. T. Wang. 1936. Notes on Orchidaceae of China I. *Bul. Fan Mem. Inst. Biol. Peiping Bot. Ser.* VII:1–2.

Teuscher, Henry. 1977. The *Cypripedilinae. Amer. Orch. Soc. Bul.* 46:910–921.

Thien Pe, Fred. 1981. A rediscovery of *Paphiopedilum wardii. Orch. Dig.* 45:99–103.

Tokugawa, Kuninara. 1967. A forerunner of white cypripediums. *Amer. Orch. Soc. Bul.* 36:92–94.

van de Graaf, J. W. A. 1972. Recent importations of some New Guinea paphiopedilums. Paphiopedilum *World* 2:74–76.

van Delden, Rex J. 1972a. *Paphiopedilum callosum* (Rchb. f.) Pfitz. *Orch. Dig.* 36:9–10.

———. 1972b. *Paphiopedilum wardii* Summerhayes. *Orch. Dig.* 36:85–86.

———. 1972c. *Paphiopedilum venustum. Orch. Dig.* 36:177–178.

———. 1979. Revival of an interesting hybrid line of *Paphiopedilum* multifloras, utilizing *Paphiopedilum parishii. Orch. Dig.* 43:59–61.

van Ede, G. 1978. Some observations on the inheritance of white and pink in paphiopedilums. *Amer. Orch. Soc. Bul.* 47:230–236.

Veitch, James. 1889. *Manual of orchidaceous plants* IV. Cypripedium. Reprint. 1963. Asher, Amsterdam.

Vermeulen, F. 1981. *Paphiopedilum superbiens* and *curtisii. Orch. Dig.* 45:177–178.

von Martius, K. F. P. 1893. *Selenipedium isabelianum*. *Flora Brasiliensis* Vol. III, Part IV, I *Selenipedium*, 6, 16, Tab. II, Fig. II.

Voraurai, Pisit. 1974. The habitat of *Paphiopedilum parishii*. *Orch. Dig*. 38:211–213.

Wallbrunn, Henry M. 1967. The taxonomists' dilemma or the evolution of taxonomy. *Amer. Orch. Soc. Bul*. 36:1077–1082.

Ward, F. Kingdon. 1938. Plants new or noteworthy. *Gard. Chron*. Vol. 104:458.

Waters, V. Hugh and Catherine C. Waters. 1973. *A survey of the slipper orchids*. Carolina Press, Shelby, NC.

Whitlow, Carson. 1986. *Cypripedium furcatum* Raf. from southeastern United States—Be it what it may. *Orch. Dig*. 50:40–41.

———. 1988a. The genesis of *Cypripedium* hybrids. *Amer. Orch. Soc. Bul*. 57:850–853.

———. 1988b. A contribution to the artificial propagation of the species of *Cypripedium*: *Cypripedium guttatum* and *Cypripedium yatabeanum*. *Orch. Dig*. 52:140–141.

Wilcox, E. C. 1971. What you've always wanted to know about *Paphiopedilum* breeding (but didn't know who to ask). Paphiopedilum *World* 1:28–34.

Williams, Benjamin Samuel. 1885. *The orchid-grower's manual*. 6th ed. Victoria and Paradise Nurseries, London.

Williams, Louis O. and Paul H. Allen. 1980. Orchids of Panama. *Missouri Bot. Garden*. 4:114–115.

Wilson, Charles L., Katherine Maxfield, and Elizabeth Livingston. 1982. *Cypripedium furcatum* Raf.—A "new" and beautiful species in the southern United States. *Amer. Orch. Soc. Bul*. 51:900–902.

Wilson, John E. 1975. Paphiopedilums move west: a history of hybrid *Paphiopedilum* breeding in the West Coast. *Orch. Dig*. 39:84–87.

———. 1977. British bulldog, Berkshire breeder. *Orch. Dig*. 41:84–87.

———. 1979a. Premier *Paphiopedilum* parents. *Amer. Orch. Soc. Bul*. 48:801–807.

———. 1979b. Premier *Paphiopedilum* parents—2. *Amer. Orch. Soc. Bul*. 48:1024–1033.

———. 1979c. Premier *Paphiopedilum* parents—3. *Amer. Orch. Soc. Bul*. 48:1143–1153.

Wilson, William W. 1971. The end of the beginning. Paphiopedilum *World* 1:24–27.

———. 1983. On the judging of paphiopedilums. *Amer. Orch. Soc. Bul*. 52:452–463.

Wimber, Dr. Donald E. 1983. *Phragmipedium* cytology—1—Diploidy and polyploidy in the hybrids. *Amer. Orch. Soc. Bul*. 52:933–939.

Wimber, Donald and John Hanes. 1985. Phragmipaphiums—Are they possible? *Amer. Orch. Soc. Bul*. 54:61–65.

Withner, Carl L., ed. 1959. *The orchids: A scientific survey*. Ronald Press, New York.

Wood, Howard P. 1978. Hunting wild orchids in southwestern Nova Scotia. *Amer. Orch. Soc. Bul*. 47:321–328.

Wood, Mark W. 1975. *Paphiopedilum victoria-reginae*. *Orch. Rev*. 84:133–143.

Yap, K. F. and T. M. Lee. 1972. *Paphiopedilum johorensis* Fowl. & K. F. Yap, sp. nov. *Orch. Dig*. 36.71–74.

Index